THE MAKING

OF THE

AMERICAN NATION,

OR

THE RISE AND DECLINE OF OLIGARCHY IN THE WEST.

BY

J. ARTHUR PARTRIDGE,

AUTHOR OF

"COALITIONS AND FRONTIERS IN 1860-1,"
"THE FALSE NATION AND ITS 'BASES;'
OR WHY THE SOUTH CAN'T STAND."
"DEMOCRACY." ETC.

"E PLURIBUS UNUM."

PHILADELPHIA:
J. B. LIPPINCOTT AND CO.
1866.

"The whole Freedom of man consists either in *spiritual or civil liberty*. The enjoyment of those never more certain, than in a free commonwealth. *Both which, in my opinion, may be best and soonest obtained, if every county in the land were made a kind of subordinate commonalty or commonwealth.*"—*Milton.*

"The Reformation made another enormous stride, when at the American Revolution the State and the Church were solemnly and openly dissevered from one another."—*Draper*, Intellectual Development of Europe.

"Not Democracy in America, but free Christianity in America, is the real key to the study of the People and their Institutions."—*Goldwin Smith.*

THE MAKING

OF THE

AMERICAN NATION;

OR

THE RISE AND DECLINE OF OLIGARCHY

IN THE WEST.

"Cette vieille Europe m'ennui."—*Napoleon.*

"Soon after the Reformation a few people came over for conscience sake. This apparently trivial incident may *transfer the great seat of empire into America.*"—*John Adams.*

"America is therefore the land of the future where, in the ages that lie before us, the burden of the world's history shall reveal itself. It is a land of desire for all those who are *weary of the historical lumber-room of old Europe.*"—*Hegel.*

"As interesting mankind the question was, shall the Reformation developed to the fulness of free inquiry, succeed in its protest against the middle ages."—*Bancroft.*

"The more a man is versed in business the more he finds the hand of Providence everywhere."—*Chatham.*

"You will think me transported with enthusiasm, but I am not. I am well aware of the toil, and blood, and treasure, that it will cost us to maintain this DECLARATION. Yet through all the gloom, I can see that the end is more than worth all the means; and that posterity will triumph in that day's transaction."—*John Adams,* 3rd July, 1776.

"The Declaration of Independence constituted a sacred pledge in the name of God, solemnly given by each State, to abolish slavery soon as practicable, and to substitute Freedom in its place."—*John Quincy Adams,* 1844.

"It is therefore very probable that mankind would have been at length obliged to live constantly under the Government of a single person, had they not contrived a kind of Constitution that had all the internal advantages of a Republican, together with the external force of a monarchical Government. I mean *a Confederate Republic.* "A Republic of this kind * * * may support itself without any internal corruption. * * * It possesseth all the advantages of large monarchies."

"Should a popular insurrection happen in one of the States, *the others are able to quell it.* Should abuses creep into one part, they are reformed by those that remain sound."—*Montesquieu.* Vol. I. pp. 165—7. Edition of 1777.

"I regret to say, that I only see, at the present time, two Governments which well fulfil their providential mission; these are *the two Colossi at either end of the world*—one at the extremity of the new, the other at the extremity of the old world. Whilst our old European centre is like a volcano, consuming itself in its own crater, *the two nations, Oriental and Occidental, proceed unhesitatingly, towards perfection, the one at the will of one man, the other by liberty.* Providence has confided to the United States of America the care of peopling and of gaining over to civilization all that immense territory which extends from the Atlantic to the South Sea, and *from the North Pole to the Equator.* The Government, which is but a simple administration, has only, up to the present time put in practice the old adage, *laissez faire, laisser passer*, to favour that irresistible instinct which impels towards the West the peoples of America."

"In Russia, it is to the *imperial dynasty* that we owe all the progress which, for a century and a half past, has been rescuing that vast empire from barbarism. The imperial power has to struggle against the old prejudices of our old Europe; it *must centralize*, as closely as possible, in the hands of an individual, the force of the state, *in order to destroy all the abuses* which would perpetuate themselves under the shelter *of communal and feudal franchises.* It is only from him that the East can receive the amelioration which it is awaiting."—*Louis Napoleon Bonaparte*—Life and Works. Vol. I., pp. 253, 254.

CONTENTS.

From page 1 to page 163 was written and printed during the heat of the American struggle, in fact, soon after the war begun. The arguments concern the particular question of American *Unity*, and the universal question of *Democracy*. The first is still considered an open question, whilst the last has to be explored by the light of this its first real precedent. That the mere tense, as to events now recent, is in the pages indicated, in the future instead of the past, will doubtless be considered a blemish by some, whilst others will consider that success establishes argument. The author can only state the fact, and submit the matter to the reader's judgment.

A volume "on Democracy," arose out of the present work, and is published concurrently with it.

PREFACE.

"Nation is a moral essence."—*Burke.*

"The Republicans are the nation."—*Jefferson.*

"A People cannot rise but by a principle or a man."—*Mazzini.*

"Future History approaches. Historical effigy will no longer be the man-king; it will be the *Man-People.* True History henceforth charged with the education of the royal infant, the People, will study the successive movements of *Humanity.* In that (ordinary) History there is everything except History. The lamp, which smokes on the opaque frontage of royal accessions, hides the starry reflection that the creators of civilization throw over ages."—*Hugo.*

"There is nothing in the world so sound as American Society. America has left behind it the cerements of the feudal system, hereditary aristocracy, primogeniture, entails, and the established Church."—*Goldwin Smith.*

"Individuality will be a term of greater comprehension, and nations free and enlightened, will hereafter become one complex Individual, as single men now are."—*Volney.*

"To realise these grades, of Individual National Genius, is the boundless impulse of the world-spirit, the goal of its irresistible urging."—*Hegel.*

"Another good expedient would be to settle colonies in two or three parts of such a (conquered) State; because if that is not done, it will be necessary to maintain a standing army there. Colonies, though nothing like so expensive, are more to be depended on and much less disgustful."—*Machiavel.* (The Prince.)

"We have done much, but still much remains. Time and time's influences are with us. We could almost afford to sit still and let these influences work."—*Sherman to Grant,* 1864.

"If Europe leaves America to Republicanism—well. If she interferes, we interfere, and the right hand of our resistance is clasped in brotherhood with the Radicals of Europe to upset every throne on the Continent."—*Wendell Phillips.*

THREE mighty problems, in which all Peoples and systems are concerned, are now, in the fulness of time, nearly worked out upon the American continent.

The making of the American Nation.

The making of the American Democracy.

The making of the first Federal Republican Empire.

A Nation is made of material Bases, Individuality and Organic Functions. By the first it exists; by the second it exists as a nation; and by the third it thinks, administrates, and acts.

A Democracy is made of a fourfold Freedom;—of School, Press, Church, and Assembly.

A Federation is made and preserved by an adjustment of relations between the parts and the whole.

Due and full consideration therefore of the American Federal Republic, has to do—

1st. With the material Bases of that nation, or its Territory, Labor, and Population.

2nd. With its national Individuality or Oneness of Ideas and Interests, of Institution, Race, Language, Boundary, and Religion.

3rd. With the completeness of its Organic Functions, that is, of its Legislature and Executive.

4th. With the origin and power of its Democratic Equality, in School, Press, Assembly, and Church.

5th. With the result,—Material, Political, and Religious Development.

6th. With the result of *that*, namely, powers of Association, which compel political Equality.

7th. With the conflict of State Rights and the principle of Inequality, with the national bases, functions, and unity.

And lastly, With the final casting out of oligarchy secured by the recent war.

THE FEDERAL REPUBLIC has been made by and depends upon the complete development and due adjustment of the rights and properties of the Individual, State, and Nation.

THE NATION has been made by the (approximate) completion of the universality of its basis, in Education and the Suffrage,—by the adjustment of its relations with the "States," and by the re-vindication of the national Sovereignty, after fifty years of abeyance.

The DEMOCRACY is being made by the completion of Individual Right,—even to the negro. By universal educational *Development*, which secures *association*, which everywhere and always produces Equality, the completion of Freedom.

The REPUBLICAN EMPIRE is established by a settlement of the Principle of Federation on natural and indefeasible grounds. It is this principle of such vast and almost boundless applicability in the future, which suggests a possibility of combination and Unity on a scale never before supposed to be practicable.

Thus it appears that "Nation," "Democracy," and "Federation," fulfil and complement each other. To a given *nationality* are confided by the Supreme the destinies of a certain portion of the Human race. Gradually a mental, moral, and religious Freedom, develops an intensest "individuality" into a universal Statesmanship, makes nation and Government one, and as a *Democracy*, gives to the People entire Freedom, and to the Legislature and Executive its collective wisdom and united Will.

There can be no true Democracy without an educated People: no complete nation that is not also a Democracy: here is at least something like finality in politics, for here are completeness of power and universality of right. Such nations and Democracies can alone enter as Units into still vaster *Federal Unities.*

Thus the making of a nation that is also a Democracy and a Confederation, involves the existence of a completer, a stronger, a sounder, a more comprehensive, and a loftier Unity, than has hitherto been known.

All nationality is a LIVING ORGANISM, and will give all that it hath for its life; but *this* organism is strong in proportion to its vast area and inexhaustible resources, to the complexity of its interrelations and civilization, and to the perfection, simplicity, and universality, of the principle of political Equality and individual preparedness on which it is based.

Democracy requires great things, and it achieves great things, but the world's future is with it. That Federated Democratic Empire has before it a mighty mission, to react upon the world, "and lead its isolated and fragmentary nationalities into a higher unity," involving order, equality, and economy of power,—Freedom, organization, and the lightening of burdens everywhere.

The material, political, and moral elements of America are now completing. Her *material* resources are unequalled. Her *political* power comes of an unrivalled material, political and religious freedom, and *as she has proved*, there is in the whole world no concentration of will so intense, all pervading, and terrible,as that of a Democracy.

The *moral* elements represent permanence and stability. The contest America has waged for national Life, was also a contest for Morality and Principle.

That making also meant the ascendency of the nationality over its two deadly foes, —*materialism* and *oligarchy*. It meant the definitive victory of national Unity not only over law-made *classes* (the vice of the old world), but over sectional and sinister interests supported by "State" power.

It is the NEXT STEP in the world-logic of History, to the English and French Revolutions, which settled on the carcases of Kings, the principle of the right divine of Peoples.

The Royal *Nation* is at last *definitively constituted*. The People sit at last in their own Purple, —with no equal yet in the world, and with no master save their conscience, their reason, and their God. Here then is the platform for a new and indefinite advance in political science and combinations, and in social and Individual well-being.

England halts for want of mature elements of Equality. America *stopped* because the two extremes of politics were both represented in her body politic, and one had got to be destroyed before the nation could advance. The majority in power and value were prepared for self-government. A Section would continue to rule over others, and meanwhile, keep those others in a state in which they could be ruled. Between them was essential war, and from the highest point of view, the nation, before it could proceed, simply had got to destroy the speciality of the section. It did its duty and destroyed it. Broadly speaking, for the nation self-government was a fact, but for the section Slavery was also a fact, and one of the two must destroy the other.

Nor was it a local question only. *It was a question whether Humanity could advance from Christianity to the first self Governed Nation in eighteen hundred years, or whether it must pass through some vast cycle of blood, ruin and reaction, of which those eighteen hundred years may have been but a fraction.*

America has done in four years a work of giants and of ages. Rather, perhaps, all nations and all time had prepared that nation for victory, as she in turn has prepared Victory for all the world and all the Future.

The work before her now is twofold. To complete the destruction of Oligarchy, and the reconciliation of Democracy with Centralisation. Each is but a part of the world involving question of the organisation of Democracy, or the reconciliation of Freedom with order. Obviously the only way to solve this problem is to give to every individual the means of learning to combine the two in himself. The freedom and the fitness for Freedom must be as universal as the concentration of power is intense.

This can only be achieved by a nation fit to receive and determined to possess *political Equality.*

The main object of this work is therefore to trace the Historical Development of that PRINCIPLE OF EQUALITY in Education, in religion, and in politics, entrusted by God to the care and final vindication of the American nation.

Hitherto the world has assumed some inherent antagonism between Freedom and Centralisation. A true Democracy has at last established itself, that not only develops an intenser Centralisation than Despotism ever boasted, but that develops, and also vindicates it, by a completer Freedom than ever before could be permitted.

Freedom had before been shown to be compatible with order. History now goes a step further, and proves that Democratic Equality is the postulate and complement of organised power, that Republican Equality by affirming individual Freedom, consolidates national Unity, and that Federal Republicanism solves the problem of the safe and unlimited increase of an Empire.

But that this principle of Equality,—the last and most important element, nay, the very essence and soul of Democracy, has been tested by a desperate contest, and an irrevocable victory, the world need not have concerned itself much about the mere "Making of the American nation," and its settlement as the mightiest conglomerate of empire History has known.

It is precisely because it is *not* a mere question of territorial expansion, but rather *a settlement by court of ultimate appeal of the final question in politics*, a question affecting all systems and Peoples, the question whether Individuality must for ever give way to Unity, whether Freedom and order can or cannot be reconciled, whether the full Development of the man consists, or is incompatible with the perfectest organisation of the State.

Hitherto Government has always been a compromise (and after some infinitesimal sort—must always be a compromise) between Necessity and Right, between Force and Consent, between Progress and Disease.

The essence of Government is order. Order must reign by force or by consent. If force is used against Right the Government is destroyed. If consent is not yielded to the Right the People perishes. Force is cheap and can be used by the Few; ("anyone," said Cavour, "can govern by martial law.") Consent to bad Government is consent to ruin. Good Government can come only of general Intellectual and moral Development.

Where the Government of the all is good Government, there only are the means and the end both answered, there and there only is Democracy,—there only is a Royal and also a loyal nation.

Broadly and absolutely, then, there are two great elements of interest in this American question; the one of intensest interest to that People; the other of universal interest.

§

Federal Republicanism,—in the true sense of it—a new element in politics, is rendered possible by new manhood and material Developments.

The State, or "State right" system, avoiding the old error of Federations,—the Imperium in Imperio, maintains the proper local element of right, energy, occupation, and dis-centralisation.

This new element would maintain the Balance between, and *has in fact* forcibly adjusted the differences of the parts and the whole, between the *Nation*, "*State*," *and Individual.*

Each State would successfully maintain and be upheld in its *just* local claims by the universal public opinion, and "locality" would thus hold its own against centralisation; each Individual, on the other hand, helping to constitute the *national* opinion and Sovereignty, would also help to set aside and coerce any traitorous abuse of Freedom and "locality," by whatsoever strength supported.

Had the American nation betrayed their trust, chaos would have reigned in political philosophy, and dismay would have smitten all Peoples.

Step by step, tyrannies had been isolated,

weakened, and destroyed, and freedom had matured and advanced towards Equality, but the last and greatest question remained,—whether Equality could ever be adopted as *a principle of Government*, or whether its existence in America was a mere creature of the hour, of the country, or of the race,—part of an immature civilisation and a scattered people. Whether the universal people do verily gravitate towards Democracy, or whether political science has exhausted itself in the mixed constitutional Governments. Whether *nations* as well as Individuals can verily reign, and whether the interests and the rights of "the All" are compatible with a "balanced" and orderly Government.

The result of the American struggle has not confounded but confirmed the conclusions of centuries.

America alone amongst *nations* has appealed to the whole and to the all. Her manhood was developed in Religion, in Politics, and in Education, and under this threefold stimulus and partnership in Democracy, the good and the bad, the North and the South, the Republic and the Oligarchy, grew together, till Lincoln and the Judgment.

And there is this further Law, which is perhaps of the essence of the question,—*those who will not appeal to the all, dare not appeal to the whole.* Those who would not serve *the People*, can only partially develop even the instruments of oppression. Tyrants who do not dwarf, emasculate, corrupt or destroy their agents, have not studied "the Prince," and may be safely trusted to destroy themselves.

Democracy not only appeals to and lives by the complete Development of national manhood, *but it cannot live without it.*

Thus, either by the comparative weakness or the positive evil of systems imperfect or bad, does the cause of the all advance.

Freedom, removed beyond the reach of the enervating traditions and overpowering influence of corporate bodies, Hierarchies, Castes, and Coalitions, hostile to it in Church and in State, develops itself naturally and irresistibly into the principle of Equality. When a nation is free, the Individuals who compose it will always use their freedom to seek after Equality.

DEVELOPMENT (the term Education is corrupted to mean mere learning) and ASSOCIATION are the means whereby mankind advances. The two together give power and unity to the People. They are the premises of which the logical conclusion is EQUALITY.

The History of the world is a struggle for and against these factors of Democracy.

§

And what is all this—but the very actual History of the making of the American nation and Democracy?—two hundred years, compressed in about as many words and seconds. Americans are a nation and search out *Unity*. Americans are a Democracy,—they will have their representation complete. All nations will follow them.

In man are the forces, and they will out. Men

who cannot *see* the necessity, of a gradually completed representation, will feel the *ultima ratio* of revolution, destroying them and their phantasies together. In politics there is no finality but with the all. Democracy is the goal of progress. The fate of selfish and perverse oligarchies, if not their blood, will be upon themselves or upon their children.

"The making of the American nation" and Democracy thus appears to solve Problems which have been propounded in vain since the world began.

These difficulties are inherent in Government, but they affect all questions as to the extension of territory, or the character and value of the nationality, and will at once be appreciated by every reader who will consider how, in every age and Government of the past, centralisation has overpowered individual or provincial rights, or how individual or local self-assertion have destroyed national unity.

Thus, from Despotism to anarchy, from excess of freedom to excess of organisation, the world has swayed, till it had well nigh settled down to disbelief in political perfectibility, and to accept the dangerous heresy—as in France, that a good autocrat is a good *system*,—in England, that a (so called) mixed constitutional Government, is not only the *ne plus ultra* of political science, but really the form of Government under which England is to remain.

At last there comes forth a true Federal Republic

which, after infinite preparation and controversy, is proved to be a nation, and as such is definitively constituted, and proclaims to the world "here is an arrangement which is not a constituted anarchy" (Hegel) like Germany, nor an oligarchy like England, nor an autocracy like France,—which is neither a compromise, a sacrifice, an interregnum, nor an expedient,—which preserves Unity and Individuality, organisation and local rights, not in spite of but by means of each other, by a NEW, but also a *true, a complete, and a natural interpretation of the rights and properties of each.*

It seems to me worth while to turn aside to see this great sight, to see how these things are done in America, and whether and to what extent, they can be repeated elsewhere.

The thing is called FEDERAL REPUBLICANISM. It implies a state of Society in which these things are possible, and it will lead to a complete re-modelling, not of the science, but of the practice of politics.

In the present state of the world's History, and of political science, when hostile Principles are still contending in the West, and conflicting hostile theories are on their trial everywhere;—when the principles of Freedom and Slavery; of the rule of the Collective Reason, or the deputed Power; of virtual and actual representation; of autocracies, Prerogatives, monarchies, oligarchies, privileges, representations, and Democracies, have been submitted to the ultima ratio of nations;—when the latest, the intensest, the strongest, and the worst of oligarchies, is smitten in its Den by the best Democracy that ever existed,—the only one that ever proved its right to exist;—when political dogmas, North and South, have been framed with absolute precision and candour, and urged with the inexorable logic of war; during such a contest, I say, of Principles and Parties, to bring into a focus, to concentrate and organise the essential FACTS respecting the nation and the cause, which occasioned, which maintain, and which will settle the controversy, is, if honestly and carefully performed, a service not without importance in the present, or meaning for the future.

It were a question for ideologists, and as such would have its value, "what were a perfect Government for perfect men?" It is a question for antiquarians, "whether Governments that are passed were suited to nations that are gone?"

The question of questions for living, fighting, and praying men, was lately, whether America was or was not ripe for Democracy; whether America was or was not a nation: With some it is still a question, whether influences which involve the future of the whole world, are or are not now to go forth upon it. Whether the nation, colonised, educated, fitted, prepared, as the child and champion of Democracy, is now to stand up before God and the Peoples, to vindicate or to betray the truth of the unity and equality of the race,—of the force that resides in the Collective Reason of a nation, and in the recuperative energies of free Institutions. Whether America is the last, and the greatest of failures, or the first, the greatest, and the only Rupublic.

The *Americans* are on their trial, not the Principles. Principles are not on their trial,—they are before and after Peoples, eternal, and "patient, because eternal."

Oligarchy has been on its trial since the world began, and has constantly been condemned and respited times without number, simply because "the world's government must be carried on." Democracy rests on Christianity, which taught the natural unity and equality of man, and the means to realise it, and, *as a principle*, Democracy can never go on its trial, till Christianity go with it.

The question in any age, and of any race and form of Government, is, "is the actual form suited to the actual race?" What is the perfect theory as applied to an instructed People, is not the question for uninstructed Peoples, nor ever will be.

Let us then believe in, and rest upon the unchangeable, while we question the questionable, and assail that which ought to be, because it can be, destroyed.

We have seen that the strongest, the completest military, social, and political organisation of oligarchy the world ever knew, has not been strong *enough* to break down the Democracy of America.

We shall see that America is fit for Democracy,

—for that rule by and for the all, to which the world tends as surely as to the judgment!

And knowing what to doubt and what not to doubt,—what to investigate in order to test and destroy, and what to examine in order to exalt and to imitate,—let us also make sure of one thing more,—that the truth can be attained respecting this American nation, and can be attained by us, now. That truth is one and indivisible, that it is made for man and man for it, that it is made to be understood by human reason, and that the collective human reason of an educated nation, is likelier to reduce it to practice, than are the units.

Democracy looks through every man back to that which is behind him—*in him*,—the Soul,—the Infinite,—God.

All other theories look to that which is *about* a man,—his property, his rank, his "qualifications." But these are only questions of *adjustment* and preparation,—as answering the question, "for what instalment of self-goverment is *this* nation ready?

§

America now attains its majority. The hour of its manhood has struck. For a complete nationality it wanted two things;—a thorough application of the principles of Freedom and Equality irrespective of skin-caste, and a more complete administrative unity.

These things the war has provided or is the means of providing. The Slave fight was a "big job." It was the fiery ordeal through which America had to pass from federation to nationality.

"THE SOUTH" has been the occasion; FREEDOM AND EQUALITY of conditions the motive power; and the various NATIONAL UNITIES, the ultimate bases upon which the movement depends.

Two centuries ago England exported that Nation and that Democracy to America,—but it was in retail, in little, in embryo. Nevertheless all but time and numbers, was furnished by this nation, for that.

Usually, Democracy does not make Civilisation, but Civilisation Democracy. There, Freedom and Religion had already made men Priests and Kings unto themselves, and thus completed and planted in the boundless West, Democracy, Civilisation, and Nationality, worked together, and each upon the other, till they produced another English nation, *without* certain institutes of Feudality and relics of Barbarism, certain forms of force or favour in Church and in State still surviving and fastened upon ourselves.

The laws,—economic, moral, and political, that govern nations, reveal, at the present epoch, no limit to American nationality Southward, until central America is reached, the region of Panama, where, whether formally or not, there will be of necessity a real neutralisation between all the living and trading nations of the earth. For Panama will become the greatest thoroughfare, and most important Highway for all nations.

I here, assume, for reasons amply detailed hereafter, that the American nation *is* ready for and worthy of Democracy, and that they are now putting beneath their feet their only dangerous foe,—Oligarchy, with its eldest-born, Slavery. For if Slavery, or any other phase of Oligarchy,—save that natural one which will rise and fall for ever with individual character and talent,—prevail in America, then, there is for it, neither Democracy nor National Unity, but Disunion and foreign alliances, and for other Peoples whose cause it represents, but a return to the vicious inane cycles of the political past.

The American nationality rests now, upon a Unity of Ideas, Circumstances, and Interests; of Race, Language, Literature, Religion, Institution; also upon the natural material unities of its mountain and water systems, and upon the powerful artificial ones, of commerce, coin, banks, post-service, weights and measures, telegraph, rail, and revenue.

The more one knows of the facts of National History,—the more complete one's comprehension of the principles of Statesmanship, the more thorough will be the acquiescence in the irresistible influence of such a combination of all the factors of Nationality.

Nor does the natural Territorial Unity of America stay with the present limits of the nation.

Northwards as Southwards must the propagandism of Freedom and neighbourhood naturally and ultimately extend.

The Lakes of Canada are moving roads,—not barriers. The races and languages of Canada are French as well as English, and as much American as either. American Eagles and English Sovereigns divide the circulation of gold, while the silver coinage is almost exclusively American. The influences that tend to unite Canada with America, if not in name, in reality and substance, may be peaceful and slow, but they are irresistible.

It is notorious how Napoleon, in a tract prepared at Ham, pointed out how a certain spot near Panama possesses all the requisites for a great world-centre of commerce.

I mention elsewhere these ideas of Napoleon III. as to Panama. Similar purposes visited the mighty mind of Pitt, who said, "you must take Panama." But see the sequel as to the necessary effects of this transit on the commerce of the world in favour of America, and see Captain Pim's "Gate of the Pacific," as to the idea that America intends to retain and to monopolise its advantages, and the consequent necessary abandonment by England of Australia, New Zealand, and British Columbia.

The leading facts of this great question have been familiar to everybody but the English, ever since the last century, when the Abbé Raynal wrote,—"Some careful observers affirm that a quiet possession of the Mosquito country would one day be more valuable to Great Britain than all the Islands which that nation possesses in the West Indies."

It is a strange comment on English "Statesmanship" that with the keys of the Gates of the East and of the West, of Suez and Panama, in the hands of her possible enemies, England makes no worthy effort at *neutralisation* of transit routes.

The master of Mexico would of course control the Tehuantepec route, and his power in respect to the other two passages cannot fail to be enormous. According to a report presented to Congress and hereafter referred to, the securing to Americans the Panama passage will give to much of the American Pacific commerce, an advantage equal to fourteen thousand miles, as compared with the old relations between American and English shipping.

"When in the History of all time," we may well ask with Buchanan (Message, January, 1861), "when has a confederacy been bound together by such strong ties of mutual interest. Each portion of it is dependent upon all, and all upon each portion for prosperity and domestic security. Free trade throughout the whole supplies the wants of one from the productions of another, and scatters wealth everywhere."

And the political standpoint is still stronger, now that Slavery is dead,—

"The question then is," says Mill (Representative Government, p. 310), "whether the different parts of a nation require to be governed in a way so essentially different, that it is not probable the same Legislature and the same ministry or administrative body will give satisfaction to them all, unless this be the case, which is a question of fact, *it is better for them to be completely united*."

And in this view it should be remembered, that, although the rebellion began with fraud and conspiracy against the Union, with Lynch law and compulsion on the majority of Southerners, and in violation of the State Constitutions,—yet the necessities of war, its intense purpose, its absolute discipline, its supreme devotion to an idea, and the habitual dedication of life itself to a cause,—may have educated many Southern partisans to a height of character in direct contrast with their cause. Let others sing the glories of the chivalry that fights for human wrongs; we acknowledge with thankfulness, that the nation of negroes can never now be used as the labour basis of the far South, —*that they are identified with the American nation, and the cause of freedom*,—that instead of being available for a future slave empire, they will carry, as they only could, a propagandism of freedom into warmer latitudes that "may be hereafter acquired" *for the nation.*

The great fighting South was the intensest concentration of Power for evil, since Satan sat on his burning throne, and his legions were still for war! It was the most complete administrative military Despotism that ever existed, but it had opposed to it the Genius and Individuality of the Teutonic race,—the Democracy, the Law and Freedom loving race, which will have before all things equal social and political conditions,—the great Puritan race which never had a conqueror and never will. The Norman race, the Cavaliers, the race that cares not for inequality, if splendidly led, was beaten in England by that other, and it has gone to America only to be still further depleted by the larger emigration of Puritans, by the Negroes, and by ever repeated additions of the German stock. The South was an Oligarchy organising a Democracy, hence its strength and its weakness. It had against it ultimately the natural race-tendency of the ideas of the majority of the American people, the greater strength of the Puritan ideal, and its superior wealth, equipment, and population.

The South was strong. It organised and fought as a Slaveholding Oligarchy only can. It led a Democracy that could fight as men of Individual thought and action do. It fails because there is such a thing as moral, industrial, social, and political propagandism, and because between it and the North, there is no adequate difference of race, language, or institution, boundary, climate, or Religion.

§

A word here upon two other subjects. First, why has the rule of the All not produced even *better* "Government" in America? Second, why have not "civil rights" been more completely acted upon there in the matter of "Equality?" I mean during some thirty years before the war.

To the first question I answer, "Democracy has failed only so far as its postulates have not been granted."

Democracy demands development. Americans have, to a certain extent, been partially educated, *uneducated*, and *wrongly educated.* As far as the cause prevails the result follows.

The South, a third part in numbers, has been *wrongly*, perversely, educated. Another large division has been *partially* educated, by and for frontier life. Immigrants are often partially educated, uneducated, and wrongly educated. In a word, Democracy fails where it is not Democracy. Other systems fail, because *they are* those systems.

This mis-development of the South has poisoned the last sixty years of National History, and the balance of parties, North and South, Democrats and Republicans, lent, from the question of President downwards, a factitious value to compromises, "availabilities" and intrigues.

This contrary principle—the principle of Oligarchy in Politics and in Society—gathered itself up against Equality, and until that mighty issue is tried *out*, minor ones must wait.

> " 'Tis dangerous when a meaner nature comes
> " Between the pass and fell incensed points
> " Of mighty opposites."

Slavery and Oligarchy not only warred directly against Freedom, but they warred against the intellect and progress of the country which was for many years organised almost exclusively in reference to this one question.

§

The same reasons might be alleged for any imperfect apprehension of the right use of Equality.

But the leading cause doubtless is that America has, throughout her entire existence, waged a war of opinion, diplomacy, or arms, for Equality, against all opponents. War for a Principle, is not favourable to criticism of it. In its mighty reaction against an Inequality of four thousand years, it has been concerned chiefly to assert Equality,—Equality the great fountain of intellectual development. And as for the last thirty years the greatest foes of Equality have been certain American factions, the question actually considered in American politics has been, not who is the ablest statesman, but who will best promote or oppose the progress of Slavery and Oligarchy. The next step will now be to distinguish and to organise, and in organising to allow to governing qualities and to governing intellects their proper and natural rank and place.

The American Declaration of Independence but enunciated the theory, its revolution but vindicated the fact, towards which all history had been gravitating—the fact of the political equality of the race. That great People has now again vindicated the conclusions of History and the Title

Deeds of the Republic. It took four thousand years, and the raw material of scores of other nations to make this royal one, and three thousand miles of sea were not too much to keep the Holy Alliance from its throat.

How, after the *principle* of Equality is seen to be absolutely safe, the practice of it may be rectified by a truer interpretation of the principle itself; how the nation will settle down after assured victory, we know not. But *this* we know, that, if at the present epoch it be found that ignorance prevents Equality from being universal, ignorance will speedily be banished, and that a universal statesmanship will reconcile Freedom and Equality, by reconciling opinion with truth. Whatever else she does, America will not go back to Oligarchy.

The results of national life are cumulative, and it is not for nothing that the Anglo-American nation has been true to the principles of its origin through every trial that the Forces of Evil have been able to stir up against it from within or from without.

There is an age for all things. Oligarchy is a necessity of the infancy of States. Democracy belongs to their manhood, and is possible as soon as the majority of Individuals possess the governing qualities.

"Order is the first law of earth;" and because until now, the world has usually seen Individuality bow to the necessities of law, it forgets that the only warrant of Law is necessity, and that *any* rule of the Few can only be provisional. Order was made for man; not man for order.

But to have established, however roughly and imperfectly, the fact, towards which all things from creation have gravitated, that a nation can exist on the Principle of Equality in the threefold relationships of man to the Spiritual, the Political, and the Social—this, were America sunk in the ocean to-morrow, or were the "chivalry" of the dark ages again to assail it, and with success,—this, I say, is the greatest (secular) conclusion respecting the Progress of the species, and the science of Human advancement, ever yet settled in Politics.

The National salvation has been worked out at the fearful cost predicted, and almost imprecated by one of the greatest of Americans.*

* Mr. Adams had repeatedly and almost alone assailed the 21st, or Gag Rule, which denied the right of petition against Slavery. In 1843 he spoke of the Government as having become *the most perfect despotism in the Christian world.*

It was only two years before (1841) that Mr. Adams had been assailed by an organised attempt to destroy his influence by a vote of censure of the House, on a question of petition, but he commenced his defence in a manner which showed it would cover the whole question of Slavery, referring to the precedent of Burke and Warren Hastings, and pledged himself to close his defence as soon as possible consistently with duty,—probably in *ninety days.* This opened the eyes of the Slave party, and they moved to table the question.

Such was the effect of Adams's eloquence on this occasion, that one of his assailants, who had risen to confront him, unconsciously retained his position like a "standing corpse," after Adams had concluded, and with no other sign of life

§

Well has it been said that, "for the first time in the whole History of the Human Race, a people

than a nervous tremor, which pervaded his system. This assailant afterwards said of another,—"Well, if Keim has fallen into old Adams's hands, *may God have mercy on his soul.*"

It was during the debate, in 1843, that an incidental remark was made by Mr. Adams, that was often quoted in subsequent years. Mr. Dillett, of Alabama, a man of age and of talents above the mediocrity of members, was speaking upon this report. Like other Representatives from the South, he appeared anxious to assail Mr. Adams. He held in his hand the report of a speech delivered by the object of his assault to the coloured people of Pittsburg, Pennsylvania. From this he read the following passage:—"We know that the day of your redemption must come. The time and the manner of its coming we know not. It may come in peace, or it may come in blood; but, *whether in peace or in blood*, let it come."

Having read this sentence, he invoked attention to it, and in order that all might appreciate it, he read it a second time; and as his voice died away, Mr. Adams, in his seat, with peculiar emphasis, added, "*I say now, let it come.*" Dillett, apparently indignant at what he regarded the audacity of Mr. Adams, added, "Yes, the gentleman now says let it come, though it cost the blood of thousands of white men." To which Mr. Adams rejoined: "*Though it cost the blood of millions of white men, let it come; let justice be done though the heavens fall!*"

These words rose from the lips of the aged patriot like the prayer of faith from one of heaven's anointed prophets. A sensation of terror ran through the ranks of the Slaveholders. Dillett stood apparently lost in astonishment, and all were silent and solemn until the Speaker awoke members to the subject before them by declaring, "*the gentleman from Massachusetts is out of order.*"—[Gidding's History of the Rebellion, its Authors and Causes. Pp. 167—9, 217—18.]

to the extent of twenty millions, have risen up and said,—'we will forfeit our prestige before the world; we will jeopard our name even as a great republic; we will run the risk even of a terrible civil war, such as the world has never seen; we will do all this sooner than we will suffer that human slavery shall be extended one inch.'"

If America fall from Equality to Oligarchy, she must fall after her greatest sacrifices for the right, she must fall through two hundred years of History, she will carry with her to destruction the culminating hopes of the future, and leave the greatest of all political problems to be solved by some more favoured nation.

Such fears respecting American Destiny are the very drunkenness of folly. Nations never die but by Suicide, and America has but just given proof of a renovated morality and life.

But the full consideration of these questions belongs to a work especially on "Democracy," in which I have attempted their discussion.

§

Now that a Democratic nation is established, the pace of politics will be a very different affair. It will be seen throughout the world that Democracy *must* prevail; it will be settled that *education* shall prepare for it.

That which alone can guarantee good and equal government in permanence, will also render impossible *that hitherto immutable political situation*, a successful alliance between the positively and the negatively bad, between those who profit by partial rule, and those who hope to profit by it.

When a sufficient number of the All possess power, that of the sections will vanish, and instead of some ridiculous sort of protestantism in politics, we shall have (politically) a wholesome *destruction* of the genus "Whig," whilst Toryism will then be outnumbered and outvoted.

In America, oligarchs and slaveholders could neither have intrigued nor fought without the "Democrats." In England the "Quarterly" preaches actual war against Democracy; but just as the South waited too long, until Republicanism and free Labour had demoralised the Border States, and cast the Balance of Power against it, so, in like manner, has Toryism already lost the day. And the eras correspond. The "Quarterly" and the Slaveholders should both have gone to war before 1832, before Equality, which has gained since then victory upon victory, was either properly organised or adequately led.

Equality and oligarchy can never long co-exist in any country. Where the bases of Development, Free School, Press, Church, and Assembly, can be made sure, there the rule of minorities is impossible, and the triumph of Equality is guaranteed by Nature, History, and God.

The principle of "Equality of conditions," which

is also the master passion of America, is the great antagonist of the South, of Secession, and of Oligarchy.

Had the war ended without a victory, this passion and principle of Equality would effectually, and in due course, by the quiet resistless energies of its propagandism, destroy Oligarchy.

It is a stock remark that Celts love Equality, but will tolerate Despotism ; and that Teutons will have Freedom, will *not* have Despotism, but will put up with privileged orders, and unequal conditions.

The perfecting mongrel breed of America will have neither Despotism nor Inequality,—but the latter they hate with a perfect hatred.

Nothing can oppose itself to the ultimate progress in America, of Freedom and Equality.

The Education, self-restraint, and Loyalty of American Democracy, are a guarantee that "equal conditions" will be abiding amongst them, and with these neither Slavery nor any other political phase of Oligarchy can co-exist.

In the American constitution Slavery existed as a fact,—Freedom as a Principle. The Nation could attain its due proportions only as the principle of Freedom should destroy the fact of Slavery,—first of the body, and progressively of Intellect and Soul.

Had Slavery not been in the *nation*, this war had not been. "The war" simply showed that the nation was on its promotion. That it was going to be neither a failure nor a suicide. That it must dispose of its barbarous and factious Slave growth, before it could prove and complement its *nationality*, and "mount up higher."

"The world hath passed me like a ship at sea," must be somewhat the feeling of all who have discussed or regarded this question, not believing in American Nationality.

Impertinence has chased impertinence, and every point raised by ignorance and kept by presumption has run its career, and died its natural death, but those questions only that relate to the present and future of the nation, remain.

"Well, he could hardly have missed it if he kept on," was the comment of a Yankee upon the discovery of America by Columbus.

The foundations of the Nation are as broad and as solid as those of the Continent, and the supposition that such a nation could be swept away or dismembered by such a rebellion, as that which has just been subdued, was always regarded by me as one of the most marvellous of all intellectual heresies. Such a conclusion proves a wide spread ignorance not only of the essential facts, and special constituent elements of the American nation, but of the conditions and meaning of Nationality generally.

I should have thought it easier far, to sail westward for ever from Europe, and yet to miss America, than, comprehending anything of what is a "Nation," and especially of the glorious proportions and majestic strength of the American nation, to assume that it could fall away in its early youth, with its world-work undone, and time-tasks unperformed.

The man does not live, who could worthily describe that Nation, or unfold its unmatched resources. But who can follow its History, from its source in the Democratic Puritanism of middle-class England,--see how it loved to think, and yearned to worship,—trace its struggles for Individual, Municipal, and National rights,—read its Declaration,—mark its spontaneous reconstruction,—read its claims upon "the immutable "laws of human nature, and the traditions of "English immunities,"—note how the Godlike contagion of its ideas swept back over Europe, till it lighted up in the North those flames of Moscow that might indeed have been "the Aurora of the liberties of all Peoples,"—mark its combination of entire Freedom with intense Loyalty, its thirty years struggle against Slavery, its final Battle for Freedom and Nationality in one, the preludes of its second Reconstruction under the auspices of its great Puritan President, and how Action and Reaction every where wait for its issues,—who, I ask, can see, and know, and understand these things, and doubt of American *Democracy or Nationality*, without doubting also of all other Histories, Philosophies, Moralities, Principles, and Facts, together?

Democrats and Conservatives, Copperheads and the South, will doubtless endeavour to reinstate the situation which formerly gave *power* to the South, and *place* to Democrats. If they succeed before the negro can receive the suffrage, they may virtually *reinstate the rebellion.*

To this end they may use the question of the Southern debt or of the negro suffrage, as a platform to unite upon, and if Southern Freedom be acknowledged without guarantees for Negro Equality, then the Principle of the war, and of the National History and life will have been surrendered.

The North however is strong enough and clear enough to insist upon Negro Equality,—the best free labour propagandism—not only as a principle, but as a material guarantee of victory. *Until that be attained no peace or settlement is possible*, and the basis of representation will remain an open question.

The life of a nation is an organic whole, and the science of politics is absolute, and as far from doubt as from fear. The American nation will be true to the principles of its origin, life and progress. To reinstate the rebellion would be but to reinstate its defeat.

A nation that has been created for Equality, organised on Equality, and that has fought the great battle of its life for Equality, *cannot* reverse its habitudes except through a process constantly repeated and indefinitely prolonged. All precedents confirm the conclusion that America will complete her *Equality* as between Individuals, her *Freedom* as between Individuals and the State, her *adjustments* as between State and Nation, her strength and *coherence* as a National and Federative Unity.

It was in 1775 that John Adams spoke of that "*alteration of Southern constitutions* which must certainly take place if this war continues, and will gradually bring all the continent nearer and *nearer to each other in all respects*." The latent war of passions and ideas will continue for a time. In that war the weapons of the North and of the nation, are, in a word, all the elements of prosperity let loose during the last five years. The march of ideas and of interests, of that Education which in the last century Jefferson sought to carry into the South, the propagandism of free labour and free thought,—*the Americanising of the South*,—is a process from which the South can never extricate itself save by cutting itself adrift from that continent. Free Ideas, capital and labour, will carry Equality into the heart of the South, and will overwhelm and destroy Inequality in the North,—the irrepressible conflict must be settled.

The Border States are now the North, and *Republicanism will be both Government and nation.*

But to glance for a moment at the highest view, it must be admitted that there is after all no finality in mere politics. Democracy is more than Politics, and has to do with manhood. The development and organisation of the whole as to the Individual, and of the All as to numbers, is the completed work of Democracy, and the energies of States have finally to be transferred from old world questions of protection of rights, to those of new developments and combinations of power. We train the material, mental, and moral manhood of nations, that, having thus worked out and *through* political questions, we may concentrate manhood upon itself.

This then is the final justification of politics, it prepares the platform upon which man may be prepared for the Infinite.

As I have said, the steps by which *nations* advance are Development,—Association,—Equality. What may be the struggles by which this progress is to be consummated, is with futurity; we behold, not in nations, but in HUMANITY, the final unity, in Individual and National Development, its preparation; and in the Federal Principle, its formal bond. And doubtless *the completion of this first nation upon the basis of individual political Equality, secures the next great step in the series along which Humanity has to advance.*

REFORM CLUB,
May, 1866.

INTRODUCTION.

"THE gradual development of the equality of conditions, is therefore a providential fact, and it possesses all the characteristics of a *Divine decree:* it is universal, it is durable, it constantly eludes all human interference, and all events as well as all men contribute to its progress.

The whole book which is here offered to the public, has been written under the impression of a kind of *religious dread* produced in the author's mind by the contemplation of *so irresistible a revolution,* which has advanced for centuries in spite of such amazing obstacles, and which is still proceeding in the midst of the ruins it has made.

I know without a special revelation, that the planets move in the orbits traced by the Creator's finger. * * * *

If the men of our time were led by attentive observation and by sincere reflection, to acknowledge that the gradual and progressive development of social equality is at once the past and future of their history, this solitary truth would confer the sacred character of a divine decree upon the change. *To attempt to check Democracy would be in that case to resist the will of God.*"

De Tocqueville, p. 21, *Introduction.*

B

CONTENTS.

In reasoning upon great national questions there are five errors against which we must guard.

By the first, men exalt the material means and issues, above the moral. They put armies before opinion.

The second, is that they make no allowance for the momentum of ideas, and of passions, in great crises. — For the logic, which having committed men to a side, carries them on to lengths they did not intend; for the enthusiasm of great assemblies and a common cause, and the passion that hurls men on to conclusions. Men who are pledged for life or death, will always *destroy or use* the men who cannot act with equal energy and decision, on the one side or the other.

The third, is to forget the *perspective* of events, and allow the present to overshadow the future, without giving to either its true significance.

The fourth, is a false ideal of that complex and marvellous thing — national life. He who knows not somewhat of the *organic whole*,—of the essential facts of a nation's history, can form no sound theory of political causation,—*has no right to any opinion*, either on its present or its future, or on the value or *relative* significance of any particular fact.

But the worst and most childish error of all, would be to suppose that the leading men of a section, however large, of a country with unity of race, language, institutions, boundary, and religion, *can, at will*, constitute it a kind of Banyan-tree nationality, and wipe out and reverse, even by an agony of volition, the results of the past centuries, or the overruling facts of the present age.

We have no ambition to write for those who assume, that because the republican "experiment" has been attacked,—therefore it has failed, or that because it is being tried, — therefore it is condemned.

The American constitution and nation, are to be judged by theory or by result. Men who judge by result must wait for it. But neither theory nor fact can possibly condemn a nation, because it has had once in its life, a three years' rebellion, which after three years is still only a rebellion.

Judged by facts which shew its strength, and considering that it started without Generals, and organisation, against a foe well led and disciplined, we may say that the sheer fighting force, fidelity, and Patriotism, of American Democracy, have done a work not unworthy to compare with the results of even Napoleon's campaigns, and this either in improvement in discipline and Generalship, the number of men under arms, the numbers of rebels put *hors de combat*, the strategic value of positions gained, or the mighty reach of territory reconquered.

In character and national morality the progress is still greater.

Why then should it be supposed that there can be two American nations, in America?

Is it an old and common thing on the earth, for a nation of one race, language, Boundary, Institution, and religion, suddenly to fall in twain at the summons of any power or interest whatsoever?

It may be said "There must be some leaven "working in the South that we know not of." We answer, this is but the delusion of those who *will* not believe that the South is defeated till they know that it is destroyed.

Let those who have studied and learnt the meaning of the word "NATION"—its tenacity and intensity, and who know by precedent, how only one or two of the above named Unities, have defied all disintegrating energies for ages, and at last conquered them—answer, — why the contrary result should happen in America,—and give their reasons.

True, there is a vague idea that North America is "too large for one nation," and people have heard men scoff at the "Heaven-invented constitution of America," till they think themselves entitled to assume that it does *not* contain any new invention in Statesmanship,—that it is *not* calculated to hold together vast conglomerations of men, and thus they make *their* false subscriptions,—as other honest and God fearing men, without being able even to define that to which they subscribe.

> " Lie nods to lie, each falsehood has it brother,
> And half the foolish thing reflects the other."

One might have supposed that the obvious and marvellous intensity of the nationality in question, and its obvious and marvellous Territorial Unity, might counteract, even with those who only regard the surface, the idea that " America is too large for one nation." America is larger than other countries !—well, and is not the nationality more intense, and the unity of territory more obvious and complete ?

But further, do we not know that the phantom nationality of the South, exactly coincides with the interests of *avarice*, *lust*, and *oligarchy*, that give to the South its desperate purpose, and relentless grasp ? The combined energies of *Proprietors* accustomed to use up the labour and life of slaves, and enabled by their monopoly to charge the balance of the Slave's loss on the rest of the world ; of Libertines who had a monopoly in Lust, as well as in Cotton, and want to keep both ; of Oligarchs who by the nature of the cotton trade, and the whole nature and necessities of their position, were accustomed to despise and *use* the common people ; —are not all these we ask, more than enough to account for the rebellion ?

And finally, were all the precedents and conclusions of all the rebellions of the world reversed, is it of no account that America is the country of the common People,—a country which this rebellion would dismember, and a people it would disfranchise; the nation, of which the great writer on Democracy, declares, that they will destroy all attempts at introducing "unequal conditions"? It is a nation of refugees from oligarchies in Europe, and *they* are scarcely the nation to offer to oligarchy an asylum *there*.

Many, however, will never learn what *is* a nation, of which every member possesses his full rights, and a stake in the progress and conservatism of the country, until the lesson is forced upon them by the success of the American nation. That lesson the world wants every way.

To others, it will suffice to remember the guarantees of freedom, of equality of conditions, of municipal rights, and therefore of nationality, which are *new and special* to America.

Either that part of the American nation, called the South, will retain Slavery, or will relinquish it. If it retain it, without the former monopolies, it will be destroyed by it. If it relinquish it, it abandons the only real barrier and speciality, that can separate between it, and the rest of the nation.

The South finds itself in this dilemma.—Of two things one,—Slavery will remain, or cease. If it remain, it will destroy the South, for there will be now no partnership with the free North, to mitigate the natural results, economic, social, or political, of Slavery. If Slavery fail, and fall away, then there will remain no distinctive interest or characteristic, strong enough to encounter the propagandism of free Northern influences, and of oneness of race, institution, language, boundary, and religion. Slavery could not *exist* without creating an oligarchy, with all its worst peculiarities, and binding it up in indissoluble bonds of interest, caste, and character, with the mean white. Slavery, in America, could not *fail*, without leaving oligarchy for execution. Therefore either Slavery will remain, and destroy the South,—or it will fall away, and leave its distinctive features and class interests to perish.

What then is the *raison d'être* and meaning of the rebellion?—The rebellion is a result, and a cause. The gradual growth of Individual freedom and national power, compelled Slavery to choose between a constitutional, and a violent Death. It chose the latter.

But the South was also a cause. The principles of national authority and personal freedom demanded their completion. What should accomplish it? The North was to be chastised for complicity with Southern crime. What was to be the instrument of chastisement? Slavery was to be destroyed, with or without the South. What was to be the agency? Vengeance was to descend on the South. Through whom? Why the completing of American nationality,—the chastisement of northern complicity,—the destruction of slavery,—the avenger of the negro,—were all to be found in the idea of NATIONALITY which held fast the South in strong delusion or in strong pretence. It visited the North with war, and the South with war, and pestilence, and famine. And Jeff. Davis *has* assisted at the "making of a nation,"—but that "nation" is *not* "the South."

The South will always command in history a strong *antiquarian* interest, but when Jeff. Davis and his three Demons pestilence, famine, and war, shall have swept the South clear, or when the thunders and lightnings of the North shall have destroyed cities, compared with which, Sodom was chaste, and Gomorrah clean,—then, also, antiquated reputations will expire by the score in England, and new reputations, also, that might otherwise have lived and flourished, will fall still-born and dead.

No man who misunderstands Democracy in America can hope either to be believed, understood, or trusted, as a leader of Liberalism in England.

It is not even true that the American "Constitution is in danger," in the ordinary sense of the words. It is contrarywise true, that no Government on the face of the earth is *less* on its trial, than is the American.

Every constitution is in danger, when the nation advances beyond it to great conquests in morality, in social science, and in Statesmanship. But even this advance is not revolutionary in America, for the nation but returns to the *raison d'être*, sanctions, and origin of the nationality, and to the Declaration, its first authentic formula.

The constitution is in danger of being saved. It is rescued from pettyfoggers, and interpreted largely and loyally, by the context of the events of that age, and the characters and interests of the founders; and shall a miserable constitution-monger tell us that salvation is "danger," and that to bring that formula up to the nation, and back to its title deeds, is "destruction?" We say there is so little truth in such assertions that it is impossible to make even good lies out of them. It were as reasonable to complain that a Sinner is in danger when he is saved, –because he is transformed into a Saint.

Those who exclaim against this danger to the constitution, either believe that Slavery was matter of municipal law, or national. If they say it was matter of municipal law only, and that the nation could not take cognizance of it, then they challenge in one breath the deepest law and fundamental right of the nation's existence, and deny to it also the right of self-preservation,—for the nation exists as the champion of freedom, and it can only continue to exist as it destroys slavery. If they say it is matter of national concern and action,—so says the North.

If they arraign Northern interpretation, they cannot arraign its action, unless they either deny that Slavery is a national danger, or that a nation has a right to save itself.

We leave such men to the superb disdain of a Mirabeau,—quoting the Roman. They taunted him with violating forms. He ended the debate and the argument, with,—"Gentlemen, I swear that I have saved France!"

How else can we address such men? It is the crime of Lincoln *not* that he thrusts at Slavery through the Constitution, but that he saves America, and vindicates Democracy.

§

But while Democracy is surely triumphing in America, Democracy in England is hesitating, inconsistent, and divided, and it is fronted by the corporate unities of various monopolies in Church and in State, and by divers relics of Barbarism, still strongly entrenched behind their strongholds of Feudality. It is branded as "uncertain, enfeebled, debauched." In this situation, the best service that can be rendered to progress in England, is to make clear to Englishmen, the Principles, meaning, and results of the great Democratic revolution in the west, where popular institutions have a clear field, and to shew that all there that tends to revolution, is of oligarchy, Slavery, and a spurious Democracy, and that Conservatism and Radicalism, order and the People, march hand in hand to the destruction of these their ancient enemies, with a step that neither hastens nor rests, and a purpose that cannot vacillate.

The great writer on American Democracy has remarked, that complex ideas have no chance, in the popular mind, against simple ones. A simple and plausible proposition, essentially false, will often be accepted rather than a complex and involved statement of the truth.

"Slavery" is one of these "simplicities." Nobody, except Mr. Spence and Exeter Hall, wants to have it *proved* that Slavery is wrong. But it is clear that the Sin of it attaches somewhere, and accordingly, partisans distribute the responsibility North or South, as their knowledge and wisdom, prejudices, or ignorance, may dictate. The question of responsibility involves dates and facts, patience and judgment, and so it comes to pass that we have ninety-and-nine men stirring up this main sewer of the South, and the hundredth, perhaps, really able to shew how the South has sinned, and how far the complicity of the North has and has *not* extended.

The "Heaven and Hell amalgamation Society" didn't answer in America, though Clay was its chairman, and Douglas its "vice." Its members quarrelled. But Democracy will have settled it all, and expelled the evil one, and started again, almost before "Civis Romanus" has discovered that the English people don't approve of interference, even in a piratical, indirect, and unlawful shape.

The Heaven and Hell amalgamation Society didn't answer in America. How should it? There it came at once into collision with human nature, and was not bolstered up by all sorts of interests, monopolies, and corporations, sole, multitudinous, or international, of Priest, Despot, or Holy Alliance. America is not tied down to the Past, by institutions that prevail by physical force, that cannot express what they mean to modern minds, and that, if they could, would speak the jargon, the superstitions, or the necessities of the dark ages.

From 1777 to 1833,—56 years,—was the lease America gave to slavery, and then the building began to fall in upon the Slaveholders. Eighteen hundred years has Europe had, since Paul preached on Mars' Hill, and Christian slaves were tortured in Nero's Garden, and, on the whole, Europe is still an inextricable den of slaves and Despots, and "non-intervention," the best that England can do to help it.

America has done evil and has suffered, but for Europe to reprove her for fifty years of compromise, as against its own eighteen hundred, is like Satan reproving Saints for sin.

When the old and badly whitewashed sepulchre shall have been first cleansed of its own dead men's bones and rottenness, it will be time enough for

Europeans to turn out and laugh at the undertakers, who are carrying the last great national sin of America to an early grave.

"Independence" is another instance of the one-sidedness of which we complain. Every body is ready to shout for it. Every body believes in it. It involves the question of nationality, which is a "jargon" or a philosophy,—as the case may be. To investigate any *particular* case is a very different matter. It requires reading, research, statesmanship. It involves that rare combination, —passion for the right, and judicial appreciation of facts and Principles.

It is our intention, then, to thrust back on the one side, the sensationists who shriek against Slavery, without teaching who fastened and *fastens* it, on the American nation, or how it is to be destroyed; and, on the other, the sensationists who shriek for Southern "Independence," without understanding that other question upon which it depends,—the question of the anti-Slavery morality and martyrdom, the morality, unity, Integrity, and Intensity, of the mighty American nation, the completest, and the strongest secular agent God ever created, and which, having set its face towards the right, cannot be crushed, dissolved, or divided, by any power human or infernal.

It will be our endeavour, for the benefit of political infidels, to shew how the puzzle of the American nationality was put together, and what it is, that henceforth they may not vainly imagine the possibility of its being taken to pieces by "the South."

In the minds of men who have won the right to

an opinion, there need be no doubt about the character and prospects of the respective forces now contending upon American soil.

Indeed the chapter on "the false nation" will soon possess that antiquarian interest, of which we spoke, as shewing that parties once existed in England, whose belief in the "nationality" and success of the South, it was necessary to combat.

Politics is a science, not guesswork. We know what is a "nation," and what is *not* a nation, by signs which stupidity or carelessness alone could not succeed in mistaking.

The science of Politics knows only three elements of national existence;—The material Unity and Ethnical force, of Geography or climate. The Man. The Institution.

In the two latter items, the American struggle is accomplishing, or demonstrating the progress of a radical revolution that will affect all Men, Institutions, Nations, and Governments.

For the "Man," the principles of Freedom and of Loyalty are being tested and complemented. The American citizen is learning to admit the equal manhood of the Black, to crush out that anarchy which calls itself Freedom, and to submit himself to that administrative unity which war demands, and which the nation needs.

The "Sovereign State," is learning, that in America, the future can contain no probable conditions of success, for a State that attacks at once the Interests of the Individual, and the rights of Government. It knows full well, that never again in America will a rebellion be backed up by a mighty and enthralling class interest, coincident with a large and well defined territory. It is the Individual who rules both "State," and nation by universal suffrage. His municipal interests are distinct from his national interests. As member of a "State," he will guard the first. As the unit of a nation he will guard the last. And as the nation increases in power and glory, his sentiment of nationality will increase in intensity and force, whilst his municipal rights will become more particular and defined.

The "Nation," is learning and teaching the world, the strength of a nation of free men and free Institutions. And the world is learning the counterpart lesson, that the era of Intervention against the Peoples is past, and that though oligarchy itself be endangered by the contagious influences of a successful Democracy, it will only aggravate and precipitate the danger, to attempt to use the People of the old countries against the Government of the people of the new. It is "Americans for America, and America for the Americans."

§

But before we get involved in the discussion of items of power so tremendous, let us pause at the threshold to take a deeper view yet of two of them. —Of the PEOPLE who constitute or utilise each element, material, Intellectual or spiritual; and of the PRINCIPLES which create Institutions, which guide or destroy men and nation, and constitute the decisive element in every contest. We have lately been told* that "the modern mind, "staggers under the weight of accumulated facts,

* Phillimore's George III.

" which it has neither the strength to grasp, nor the " sagacity to methodise," yet above the tempest of Battle there, and the unresting sea of speculation here, there is a *science* of Politics,—there are, thank God, Principles, which stand like the everlasting mountains, and there are facts that fit beyond dispute the precedents of the past. These principles of Statesmanship and morality, stand above the turmoil of the present,—

> " as stand the Stars o'er thunder,"

and no man bent on the clear seeing, strong feeling, and whole telling, of the truth, and who studies causes and not results, need mistake *igni fatui* for principle.

The answer to the question, " what is a given " nation ?" depends on the answer to another question,—" what are its MEN ?" Every man sees how the strength of a nation, at any given time, must depend upon the average strength at that time, of the Individual man. Its character upon his character. Its Intellect upon his Intellect. Its highest, completest, sublimest efforts, upon his spiritual elevation and power.

But the net political result,—how a full proportion of Physical stamina and strength, of Morality, of Intellect, of Spiritual energies,—all working together, must bring about *such a grand total of power, purity, and completeness*, as the world has not seen yet,—this the world is not prepared to appreciate, precisely because, perhaps, it *has*, as yet, neither seen nor possessed these qualities in a really national sense.

Yet the possession of these qualities in due proportion and subordination, is manifestly the crucial and absolute test of the value of any given nationality,—they *are* its past,—and will *create* its future.

For to know the momentum of a Nation's progress, —Its force of will,—Its moral power,—Its strength in relation to the opposing forces, and to other national entities,—volitions,—progresses,—forces, to know these things, or, in other words, to know aught of the *future* of a nation, we must ascertain *the proportion between all the other qualities and forces of that nation, and that central force which moves and actuates them, namely,—Character or Principle.* This is not anatomy,—but Life. The soul, not the accidents of a people.

The Bases, the Unities, the organic Functions of a nation,—all these should grow, consolidate, and mature; but the spiritual part of a nation, its character, its moral power, its generative force, grows by constant destroyings and constant new creations. It is a battle always beginning, never ending.

The one absolute question for the *future* is,— "Does the spiritual advance with the material?"

If not,—the mortal poison of materialism may but feed upon its strength.

If not,—all the "Unities" may be unities in decay, despair, Death.

If not,—the very strength of its "Executive" may do execution on itself, and its "administration" may administrate Suicide.

Schools, suffrages, institutions, are but means to an end. The end is the advance of the People in spiritual energy and initiative. This is the end of national life. It is also its eternal recommencement.

Without this,—material advancement and appliance; the just balance between the Individual and the Nation; the honor of Nation and Government before the world;—all these have neither guarantee nor aim; *raison d'être*, nor use.

In this matter of Principle, the North was defective, but it has purged its crime, and reversed its action. The South remains inveterate and desperate.

Neither nation, nor constitution, can at any time be more or less than its Men make it. It is only when manhood is shackled or debased by constitutions, that "constitutions are in danger." When the million-folded man-power of a nation elevates itself, it is only the inadequate, the antiquated, or the dangerous part of the constitution, that can be in danger.

The real ultimate question, therefore, is after all, —"*Can the general common people add the fore-*" *thought and self restraint of Legislators, to the*" *energy of a Democracy?*" We can only say they have the best guarantees for this consummation in America, — Education, responsibility, habit, and property. We reply, with De Tocqueville, "it is" by the enjoyment of a dangerous freedom, that" the Americans learn the art of rendering the" dangers of freedom less formidable."

Since the feudal times, how has the number multiplied, of men capable of that combination of self restraint, and energy, which is the secret of dominion! Formerly, it was assumed that only a handful of Gentles,—Statesmen, Churchmen, and Warriors, were thus competent. But what more or what less than these same qualities, have the thousands of the "middle classes" that succeed them in England, or the tens of thousands of the "Common People" in America?

The People's Government there, seems to us to display at least as much submission to authority, as many sacrifices for freedom, as intense a nationality, as *any* Government of their masters.

As long as there is Government by the all,—as long as that Government is wielded, according to the necessity of the situation, for progress and Freedom, we care not though they manufactured constitutions as fast as Greenbacks,—the national life will still progress, and its guarantees will still remain.

But we waste words in arguing this. Man is but a pupil in social science till he has learnt how to govern himself. If the Individual man cannot become fit to be intrusted with his own political destiny, how *can* it be guided and secured? The Americans have already solved the problem, but if it were insoluble, what becomes of human nature and responsibility?

As then the only ultimate question about the fundamental principle of Democracy is so easily answered, it is not a matter for doubt, but for political Infidelity only.

It is thus a question between Democratic and Oligarchic Institutions, and Slavery is only a part of that question.

§

The canker of a long peace,--a peace that was not peace,—a false and adulterous peace,—a peace of compromises and degradation,—a peace that lowered and debased the material, Intellectual, and Spiritual energies of the nation, could not destroy it. If *that* could not, what can?

Such a peace was essential war against the Nation and Society. If it could not destroy the Nation, the Nation will destroy it.

And now, though even the present generation of Americans *consent* to separate,—of two things, one—either the nation, North and South, would gradually fall away, and as a nation perish and decline ; or the propagandism of free labour, of equal political conditions, and of nationality, would gradually supersede, plant out, and destroy "Secesh," with its oligarchic Institutions, its slave labour, its surrender of American soil and influence, and its alliances with the alien.

The present generation arose from out the infamy of the last. The next would have a less steep ascent, and fewer difficulties. The enemy would be without and not within, and all influences would fight for reunion.

Give it but time, and "Squatter Sovereignty" alone would be more than a match for the South.

American Slavery has an epic to itself, and yet is but an episode in the mightier epic of American freedom.

Its episode of eighty years shews its dealings with Man, the *primum mobile* and *ultima ratio* of politics. How it debased him in all his relationships, social and political, and how he, having risen against the wrong, and cast it off, reversed the process of degradation, set right his position and relationships throughout, and ascended to greater heights of citizenship, and freedom, than those from which he had fallen.

The present war is, in fact, the nation's salvation. It rescues it from two mortal dangers,—*materialism* and *slavery*. Had Slavery not been identified with a certain territory and interest,—had it met any other foe than a free democracy,—had it been possible for slavery to amalgamate with the North, the fate of the Nation had then been sealed. Servile vices, (idleness, carelessness, deceit, cowardice, stupidity,) matched by those of the tyrant, (cruelty, avarice, violence, lust, and war,) *would have sunk and lost the American nation, as they have sunk and lost all nations that ever tried them.*

The subtle social and political poison had then decomposed the nation, and eat into its heart, like rottenness into Death.

On this pivot turned, the future of the people, and the fortunes of the Western world.

As God would have it, Slavery could not be domesticated North. Southern genius, leisure, culture, and intellect,—the specialities of the actual Cotton trade, and of Northern Democracy, Puritanism, and Religion, guaranteed war, and not peace. The non extension platform of 1860, claimed life and freedom for the North, whilst the South incorporated essential disease and death into its constitution.

And so the world turns the other way. It is the Slave faction, and not the American nation, that is to be destroyed.

Why then, in conceding national morality to the Americans, deny them its just consequences, or assume that Destiny has a quarrel against them. Why attribute to them the blindness which would keep apart, when their interest is Union, or to their Government or the rebellion, the power to resist the irresistible? The Americans must truly become another people, before any Government there could defy opinion, or challenge the constitutional conditions which express its changes or enact its will.

It is not in the power of any one, or two, generations, to resist or supersede causes and influences so deep-seated, so prolonged, so unanimous, and so universal, as those which have made the American nation, and assured its Nationality and Independence. History contains no example of such a change, and History never before knew either an unity so strong, a sympathy so complete and electric, or a freedom so universal.

It is equally true, that neither slaveholders, nor their followers, and victims, have any pretence to nationality apart from the American nation. It is equally true that their ascendancy can be but temporary, and that the interests of Slave, mean white, and master, are utterly, and absolutely, and essentially, irreconcileable.

The theory of faction and treachery, accounts for all the South has done, or can do.

§

The phrase "United *States*" of America, has a good deal to answer for, and is but another instance, of how much there is, for the majority, in a name.

The completest Nation,—the intensest Nationality under the sun, remains in the European official mind, "as it was in the beginning," scarcely more than a mere league, or association of States, although it has long since surpassed every other nation in all those free and equal conditions of thought, operation, activity, progress, and manhood, which alone are the factors of nations.

The main twofold result of the present contest is obvious, namely, the completion of national Unity, and Individual freedom; the former, through habits engendered by the enforced centralisation of war, the latter by the removal of slavery, its interests, and associations.

Great must have been the pre-existing force and depth of national feeling, great and long matured the strength of Principle, and elevation of character, that took the open issue of abolition at the risk of Disunion.

There is no parallel prima facie case for Southern "nationality." The Slave interest was exactly coincident with the revolt, and it involved intense caste prejudices and overwhelming material interests, which seized upon and absorbed all the resources of the South, and subjected them to the matchless discipline and genius of the two hundred thousand aristocrats who overruled the Union majority in the South, and made the rebellion.

The Slave interest is not "national," for it is contrary to the laws of economics, as well as of morals, and of Statesmanship.

The Slaveholding oligarchy can shew no credentials of national delegation, for the majority was against them, and the strongest passions and primary ideas of the whole American people are those of equality, freedom, nationality and independence, each of which the South would undermine and destroy.

Under any possible circumstances, other than the actual ones of long treasonable preparation, and early success, the idea that the American country and nationality could be permanently affected by an immoral fractional interest, however strong in arms and discipline, would never have been accepted as matter of debate.

Nor, in the last resort, would it be simply a question, whether citizens at all times, and in all places, and in all reverses, would voluntarily support the Government.

The People have elected a Government, voted a war, and created an army, and now the war has a life of its own, a will of its own, a way of its own. It is a life within a life, a power, for a term, above a power, a will, for a term above a will. Unless the *general* will of the people turn against the war, there cannot even be a crisis.

§

There are recognised tests, of strength, and of nationality, which can only be applied by observation of the present, or analysis of the past,—by witnessing present action, and examining History, and chiefly by the latter.

American nationality must be vindicated in respect of;—

Its Territory,—or Geographical Unity.

The "Man,"—his Freedom, Character, and Power.

The "Institutions,"—their Balance, and their adjustment to the National Life.

The Individuality, character, will, resulting from these, and constituting the Unity or aggregate National life.

First; we shall shew,—the Geographical Unity of America, in the chapter so headed.

Second; that Man, the *primum mobile* and *ultima ratio* of all things Human, attains, in America, *his greatest average value*, and mobility, so to speak. That he is completer in himself, and of more effect and value for social or political combination.

Third; the *peculiar Institutional Balance*, established by the "Sovereign State," and by the "Constitution and Genius of America," between the Principles of Freedom and Authority, *i.e.* between the Man and the Government.

Fourth; that America has, on the whole, been conspicuously faithful to the true Principles which are its inner political life, and for the vindication of which it was created,—the principles of Freedom and Democracy. That it therefore makes its title clear to political immortality.

Fifth;—*the result* of these perfected and balanced materials, upon the American nation.

While therefore these pages will prove that the South has no elements of nationality, our chief concern is with that great nation which *it* will assist to establish on eternal foundations. For we find that in the light of those great principles which preside over the destinies of nations, and the evolutions of centuries, and which are indeed of the substance of the future, the Slave power is being used to punish the complicity of America in the

Slave system, and to bring out into greater distinctnesss, and power, the great principle of American nationality,—as involving Individual freedom, administrative centralisation, popular Government, and national morality,—a combination of which America is the chief exponent, and which will crown the glorious edifice of her Democracy.

When the South has done this work, it can have no other. It will fall into contempt, or be dashed into pieces like a potter's vessel.

§

In collating the Facts, which constitute the History of the American nation, and discussing the Principles upon which that nation is to be judged, we have chiefly regarded those which illustrate the process of the growth and consolidation of the central executive, and also of the Freedom and Morality of the Individual, (the unit, there, of Government, as well as of the State.)

The making of the American nation has involved the development and Union of its three great constituent forces and elements.

1st. *Individual Freedom and Equality* as a matter of Economics, and Statesmanship,—of conservatism, of morality, of material prosperity and of political value.

2nd. *Democracy*,—which will secure the power, and Balance, and Unity, of the Government, as a pledge of the power of the people, and as a defiance of intervention from without, and which renders hopeless any insurgent oligarchy, either now, or in the future.

3rd. *Principle*, which has now for forty years,

conducted against Slavery, a war of protest, agitation, martyrdom, and arms.

These forces, deeply rooted in the History, Laws, manners, customs, opinions, and Constitution, of the American nation, render the essential future of America a settled question.

With Freedom completed and balanced,—Democracy rid of its only dangerous enemy, and Equality purged of its only contradiction and weakness, the American nation may be regarded as made,—a glorious and completed agent for the future good of that Continent and the world.

We have been brief where we could, and ample when we must. In some cases mere summary or suggestion of detail, well and generally known, suffices, in others it has been necessary to insist on facts admitted, but scarcely recognised, or recognised but not appreciated.

For instance, in discussing the American Constitution, there are three points on which we would insist again and again.

1st. The *quasi recognition of Slavery*. This has often been denied by the prejudiced portion of the Anti-Slavery party, who therein deny one of the most glorious results of the war, for undoubtedly one of the greatest of the "labours of Lincoln" will be the expunging of Slavery from the Constitution.

2nd. The peculiar political effect of the third great constituent element in American politics, is,—"The *Sovereign State*," which completes the Balance of the Constitution and is the vehicle for one of the intensest passions of America,—the passion for equality. This effect everybody admits, and few appreciate. Otherwise how should we hear so much of the "danger of Despotism" in a land which contains that momentous element,—34 armed and organised nuclei for provincial Independence and Freedom,—How should we hear so much of the "want of a new centre of ambition for active and turbulent Intellects,"—when 34 such centres already exist, of the average size of European kingdoms? &c. &c.

Some men insist on a controversy between the State and the Government (as others, between Free will and Destiny) but there need be nothing but harmony between them.

The 3rd point respecting the constitution, is notorious, but apparently often overlooked by learned and conscientious writers, who treat of it as fixed, rigid, and unalterable. They *will* forget that as the nation possesses legislative functions, it can, in a legitimate way, amend and alter the constitution, and moreover that were organic change essential, there is, apart from the sectional Slave interest, no reason why,—in a country where nothing is deemed venerable that can be improved upon, in a country of the most equal conditions of knowledge and of property, and of the most intelligent political constituency, and the most thorough political organisation also,—such *organic changes should not be peaceably and thoroughly carried out.*

We have said that we are not going to prove Slavery an evil. De Tocqueville said in substance all that has been said since on that score, and there is a proverb beginning—"The more you stir," which always forewarns me from that topic. Persons ignorant of such things should repair to elementary schools. If a man really believes in Slavery, the only way to convert him were to sell him into it. Some men can neither feel, think, nor act, without stimulus, and in this country, the "stirring" has been done so well and vigorously, that we should think even "evangelical" nostrils have had enough. Slavery has certain economic and political results, and with these we, and the American Union, and nation, have to do, because abolition will rid the Union of those results, and because the effort to cast out Slavery will elevate, strengthen, purify, develop, and reconstruct, the nation.

Nor do we want to shew the connection between Slavery and the war. It is self-evident, and is affirmed by secesh ordinances, and by the leaders on both sides. He who doubts it has no right to any opinion on the subject. He has not examined it, or if he has, he is, politically, past printing, preaching, or, praying for.

For our investigation, there is no need of authorities on doubtful points.

We want only and always, History, Insight, and Common Sense.

And the History with which we have here to do, is of two sorts; First, that which is matter of common agreement,—which is not controverted,—the great outline facts, of American settlement, and progress. Second, the history of the rallies, divisions, reactions, and objects, of parties, as affecting the essential character of the nation, or its sections, and the relationships between the Individual, and the Government. This is a mere question of Platforms, formal records, division lists, &c. For these things we rely on "Parties and their Principles," by Holmes,* whose work is scarcely more (and as such *most* important) than a dry impartial record, or Hansard analysis. It extends from the year 1787, and the great division on the Slavery question in North Western territory, to the recent "Dred Scott" case.

History (whether of man or nation) is an organic whole, shewing the Life, Individuality, character,—Destiny. It really contains the present, and the future, as well as the past. For Destiny itself is but the last inevitable step in a Syllogism, of which the major premiss is Principle, and the minor premiss History.

In the main, therefore, we must rely only on the plain and intrepid use of our senses, and on the great primary truths of human nature, and if any man can get round, or above, or beneath *these*, he is welcome.

With regard to this Book, of course it will be easy to discover faults in plenty. Our object is to take, on behalf of the Truth, herein, as many blows as may be necessary, and to give as many and as hard as we can. The rules of the ring are better out of it than in it. Train well. Hit hard, and fair,—and keep your temper.

Reviewing, of course, every rational man would welcome. We complain, only, as that great profession complains, of liars, who are *not* "reviewers," men who not only attribute to an author assertions he has not made, but who reverse his meaning, and garble his phrases. Such men are

* "A manual of political intelligence, exhibiting the origin, growth, and character of national parties."—*Arthur Holmes.*

found up and down in literature, but they cannot succeed even in disgracing the profession. They can destroy nothing that would not fail without them. They are mere obstructives and *figurants*, —*filles de joie*, ready to prostitute themselves in ink,—eunuchs of literature, without any generative force or reproductive intellectual energy.

We repeat that we can come to no other conclusion, than that the American Nationality, Freedom, and Unity, are the least reproachable, and the mightiest secular agents, God ever created on this earth.

True, it may be objected, and "it is part of this "very strength that is now divided against itself."

We reply that here is the key to the whole question, and that when a portion of a nation contends with the prevailing genius and dominant principles of the nation, with the larger numbers, the loftier principles, the truer economics, the purer religion, the more comprehensive material unity, and with the national unities of race, language, institutions, religion,—for the sake of establishing an oligarchy, schism, and a false labour system, —that portion of the nation simply denies the law of its own existence, and repudiates the source of its strength. It seeks the dismemberment of the whole, but will only consummate the suicide of the part.

The South wants to be a second American nation, plus oligarchic and slave institutions, but, inasmuch as American nationality means republicanism and freedom, the South must either affirm those principles and remain part of the nation, or deny them and die.

The South is a *reductio ad absurdum.* If it could destroy so much of American nationality and freedom, as to allow of oligarchy and slavery, oligarchy and slavery would destroy it, and it would be swept from the earth by the arms, or supplanted by the influences of the true American nation that surrounds it.

If these things be so, the war will have achieved all that the North wanted for itself, and all that the war demanded against the South.

1st. It will have destroyed the most formidable enemy the Union ever had.

2nd. It will have completed American freedom and nationality, elevated the Individual, proved the strength but settled the limits of the Sectional State power, and strengthened the Unity, and centralisation, of the Government.

3rd. It will have purged the constitution of Slavery, purified the national morality, and cleared the national character.

4th. It will enable North and South to return to a complete and unqualified Union, after extirpating the Slave faction, the enemy of both.

It *completes the nationalisation* which began two centuries ago, which has been the prevailing tendency, and is the permanent destiny of America;—which was the work of Washington, and is probably to be the greatest secular fact of all ages.

BOOK I.

THE CASE STATED.

GENERAL QUESTIONS.

THE ENGLISH STANDPOINT.

AMERICAN NATIONALITY AND DEMOCRACY.

"MARES' NESTS;"
OR, JOHN BULL AND THE CHIVALRY.

"The time cannot be foreseen at which a permanent inequality of conditions will be established in the new world."—*De Tocqueville.*

"You are deceiving me or yourselves. The —— people is *not corrupted by the political opinions* of Europe, and *therefore* its fate does not depend upon a Battle."—*Napoleon* the 1st to Joseph.

"If *republican principles* are to perish in America, they can only yield after a laborious social process, often interrupted, and as often resumed; they will have many apparent revivals, and will not become totally extinct till an *entirely new people* shall have succeeded to that which now exists."—*De Tocqueville,* 429, Vol. 1.

"They will not endure aristocracy. All men and all powers, seeking to cope with this irresistible passion (for equality) will be overthrown and destroyed by it."—*De Tocqueville.*

CHAPTER I.

THE CASE STATED.

THE QUESTION.—THE FORCES.—THE SITUATION.

CONTENTS.

THE Making, and the Un-making of Nations, is in the Man, the Institution, and the Government, and in the dealings of these with the material Bases of Power.

All considerations on the American struggle depend ultimately, upon the answer to these three questions;—First, "What is a Nation?" Second, "What is the American Nation?" Third, "What

" is the force that assails it, and which of the two, " commands more completely, those motives of " action, and influences, which affect Individuals, " Associations, or States, and ultimately, the Na- " tion?"

It is this last question that we propose to state in the present chapter, and it involves also the question of " the Forces" or Interests and Principles, that uphold the North, and of " The Situation," or absolute nature of the Crisis.

But the enquirer must first clearly define to himself, whether he seeks the Comparative, or the Absolute,—whether he merely wants to know which of two powers is the stronger, or which of two rivals is the real Nation.

For there are two kinds of tests, whereby a pretending nation or power may be judged. One or other of them will be relied on, according as the enquirer is an expert or an ignoramus, in political science, or as he proposes to decide between rival nationalities, or only between two powers, neither of which may be a nation.

It is necessary, therefore, at once to come to an understanding as to what these tests are, what they are worth, and why they are to be rejected, or how employed.

If we only enquire which is the stronger, we may estimate the *actual results* of the war, and the present military situation.

But if we want to know which is the real nation, we must consider the *characteristics* of nationality; and apply its all comprehensive and exhaustive tests. The prizes of victory are included in the "material bases,"—Territory, Wealth, Population. The "Military Situation," results, of course, from the Nation's Bases, Functions, and Life, and these again correspond with the ultimate "Forces" Material, Intellectual, and Spiritual.

Of Facts concerning the American rebellion, and of vague speculations upon their results, the world has had enough and a nausea.

What is wanted now is to know what can be determined, and what cannot,—to bring the undoubted facts of the case, in juxtaposition with unquestionable Principles of Statesmanship, and see what they have to say to one another,—whether the future of America, is altogether an open question, or which, out of several alternatives in the broad issue of her Destiny, has got to be chosen.

The alternatives are few, the essential facts clear, and the Principles eternal. The general issues ought not to remain obscure to those who know that the history of a Nation is an organic whole, who see how Principles do laugh.

> "Their fierce and infinite laugh at things that cease,"

at the phantom victories of their adversaries, or who believe in progress, in the Peoples, and in God.

It is curious to see how believers in the old system of Government by the one, or the few, look upon what they term the great "experiment" of Government by the all.

They were always surprised that Democracy could walk. They always expected to catch it tripping. They always supposed, that once down, it could never get up again.

And now, that it has been attacked by certain rebellious provinces called "the South," which, in its essence, is a mixture of avarice and oligarchy, they say, the *Democratic* "*experiment*" has failed, and the *Constitution*,—Heaven save the mark, is for ever gone.

It were a truism to assert that the Man,—the Individual, properly educated, has in him the nucleus of all just Laws and Constitutions, and it cannot be denied that America supplies the grand desideratum, and has taken the false traditional systems out of his path and given him a clear field. The natural inference can only be missed by those who regard results, and not causes, and who are intent on the actual *Military Situation*, and *actual achievements*, without regarding the *ultimate forces.*

But this question of ultimate forces, is identical with the question of "Nationality," for faction, however strong, only survives the fortunes of war to fall before the disasters and disruptive agencies of peace.

The materials of, and the agencies in, the Making of a Nation, and its outward and visible signs, cannot be matter of doubt or debate.

There must be adequate territory, sufficiently connected together,—adequate and united population, sufficiently brave, moral, industrious, orderly, —and institutions fitted to express, control, protect, unite, and elevate.

The *Un*making of a Nation, is in the want, more or less, of these conditions of Nationality.

A scattered and disunited territory, with no defined boundaries, inadequate, disaffected, or depraved population, and institutions, that conduce to repression or anarchy,—these defects are the "unmaking of nations."

Let these truths test the issues of the great quarrel in the West.

The South claims part of the Territory, and Population of the Union. But in its origin, composition, and end, it is essentially oligarchic.

Of two things,—then,—one;

Either these belong to the North, and the Southern revolt will end in extirpation of Slavery, with its anti-national, and anti-democratic tendencies, interests, and classes,—in the completion of the principle of Individual freedom,—and in greater administrative unity, and centralization,—in other words, (for all these things were yet inchoate in America)—in the "Making of the American Nation;"—

Or;—

In the unmaking and dismemberment of that Nation by the South.

The contest *must* be treated, either as a phase which in the fulness and completion of the National American life, must have arrived some time, and ought in fact, to have been expected and welcomed, —or as a first warning of National decay and dissolution. If deprived of the free use of its mighty river system, of a third of its population and wealth, and of its relative power and prestige, Democracy might as well never have created the American Nation.

We prefer to take,—and to prove, this contest to be *not* the dismantling, but the crowning, of the glorious edifice of new-world Democracy.

§

In this particular struggle, it were even possible for the South to overcome the armies of the North, and yet to be, after all, no "Nation."

Victory does not establish nationality. Public opinion is the *last* arbiter.

On the other hand, the nationality of the North being admitted, Northern victory implies, for itself, merely the suppression of a revolt, but for the South,—annihilation.

"Southern nationality," has got to be *proved or won;* Northern nationality to be disproved or triumphed over. The South has done neither.

The result of all this is that Southern advocates have to prove;—

1st. That the South can repel Northern "Invasion."

2nd. That the South is a Nation.

And Northern advocates have to prove,—

1st. That the North will quell the present "rebellion."

2nd. That those two great prizes of Victory,—viz., the *Territory* yet held, and the *Population* now overawed and used by the South,—must return to the American nation. Because with respect to the former, the North has such inextricable interests, such natural advantages for attack, that it would not and could not relinquish it. And because, as influencing the latter, freedom and equality of conditions, democratic institutions, and the union, are the master passions of all American citizens. Unless therefore *they* can be uprooted, and the American nature and nation entirely changed, sectional independence, Slaveocracy, and the Slave

Trade, must be destroyed, for they are contradictions in terms of the American existence and nationality.

The essential meaning and result of the rebellion, if it succeed, would be Disunion by means of oligarchic institutions, and influences. The result of Northern success, would be union and democratic institutions. We contend that disunion, with permanent oligarchic institutions, is impossible in America, but disunion with democratic institutions, would be disunion only in name.

If then it be proved, that Equality of Conditions must, in any conceivable event, be maintained in America, it is proved that the rebellion has failed.

Again, if the South be a Nation, the material or *Geographical Unity* of America is defective. If that material Unity is complete, then the South wants that territorial basis, without which a nation cannot exist.

There is also another difficulty for Southern enthusiasts to overcome. Is it possible in this world of Law and of God, that a great nation be dismembered and destroyed at the end of a long agitation, martyrdom, and struggle against its master sin, and *by and on behoof of those who tempted it, and were indeed the chief sinners?*

When the Devil cometh out of a nation, it may be torn sorely, but it is that it may *not* be destroyed.

Having thus stated the case as between North and South, we come now to the summary of the Forces and Principles contending on the side of the North, and the fate and comparative power of which we propose to examine.

§

THE FORCES.

Principles and Parties.

We say then that the South can not stand, and that the *present* struggle will prove it,—and *that*, whether, it be settled by the sense of the majority, or by war, or whether by the gradual replacement of Slave labour by free, or whether North and South in their death-grapple, topple together headlong into revolution.

Because the rebellion assails the fundamental Principles of American existence,—material, political, social, moral;—the marrow, the heart, the essence, the soul, the spirit of it.

It assails,—

1st. American NATIONALITY. Nationality is the intensest principle and passion that animates communities,—for it is man's instinct of self-preservation million-folded, and of all nationalities, the American is the intensest.

2nd. American DEMOCRACY, rightly so called. Government by and for the all. General equality of conditions.

3rd. National American INDEPENDENCE. The Statesmen of all countries find America too strong.

4th. STATE SOVEREIGNTY. The South denies the personal rights of the Individual;

violates the constitutional rights of the Majority; and is, not only from the necessities of war, but in its nature, by its origin and genius, and by its acts, a Despotism. It therefore is unfriendly to Sovereign State rights. The narrowing circle of Slave States *live* upon that which injures the life of the other States. A false "Democracy," and a false "State Sovereignty," plotted together against the North, but People and States repudiate the crimes, the mistakes, and the dictation of that which, even in the South, is only a section.

5th. The MATERIAL INTERESTS of the American people, in American Unity, Free soil and Labour, and also in the four preceding items. These material interests are backed by forces constantly increasing, and now arrayed against the Slave interest. They are mentioned in detail under the head, "Reconstruction." The Population which will wield them, increases faster than that of any other country in the world, and if it were as dense as in England, would amount to Twelve Hundred Millions, and to nearly half that number, if as densely settled as Massachussetts.

6th. The GEOGRAPHICAL UNITY of America.

7th. To these must be added the force of PRINCIPLE. For we contend that the North wars for the restriction and extinction of Slavery, that the South had neither a constitutional, nor a revolutionary right to revolt, and that it revolted to maintain Slavery.

These Influences, Principles, and Powers are each of the mightiest the world has yet seen, and they present obstacles, material, moral, social, and political, — obstacles internal and external, to Southern nationality.

They are all fully treated of in the sequel.

In all contests, the first question always asked is, —" Who and what are the Parties?" and the second —" Which of them will command the preponder-" ance of forces, material, intellectual, and moral,— " of sentiment, of organization, and of battalions."

A third question, — " What are the Principles involved?" is usually *not* asked, although the answer would at once unmask the real forces, shew the powers and pertinacity of the agencies at issue, and determine every essential question, save that of time.

For the main question now is, and always is in great contests,—" *Is there enough power and urgency* " *of the spiritual sort, to use, to energise, and to* " *organise, whatsoever power there may be of the* " *material sort.*"

But it is not enough to know that certain Principles contend,—that one of them is true, and must triumph, the other false, and to fail; we want to know further;—

Whether the relations of the actual contending parties to each other, and to the Principles for which they contend, are such, as that the issue *will be fought out by them* NOW?

The answer to this question,—" Can either party " avoid the extreme controversy, the *experimentum* " *crucis?*" depends on " The Situation."

We say, that the American quarrel must be fought out,—that the combatants *cannot* retire from the contest. That the Principles, and the Situation, involve the destruction of the Unity, the Nationality, and the Institutions, of the North,—or the defeat or extermination of the Slaveholders, their faction, and "institution." At the end of this struggle, there will remain neither a Slave empire, nor a mere Federal Government, but either a score or two of rabble States, or a completed American Nation, with an infinite expanse of territory, and soon, 200 millions of population.

§

THE SITUATION.

Relations of Principles to Parties.

Having pointed out the forces engaged, the next question arises,—"Can either party by declining "the contest, leave it undecided?"

The negative of this question is but a truism, if what we have just stated be true. The Situation is one that admits of no compromise.

Every situation has its logic, and the logic is Destiny to those involved in it.

The logic of War is to beat, or be beaten; to draw all things and men irresistibly to the one side or the other. War avails itself of all the powers, resources, and passions, of a nation. It treats doubt as treason, and indecision as treachery. Its logic is inexorable, and every step leads peremptorily to another step, and still another, until the conclusion. War has a beginning, two sides, and an end.

The logic of peace may for individuals, be compromise, evasion, postponement. Nevertheless it for ever silently prepares, for Parties, and Peoples, the ultimate alternatives of acquiescence or dishonour, Principle or Defeat.

There are "tactical" contests that are not war, that have all the evils of war, and none of the advantages of peace. Diplomatic wars. Mechanical wars. Wars without principle or issue; that Diplomacy begun and Diplomacy may end; that came from hypocrisy and insincerity, and terminate in evasion, and doubt.

They begin in falsehood; continue in murder; end in,—nothing.

There are "wars of Principle," that appertain necessarily to an epoch. That outcome from the striving spiritual *life* of a nation. That must come. That are "irrepressible." They cannot be avoided, and must be fought out. They have their natural laws, their normal conditions, their inevitable unalterable issues.

They begin in Truth; the battle they set is for friends a sacrament, for foes an execution, for Humanity an epoch.

The Crimean war was a sham war. The Allies waged Peace upon Russia. They dared not pronounce the name of Poland, for thereafter each of them might want Russia against the other. It ended in Circassian Blockades, in Black Sea "Neutrality," and in "non-intervention."

The war of America upon Slavery is a real war. It is part of the great battle for equality. Its logic is not to halt, or to temporise, but to beat or be beaten. America has pronounced its "Poland," for the origin, development, and issue, of the war is abolition. It comes of the eternal feud between right and wrong. It leads somewhither. It means something. It could not be avoided. It must be brought to an issue. They who believe in God and in human nature, will interpret the issue one way. They who believe in the Devil and anarchy,—another.

But all the fools on the one side, and all the devils on the other, all the doubters and imbeciles, democrats, and copperheads, north, and all the foam and fury of slave drivers, south, can now only precipitate, or deepen and aggravate the issue, prepared for 80 years.

> "The mills of the Gods grind slowly,
> But they grind exceeding small."

The result has passed beyond the control of the combatants. It is a war of "Principles." It is gradually drawing the whole heart and energies of the North into it. The North has progressed an epoch in two years. The North arms negroes, and the South hangs them. According to the *Times* correspondent, over 700,000 of them have already been emancipated. But this is not all. Black and White, approach the sacrament of a common political Faith, and a common ordeal and a common nationality. Freedom has had to overcome, first prejudices, and then treason. The march of opinion has been more steady, relentless, and powerful, than the march of armies, and it promulgates its laws amidst the thunders and lightnings of battle.

Statesmanship and a crisis, have done in the South, what Necessity and Principle, have done in the North:

There were irresolute men in the South. Statesmen took an advanced position, knowing that the logic of the situation, must drive the herd to follow. For it is nonsense and imbecility to hold property in man, without holding also the right and the power to maintain it.

There were irresolute men in the North, as everywhere else, but the logic of the South soon became their necessity, for it demanded that the North itself should become a slave.

And the logic of the Situation, which dominated both, was this—

"If Slavery be allowed, the Declaration and
"the free heritage of the People must be disallowed.
"If Property in man be a Principle, then it is
"Property everywhere, —by water as well as by
"land,—in the Territories, as well as in the States.
"What's right is right, and Felony can't be Pro-
"perty, or Property felony."

The North, therefore, had to accept the external Slave trade, as well as Slavery,—to defy all nations on the "right of search",—to repress abolitionism, —to swallow Dred Scott cases,—to be the servant, soldier, and slave, the drudge and the tool, of the South,—or gradually to unite against its aggressions, and ultimately to fight for the right, one and indivisible.

This was the question. "Could the Nation be "committed to an Anti-Slavery War?"

"The Puritans from Abraham's bosom" worked at it, and necessity and the South, worked also. Once solved, the rest was easy. The Situation once probed, the issue once understood and joined, there could be but one solution. The ultimate result, was from the first, to the Statesman or the believer, but a stark, staring, blank, palpable, insurmountable, truism,—but it has taken three years already, and may take more, to work it down and out to the level of all the fools and infidels in the North.

That done, all is done, and now, two years after the South resorted to the most ruthless conscription that ever swept over a desolated country, taking striplings and patriarchs alike, now Lincoln has behind him, not a congerie of States, but a nation growing day by day, in Unity, determination, and power.

Whether, then, we consider the material forces, the great Principles at issue, or the spiritual forces that are arising to inspire and lead the Battle, we can come to no other conclusion than that the South must submit, or that the parties must contend to the last.

If one be more than three,—if the national instinct of self preservation be replaced by an instinct of suicide,—if a high heroic spirit of self sacrifice leads to national perdition,—then the North will fail. If not, not.

It is the South that denies and destroys itself. It began by asserting the right of Secession. It is evident that without nationality, secession must kill secession. It began by asserting the expediency and the principle of slave labour. It ends by vainly wishing to turn the labourers into Soldiers to fight for their freedom. It began by denouncing all interference with the natural and Christian institution of Slavery. It ends by trying to persuade the Slaveholder to allow his nigger to fight for the right of destroying his "property." It has for three ages degraded the whole Southern White population by slavery. It now would elevate the whole Black population at one stroke to the dignity of preserving their tyrants by arms. It started to maintain Slavery, and *in order not to be beaten, it must destroy that for which it exists.*

Thus Suicide, Individual, Political, and Moral, closes the scene over the South.

Squatter Sovereignty, and free labour and opinion, are the likeliest weapons to decide the contest, but however that may be, it is a war of principle, a war of essential and irrepressible antagonism.

The beginning of the war was abolition. The sides are Freedom or Slavery, the end cannot be compromise. It will be a Government by and for the all, or *of* the all, by and for the few.

That is the logic of the Situation,—and it is absolute.

CHAPTER II.

GENERAL QUESTIONS

INVOLVED IN

THE AMERICAN QUESTION.

DEMOCRACY AND CHRISTIANITY.
LESSONS OF THE FOUR GREAT REVOLUTIONS.
SOLIDARITÉ OF PEOPLES.
REPUBLICANISM, FEDERATION, AND AMERICAN NATIONALITY.
FUTURE ENGLISH ALLIANCES.
THE ANGLO-AMERICAN RACE.
SLAVERY AND OLIGARCHY.
FREEDOM OF THE OCEAN.

"The organisation and establishment of Democracy in Christendom is the great political problem of the time."—*De Tocqueville.*

"That Providence has given to every human being a degree of reason necessary to direct himself in the affairs which interest him exclusively, is the grand maxim upon which civil and political Society rests in the United States."—*De Tocqueville.*

"And thus of necessity, by reason of the existence of some few really free states, will the empire of civilisation, freedom, and with it universal peace, gradually embrace the whole world."—*Fichte.*

"In a word, free states, I think, must ever look with suspicion on an absolute monarchy."—*Demosthenes.*

"The day will come when a single fibre left of this Institution will produce an hereditary aristocracy, which will change the form of our Government from the best to the worst in the world."

Thos. Jefferson.

"Between North and South, there is at this moment raging a controversy, which goes *as deep as any controversy can, into the elementary principles of human nature,* and the sympathies and antipathies which, in so many men, supply the place of reason and reflection. The North is for freedom; the South is for slavery. The North is for freedom of discussion; the South represses freedom of discussion with the tar brush and the pine faggot."

"*Times,*" January, 1861.

E 2

"The issue (of the war) is to them (the South) one of life and death, and whoever raises it hereafter, if it be not decided now, must expect to meet the deadly animosity which is now displayed towards the North.

"The success of the South,—if it can succeed,—must lead to complications and *results in other parts of the world*, for which neither they nor Europe are prepared. Of one thing there can be no doubt, a Slave State cannot long exist without a Slave Trade. The poor whites, who have now to fight, will demand their share of the spoil. The land is abundant, and all that is wanted to give them fortunes is a supply of slaves. *They will have that in spite of their masters*, unless a stronger power than the Slave States prevents the accomplishment of their wishes."—*W. H. Russell.*

"*Monarchy* had no motive to emigrate. * * * The *Feudal Aristocracy* could not gain new life among the equal hardships of the wilderness. * * * * *Priestcraft* did not emigrate."

"The settlement of New England was the result of implacable differences between Protestant Dissenters and the Established Anglican Church. * * * Nothing but the wide ocean, and the savage deserts of America could hide and shelter them from the fury of the Bishops. * * * *An entire separation was made between State and Church.*"—*Bancroft.*

"The relations of the rising colonies, the representatives of *Democratic Freedom*, are chiefly with France and England, * * * with the Parliament of England which was the representative of aristocratic liberties, and had ratified *Royalty, Primogeniture, corporate charters, the Peerage, Tithes, Prelates, prescriptive Franchises, and every established immunity and privilege.*"—*Bancroft.*

"Their Independence would agitate the globe, would assert the *freedom of the Oceans as commercial highways*, vindicate power in the commonwealth for the united judgment of its People, and assure to them the right of a self-directing vitality."—*Bancroft.*

"England became not so much the possessor of the valley of the West, as the transient trustee, *commissioned to transfer it from the France of the middle ages* to the free People who were working for Humanity a new existence in America."—*Bancroft.*

"If Europe leaves America to Republicanism, well. If she interferes, we interfere, and the right hand of our resistance is clasped in brotherhood with the radicals of Europe, to upset every throne on the Continent."—*Wendell Phillips.*

CONTENTS.

GOVERNMENTS and Peoples.—The foundation of all stable systems.—Christianity in relation to the Principles of conservatism and radicalism.—The five stages.—Christianity, the printing press, the English, American, and French revolutions.—Solidarité of Peoples.—Democracy, the problem of all ages.—The crowning victory of Democracy.—Manhood.—Representation.—Nationality.—Association.—The fundamental Principles of the four great revolutions.—American Puritanism.—Providential education of the Peoples.—Democracy of the future.—Oligarchy in America.—Aristocracy "revolting."—England not with them.—The bases of anti-popular Policies.—America drills.—The army of the future.—Universal questions.—English questions,—India, Canada, and Cotton.—Universal popular reaction.—The perils of England.—The tendencies of anti-English policy.—Slavery a part of Oligarchy.—Fate of Democracy.—The Exodus of Oligarchy.—Essential antagonisms in the future.—The political Unity of America.—The Principle of Federation.—Tremendous import of the general issues.—Number and inveteracy of the questions.—The interest universal.—The Settlement absolute.

FOR four thousand years the People had had experiments of Governing tried upon them.

Government by the few had repressed the life and energies of the many. Government by the many had resulted in anarchy. Scarcely ever were freedom and authority united, and never for long, or thoroughly.

On the whole, it cannot be concealed, that certain brilliant exceptions only proved the *rule* of Government to be neither good, nor indifferent, but after the average and alternating fashion, of Priest, Beast, Fool, or Devil.

The Priest ruled men's Bodies by misleading

their souls. The Beast ruled their souls by embruting their Bodies. The Fool attempted to make the past fit the present, and to hand down the present to the future. The Devil had only to combine and perpetuate the faults of his brethren.

America asked the question propounded by the same race in England. Is this state of things fated to be eternal? Is it of the nature and essence of Government, and of man, that Governments shall be unstable and *farmed* by families, factions, or individuals?

Eighteen hundred years before, Christianity,—the soul of all revolutions, as of all conservatism,—had already answered this question. If the Soul be immortal, *its* welfare must be the rule of action,—not that of State anatomy, of a class, or of a system. The culture, character, and Destiny of the Individual, must be the foundation of all social and political systems.

The value of the individual,—of the unit,—this great principle,—the very savour and salt of all true conservatism, and the root itself of Radicalism, were destined to decompose all systems opposed to it.

Absolutism, Priestcraft, Oligarchies,—all that did not allow of, or that could not consist with, the freedom, morality, intelligence, self-government and progress of the MAN, were but as so many forms of a more refined or postponed anarchy,—so many lies or half lies, that must of necessity fall away, as this single central truth should be proclaimed and accepted.

This Truth taught the Man to govern himself,

by principles of self-government and restraint that would not conflict, but coincide with, the rights of others, and the just authority of the State.

But this Truth had first to be revealed, and then propagated. It must be gradually taught by precedent, and commended by example, as each great epoch brought its lesson and its moral.

Christianity, we say, made this change possible. The Printing press made it practicable. It gave an impulse to propagandism, power to public opinion, and a basis to the Principle of popular association.

The English revolution made the first precedent of representative Popular Sovereignty.

The Americans, upon a wider bases of popular Sovereignty, established the principle of National Independence.

The French sought upon these principles the Union of all Peoples against all tyrannies.

The present contest is the result of a great national movement against an insurgent oligarchy. It is not a revolution, but a reconstruction upon the principles of the revolution. It affirms Authority and Freedom,—Democracy, Morality, and Nationality, at once.

The friends of Slavery are the foes of all true nationality and popular propagandism. They resolve themselves into two classes,—Oligarchs and Anarchists. Those who do not believe that the People can ever be prepared for self Government, and those who plot that the self Government of the American People shall now end.

But with "non Intervention" against Peoples,

they may plot but they cannot execute. *They cannot combine*, and are little likely to succeed in destroying and reversing the results of all the blood and enterprise of the three great revolutions of the world, or in bringing back the era of revolutions, and the old-world cycles when the Individual and the State contended.

The question of all ages has been how to complete and maintain a Nation by the Principles of Democracy.

The effort, and test, and progress of civilisation, is how to involve ever a fuller complement of the national intelligence and will in the Government, and thereby to build upon the broadest base, and to achieve the good of a greater and ever greater proportion of the all.

Democracy is the self-government of Peoples, and self-government is the crowning victory of morals and of Statesmanship.

Freedom generates self-command; self-command justifies freedom.

It is the double problem of the best Government and the broadest base.

A good autocrat is a bad principle of Government, for Kings must die, but nations are eternal.

To set for the universal national life, the Hazard of the Die of a single life, is but gambling on a magnificent scale. Autocracy is better than anarchy. Oligarchy better that autocracy. But oligarchy, autocracy, and anarchy, are alike weak, vicious, and incomplete, and Democracy *is* that towards and of which all other forms of Government are but approaches, delegations, and assumptions,—the will and the well-being of the universal people.

When the History of the World began we know not, but we know that the reign of the People was made possible only by the Christian religion, and that the History of "the People," began with the history of America.

The first revolution levelled the exclusive pretensions of Judaism, revealed the infinite in Man, made right co-extensive with the Soul, and evoked therefrom the energies of Progress, and the necessity of Law.

Other revolutions are but the completions, or developments of the first.

The second revolution,—the English, asserted the rights of man under the principle of representation.

The third,—the American, established the rights of "Nationality," and combined the two fundamental conditions of national life, namely, freedom, and executive efficiency. The one by the reconstruction of 1787, the other, by "the Declaration."

The fourth,—the French, established, and sublimely yearned and fought for the crowning Principle of Democracy, its cement, its guarantee, its Unity,—the "Solidarité of Peoples,"—the right and the necessity of Democracy all over the world, to stand by its order.

And all three, we say, are based upon Christianity, which teaches the infinite value of the Soul, and its personal and relative duties and rights.

Manhood. Representation. Nationality. Association.

Christianity taught the rights of man. The rights of man involved the rights of nations. The rights of nations involve the duties of protecting them by international association.

And these things, as they spring from Christianity, must partake of its nature. Democracy must be intelligent and self-restrained, or it can neither understand its relative duties, or maintain its own rights.

It is here that the general Intelligence and conservatism of the American comes in with decisive weight. *In republics* man must be educated to self-restraint, and respect for law, the embodiment of the social compact, and of the will of the People. Without this, republics cannot exist.

"This Government, the offspring of our own choice, completely free in its principles, and containing within itself a provision for its own amendment, has a just claim to your confidence and support. Respect for its authority, &c. are duties enjoined, by the fundamental principles of true *liberty*." *

Nationality always asserts itself. But it is when nation helps nation, that we have the crowning victory of the People,—a power of organisation and self-denial, that ensures the ultimate, though gradual, triumph of Principle over force. The growing solidation of the Peoples, and an increasing division and distrust among Despots, are the natural results of the universal, social, and political progress of the masses.

This question is profoundly stirred by the conflict in America, and the contradictory sympathies and endeavours of Governments and Peoples, in relation thereto.

* Washington's Farewell.

It behoves, now, Democracy to be consistent, calm, clear, and resolute. It must take its stand on the fundamental principles of Christianity, and the three other great revolutions of the world, for they furnish, each a step, towards the final logic of victory.

In revolutionary epochs all fear of consequences is cast off,—Thought is free, and passion wings it, passion,—sentiment,—without which nothing is ever thought out, or fought out, without which mere Intellect has no generative force, without which no great deeds are ever done. Then are first principles established, and we witness the greatest efforts of the most majestic attributes of Man.

The central thought and life of each of these revolutions, (however diversely time and circumstances may have influenced its development) was the same—the value of the Individual Soul. De Tocqueville (let us repeat it) says of American puritanism, that it was—

> "Not merely a religious doctrine, but corresponded in many "points with the most absolute Democratic and republican "theories. The General principles were all recognised and "determined by the laws of New England. The intervention "of the people in public affairs, the free voting of taxes, the "responsibility of authorities, personal liberty, and trial by "Jury."

The Charter of Frenchmen;—the Declaration of the "rights of man," was nearly coincident in point of time, and is identical in substance, with the great settlement of American liberties. It declared all men free and equal. It declared the responsibility of all officials to the sovereign people.

Their right to change the Government, and to meet in public assembly. Their right to prompt justice, to authentic trial,—and to freedom of worship and of the press.

Except in America, these Principles have everywhere been defrauded of their victories. Nowhere else is responsibility to the people, and representation of the people, completely carried out, and universal Democracy has long looked to America for the grand moral impulse.

The complete realisation of the principle of Democracy, belongs inevitably to the providential education of the Human race. Soon or late, it must come, and we believe it is coming now.

Broadly stated, Autocracies and Oligarchies tend only to complete the few. Representative Governments tend to complete the many. Democracies tend to complete the all.

In whatever epoch, or with whatever "enlightenment," Man will not be governed for himself, till he is governed by himself, he cannot become a creature "looking before and after," in politics, except by the *exercise* of those faculties of self Government, in respect of all his relationships, here and hereafter, which are his right and his duty as Man.

All this, we think, is absolutely plain,—from the laws of human selfishness, the necessities of social order and advancement, and the capabilities of the Human Soul.

For in a measure it may be said,—that Autocracy at its best affirms little but the fact and necessity of Order and Law,—that Oligarchies and partial representations are a *compromise* between Law and Freedom,—and that all tend (as the firmamental universe through space) to some point of final adjustment of Law and Freedom, Order and Authority, the Man and the Institution, to be reached by the Democracy of the future.

The Logic of History is as simple and sublime as it is absolute; at every stage, from Cæsar to the Citizen, from the autocrat to the broadest based democracy, the two conditions of all organised life have had to be realised, or the system that could not realise them has been destroyed for want of them. Thus, from cycle to cycle, has the world been put back or forwards, to learn the needful lesson, or take the rightful prize. Order and Progress, Loyalty and Right, Conservatism and Radicalism, are the positive and negative poles of politics, but really own one life and law.

The two must be equally present in every completed revolution. Despair may begin a revolution but it cannot end it. And wherever a yet larger number of men are prepared by self restraint and energy, by that mutual trust which can alone render combination against authority possible, to take the next step, the nation will always be the stronger and the world will always be the better for the change.

Thus the fight of thought, of agitation, or of arms, will be fought in every nation, as larger and still larger numbers of qualified men knock at the doors of power, and from autocracy to oligarchy, from oligarchy to representation, from representation of the few, to representation of the all, will nation after nation be completed in politics and in men.

§

But the same energies, habits, principles, that enable individuals to combine against domestic wrong, will impel nation also to combine with nation against their oppressors.

This battle of the future is scented from afar by all parties, who see in the freedom, and loyalty, and union, of Americans, their own representative or antagonistic forces.

Accordingly, the Aristocrats all over the world are "revolting!"—In America by arms; in Europe, by opinion, although the letter of the law, as well as the spirit of equity, is against the South.

The Aristocrats are at last "revolting!" It is an instructive spectacle, and Gentlemen who never before approved of revolutions, have now acquired a holy horror of repression, and will carry it with them to their dying day.

The great Democratic nation is in danger of succeeding. It is being "made." This is the heart and essence of the American question, and it is the head and front of the North's offending, for in the perfectibility and progress of the People, the oligarchs of all countries believe and tremble.

The third great stage of the conflict between Democracy and Oligarchy has arrived.

The Solidarité of Despots has destroyed itself by its own extravagance and Obstinacy. It exists no longer. The People bid for the premiership of the world, and parvenu Emperors bid against Legitimists for their alliance. Legitimacy is "demoralised." It has gone on tick to England for eighty years, but now its accomplices here are revoking their suretyships, and its securities are beginning to be overhauled.

The Solidarité of Peoples is completing. Their power has broken down the old monopoly of Statecraft, and ventilated the fœtid recesses of Diplomacy.

The first and second stages of the conflict are at an end. Holy alliances against Peoples are no longer the certain and safe events they were, and the great fact that England, formerly the heart and soul of those alliances, is now at least *not with them*, has made itself duly felt.

The beginning of the end is at hand.

Legitimacy is divided against itself. The dogma of "Non-Intervention," a wonderful doctrine, neither moral nor Statesmanlike, which half betrays and half helps the right, is gladly preached and accepted by those who know what will follow when the People shall intervene for the People.

The third stage approaches, and will end in favour of Democracy, this balance between the past and the future. The Peoples contemplate Intervention on the right side. Intervention *for* the Peoples. The Union of the Peoples for common objects, with or without, against or by means of the Governments. The destruction of those popular jealousies, and of that ignorance, which were the basis of all anti-popular policies. When reaction is seen to be hopeless, it will become identified with revolution, and will array against it all true conservative instincts.

This Solidation of the Peoples,—their essential, active, material, triumphant, Unity, has already had its baptism of blood, its discouragements, and its triumphs. It arose in 1790, (as one of those manias by which, according to Plato, the soul ascends to God.) It gave its impulse to all nations, and it fell, to rise again.

Whenever the Solidarité of Peoples is completed, and meets that of Despots, there must be the real final struggle.

The mightiest leverage is in America, for there Democracy is entirely at one with conservatism.

America is the most advanced parallel of approach,—the most dangerous sap,—the only complete and substantive platform, from which the great guns of Democracy can assail, for the benefit of mankind, the strongholds of absolutism.

But there will be a Solidarité of Citizens, as well as of Nations,—within, as well as without,—for democratic, and national, as well as for international, objects. That Solidarité is called Association. This power has been one of the mightiest in America, and the English People are learning it fast, and are applying its leverage to Political, as well as to social problems. *With the British Constitution for fulcrum, and Popular combination for the lever, even the political world of England may soon be moved.*

While America, then, drills and completes herself for the conflict she will probably be called to sustain with Europe, against some form or other of Aristocracy, be it remembered that unless chaos come again, the army of the future will have to be assembled beneath the banners, and under the moral sanction, of American Democracy triumphant.

The intelligent will and action of the all is of necessity the goal of the political future. Education is the road to it, and universal suffrage is its expression. Progress and safety, together, are the object of all Statesmanship. Progress, without enlightenment, is the dream of fanatics, or madmen. Safety, without progress towards the universal rights of the People, is the fiction of those whom the universal People are destined to crush, or to banish from all share in practical politics.

By Oligarchy we mean Government *by and for* the few, for whatever may be said to the contrary, Government always stands by its order, and Government *by* the few will always be Government *for* the few. But inasmuch as few Governments are Democratic in theory, and all are oligarchic in practice, this American question is a question for all nations.

America deals with the facts of the rebellion, and the principles that energise and direct it. Europe has to do with the moral effect of the results of the contest, and with its principles, which are universal.

§

The Battle of God in the West, has for its issue three causes triumphant, each in its order. 1st.

The right, the capacity, and the earlier practice of self Government by the Peoples everywhere. 2nd. The vindication, by American Reunion, of this Atlantean Statesmanship that teaches man to believe, *politically*, in himself, and in God, and to look to the universal people, to bear up in economics, in politics, and in religion, the adamantine pillars of a State. 3rd. The enfranchisement of the particular negro race, which constitutes about an eighth of the American population, and which represents the rights of labour all over the world.

The political future of Man. The permanence of the American Union. The freedom of the Slave. These three are a cause one and indivisible. Without the Slave free, the Union goes, and if the Union goes, ALL go, for this generation. The cause of the North is the cause of the World. The World sees it. The World knows it. The World's opinion sides with the North, and every throb of the Hell-drum of the South, as it calls more than the "first male" of every household to execution, proclaims the Exodus of the African, and summons the manhood of every nation to ask where and what are its rights, and *how it is* that everywhere the Press and the parasites of the few, hate the North, and would make war against it.

For the World, the question of self-Government by the Peoples everywhere. For England, the questions of the future of the great Anglo-Saxon Continent; of India, Canada, and the Cotton felony and famine. For America, the questions of free labour, of free and centralised Government, and the Union sooner or later restored, and enlarged. Such, and of no less awful magnitude and importance, are the questions directly affected by every act done, and opinion expressed, for, or against the American Union.

Historians will undoubtedly point to the present crisis, as the period whence an *universal* popular reaction set in,—when the great *In*dependencies of England began to assume a new position with regard to her,—when the importance of India was immensely developed. Were it not for the almost personal interference of our Democracy,—our nobodies, and our unpaid Clergy, it would almost have appeared that the consolidation of the American Union, whether completed by the sword, or begun afresh *a pas de géant* by peaceful influences, the vindication of its constitution for conservatism and progress,—the sympathy of Canadians for her heroic struggle,—the contempt of the world for the conduct of some anti-English leaders of the English oligarchy and press,—the bad political company into which the results of the cotton felony threatened to drag us,—and our inveterate vestry statesmanship, petty policy and mighty exhausting expenditure, had all combined to jeopardise our moral position, and relative power before the world, and involve us in another great war against the cause of Freedom.

Great as is the struggle, and great as are the results of all sorts already realised in this American warfare, it cannot be allowed that these things are aught or less than a speck in that mighty system of means, influences, and issues, which America sets before the world.

Thus the questions at issue in America are not to be circumscribed by even the widest limits that have generally been set for them.

The question is not between Freedom and Slavery, in the limited acceptation of the terms, for Slavery is a system of oppression and suicide, and will either be destroyed, or fail. Slavery is doomed, and is not a question, but an irritation only.

The outside question is whether the principle of treason and unjustifiable revolt shall triumph in the new world. But the essential question, in its largest and completest aspect, is whether that system of balanced right between man and man, and between the Man and the Government, established and preserved there for 80 years, shall be rebuked and degraded before the world,—whether the great Anglo-Saxon race, and the tributary races it has assimilated, and those free institutions, in religion and politics, for which the world's martyrs have fought and died, shall now have on their side, a great, a successful, a united, and advancing People, *to fight the battles of the future*, and to stand by the side of the veritable English people, in the essential contests that must come from essential antagonisms, in the History and emancipation of the Human race.

The greatest facts not only of the present era, but in the secular history of the world,—are the spread of one race over the whole of one Continent; the Federation of many separate states, each of the average size of an European kingdom, under one Government; and their existence, and probable continued existence, under Institutions really free and democratic.

The tremendous import of the general issues; involved in this special issue between Slavery and the constitutional Government of America, may well stagger the apprehension of those who do not advance to them full panoplied with Principle, and with a proper sense of responsibility. But it should steady the minds of those who do thus advance.

Let us repeat and emphasize these issues;—

They are, for the World, the question of self-Government by the Peoples everywhere. For England, they affect, more or less deeply, the questions of Democratic Institutions, of India, Canada, and the Cotton Felony and Famine, and of the Anglo-American Continent. For America, the questions of free labour, of territorial Integrity, of free and centralised Government, of the Union, sooner or later restored and enlarged, of Nationality and Independence.

The political future of Man.

The Permanence of the American Union, and the integrity of its nationality.

The freedom of labour, and of the Negro.

These questions have their full meaning at home as well as abroad, for there really exist in England but two Parties,—*The party that believes in and is prepared to trust the People, and the party that does neither.*

The number, the magnitude, the inveteracy, of the questions involved, and the essential and intimate relations of the two parties to them, account for the interest mankind take in the struggle, but they also demonstrate the folly of expecting that anything less than an absolute settlement of the Situation is possible.

CHAPTER III.

THE ENGLISH STANDPOINT.

THE ANGLO-SAXON CONTINENT.
PANAMA.
CANADA.
INDIA, AND THE ENGLISH STAPLE.
OLIGARCHY AND DEMOCRACY.
THE CONSTITUTION UNBALANCED.
LAND TENURE.
POPULAR ASSOCIATION.
THE REACTION REACTED UPON.

"The two or three main ideas which constitute the basis of the Social theory of the United States were first combined in the Northern British colonies, the States of New England.

"In England the stronghold of Puritanism was in the middle classes, and it was from the middle classes that the majority of the emigrants came.

"The general principles which are the groundwork of modern constitutions, were all recognised and determined by the laws of New England.—The Americans are a very old and enlightened People, &c. *That portion* of the *English People,* which is commissioned to explore the wilds of the new world."—*De Tocqueville.*

"Already (1690) the plebeian outcasts, the Anglo-Saxon emigrants, were the hope of the world."—*Bancroft.*

"That the first adventurers and settlers of his Majesty's colony and dominion brought with them, and transmitted to their posterity and all other his Majesty's subjects since inhabiting, all the privileges, franchises, and immunities, that have at any time been held *by the People of Great Britain.*"

Resolution in Virginia Assembly, 1765.

"That the inhabitants of the English colonies, by the immutable laws of nature, *the Principles of the English Constitution, &c.* have certain rights."

Resolution of 12 *Colonies at Philadelphia Congress,* 1774.

"Permit us to be as free as yourselves, and we shall esteem a Union with you to be our greatest glory and our greatest happiness."

Address of Congress to the People of Great Britain.

"*Representation and taxation* must go together; they are inseparable. For genuine sagacity, for singular moderation, for solid wisdom, manly spirit, sublime sentiments, and simplicity of language, the Congress of Philadelphia stands unrivalled. * * * America has all the reason in the world to believe you mean her death or her bondage. I pledge myself never to leave this business."

Lord Chatham, in the Lords, 1775.

"The idea of *virtual representation* is the most contemptible that ever entered into the head of man."—*Mr. Pitt*, 1766.

"When a nation modifies the *electoral qualification*, it may easily be foreseen that sooner or later that qualification will be entirely abolished. There is no more invariable rule in the history of Society."—*De Tocqueville.*

"Should Angels and Archangels come down from Heaven to govern us, public liberty must be in danger whenever a free constitution is dependent on will; and a free constitution is dependent on will, whenever the will of *one estate can direct the conduct of all three.*"—*Bolingbroke.*

"The English Government will be no more, either when the Crown shall become independent on the nation for its *supplies*, or when the representatives of the People shall begin to share in the executive authority."—*De Lolme.*

"Besides these more general questions England has some of her own. Foremost among them all is the suppression of the *Slave Trade.*"—*Castlereagh's Instructions to Wellington for Congress of Verona.*

"Almost all ancient legislators, especially Moses, grounded the success of their ordinances concerning virtue, justice, and morality, upon securing hereditary estates, or at least, *landed property*, to the greatest possible number of citizens."—*Niebuhr.*

"It is of the nature of property to run into large masses. Public laws should be so constructed as to *favor its diffusion* as much as they can."—*Paley.*

"If men are to remain civilized or to become so, the art of *associating* together must grow and improve, in the same ratio in which the *equality of conditions is increased.*"—*De Tocqueville.*

CONTENTS.

English Puritanism.—Freedom and Law with the North.—The Anglo-Saxon race, History, and Continent.—Root of American nation, and of Slavery—Panama, and English Commerce, and Napoleon. — Policy of England.—America, France, Russia, and the South.—The chief seat of Anglo-Saxon power already transferred to America.—England will want American alliance.—Perspective of Events. — The English Cotton Felony and Compromise. — Imperial Statesmanship. — Intermeddling in Europe and neglect in India. — The "London Cotton Plant" story of the trade as affecting prices in England. — English monopoly depresses India, and elevates the South.—English subsidy to the South.—Ten millions per annum to Slaveholders.—Rise in value of Slaves and Plantations. — The great Tory reaction from Charles II. to the Reform Bill. — The reaction reacted upon.—Fraud, compromise, and postponement, its chief weapons. — Recognition of South as Belligerent. — Hungary, Poland, and the South.—Who governs England?—Middle class partially retrograde.—Upper and "lower" classes advancing.—Murder and non-Intervention.—The European situation.—The cycle of results.—Democracy in England.—Theory and practice of the English Constitution.—Representation, and Foreign Policy.—Reaction.—Primogeniture.—Law of progression.—American progress and English policy. —"Recognition."—The army of revolt.—The great representative class abuse.—English Policy in a transition State.—English Democracy waits the momentum from American successes.—A word to the wise.

THE *sangue azul* of the world,—the bluest of all bloods,—the conqueror of conquerors,—the old Puritan English blood, and brood, now fights and wins its third great battle. The first, established on the body of the Stuart the fact of popular Sovereignty. The second, settled the theory, and went far to establish the fact, that human Government exists for the diffusion of equal happiness, and the vindication of equal rights. These two were struggles for the principle of freedom, the present is for those of freedom and authority combined. The first were against great odds. The present has on its side the great preponderance of material, as well as of moral power.

Not, as heretofore, with authority against right, but against authority,—against law, against the letter as well as the spirit of right, have the representatives of the world's oppressors at last to contend.

Freedom and law are one in Northern practice, —in Southern practice,—anarchy and oppression.

To this pass has the world's cause come, but it has reached it through a stormy road.

The third great struggle of the Puritans now culminates. The cause was adherence to Principle. The champions are come of the great English revolution. There is no great question which the issue will not decide, for it tries over again, and as in a court of last appeal, all the great spiritual controversies which before have shaken the world.

The rights of representative Government was the issue against the Stuart. The rights of Nationality was the issue against George the III. The present contest includes these, but it is deeper down. It is for conservatism as well as for progress. Not only will it settle the right of the universal people to representation, and of the Americans to nationality, and also their power to have them and to hold them, but it will teach the enemies of mankind, that the People know what is freedom and what license, and the bounds between them. That they will not allow license to slave drivers, because it is called "freedom;" an unnatural separate existence to rebels, because it is called "nationality;" or anarchy to "sovereign states," because it is claimed by "Democrats." Freedom and Law are at last balanced, and Despotism and Anarchy are proved to be one.

A nation is the mightiest Integer in this world's combinations. It is not easily made. It does not easily die.

Of all the mighty nations in the world the American nation is the most progressive. It grapples with its roots the heart of the Anglo-Saxon traditions and nationality. It will reach from the Gates of the Pacific to the Pole and from the Atlantic to the Pacific.

It increases its Population by half in ten years. It increases its wealth at a rate unknown before. It is the country of equal social and political conditions. It has now overcome the deadly temptation of partnership in Southern shame.

The root of the American nation, is as concerning the flesh, in the Anglo-Saxon race; as concerning the spirit, it is of the Puritans.

Other breeds are there, and other spirits, but the blood and the speech of the English stock, rule, and it is by the sword of the spirit of the Puritans, that the great nation must conquer.

The root and Principle of Slavedom, is aristocracy in its worst sense. The assertion of the special and exceptional rights of the few, and the denial of equal spiritual, mental and physical rights to the many.

It is the exact contrary of American Democracy and race, of the Puritan blood and politics,—of the love of the People, and the fear of God.

America is England plus a larger sphere, a clearer stage, and democratic institutions. Americans enjoy the rights Englishmen have fought for, but which are there set forth in express declaration, and cleared of all doubt. The strength of the branch proves the vigour of the tree.

American questions are English, almost as much as they are American. The English are for America, and the opposition to the *People* of both countries by the anti-English faction that was beaten once for all by Cromwell and the Ironsides, proves it. The Continent may be called the Anglo-American, or ANGLO-SAXON CONTINENT. The race, the Anglo-American or Anglo-Saxon race. American History is but the continuation of English History upon a vaster area, and a clearer stage. The Great Federation is a vindication of that union of freedom with self-Government, which marks the Manhood of nations, and which marks as yet few but the English. Democracy is the principle towards which all free nations must tend till it is attained, inasmuch as they tend towards universality of rights and enlightenment, which are Progress, which tend to Unity, and which constitue the only alternative of revolution.

§

But although everything in Morality, Policy, and Commerce, pointed to an alliance with the North, we have left the chances to others, and through the sympathies of our rulers against the Integrity of the Northern Continent, have offered a dangerous opportunity to Napoleon.

Napoleon, as is the trick of his race, seizes now, a hundred years before the age, the "Gates of the Pacific," at Panama, even as his predecessor seized the Key of the East at Suez.

It is a mechanical success, and is not intended either to menace or insult any great national forces or principles in America.

If the people of one nation were ever to be safely led against the people of another living nation, three thousand miles from the base of operations, this is not the "epoch," nor are the French the nation that could be led with impunity against a brother nation, fighting for freedom, for Democracy, and for good Government.

"The Gates of the Pacific" might seem a glorious prize to a mere Soldier, but Napoleon knows that there are prizes still more inciting and glorious to Americans,—the prizes of American Nationality, Unity, Independence, and not only so, but that the servants of these, could put into the field the "stronger battalions."

Panama will doubtless be the great thoroughfare for the commerce of the future. Napoleon may hold it for civilization, or exchange, or neutralisation,—he can scarcely attempt to hold it for conquest.

But Panama is a mechanical, a tactical affair only. Napoleon means not to menace or rouse the invincible energies and immortal hate of the American nation. It has nothing to do with the deep permanent things of the Western world.

It only constitutes a makeweight in European (Austrian) compromises, or the most splendid prize in the world wherewith to negociate with that power in America that shall ultimately conquer.

Panama is indeed a marvellous instance of how a profound intellect discovers at the ends of the earth, instruments of his will, and threads that can be woven into the warp and woof of policy.

Panama is held *for* the Americans whenever they can redeem the pledge, but it may be held *against the English.*

It is the furthest parallel of approach against her commerce and authority in the West, just as Suez in the East.

These are "far off," it is true, but they are lines of circumvallation, through which England *will have to pass*, for the nearest and best approaches to her mighty "Independencies," and to her mightier trade.

The most obvious view is that the Isthmus is a makeweight in Austrian compromises. This is not unimportant. But it does not vitally concern England, and it must be remembered that *whoever* may hold the South, whether Confederates or Federals, they will not be friends of England. Till Canada is annexed, there will be jealousies about that territory. If the "South" dies out, it will be what it always has been,—part of America. Should it succeed, our Government will have incurred the enmity of the greatest naval power in the world, and also of its friends and allies.

The policy of England has again been Isolation and barrenness.

§

Thus to the Government of the future, the safety of the Union, the freedom of the Slave, the right administration of India, the safe settlement of the Cotton question, the future of Canada and our relations arising therefrom with the United States, there must be added other questions of our position and policy in relation to the key of one of the world's greatest thoroughfares.

The great seat,—startling as the assertion may seem,—*of Anglo-Saxon power*, *is* ALREADY TRANSFERRED *to the American Continent*, and we see no cause for alarm, no omen of misfortune to England or the English, when we look in vain even to the Canadian lakes or rivers, for an ultimate barrier against the unifying power of natural and social influences and propagandism, which may cause the great American Anglo-Saxon races to flow into one Confederation. Family and personal virtues, have given them power to multiply, and spread, and subdue nature. Peaceful pursuits have taught them to manipulate its products. Their strength and stamina have enabled them to resist, alike, oppression and assimilation. Why should the Anglo-Saxon race go to pieces or remain in fragments, as all other races are coming together? The pride of our common race, origin, and history, and the future world-wide interests of freedom, and popular institutions, may be better vindicated, and more deeply involved, than we now suspect, in the widest theory of American Unity. The Canadian lake chain is no barrier, but the contrary.

Commerce, intermarriage, neighbourhood, association, language, race, religion, and boundary, all tend, soon or late, to draw together the *great English Continent*, in everlasting bonds of interest, sympathy, and love. In this process, it is not English territory that would be absorbed, it is the great English race that would unite. Nor must it be forgotten, that that race, having conquered and utilised America, would by natural tendency, join with the nation of their Father's home, in the reciprocations of peace, or, if needs be, in the sterner alliances of war.

Time will settle these things. The only impolicy, as regards America, is that which would give to time, vengeful and rankling memories to assuage, instead of mutual connecting links, and interests, to multiply and confirm.

War with America would be truly a civil war, and a "Statesmanship" that rejected the natural staple of India, and considers it "natural" to form an alliance with the Slaveholding South to get that self same staple at a higher price, is a policy which it will now be impossible to impose on the English nation.

Slavery must go, for it is not self-supporting, and the free nation on whom it leant, has cast it out, and off. *Other questions must come*, and when they come, where will be the balance of righteous power, and will England be prepared, and will the empires she has given the world, be willing, ready, and whole, when something *will be* in question?

Every agency will then be wanted and worked on the one side or the other. *The English Govern-*

ment may want America then. The world will want America then. And now, every individual man and woman in England, should realize that he and she both feel and want America's influence now, and should see to it that Governmental action shall not have made communion of action impossible, between Englishmen here, and Anglo-Americans there.

A home in America has proved the most valuable thing on earth to fugitives of all nations.

The influence of American freedom, is the most valuable influence on earth to the oppressed or depressed of all nations, who remain where they are.

Next to the Christian Religion, of which America is the most influential advocate, the American Government and constitution is the most precious possession which the world holds, or which the future can inherit.

§

An enthusiasm that acts in the present, and an appreciation of the whole far-reaching character of the crisis,—qualities elsewhere oftener found separate than together, are part of the political character of the American people, and we must try to appreciate them. It is our first duty as onlookers to estimate the true character and just perspective of these great events.

In the life of a nation, even were it a small one, and of a race, were it ignoble, eighty years are almost as one day, and three years a hardly appreciable point of time. In crises so stupendous as this, man reaches a stage when passion, and vengeance, and immortal love, and fixed eternal hate, lift human nature to heights, and sink it to depths, unintelligible to the ordinary "practical man." Accordingly, the friends of the South in England, have already proved themselves the only unpractical men. They exult over the Southern "nationality," which is but a faction, and ignore the American nationality, the intensest yet created. They are in fact the only utterly hopeless partisans. They talk about "the needful," and "Bankruptcy," and "Wall Street," and "the price of Bullion,"—doubt whether negroes will fight for freedom, or whether, because a certain State is a manufacturing State, it will not join secesh,—for the sake of monopoly "in woollens," for example. They forget that when battle is once begun the noblest and truest faith will always last and fight the longest, and "gain definitively the last victory."

America, just now, has got the measles. She has been passing through the diseases of childhood,—and as she throws the disease outward, the process will ultimately strengthen and purify her infant constitution. But, lo! all the state quacks of Europe are talking of her unnatural growth and proportions, prophesying of decay and amputation of members, or taking up their parable concerning atrophy and exhaustion,—while all the while the patient is only conscious of a healthy and desirable outcome of impurities, worked out at last by an athletic constitution to the surface, and soon to be worked off it.

This is about as it should be. *There* is no want

of farsightedness. The Diplomatists, who, in any European war, would seek to commit this country on the side of Legitimacy, against the peace and the interests of the People, tremble at the success of the American experiment, and would recommend to America the right divine, not of rulers but of rebels, and the Sovereignty, not of Legitimate authority, but of revolting states. In America the rebels are the Oligarchy, and an Oligarchy, though a rebellion, is always right!

But the crisis of the Northern life is already past, and the suicide of the South goes on swimmingly. No nation, true to principle, ever yet foundered in stress of battle, or in any lesser trial. The South imagined that the North would not dare to emancipate, or that it was not pure enough to desire emancipation. It rested also on the broken reed of European convulsions, recognitions, and interventions.

The course of this struggle has pointed a moral at which the whole world has turned pale. For eighty years, England and America have attempted, in the face of that world of which they have been the greater part, to compromise a felony,—and they have failed. The natural laws that govern the universe have indicted these two countries, and prosecuted them to conviction. Civil war and industrial bankruptcy are the penalties.

Compromises in Northern politics, and in English cotton trade, have well nigh got the world between them into a dead lock. Morality now has demonstrated itself to be also Statesmanship and Finance, and the question now is, not whether the world will attend to the Slave question, but whether it will settle it so that it shall not arise again to confound us,—settle it in accordance with the principles of commerce, philanthropy, statesmanship, and religion. The question has gone the old established round and come back to the old foregone conclusion. Principle came at the first as a choice, next as an alternative with defeat, and lastly as an avenger and a doom. The two stages of hypocrisy and compromise, and then of constitutional warfare, have passed away, and the stage of open war has come. Freedom and Slavery, slavery and trade,—two essentially antagonistic principles, have been pretending,—the greatest organised hypocrisy the world ever saw,—to live together in unity, and now the farce is over and the piece damned. The Slaveholding states have been the great moral teachers. The North has learnt that in all compromises the *right* is in danger of losing,—has already lost its best vantage ground. The North has chosen principle instead of defeat, and learnt how to do, as well as for what to die. The Emancipation Act propitiates the principle of justice, and settles the ultimate issue of the war. A policy of Despair has urged on the Slave power for forty years, and it has yet to conduct it to its end.

But has England,—the England of Lancashire, of Canada, and of India, no remorse to bear, no folly to recant, no lesson to learn, no policy, industrial or Imperial, to undo and to reconstruct? We have had India now long enough, *if we had had also a* MAN, unhanded by manikins at home, and Lilliputians at Calcutta, to settle the democratic rights there as to land tenure, and reconcile them with the feudal rights. To adjust law practice to the traditions of the people, and to natural equity, and to bear ourselves as a Christian nation, in a manner neither inconsistent, aggressive, nor weak.

But the old moribund traditions,—partnerships old and new with "Chivalry" against mankind, are yet we fear of more living weight in the English cabinet, than all the majestical future of Imperial interests, or of Anglo-American and Anglo-Saxon destinies, and Indian rights. As Earl Russell said,—"They have no time to examine great questions!" Still Statesmen called "English" exist as little better than watch dogs of the Rhine, and as guardians of the interests of those 38 infinitesimal blasphemies called German States. In foreign affairs they care more for an acre on the Rhine, than an Empire in the East, and all their philosophy, and all their function, has been till lately, how to govern the world so as to obstruct the territorial unity of France, and how to uphold the mechanical structure called the Austrian Empire, at the price of Italian unity, and Hungarian freedom. It seems true that till these men,—the last of them, are clean gone for ever, the industrial necessities and opportunities of this country, and the opportunities of India, will not be made a primary object of Statesmanship.

When the last of the "Austrians" is gone, the English Empire may have a chance, but till then, Imperial Statesmanship, must, we fear, be left to individual Statesmen, inadequately sustained by public opinion.

Until Englishmen will resolutely attend to their own essential needs and greatest interests, and to the rights of our great dependencies, the opportunities of empire will be lost, the claims of subject races to justice and intelligent Government will be mocked, the resources of the world will be undeveloped, revolution will menace order in the East, and collapse threaten industry at home, and above all, the great lesson now taught us by America will be unrecognised and unlearnt.

It is, after all, a coincidence, not strange but most emphatic, that politicians amongst us, called, with no complimentary intent, "American," should be those same men who *have* time to examine great questions, who have accordingly comprehended the great dangers and opportunities of India to England, and tried *before* the danger came, without ceasing, as without success, to awake the nation to a sense of them.

Adjustment of representation to population, has done much to save America. It has made power commensurate with right. Could English policy be much meaner, narrower, or worse, with some such conservative-democratic element. Is it a fact, that England has lost the art of Empire, or that Englishmen yet remain unrepresented? The West salutes the future with a policy of reconstruction and hope. Is it that *our* constitution is unbalanced,—that for ourselves, and for the West and East, we seemed so long incapable of moving, and of forcing obstructives to move themselves out of the nation's pathway, and to occupy one of the most splendid positions in the world, for something less fatal than the repudiation of all foresight in Government, and all prevision in Trade.

§

Nothing but English Statesmanship could have transferred the Cotton trade from India to the South, and it is owing to that that Murder and Cotton have grown together to the harvest there for 80 years. Enterprise and Freedom created the South, and partnership with free states and free men has sustained it, and in 60 years multiplied its staple, from 5000 bales to 5,000,000. The Northerner, Whitney, invented for the South the Steam Gin. Free men invented, and free labour made for it, railways and steamboats. The North found, for the South, capital, of which the South repudiates the interest. England found for the South a sum of £25,000,000 invested in American railways, and for some years kindly made an annual present to the South of a cool £10,000,000 in the way of unnatural and extra price for Cotton.* Finally, for the South, African Slaves have worked, and the South, hitherto, empowered by political partnership with the North, has kept the Slave a Slave, and has had leisure to plot politically against the well being of its neighbours and dependents.

In 1806 the West Indies contributed about 30 per cent of the Cotton that came to Liverpool.

* It was calculated in 1856, that an advance of one farthing per lb. on the consumption amounted to nearly a million sterling.

They now send ½ per cent. The West Indies were governed by English proconsuls, but were not in social or political partnership with a free nation. The destruction of that country enured to the benefit of the South.

In 1806 India sent us 7,787 bales. In 1818, 247,659 bales, or 1-6th more than the South. In 1856 it sends us 463,000 bales, while the South sent us 71 per cent out of our whole consumption. And what was the cause of this? From 1834 to 1848, the East India Company,* having received £300,000,000, for the development of Indian resources, spent on its roads, irrigation, &c. £1,400,000, little more thon 1*d.* in the pound. Englishmen, neglecting the warning of the Statesman, Bright, who, in 1848, moved for a Committee upon the growth of Cotton in India, allowed their Government, to allow the East India Company, to allow their Directors, to strangle India, by withholding transit facilities, land rights, &c. and so, forcing back and down the struggling and rising commerce in our National Staple. *Thus* has the South prospered.

But in 1860 two causes arose to destroy the South, which through the follies and crimes of the world had swollen to unnatural proportions and suicidal insolence.

Politically the South wanted more Slave States, mechanically made, to counterbalance the votes and power of Free States, naturally arising. Economically the South wanted more Slave States to feed the land waste of her barbarous system.

* Evidence of Mr. Mangles, Chairman of the Directors.

The South by violence, conspiracy, and perjury, would have cut up the free territory for these base needs and uses, but the North stood at bay.

Hence Secession, civil war, and destruction of Cotton, and ultimately, of the political structure of the South. In 1844-5 cotton was about 4*d.* In 1846-7 it rose to 7*d.* and 9*d.* In 1858, the monopoly which England had conferred upon the South, told fearfully against herself. India was wanted. Cotton rose 3*d.* a pound, and about £7,000,000 sterling went out of the pockets of John Bull and into the pockets of the "Chivalry." England that ransomed her own slaves at £20,000,000, pays with one hand £1,000,000 a year to stop the Slave Trade, and with the other pays the South seven to ten millions a year, to raise the value of Slaves, and plantations, and Slave produce,—thus practically enabling it and forcing it, to secure fresh slaves from Africa, and paying in increased price of Cotton, the insurance dues on every Slaver that sails.

Liverpool, built, like the South, with blood, began, like it, to totter. Cotton is up. India and England down. The murder is out. Its partnership with Cotton, and England, and Slavery, and America, at an end. Morality has strangely turned out to be economics, and might, had any body tried her, have turned out to be Statesmanship. And now after a circumbendibus of eighty years, and by way of India, Lancashire, and Eastern and Western America, the rogues have turned out to be fools, and the prospect of outwitting nature and God, only a gigantic hoax, in which each member of the partnership suffers exactly in proportion as he has sinned!

The People of America will see to it that the Slave power does not repeat its treason. Will the People of England see to it that their Statesmen do not repeat theirs?

§

The History of England, from Cromwell to that curious measure, the Reform Bill, is the history of the great Tory reaction, counteracting extensively all that has been good and progressive in England, and using its power against all that is good and progressive abroad. It is the history of the conquest and degradation of the English People by a clique and a faction. The history of England during the time of Cromwell, and also since 1832, is the history of the successful struggles of Democracy and Puritanism, against the influences of the reaction.

It was the great conservative reaction that brought back the sanguinary and lecherous Stuart to succeed Cromwell, the "first of Englishmen," and that made the next hundred years a blank in English achievements.

George III. and the reaction followed even to America, the political progress of the great English revolution, and would have strangled the Hercules in the cradle.

The reaction, and George III., assailed the republic of France, declared their determination to uphold Austria and the French king, drove the democracy of Paris mad, and created the spirit that welded the French nation into one,—that created Napoleon, and made his career possible.

But now the influence of faction is less,—that of the People, more.

The influence of great towns is augmenting, that of great lords is decreasing.

The influence of the many is more; that of the few, less. Oligarchy declines, Democracy advances.

Fraud, where it can, succeeds now to force. Still Secret Diplomacy does sometimes by stealth, evil, that would otherwise be not only infamous, but impossible, and hastens, *where it can*, to delude, or forestall opinion.

The Reaction is so far reached upon, that fraud, compromise, and postponement, are now its chief weapons.

Though the Reform Bill was a dishonest measure, giving to feudality in the counties, what it took from corruption in the towns, yet the popular reaction it stirred, has been a power ever since, and if a righteous struggle can but last, the Democracy and Puritanism of England are always aroused to the help of the right, and sometimes checkmate, sometimes overpower the foe.

The Oligarchy of England "recognised" *as Belligerents* the Oligarchy of the South, in a few weeks after their rebellion against Democracy and freedom began.

The Democracy of England would have "recognised" the pirate ships by destroying them.

But Public opinion,—English Democracy and Puritanism,—bestirred itself. They could not however undo the quasi "recognition," and "Belligerents" can claim the right to buy contraband of war. And the Government that prosecuted Kossuth, and that prosecutes recruiters for a nation centuries old, so far irrevocably secures in a few weeks, and against the will of the English people, the immunities and advantage of English markets, for the friends of Oligarchy and Slavery, to use against Democracy and Freedom.

Thus they tempted the South to goad on the North to war against us. Thus they tempted the South to stop and challenge on the high seas all the English marine, lest it carry "contraband" to its enemy, our friend, and blood relation.

The question clearly remained for us to answer, —"Who governs England,"—"where is the sovereignty of the People?" asserted by Cromwell, and transplanted by us to America. Oligarchs fain would have forced us to destroy it there, as well as as in France, and hastened to yield advantage to its deadly foes.

The friends of progress, of improvements in the practice, and of initiative in the science of Governing, are of two classes. The People with reason undebauched and instincts uncorrupted; and the higher classes (in every true sense of the expression), whose completed culture, ample leisure, and disciplined reason, enables them to comprehend human questions in their historical Integrity, and to apply the world-logic of events to politics. The "great middle class" of England, too much affected by the mortal poison of materialism, too exclusively occupied with trade and professions, apes mechanically a conservatism which many of their betters have abandoned, is "educated" out of sympathy but not up to faith, is refined enough to sneer, but not strong enough, in head, or heart, in fortitude, in enthusiasm, in leisure, in generalisation, or in ideas, to *believe.*

Well then, if the centre of England is so far demoralised and weak, the flanks must wheel round, and cover it, and hide it, in the day when *English* opinion has to be expressed before the world.

The People scent their own battle, and will see to it, that *their* country, *their* strength, *their* repute, *their* future, is not prostituted by figurants of State-craft, and *filles de joie* of policy, for Southern uses,—by the same criminal and inane crew who assisted at the destruction of Hungary, and the "neutralisation" (?) of the Black Sea,—who put, and so long kept, Austria in Italy, and have at various times prevented the resurrection of Poland.

The shrieks of Poland resound for the fifth time throughout Europe. Why does England crouch still, at the feet of the Czar, in company with Austria the jackal of Russia, and Prussia, "*bien bête et bien fausse?*"

Because the dead old George, and the dead old Tories of the Holy Alliance rule us still. Because we inherit the results of their deeds. Because we have left Europe practically unbalanced, between Russia and France. Because we fear the strength of France if we aided her to intervene, and the weakness of Russia if Poland were re-established!

The public law of Europe means license for barbarism and physical strength, and the purest, if not the wisest politicians, advocate neutrality between right and wrong, because, without neutrality, there would be complicity. Europe still suffers many of the wrongs and the mistakes saddled upon it by the great wars against progress and democracy, and is incapable of demanding of Russia, the fulfilment even of her distinct undertakings and guarantees entered into for valuable consideration, and of the plainest requirements of common sense, and international adjustment.

Europe cannot or dare not pronounce the name of Poland, and looks on while Prussia assists Russia in murdering her. The reason why, is that eighty years ago England went to war for legitimacy, Austria, and retrogression, against France, and Democracy, and is still bound by a thousand ties in that direction. Intervention brought us within a cycle of results of which some are not yet developed, and others not yet passed away. "Non-intervention" is the philosophy and the policy with which we salute the victims of *that* intervention, and the phrase, "the right, not the duty to intervene," expresses the Christianity and wisdom, that caps the anticlimax of imbecility and dishonour.

Democracy in England did not at first become articulate on secession. It has spoken partly through Trades' Union, and partly at the instance of various societies friendly to the slave of *colour;* but as a political question affecting every living soul upon the earth, both in principle, and in most intimate results,—especially the rights of the all against the usurpations of the few,—the People of England have scarcely delivered themselves adequately in support of their natural allies in America.

But the English Lion only slumbers. His last repast was of a class abuse of strictly economic laws. It is thirty years since he made a mouthful of a great political wrong. Let then his keepers take warning from the social law expounded by De Tocqueville, p. 67, vol. 1. and already quoted.

"When a nation modifies the electoral qualification, it may easily "be foreseen that sooner or later that qualification will be entirely "abolished. There is no more invariable rule in the History of "Society. For after each concession, the strength of the Democracy "increases, and its demands increase with its strength."

And now the just opinion and self restraint of the Democracy of England and of Lancashire, have immensely increased the *strength*, and fortified the position, of that Democracy for the coming reaction.

§

Every Government ought to be, or to be in the way of becoming, Democratic in its principles,—because, in every country, good Government tends to make the vast majority educated, and orderly,—conservative and free.

The only lasting conservatism,—the only conservatism that can be conserved, is the conservatism of a true Democracy.

Every Government, therefore, that opposes obstacles to the physical wellbeing, and intellectual and religious culture, or the adequate representation, of the People, is a Government of ignorance, atheism, and revolution.

We are not of those who would have Democratic

Institutions thoughtlessly adopted, but the essence of Democracy is Government by the public opinion of an instructed People, and we hold it to be the duty of all—of Kings, Lords, Commons, and Press, to work together for the advent of Democracy to power. Every man who does not so work, does, not so much postpone Democracy, as precipitate and aggravate revolution.

This is the answer to those who may ask "would you apply American institutions to this country?"

Remove every corporate, fiscal, or other unnatural obstacle, from the path of knowledge and religion, and then, let any Institutions come that may. For an instructed minority to dictate to an instructed majority, is,—not monarchy, oligarchy, or representation,—but a triumph of physical force over ideas.

The Georges sent this country galloping towards a republic. It is the greatest praise of Victoria, that almost every element of irritation, save that of an unbalanced constitution, has been removed, but as our good Queen reigns without governing, the usurpers who wield her functions, to deny the People their rights, have an abundant interest in withholding the suffrage from those who, at once, *understand*, and *condemn* their policy.

If in *any* country, the power of an instructed and orderly majority, does not, through whatever fictions or forms, rule that country,—its Government, either past or present, is judged, and is condemned.

But what are the facts about "Institutions" in England?

Does the Monarch rule?

Do the Lords rule?

Do the Commons either rule or represent the People?

The first is perhaps too much a formality, the second is very much an obstruction, the third is six-sevenths of a farce.—For the theory is that Lords and Commons are distinct estates and powers, and that the Commons represent the people. The fact is that only one million out of seven have the suffrage, and that the representatives they return, represent the Lords more than the People. The Principle, is that enunciated by Chatham an hundred years ago, in both houses;—"Representation and "taxation must go together. They are inseparable. "The idea of virtual representation is the most "contemptible that ever entered into the head of "man."

The grand desideratum is that theories and procedures should be ruled by the fundamental principles of the British Constitution.—That the balance of the Constitution be restored, and that the COMMONS should represent the veritable People and their interests.

To decide what is in England the ruling power, would require an investigation into the various branches of administration, of internal, external, and colonial questions, the discussion of which, is not the object of this Book. Sometimes it is public opinion *dis*tempered by Lord Palmerston, jockeyed by Mr. Disraeli, or "stemmed" by Lord Derby. In some cases it is one or other of these Gentlemen, driven along by Public opinion like thistle down before the whirlwind. In some, public opinion knows nothing of the matter in hand, till it is out of hand. In some, the dead old George III., and even his "dogeship," George II., rule us from their graves, by force of old-world connection and traditions. In some the true People do, and undo, at will.

One special element, disturbing the balance of social and political forces in England, has received some attention of late. We refer to our peculiar land laws. The genius of John Bull, as yet developed, is to insist on liberty, but to tolerate inequality,—nay, rather to like it than otherwise. The operation of the law of primogeniture, which is neither original Saxon, nor even Norman, has, in concert with the enormously increased price of land, created an oligarchy, constantly increasing in wealth, and decreasing in numbers, and which, up to the time of the Reform Bill and of the Repeal of the Corn Laws, ruled England absolutely.

Saxon England distributed estates amongst all the sons without primogeniture.

Norman law gave the eldest son the best estate, the *primum patris feudum* only, but as a law of conquest and precaution it parcelled out England amongst its conquerors, and limited the English estate from father to eldest son.

The holders of these fiefs, were, when English population was about two millions, as one in forty. Now they are only as one to two thousand, and, subject to disposition by the testator, all his land in the three kingdoms, and in the colonies, goes to the eldest son.

Thus is the Norman conquest perpetuated and intensified over Englishmen.

This oligarchy has sometimes stood between the Throne and the People, to the advantage of the latter. For the last eighty years it has joined the Throne against the People, or stood between them to the disadvantage and prejudice of both.

It would soon become a question, whether the growing numbers of the People, without the growing rivalry in wealth-power created by commerce, would not, in due time, make primogeniture a kind of *reductio ad absurdum.*

The weakness of the Anglo-Saxon race for inequality, provided it be tempered with liberty, has been most dangerously tampered with and aggravated by the grasp which the Conqueror still lays upon the land of the English, and by the thousandfold oligarchic influences built upon that foundation.

It requires but a short resumé of Anglo-European events, to show in what position the People and the Government really stand to one another and the world, and to prove that power should not be so much where it is, and should be more where it is not. To prove that *the constitution is unbalanced*, because the principle of representation which is the basis of our liberties is not enacted, and that inasmuch as the People do not really elect, representatives do not really represent. To prove that had this principle of the Constitution been enacted, the great measures which have weakened the national strength, tarnished the national honour, perpetuated the ignorance, and impoverished the condition of the People, by unjust and unnecessary wars, and by wars on the wrong side, would have been reversed.

The first American war, against which Chatham and Burke thundered, was not a People's war.

The war against the Republic of France was a war by an oligarchy and an autocrat, *for* Legitimacy, *against* the People.

The Russian war of intervention against Hungary would have led the English *People* into war for Hungary, but English policy was for dynasties, and not for Peoples.

The Crimean war was popular, for the People would have made it useful. The People would have pronounced the name of Poland, and would not have been content with immaterial Guarantees, —with Black Sea "neutralisation," and Circassian blockades.

The Italian war found us neutral, or talking about English Interests in the Adriatic, because our diplomacy, which had put Austria into Italy, could scarcely be expected to drive her out for the sake of the Italians.

We have deserted Poland from 1772 until now, from jealousy of France and alliances with Russia, arising from the necessities of our position as enemies of the People, and allies of reaction.

What, we ask, on all these great questions, would have been the policy of the People?

Would it not have been conservative for Europe, and destructive only of those powers and influences which cannot co-exist with real peace, or with any definitive settlements?

The responsibility for these things must rest either with THE PEOPLE, THE MEN, or, THE SYSTEM.

The PEOPLE have struggled for representation. The honest part of the Reform Bill would have given it to them, the dishonest part gave it back from them. True, the religious, or rather "evangelical" section of Englishmen, may have neglected citizen duties in the *haute politique*, but the cause we seek is not here.

Is it then the great representative MEN? They have been parties to all these European transactions. Was it connivance or Imbecility? Shall one say, for instance, of Lord Palmerston, that his prodigious energies have been willingly and mainly employed in withholding that which must inevitably be granted, and in upholding that which must inevitably fall, or, as such are the actual results, shall we say that he has been overruled and used, and has weakly preferred a spurious, and class-popularity to fame?

Or shall we say it is "the SYSTEM" that "did it all?" The question then is, who wants the system and who upholds it?—This system which lets these "creeping things" of office

"Get up into the ark."

§

The first stage in the downward course, and it has been a long one, was wrong doing. For eighty years Diplomatic England was little else than the procuress of Austria. For eighty years dealt she at the body of freedom her deathful stabs, and but for the unrepresented masses it had gone hard lately, that she did not run up her flag side by side with the black infernal flag of the Slaveholder, and range it against the great republic of the People.

The second stage was publicity. The world now *knows* these things.

The third stage was contempt, isolation, neutralisation, and rigid "non-intervention."

The fourth stage must be reaction, or destruction, or decay.

We think we see symptoms of a mighty reaction for freedom, representation, and a just foreign policy,—of a time when the People shall be represented, when Lords and Commons shall be really distinct powers in the State, when we shall no longer be glad in order not to be infamous in our Diplomacy and our arms, to take no side at all, and to allow the mighty heart of England to throb in vain, and her mighty arm to be shortened.

The nation must in time abdicate its place, or show its servants that it is Sovereign:—

> "The Problem solving in Politics always is, how Power shall "be developed, or how the Policy and the Politicians shall be "destroyed."
>
> "The development is an Imperial question,—Providence "secures it for the whole."
>
> "The destruction is a provincial question, each country may "settle it for itself."

§

Granted that America, by force of her own race, appliances, and institutions, and by assimilation of picked men (colonists) of all nations, shall continue to progress at the present ratio; granted also that European policy be one of short-sighted jealousy and intervention, and Europe may soon be waging a war 3000 miles from its base of operations, against a power that, acting on the defensive, might as well, for all practical purposes, be *infinite.*

For according to the outworn policy that suckled the fools of the anti-French era, and long maintained, at the charges of the English exchequer, and to the dishonour of the English nation, the vermin of legitimacy in Europe, we ought, long since, to have found our natural ally in the South, which seeks to divide a possible rival, which represents "interests," as opposed to rights, and the few, as opposed to the all. And we ought, long since, to have declared war against the North, the natural enemy of the classes that rule us, for do we not there perceive a great rival maritime power to be humiliated, a democracy which, if it succeed, *will propagate its virus through all institutions*, a nation of rival manufacturers, and a people who believe not in the "balance of power" for Europe, and who will not allow the "Balances" to be set up by Europeans in America?

This is the animus of all attempts to "recognise" a country that does not exist. If a faction, a minority *in* a minority in the North, had waged war against the Union for freer institutions, we should have had no motions for recognition.

These 190,000 slaveholders, polished, skilful, capable and strong,—with their train of slave-brokers and slave drivers, their black harems, their devil's chaplains, and their devil's huntsmen, and their millions of mean whites helping them, in the name of nationality, to tread down one nation that they may assail the organic life of another,—these "seekers of a country" have, forsooth, "sympathisers." The sympathy shown them but lifts the curtain from *that mighty army of revolt* existing in all countries, which views with terror, ludicrous, abject, but malignant, the approaching destruction, by and for the people, of the last *great representative abuse of class privilege* that exists in America. The North has destroyed all other class interests, and has set the individual and the nation free to run a career, without special class and corporate interests to handicap them in the world-race. Slavery is a class interest, and class interests throughout the world stand by their order. The order of the few against the all,—of power against right,—of caste and class against principle,—of privilege against the multitude,—of the isolated against the universal. Such is the motley and multitudinous host set against those who to-day fight the great representative battle of the human race.

This is the battle of the Peoples every where, but it is the special battle of the American people, —the price and the crown of their unity. If they fight it not out, they will be divided, degraded, reviled, and accursed amongst all Peoples, and to the end of time.

Fortunately, English policy and power is in a transition state. Fortunately also, that diabolic jest called Secret Diplomacy is passing away. The collision *may* be avoided.

There are but two parties in England. The party that believes in and trusts the people, and the party that does not.

There are but two parties in America, and they are virtually the same.

The same party and principles divide the two countries and policies. But America is in a crueller crisis, and England has no corporate anti-national and anti-popular power, so strong, so logical, so consistent, and so desperate as the Slave power.

Government by and for the all, or by and for the few, is the question with both, but England proceeds with less speed, and they say, with greater safety, to place her centre of authority and representation nearer the real centre of her political gravity.

The masses may be *blindly* drifting towards a great constitutional conflict, but they are none the less approaching it. The situation exhibits all the presages of such a conflict, and explains the present paralysis of parties. There is popular contempt of official supineness; there is official blindness with regard to popular progress and strength. There is a determination on the part of certain leaders to stem the tide of Democracy, and on the part of others there is the fear to lead it on. Meanwhile the power and intelligence of the unrepresented people accumulates behind these obstacles. They are thinking, perhaps, that in the matter of American Democracy,—of recognition of a pirate Empire of six weeks standing,—of *non* intervention and *non* recognition of an ancient nation now being slaughtered before the eyes and within the hearing of Europe,—and in the matter of Domestic reform, Democracy could scarcely cost more, or do the work worse. The oligarchy cannot much longer combine pity for the misfortunes, and admiration of the self-restraint, with denial of the rights of the masses. And the masses are learning fast and well the grand lesson of Association,—of political, as well as social, co-operation and combination, which America has so long practised, and which so many of the speciosities and dilettanti of English political life, are ignorantly helping the masses to achieve.

Thus English politics stand still, awaiting the mighty momentum which American Democracy triumphant will impart to its English counterpart.

The question of the Freedom of the Ocean we cannot here discuss. England has for ages made her might the right and the wrong of the maritime world. "Against what shores have not the bloody prows of our vessels dashed themselves?" America, especially, remembers that as long as we had the power to compel it, their vessels knew but one path, the path that led to England. Since their marine arose to power, there has existed a second might and right upon the ocean, and freedom and law are gradually growing out of the change.

It is long since in time of full peace we seized merchantmen of the French to the value of thirty millions of livres, and took captive eight thousand of their seamen, but even now we hear that tame Corsairs in the Commons send out English Pirates to prey upon American merchantmen, and dare to boast of the outrage in the Halls of Legislation.

It is perhaps time that the opinions urged by Chatham and Burke, in 1766, upon the English Parliament on behalf of America, and in favour of actual representation, should be acted upon on behalf of England. Thus the influence and good offices of English Statesmen may be repaid, after a hundred years, by the American nation.

Let us here repeat,—actual representation, and a separation of the different Estates of the realm, are of the essence of the British constitution.

"Whoever," said Chatham in 1770, "understands the theory of the English constitution, and will compare it with the fact, must see at once how widely they differ. We must reconcile them to each other, if we wish to save the liberties of this country. The constitution intended that there should be a permanent relation between the constituent and representative body of the people. As the House of Commons is now formed that relation is not preserved, it is destroyed."

It is still almost as necessary to quote Lord Coke, as Otis found it in 1765;—"that it is against Magna Charta, and against the franchise of the land, for freemen to be taxed but by their own consent." We have still to wish, in the words of Lord Camden, in an American Debate in 1766,—"that the maxim of Machiavel was followed, that of examining a constitution at certain periods according to its first principles; this would correct abuses, and supply defects; and that the representative authority of this kingdom was more equally settled." We have still to better the instruction contained in the famous "Bedford Protest" in the latter year, and signed by thirty-three Peers, of course including a goodly sprinkling of Bishops, that "the plea of our North American Colonies of not being represented in the Parliament of Great Britain, may, *by the same reasoning*, *be extended* to all persons in this island who do not actually vote for members of Parliament." Without endorsing this idea to its full extent, we have still to combat the old Tory doctrine that representation is not in the Bill of Rights, and that Parliament holds power not as a representative body but in absolute trust. The fact is that the Commons represent the Peers, and that the masses have no suffrage. Chatham recommended the liberal aristocracy to join the People. But whether they do or not, political science has now armed the People with a new weapon, which will replace Prerogative with popular sovereignty, and Privilege with equality of conditions. *Thus with the true British constitution as fulcrum, and the Principle of Popular* Association *as lever, the battle of the People and of the Constitution may be fought and won.*

A word to the wise is enough. It were pity to waste even that word upon men who are neither good enough nor bad enough for practical purposes,—who show their hatred of sin by backing up the sinners, and their political honour by prostituting it to the Slavedriver or the Austrian,—who have no mental generative force, whether for good or evil,—who claim for *single* events, that "they establish a principle,"—and whose ill-digested facts, and faithless philosophy, recognise, and would have England recognise, *that Nightmare of felons and fools*,—a permanent Slave Empire!

CHAPTER IV.

AMERICAN NATIONALITY AND DEMOCRACY.

THE ARGUMENT.

"The spirit of nationality is at once the bond and safeguard of kingdoms; it is something above laws, something beyond thrones, —the impalpable element of the inner life of states. But anti-nationality is the confusion and the downfall of kingdoms,—it is a blight and a mildew to the heritage of the people."—*Burke.*

"One event at least is sure, at a period which may be said to be near, the Anglo-Americans will alone cover the immense space between the Polar regions and the Tropics, from the Atlantic to the Pacific. * * *

"One hundred and fifty millions of men will be living in North America, *equal* in condition, the progeny of *one* race, owing their origin to the *same* cause, and preserving the *same* civilization, the *same* language, the *same* religion, the *same* habits, the *same* manners, and imbued with the *same* opinions, propagated under the *same* forms. The rest is uncertain, but this is certain; and it is a fact new to the world,—a fact fraught with such portentous consequences as to baffle the efforts even of the imagination."

De Tocqueville, pp. 453-6, vol. 2.

"*The Sovereignty of the People is the last link in the chain of opinions which binds the whole Anglo-American world.* That Providence has given to every human being a degree of reason necessary to direct himself in the affairs which interest him exclusively, is the grand maxim upon which civil and political society rests in the United States. The father applies it to his children, the master to his servants, the township to its officers, the province to its townships, the State to the provinces, the Union to the States; and when extended to the nation it becomes the doctrine of the Sovereignty of the People."—*De Tocqueville,* 428, vol. 2.

"The Union is an accident, * * * but the *republican form of Government* seems to me the natural state of the Americans, which nothing but continued action of hostile causes, always acting in the same direction, could change into a monarchy."

De Tocqueville, p. 424, vol. 2.

"Government is founded, not on force, as was the theory of Hobbes, nor on compact, as was the theory of Locke and the Revolution of 1688; nor on property, as had been asserted by Harrington. It springs from the necessities of our nature, and has an everlasting foundation in the unchangeable will of God. * * * *This supreme power is originally and ultimately in the people;* and the people never did in fact freely, nor can rightfully make an unlimited renunciation of this divine right. Kingcraft and priestcraft are a trick to gull the vulgar. The happiness of mankind demands that this grand and ancient alliance should be broken off for ever. * * * To bring the powers of all into the hands of one, or some few, and to make them hereditary, is the interested work of the weak and the wicked. * * *

"*There can be no prescription old enough to supersede the law of nature, and the grant of God Almighty,* who has given all men a right to be free.

"The grand political problem is to invent the best combination of the powers of legislation and execution: * * * but the first and simple principle is EQUALITY and THE POWER OF THE WHOLE."

"The colonists are men; the colonists are therefore freeborn; for by the law of nature, all men are freeborn, white or black. No good reason can be given for enslaving those of any colour.

"Nor do the political and civil rights of the British colonists rest on a charter from the crown. *Old Magna Charta was not the beginning of all things;* nor did it rise on the borders of chaos out of the unformed mass.

"*Acts of Parliament against the fundamental principles of the British constitution are void.*"

"The world is at the eve of the highest scene of earthly power and grandeur that has ever yet been displayed to the view of mankind.

"Who will win the prize is with God. But *human nature must and will be rescued from the general slavery that has so long triumphed over the species.*"—*Otis*, on the American Crisis, 1764.

"Otis was a flame of fire; with a promptitude of classical allusion, a depth of research, a rapid summary of historical events and dates, a profusion of legal authorities, a prophetic glance into futurity, and a rapid torrent of impetuous eloquence, he hurried away all before him. *American Independence was then and there born.*"—*President Adams*, on the speech of Otis against "writs of assistance" in 1761.

CONTENTS.

Conditions. — American nationality, freedom and Democracy.—What is a nation ?—What is the American nation ? —*Prima Facie.* — With compensation or without.—Democracy and the South.—The South a faction.—Six reasons.— Precedents, Facts and Analogies. — Objections answered. — " Strength of South."—Bases of national movements.—Principle or Interest.—Internal and External Strength.—Individual, State, Nation.—Relation between them.—The Tests of Peace. —The strongest Principles and greatest numbers.—" Statesmanship and Unity " of South.—Dilemma of South.—Slavery and Decay.—Freedom and Democracy.—Election returns.— Secession a minority in South.—Irreconcilable Interests.— War of Principle and " live Stock."—Southern results so far.— Argument from Strength ; Material, Intellecual, Spiritual.— Argument from nationality. — Elements of. --Questions of GEOGRAPHY, HISTORY, CONSTITUTION, PRINCIPLES and NATIONALITY.--The making of the Nation.—Leading characteristics of America.—Unity and Community.—Six points.—The Royal Nation.—The South *per contra.*—The five monopolies on which it has lived.—Mean Whites, Slaves, and Despots.—Secession kills Secession. — Narrow basis of South. — Universality and oneness of America.—Who shall separate ?

" If the men of our time were led by attention and observation, and by sincere reflection, to acknowledge that the gradual and progressive development of *social equality* is at once the past and future of their history, this solitary truth would confer the sacred character of a divine decree upon the change. *To attempt to check democracy would be in that case to resist the will of God.*"

De Tocqueville, p. 21, Introduction.

WE have shown how we propose to prove that the South is no nation.

But it were a poor thing to establish only the nationality of America. It is our business to prove, that America possesses all the elements and conditions of nationality in such complete and magnificent development, as to make it *the royal nation of the future*, and to carry it beyond all shadow of present parallelism, even with the great English nation that gave it birth, that colonized it with its best men, and laid the deep foundations of its glory in the common law, and traditionary rights of Englishmen.

During the greatest era England has known,—the era of Sidney, and Raleigh, and Elizabeth, and Burleigh, and Milton, and Shakespeare, and Blake, and Cromwell—England sent forth many of her noblest, to reproduce and magnify herself in the great Anglo-Saxon Continent of the West.

We propose to discuss in this chapter certain general considerations respecting the conditions of American nationality; to state the specific form of *proof* which those considerations ought to assume; and also to institute a comparison between the characteristics of the Slave faction, and of the American nation.

The present epoch has to do with American nationality, and its struggles to complete itself against treason, sectional action, and oligarchic influences. American Democracy represents authority, nationality, and freedom. Its natural enemy is oligarchy, in the form of Slavocracy, attacking nationality, democracy, and order, all at once.

There is, therefore, first, the question of nationality and its guarantees; and secondly, the question of its character and conditions, as they exist in America.

The general questions which thus challenge the judgment of mankind, as the main items of the "American question," strictly so called, assume the following specific shape:—

1st. Can America reunite?

2nd. What political future is to rule her (to be) enormous population, and the vast territory which it will inhabit? How will the war test leave her Institutions? will the People remain masters, or is Government by and for the all a problem still receding into futurity from the passionate grasp of the million—still mocking the prescience of philosophy, and the hopes of those who believe in Man?

3rd. The Slave Trade, as a main feature of one of the contending systems.

In other words, *what of American Nationality, Freedom, and Democracy, as opposed to a divided nationality, and a government by and for the few, whether it be termed slaveocracy, monarchy, oligarchy, or Despotism?*

It must be borne in mind, that the complete answer to these questions depends upon the answer to the three questions before stated, and which it is the object of the whole book to answer, namely,—"What is a Nation?" and "What is the American Nation?" and, "What is the South?" But, we think that a conscientious attention to certain general considerations on the conditions and characters of American nationality might have saved Secessionists a good deal of inane talk about Independence, and Englishmen perhaps, all attempts at a third great war against republics, and popular institutions.

We have seen that the Americans, though a young nation, are an old people, and an old Democracy. "A Democracy," says De Tocqueville, "more perfect than any which antiquity had "dreamt of, started in full size and panoply from "the midst of an ancient feudal society." The same great writer also remarks,—"The Americans "are a very old and enlightened people, who have "fallen upon a new and unbounded country, where "they may extend themselves at pleasure, and "fertilize without difficulty. This state of things "is without a parallel in the history of the world." They are, "That portion of the English people "which is commissioned to explore the wilds of "the new world."*

When therefore we behold an old and strong nation, disturbed by rebellion, we naturally at first sight, conclude that the disturbance is but temporary.

If we find that the country is peopled by one race, governed by uniform institutions, animated by one political genius, speaking one language, worshipping one God, settled in a compact territory, with well defined boundaries, we conclude that the cause of offence must be strong, deep-seated, and desperate, indeed, that could crown such a rebellion with success.

If we discover that the rebels had constitutional modes of redress of grievances, to the use of which they were open, and free, and invited, we

* De Tocqueville, pp. 66. 68, v. 3.

stand amazed at the profligacy that should reject constitutional opposition, and appeal to arms. And this feeling would become still stronger, if it appeared that they constituted a leading and powerful party in the State.

But if it be seen that a rebellion *à priori* so causeless and hopeless, has in fact been already driven from some of its chief positions for offence, defence, and commissariat, and that these defeats have been sustained notwithstanding a long preparation of plans and amassing of monies and material, and notwithstanding that military genius has disciplined, organised, and led the whole,—then we are reduced to ask what can possibly have brought about such an undertaking, and what now can possibly avert its total failure?

Nations with real rights and real grievances, with no hope of constitutional redress, separated and alien in language, religion, race, territory, and institutions, have rebelled and failed since the world began. Why shall these rebels,—whose cause apparently reverses all known conditions of success, and includes all known conditions of ultimate failure,—why should *they* hope?

Probably the truth is they do *not* hope. Doubtless *despair* enters largely into their calculations. Doubtless their rebellion is but a phase in the essential progress and discipline of the mighty nation that bore them. But as their friends in England hope or pretend to hope, for them, we will shew hereafter that the circumstances which occasioned the rebellion will destroy it.

We say then, 1stly, Slavedom saw the natural

superiority and steady progress of free labour, free votes, and free institutions, and saw in them its *Executioner. The Slave Interest must do, or die.* It might as well do, before the dying.

2ndly.—It was led by 200,000 men who had amongst them many of culture, leisure, and genius. Their prestige, reputation, fortunes,—all, were set to win or lose by Slavery.

3rdly.—They were followed by some 6,000,000 "mean whites," identified with them by prejudice, material interest, pride of race and party, and by necessity.

4thly.—They were supported by Slaves who had neither energy, union, resources, opportunity, or will for freedom.

Thus the 200,000 Slaveholders have an absorbing interest in supporting Slavery, and an extraordinary concentration of power enabling them.

We put aside here the Southern constitution, which declares, "that no law against slavery shall "be introduced," and consider only military necessities.

The South will either retain Slavery or not.

If it do not retain it, it would Compensate or it would not compensate. It cannot dare entertain the project of compensating the owners of three and a half millions of slaves. That would make the South too dear a place to live in. Free labour would repudiate the obligation, and the men who alone can assume it, are already experienced repudiators, and would not be trusted. The Slave constitutes near half the population of the South, to free him, and promise to his masters compensation, is but to establish the alternative that he shall either remain, and, in some way or other, pay his own ransom, or run away to avoid the impost.

But without compensation, what is the prospect? The North compensates,—the South does not. The North only wanted to limit Slavery and keep it out of the "Territories." The South uses up the Slaveholders, and wages a desolating war to destroy their property, and institutions, for the sake of which the war was commenced. The North would have proceeded by order and vote. The South seceded against its own majority, and occupies regions, some of which Richmond papers now describe, as "reeking with disaffection."

For what then are these enthusiastic Southerners going to remain true to the men who have passed upon them the greatest practical joke since the world began?

Are they to remain in allegiance to the men, to the Institutions, or to the mere "idea" of fractional Southern Independence?

"The men" have deceived them. "The Institutions" are oligarchic. The Independence, even though bolstered up by Frenchmen, would be absorbed or destroyed by the greater American nation.

Why? For what reason? By what inducements? How should they—could they,—or would they remain with a party that has jeopardised American Independence, exchanged a republic for a Despotism, and a servant of the people's choice, for a self elected Dictator?

§

The South argues that it is, or will become, a nation, and that its Battle for Independence proves it.

The North argues that the South is no nation, because :—

1st. The ethnical elements (white and black) are unreconciled and unreconcileable. Two hostile and essentially different races do not constitute a nation. The South is *divided* by races.

2nd. As concerning even the white race South, the non-Secession votes were in 1860 in the majority, the "Union" and "Squatter Sovereignty democrats" polling together 138,000 more than the Secesh candidate. A "nation" is not a minority on its own ground.

3rd. All the interests of the South in Separation have disappeared, save those of the few remaining actual Slaveholders, and the civil and military chiefs. All permanent interests of the South are towards re-union, which guarantees a freer Government, national Independence, and a loftier sphere of ambition for great and good citizens, both in the central Government, and in the various offices of the great sovereign States.

4th. The North is in military occupation of by far the greater part of "Southern" territory. Especially of the great river that bisects it, and that interpenetrates it by its confluents; also its fleet commands its coasts and seas.

5th. The Unique Geographical Unity,—the most remarkable of any country, in fact the most remarkable material arrangement, bearing directly on politics, in the world,—renders *permanent division impossible.* This division can only be thoroughly appreciated by men of culture and intellect, who know the vast influence of climate, mountain ranges, and rivers, on the political destinies of races.

6th. The Unique political unity, wherein a variety of causes unite to make the American nationality the strongest, compactest, and intensest, yet created, —absorbing all others that enter it, and little likely indeed to let go or lose either by influences or arms, any part already incorporated with it.

Upon this Statement there are, in the first place, several things quite obvious and incontestable.

1st. The intense, the disciplined, and the long-prolonged unity of feeling, interest, and action, in the ruling race South, guarding its interests against the North, and against the Black; together with the actual subservience and degradation of the Slave, and the genius for command and organisation amongst the Whites, are more than sufficient to account for any apparent unity during a three years' fight.

2nd. That civil wars have repeatedly been desperate, and much longer than the present one, without ultimate division.

3rd. That if ordinary precedents of successful revolt were all for instead of against the South, it might be assumed that an old nation, with all the "unities," can certainly not be disintegrated by a three years' fight, properly denominated a civil war.

4th. That American unity,—strong enough in 1777 to resist the war of George III.,—deliberately reorganised and constituted a nation in 1787, with executive, administrative, judicial, and legislative unity,—has, during the last ninety years, and owing to general equality of conditions, and various circumstances lastly mentioned, *grown in consolidation and nationalty at a rate out of all proportion to any other precedent.*

5th. To erect in America a duality of power, similar to that which Austria and Prussia constitute in Germany, is impossible. The Duality would be only nominal. The one American nation would remain one as regards the world, and one in Democracy and institution. Any such change would involve one of two alternatives,—either the Southern Government, essentially an oligarchy, will overturn the Independence of the Sovereign States, and form an Empire, or that Independence will remain intact under a change of name. The first result, all precedent, authority, and argument, forbid. The second would be no real change as regards the outer world, and as regards America would for reasons hereafter given, leave the essential Unity unimpaired, and without any permanent influences to undo its nationality. America would never for long allow the flag of Democracy to be prostituted to European Diplomacy, nor Government by the few, to deny and undo her opinions, manners, and laws,—her very History, Principles, *raison d'être*, and Life.

Oligarchy would be a failure. Double Democratic Government a phantom or a Lie. The worst and most hopeless of all failures possible in America would be that of any party allying itself with foreigners against American Independence, Integrity, or Nationality. The bayonets of the Allies that thrust back the Bourbons on the French *destroyed* the Bourbons for the French, and any similar party in America would be destroyed before it could announce its projects.

6th. Were all these considerations reversed, a true nation is never to be despaired of; reunion can *never* be hopeless where the race and the boundary are one. The Unity of the German race has always been relied on to accomplish an unity of Institution, — although Germany contains two armed, equipped, and organised powers, one of them old enough to be the heir of the Cæsars,—and though German State Sovereignty is more like American State Sovereignty in its divisions and severalty before the English war, and contains a Democratic element, but indifferently organized and led.

Germany contains a Kingdom, an Empire, thirty-six Sovereign States, two religions, and three varieties of Institutions, and yet it will doubtless one day be one, *for its race and boundary are one.*

America has every bond of Union known to History, or the philosophy of History. Is it wise to speculate on its Disunion?

§

It is not, however, to be denied, that with an adequate territory and population, and a centripetal force, greater, for the time being, than the sum of the centrifugal forces, the making of a nation is not a hopeless question. Notwithstanding all deficiencies of morality, or industrial effort, the nation *may* hold its own, and await the chances of improvement and consolidation.

Can it stand? is the question. Is it strong? And morality and industry enter into the calculations, because they are elements of strength.

But it is not enough to say that because it has a competent territory and population, the South has but to will to be free. We grant the truism implied. But *the will depends on Principle and interest, and the interest must be permanent and general, and the Principle strong and universal*, or it affords no support for *National* movements.

"Independence," without this proviso, were but a phrase, signifying the figment and crotchet of a faction, and having nought to do with the symbol of a nation's Unity or will.

To establish the idea of "National Independence," shew us first your "Nation," and therein, the material power which is to achieve independence, and the *national* ideas and interests that are to sustain the national will in the struggle.

To talk of Independence as the "cause," before this is shewn, is neither to deceive others, nor to deceive yourselves. It is a begging of the question.

Policy and arms, opinions and material forces, are the weapons in all wars.

If the South conquer, it must by the first, divide and paralyze Northern Will, or by the second, repel its armaments.

But the same course is open to the North. It also may divide to conquer; it also may present inducements to paralyze the Southern Will, or they may be presented by the evil necessities of the South itself.

Thus the question, — "Can the South stand against outward foes?" would be followed, were it met successfully, by the more formidable question, —can it stand against internal foes? and we have to ask of the South the double question,—1st. Can it defeat Northern arms? and 2nd, after victory, would there be and remain a central power of cohesion, adequate to resist the forces of dissolution, and of alien internal interests. In other words, would the interests of the People, and of the separate Sovereign States tend most *to the old Union, to the new Confederation, or to a still further subdivision of authority?*

The simplicity and energy of a Despotism, might for a time be possible in America. But an educated well-to-do people, bred to use and trust opinion, as the ultimate power, is naturally suspicious of the professional arbitrament of war, and regards it as a clumsy and ineffective settlement of internal questions.

And so let peace return,—let the Slave power only die the gradual death it was dying before the present war, and which political economy and human nature guarantee to it,—let a war against intruding foreigners arise or be forced on, or any serious impeachment of the Monroe doctrine be attempted, and the *nation* would again appear. There are two things which will for ever prevent a long-lived Despotism in America. The "State" organization, and the Individual. Of the three powers that rule America,—the national Government, the Sovereign State, and the Individual,—Despotism will always meet with two, ready organized and equipped, to oppose it.

Slaveholders, "State rights" men, Copperheads, and Democrats, constitute the party of the South.

But they are not a fixed quantity. They will be led by interest or principle, towards the North, and the question is, "Can the interests and principles of the rebellion tempt the adherents of American Unity, Nationality, Freedom, and Democracy?" — "Which is impelled by the stronger motives of action, and can command the greater numbers?"

The weapons of the North are free labour, Democratic Institutions, and a territory, a race, a religion, and a language, one throughout the Continent.

The weapons of the South are Statesmanship, Generalship, and an unity of interest between Leaders and People, covering exactly the same ground at any given time as the slave interest.

In arms, the materials of revolt, will be made the most of.

Its policy is clear, and so is its failure, when we know how many of the 4,000,000 Blacks have already left the South and joined the North,—that the North is converted to emancipation, and is baptized with the Negro in one baptism of fire,—that men naturally and always seek equal conditions of existence—that if Slavery last, the blight it casts upon all but the privileged classes in the South will continue,—and that, if Slavery comes to an end, the rebellion must end with it, or change altogether its declared objects and policy.

Such is the Problem the South has got to solve. Such being the weapons and the policy of the respective parties, let us see what materials there are in America, to which they can severally address themselves.

The motives that animate the *Slaveholders* are indeed of the strongest that can animate any body of men without Principle,—Property, Station, Interest,—the habit, the ability, and the ambition, to command. But the Slaveholders cannot number over 190,000, nor their followers over 5,000,000. The Slave Barons will fight to the end, but Slavery being notoriously injurious to all the interests and rights of labour, the rank and file cannot be expected to follow unless under the lure of an indefinite extension of the Slave area and Slave trade, and these would bring their own punishments and their own overwhelming antagonisms.

Of State rights men and Democrats, it is evident that unless personally involved in the Slave trade, they have four of the strongest of human motives to draw them to the side of nationality, freedom, equality, and Independence. Material interests would range them against Slavery, and under any fair dealing with State rights, their inducements to deny their country would be slender indeed.

It is the fatal position of the South that it must choose between Interest and Principle. It cannot have both, and the one that it chooses will be destroyed by the other in the South, and be overmatched by its contrary from the North. If it choose "Independence" as its principle, that will be overmatched by "Nationality," which is a passion and a principle with every American. If it choose Interest, it must come to the Slave trade, and defy the Principles of freedom, and democracy, and all the forces of their propagandism.

If the South be slave, then its Industry will decline or perish, for its monopolies are gone. If the South be free, then its Industry will live, but its Institutions *cannot* remain oligarchic.

If it be said that the South stands, and will stand, because it can govern, do, and dare ; that it moves as one man, and vibrates with one passion, and is *therefore* a nation,—we reply that the precedents and probabilities are all the other way; that a few years war never *yet* placed a fixed eternal gulf between men of the same race, and language, and boundary; that every such nation that has been rent by such wars, (the thirty years' war for instance) has survived them; that passion subsides ; that interest in the long run governs the course of nations; and that there never yet was a Government that could not find and apply a leverage adequate to shake such an heteregeneous edifice as the South (to say nothing of the crumbling of its corner stone). Further, *we know* that in the South Union movements were from the first put down by force, and that (as we shall shew hereafter in detail) an analysis of the election returns proves two things, the Union of the North in 1860, and the Disunion of the South. The Slave party in "convention," split 16 to 17, on the question of "Squatter Sovereignty," or a complete Slave code. It adjourned in order to agree, but the split remained, and Lincoln entered through it. The North plumped for Lincoln in the electoral vote. His majority on the whole popular vote over the Slave democrat, was 1,009,657, or more than two to one. The Slave Democrat polled only 72 *Southern votes* against 48 on the electoral vote. He polled, on the popular vote, 500,000 *less* than the other *Slave Democrat candidate.*

Finally, this ultra Slave faction, a minority in a minority, passed in South Carolina in four days after Mr. Lincoln's election, a secession convention Bill, vainly hoping that the North would at once repudiate him; South Carolina for some time stood alone for war and secession, every other State having given a popular vote against it; the escaped slaves demonstrate how far the black nation, 4,000,000 strong, is party to "Southern Unity;" and the 5,000,000 mean whites, *must,*—when the bond which Slavery creates out of a common greed, a common hate, and a common fear, is dissolved by emancipation,—have interests, political, social, and industrial, hostile to the Slave Barons, their masters.

War, we repeat, must be carried on either for Interest or Principle. It is not in the mass of human nature to wage war long for mere pride, vain glory, or hypocrisy, the South never waged their war for freedom, and in the Union it had not only freedom but even license.

There was an immense live Stock down South. The South called it "chattel;" the North, "man." The Southern masses fought for power to retain and multiply their live stock, and for territory to turn it out in. The oligarchs fought also for political power over the masses. They would lead their middlemen, the mean whites, against the free North, and ratify the bondage of the Slave, *for a consideration*, and the mean white, must stay where and as he was, or attempt to dissolve the partnership.

Here are no elements of "eternal war." It is a fraudulent and delusive compact, a case for the police. Men will fight for a time for their "chattels," but with the chattel, goes their cause of fighting. The few will fight on for power, and vengeance, but the many, if they have not a high principle to sustain them, or strong interest to induce them, will gradually fall away.

Once it is seen that the Slaves are going and gone, that the "Stock" involves a ruinous sacrifice, and it will be seen that there is no more "principle," no more "interest," no more "Patriotism," no more "Independence" at stake in the Slaveholders rebellion, than there would be stuff for the making of a respectable "war of Principles," between the "Little-endians" and the "Big-endians" of Gulliver.

The naked question will then stand confessed,—Can the military despots of the South complete its ruin?

§

The conclusions to which we are irresistibly led by this general inquiry are, firstly, that not only will the American nation reunite,—it *cannot remain separate.*

2nd;—That the American constitution, a new thing in Statesmanship, affords guarantees for the freedom of the Individual and the efficiency of the Government, never before approached in practice. Though called a republic, it radically differs from all preceding republics. One thing alone impeaches the Institutional Unity of America, and that it is supposed by all the world will vanish during the struggle. Further, that foreign Intervention on behalf of the Slave faction, would only sting the American nationality into ten-fold intensity and power.

3rd;—That the Slave trade and faction, even in its prime, appears, in the light of History, and to those who have gained the true perspective ot passing events, already, but a filthy and blasphemous dream,—but a moment in the History of America,—but a speck in that mighty system ot influences and means, which concurred and concur to *make* the American nation.

But none of these things are here taken for

granted. If they are not inexorably proved, the fault is with the author's ability, not with his intention.

§

We have now to show, in outline, the mode of investigation, and specific form of proof we apply. It is "exhaustive," it has been arduously and conscientiously carried out, and will afford the readiest means of checking, and (if wrong) of controverting its conclusions.

To argue from isolated *results*, (a battle, victory, or defeat) is quackery. To understand *causes*, is political science.

It would be easy to add up on one's fingers, the elements of *success in war*, and to decide which party is the stronger.

In all great contests the elements of success are the Material, the Intellectual, and the Spiritual. The first, for the basis, the second to organize and lead, the third to energize and inspire.

1;—The Material,—armies, equipments, food, monies, ships, men liable to military service, railways, natural boundaries, climate, mountain, and river, &c.

2;—The Intellectual,—Generalship, Statesmanship, discipline, and organization, &c.

3;—The Spiritual,—the supreme motive energies, leading and inspiring the material and Intellectual.

Compare then the elements of success, North and South,—their numbers, value, and power.

Of the first, the North has an overwhelming superiority.

Of the second, the Statesmanship of Lincoln shows to no disadvantage, for it is victorious. Southern Generalship, though so brilliant, loses its hold of territory, and Northern discipline is becoming complete. Moreover, against a true nation, military genius never finally prevails.

Of the third, the highest motive energy of the South, is the idea of "Independence," but it is an idea contradicted by Slavery, and by the principle of secession, and hampered by oligarchy, which affronts the intensest passions of the American People.

Independence, nationality, a true labour system, Democracy, and Equality, and, above all, and essential to all, a determination to destroy Slavery, —these are the ideas that lead the North.

The motive energy of the South, is the wish for Independence to perpetuate Slavery, — which is oligarchic, Despotic, immoral, and unprofitable,— by the destruction of the great republic which offered it all legal redress, — by introduction of foreign alliances and arms, — and by undoing and denying the spirit of the Great Declaration and of the Constitution.

Compare these forces, North and South, noting their respective order and value.—The result is the result of the war.

But the object of this Book is to prove that this contest is "the making of the American nation." And we have seen that, according to some, the North may beat the South now, and yet the South must ultimately become a nation; according to others the South may beat the North now, and yet not possess the elements of permanent national life.

The strength, gallantry, genius, endurance, and resources of the South are admitted, but the admission does not admit the nationality. The question is, is the South a nation, and can it undo the nationality of the North? The question further is, of *what kind and degree* is the American nationality.

A complete nation is one that has complete and whole its MATERIAL BASES, ITS INDIVIDUALITY, AND ITS ORGANIC FUNCTIONS.

By the first it exists; by the second it exists as a nation; and by the third it thinks, administrates, and acts.

The material Bases of a nation, consist of its *Territory*, *Labour*, and *Population.*

The Individuality or Unity of a nation, consists of a oneness of circumstance, ideas, and interests, and this results from a oneness of *Institution*, *Race*, *Boundary*, *Language*, and *Religion.*

The organic functions of a nation are its *Legislative*, and *Executive.*

We have then to investigate, as the nation's bases, its MATERIAL UNITY, its Geographic, Strategic, and climatal conditions, its Labour system; and its Population.

The Geography of a country,—its climate, mountain and water system,—powerful in social, commercial, and military affairs,—unchangeable,—inviting, enabling, or preventing intercourse,—can, as an ethnical force, hardly be over-estimated in any country. In America the river system is of colossal development, and unites with climate, and mountain, and rail, and telegraph, in all the emphasis of five-fold power, and with all the distinctness of a predetermined plan, to prepare a fitting material unity for the mighty American nation.

Its HISTORY, revealing, from a whole view of the nation's life, its genius and character, its Individuality and soul; and shewing also the *Principles* that now contend upon its soil, and the manner of its past and present dealings with those great factors of nationality.

Its CONSTITUTION, showing its organic and Legislative functions, and especially the peculiar relations established by this new invention in Statesmanship, between the Individual, and the nation, and between both, and that third element of power, peculiar to America, — namely, the "Sovereign State."

The nationality of the North being admitted, and that of the South in question, there must be this difference in the application of the above tests to the one and to the other, and in the conduct of the argument,—*the nationality of the South has to be rigorously tested at every point—that of the North has to be tested only in regard to those elements of nationality which are claimed by both parties.*

These are; -- 1st. the *territory* in military occupation of the South. 2nd. The *Population* within their lines. 3rdly. The *political principles* that animate, not only that population, but the whole nation, and which will really decide this contest.

These subjects remain for treatment in due course.

What then are to be the results of this appeal to arms? We undertake to show in the sequel, that the South is not a nation in any sense, material, moral, or spiritual.

Of all the arguments upon which this conclusion is sustained, those *from* the geographical unity of America, and *to* the intense character of its nationality, are perhaps the most important, though they are the least explored, and, in fact, have never yet been adequately expounded.

§

In comparing the characteristics of the Slave faction, and its great antagonist, the reasons for belief in the ultimate triumph of American nationality, Freedom, and Democracy, have always appeared to the author to rest on demonstrations as incontrovertible as any of those accepted facts in nature, or truisms in morals, upon which universal belief reposes, and from which universal activity springs.

To know that the history of America for the last thirty-five years (nearly half the nation's life) has been the history of a protest against Slavery, always becoming more emphatic, practical, and strong,—a protest so effective, as to procure at last a majority, and so earnest, as to engage in war to enforce it;—to know this, ought to enlist the sympathies, engage the hopes, and command the confidence, of any who comprehend what is moral force, or who "understand their own epoch," or any other.

To know for what the South contends, and that Slavery means, as essential a contrariety of interest between the millions of mean whites, and the thousands of the ruling Whites, as it does between the latter and those who are more especially their "slaves,"—to know this ought to at once expose the fiction and falsehood of Southern "nationality."

To know the special geographical unity of America, its great rivers, its mountain ranges, its climate, and its railway and telegraph system, ought to suggest to all, in favour of the *political* unity of America (even west of the Rocky Mountains), a *prima facie* case of peculiar strength.

To know the extraordinary force of the American nationality, the rapidity with which it assimilates, the tenacity with which it holds; to know the universal, intimate, and essential interests for which the North contends, and how for their sake its Democracy submits to the necessities of a central will and organization; to know these things ought to rally the force of all the precedents of the past around the conviction, that without extermination the North cannot be conquered.

To know these things,—the moral forces of the North, its elements of essential unity, as contrasted with the essential contrariety of the South, its superiority in food, money, and numbers, its geographical unity, its fleet, bisecting "Secesh" through the Mississippi, and threatening it everywhere,—to know that the strength of the North is of a nature to increase, and the strength of the South of a nature to decrease,—to know these things ought to have at once secured the unhesitating unanimous verdict of any who are capable of appreciating them.

But above all these considerations, each bearing so remorselessly against Southern pretensions, rises that of the History, if it be regarded as a whole, with its thirty years of determined agitation, leading straight to Freedom or War. The History of this great Slave fight should be noted with especial attention, for it is the history of the completed freedom of the individual, and of the subordination of the insurgent State Sovereignties to the national unity. It is therefore the history of the strengthening and elevating of the units, and of the consolidation of the unity, or in other words, it is really *the history of the making of the American nation.* If we are to despair of America, we must reverse our conclusions, and deny our belief in History, in human nature, and in God.

It is believed that a simple categorical statement of the material and moral elements of this nationality, and the history of their development, ought to do more than anything else to settle English opinion on American questions.

§

But let us here summarily compare the broad and natural, and impregnable foundations of the North, with the narrow and artificial bases of the South.

The following were the temporary, unnatural, and abnormal conditions, or rather MONOPOLIES, of Slavedom.* They are gone, and Slavery must follow. But for them it could not have continued.

1st. The Cotton monopoly. The South would get rich on Cotton at 3½*d.* Since 1844 it has gradually risen to 4*d*, 7*d*, 9*d*, &c., and England has for some time lost £10,000,000 a year by dependence on the South, because English "Statesmanship" has secured the South against competition.

2nd. The Slave interest, through its connection with the Union, used it politically, for fugitive Slave laws; commercially, for capital, transit facilities, &c.; and mechanically, for inventions, such as Whitney's cotton gin. The South has used the Union and plotted against it. The South has never stood upon its own merits.

3rd. The South lived on the premature wasted life and unpaid labour of the Slave, and now declares the revival of the African Slave trade to be politically necessary in order to occupy the "territories."

4th. Southern culture admitted neither of rotation of crops, nor skilled labour, and lived on a

* Professor De Bow gives the aggregate number of Slaveholders at 347,525 in 1850, and Mr. Helper, gives the following classification:—

Actual Slaveholders	186,551
Entered more than once . . .	2,000
Non-Slaveholding Slave-hirers . .	158,974
Total	347,525

costless territorial expansion, through an indefinite area of unexhausted land.*

5th. By a compulsory labour system, degrading the principle of labour; by the creation of a "high and haughty spirit" of skin caste; by constituting the holding of Slaves, even of one or two, the badge of aristocracy; by training the whole white population in habits of associated command, maintained and maintainable only by physical force, and in all those military characteristics which belong to a despotic oligarchy in danger; by all that political situation, which left no alternative between aggression, or submission and decay;—by all these circumstances there has been gradually created in the South, in the space of fifty years, an immense mass of material, by no means raw, for the Southern armies. Thus it comes to pass that these men, united and nerved by political and social passions of terrible force; struggling for a national "industry," as well as for political preponderance and existence; with the pride of an aristocracy, and the wants of a democracy; equipped with all the appliances of civilization, and inflamed with more than the ferocity of savages; are so fitted for fighting, that but one other class in all the world can excel them in it. They are fit for fighting and fit for nothing else.

Such is the Genesis in Trade, in Politics, and in

* "Slavery cannot be confined within certain limits without producing the destruction of both master and slave. There is not a slaveholder in this house or out of it, but who knows that whenever confined * * * * it is only a question of time as to its final destruction."—*Judge Warner, of Georgia.*

Power, of the the Southern revolt. It is the mightiest and completest *class interest* ever known, but manifestly sectional, unstable, narrow, and revolutionary, vainly looking for intervention from Europe, or for disunion in the North. It denies the principle of authority and the principle of individual right, and therein denies ultimately the principle of its own existence, strength, and unity. Its Slave system will either stand or fall. If it is to stand, the "political" superstructure must fall, and be sacrificed to it before free competition. The Slave empire has within it the seeds of organic disease and inevitable death. Either the revolt will be itself revolutionised by the conversion of the slave man into the free, or free trade in labour and in Cotton, will once more vindicate itself. The South works with borrowed capital, it works with stolen men upon a desolated soil, and without the skill and energies of freedom. It will become either a wilderness or a re-construction, for the laws of trade are the laws of human nature and of God. Thus much for the Labour question, and the individual right question, but neither is the principle of authority mocked. Southern "Sovereign States" have been supplied with a precedent, they will soon or late be supplied with the motive, and Secession will kill secession.

§

To live, Secession must not only destroy the armaments of the North, it must destroy also those material, moral, and intellectual conditions which have made the American nation, and would remake it, and of which UNITY of will and COMMUNITY of spirit are the leading characteristics.

Thus the Geography, the mechanics, (mechanical facilities and appliances), the institutions, the material interests, and the universal Statesmanship of America, all operate in one direction,—to make *unity* and *community* its leading and abiding characteristics. This is well known by the South, which does its possible to countervail it, and by all *intelligent* haters of freedom, and lovers of the South in Europe.

1st. The mountain ranges which elsewhere combine with climate, to separate the earth into zones or belts from East to West, are not so placed there. They run from North to South, and are tapped at frequent openings.

2nd. The river system, which widens as the Continent widens Northward, connects the whole with its various conditions of climate and production.

3rd. Always excepting the 190,000 Slaveholders, there is an equally conspicuous absence of inveterate corporate and class interests, obstructions, influences, and institutions in Church, in State, and in land tenure, which everywhere else create artificial obstacles to the communion and intercourse of men, to the acquisition of property, to the fusion of races, to the union of interests, and the progress of civilisation.

4th. Whether for ideas, men, or things, transit facilities are cheaper, more numerous, more profitable, swifter, and more universal, than the world ever knew before. Banks, Telegraphs, the Steam press, the Steam boat, the Postal service, the rail, and revenue system, &c., perfect the vehicles of national sympathy, exchange, and interaction.

5th. The equality of man politically, the universality of suffrage, the existence of a mighty uniform class with equal intelligence universally diffused, and the stake which almost every man possesses in the representation, in the progress of the country, and stability of the Government.

6th. The marvellous power of their habits of political, industrial, intellectual, and moral *association.*

Thus as to the meaning of Providence foreshown in the Geography of the New World, and verified by partial analogies in the history and Geography of the Old. But America is prepared for maturer races, a later epoch, and a prepared civilisation. *There* are no barriers from West to East, and the great river system takes a like direction, or departs from it only to bring fresh regions within the scope of its influences. The great idea to be obeyed and sought out in America is evidently that of *spreading*, *sharing*, *uniting*,—not of dividing, isolating, or confining.

These influences, whether in peace or war, demand especial notice, as they must effect special results.* It is not for nothing that the hand that divided Europe and Asia, North and South, by natural barriers, and into numberless nationalities,

* Strabo said of the then thinly inhabited Gaul, that the course of its rivers showed it to be destined for the home of a single nation. All men who have known how to understand and use the situation have availed themselves of these influences.

and that kept back the mighty West until the fore-fixed time, has placed no such barriers on the American continent. That is a place prepared for all peoples and nations, who are becoming one by a process of amalgamation more rapid and complete than was ever known before. This crisis is the making of the American nation, because it has proved its possession of all the qualities and forces, material, moral, and spiritual, which go to make up a nation.

For ourselves we cannot but see in the thirty years virtual, preceding the three years actual Battle against Slavery, the crowning victory of the highest attribute of American nationality, adding to all the other attributes that make that nationality the strongest and intensest in the world, a loyalty to Principle, which will keep it at one with God's purposes in its progress and futurity.

The salt of America has been enough to savour even the South.

We see no incongruity in the completest and intensest nationality, being set to occupy the largest, and also compactest, territory.

We see in the great civil war, precisely the means,—the only means, that could have prepared America for the "weight of Glory" that the future and God hold out to her. The only means that could have drilled her Democracy to maintain against the Devil and all oligarchs and oligarchic powers, the integrity of the American Continent and nation.

Why should not the greatest nation utilise and hold the greatest Continent?

Why should not the purest People work out for man the greatest problem of the future?

Why should not the only Democracy in the world realise the hopes of all ages? Why should not this Royal nation enact the thoughts that have flushed the purple visions of earth's greatest Intellects?

UNIVERSALITY and ONENESS are written on the Geography of America by the hand of God,—Were imprinted on her indelibly by that glorious Statesmanship that would not obstruct human nature by imposing the past on the future, nor divide the nation into close corporations with hostile interests, nor weaken by swathing it in murderous bonds and old-world formularies. Miracles in mechanics also, help to enact and confirm political institutions.

The soil and the nation,—the body and soul, of America, are thus one by a thousand influences,—one in interest, in intercourse, in sympathies, and in politics, as nation never was before.

Who shall separate them? What can disunite them? Assuredly *not* that 190,000 head of Slave-holding carrion in the Gulf States, that "lives in the saddle and is sparsely settled" over that region,—that exists on the unpaid labour, and wasted lives, and degraded souls of other men, — that reduces prostitution to a science in economics,—that is accustomed to sell its own flesh and blood into slavery, — and that is called "chivalry," by newspapers, which, on the question of Slavery, have been the common houses of ill fame for all the world!

CHAPTER V.

"MARE'S-NESTS;"

OR

JOHN BULL AND "THE CHIVALRY."

BEGGING OF QUESTION.
CONTRADICTIONS.
SERVILE WAR.
SLAVERY AND BIBLE.
UNITY,—"DESPOTISM."
DESPOTISM,—"UNITY."
RIGHT OF SECESSION.
SLAVERY PROFITABLE.
SLAVERY AND NATIONALITY.
CONFEDERATE "BONDS."

" I sing how casual bricks in airy climb,
Encountered casual cow hair, casual lime;
How rafters borne through wondering clouds elate,
Kissed in their slope blue elemental slate,
Clasped solid beams in chance directed fury,
And gave to birth our renovated (Drury)."

" I swear to fear, revere, and serve God; to suffer death rather than renounce Christ; to maintain the rights of the People, the widows, and the orphan; to offer no wilful or deliberate offence to any one; never to be engaged in any transaction for the pure love of gain."—*Oath on taking the degree of Esquire.*

* * "En obant de vous tout orgueil. * * Soyez loyal en faits, et en dits. * * Soyez secourables a pauvres et orphelins."

Mother of Bayard to her Son.

" Sez John C. Calhoun, sez he,
'Human rights airnt no more
Right on this 'ere floor,
No more than the man in the moon,'—sez he."

Biglow Papers.

MARE'S-NESTS.

"In short I firmly do believe in Humbug generally,
For it's a thing that I perceive to have a solid vally;
This hath my faithful shepherd been, in pastures sweet hath led me,
And this 'll keep the people green, to feed as they have fed me."

In the "Carnival of Cant" of Slaveholders, the following theories and contradictions have been running a muck at each other and at everything else that is intelligible.

The "begging of the American question," is a feat sturdily persisted in by the friends of the "Chivalry" or in the interests of Slavery, after many exposures. It is not to the credit of the leaders of English public opinion, that the impostures require now even a slight notice.

It is asserted that the 6,000,000 whites, South, are a nation, and therefore cannot be exterminated, and that *because* they cannot be exterminated, they cannot be subdued. That this rebellion, though to maintain Slavery, is a glorious undertaking.

It is asserted that the 4,000,000 negroes, South, are not a nation. That they ought not to be emancipated till convenient to the white nation. That for them to fight for freedom, would be a bad war, *because* it would be a "servile war."

It is asserted that "the South is an aristocracy." That an aristocracy ought to lead, that chivalry must conquer, and that a war to set them in their proper place, is a war of nature and necessity.

It is asserted that Slavery is sanctioned by the Bible, and that therefore it is a divine institution,

L 2

for which religion permits or demands an armed propagandism.

It is asserted that free labour will not pay; and that white labour cannot last in the South.

Other such assertions as that "Slavery has nothing to do with the war," are relegated now to very low-art tumblers in the political sawdust. They pay no longer, for even "the gods" know that they are lies, and nothing more.

The fashion that speaks of Unity in the North, as "Despotism;" and Despotism in the South, as "Unity;" is to be set down as an instance of that rare and unhoped for good fortune which sometimes favours the most audacious speculators on the folly of mankind.

The "strategists" who talk of the advantages accruing to the South, from "moving on interior lines," now that it is driven into a corner, and cannot move on the exterior lines, have also met with their share of appreciation.

The Three assertions or propositions,—that the Bible authorizes Slavery; that free labour will not pay in competition with Slave labour; that the right of Secession is inherent in Individual States, need no repetition, for they may be said to commit suicide directly they are clearly formulated.

The BIBLE indicated to the Jews certain modes by which the evils of Slavery, as practised by surrounding heathen, were to be mitigated and reduced to a minimum, as far as was possible to the civilization of that age. The Bible lays down concerning Slavery no *principles*, but authorized, through Moses, certain administrative reforms, changing slavery into servitude. But the whole scope and purpose of the Book, and of the religion of human nature and of God, is to make men free in the Truth, by binding them under one law of equality, brotherhood, and lovingkindness, — members one with another in Christ's body, the Church. To charge, then, *Slavery* upon this system and this Book, is not merely a lie in terms,—it is a generic lie, a lie against their whole genius, scope, nature, and tendency, as well as against their particular inculcations and commands.

It is an indignity to Truth and Honesty, — it is a complicity with charlatans against the value of evidence and reason, to apply its rules and formulas elaborately to transparent falsehood. It matters little, comparatively, that there exist in a State a certain number of Liars. It matters infinitely more that palpable Lies should be habitually deferred to as arguments, examined as one-sided truths, or treated with the honours of controversy.

It is far better to meet flat falsehood dogmatically,—*to tell the Dog he lies*,—and to pass on about one's business.

With regard to the phantasy that man free, is not equally equipped for LABOUR with man enslaved, it involves the same falsehood, the same doubt of God and man, the same impious impeachment of the ways of God with man. *La mort sans phrase* is the only answer that reason can give to such sophistry. Without argument, we may repudiate once for all, the idea that *any* contradiction of the laws of God and of nature, can be permanently profitable to *any* participator in the transaction. The superiority of free labour, as shewn by its results in America, has, however, been demonstrated *ad nauseam.*

The Principle of "STATE SOVEREIGNTY," when brought to mean individual State license and national dissolution, is matter, not for argument, but for contempt and ridicule against those who uphold it in theory, and for a war of execution against those who uphold it in arms.

But supposing it granted, for argument's sake, that every thing relating to the supposed internal interest of each State, is to be absolutely settled by such State. Is there to be argued from this doctrine of severalty of interest, a community of crime, a sufferance of aggression, and a complicity in national suicide? The acquiescence in an organized system of barbarous cultivation, depending on organized crime, that must spread or die,—*the one law of whose existence is aggression, and evermore aggression?* We say such "State Sovereignty" would make each State despotic over the fate of the Union; would be a reversal of the natural relationships between Republic and State, making the State supreme, and the Republic itself a slave. The assertion, as regards America, of a constitutional right to nurse and aggravate a desperate organic disease in the republic, or as regards the world, to constitute that incomparable nuisance a Slave empire, is an assertion which certainly does not deceive those who make it. If right, or reason, or religion, remain upon earth, then the right to constitute or to extend an empire founded upon the unmanning of man, is not the doctrine of men, but the doctrine of Devils, and as wrong in every economic or statesmanlike sense, as in morals, and religion.

§

The argument for "NATIONALITY" founded upon Slavery, is also a contradiction in terms. Nationality depends upon Freedom and Law, upon the strength and virtue of the Individual, and the coherence of the State. Slavery opposes both, and will destroy them or be destroyed by them. At the early stage, Slavery may only encounter individual and municipal rights, but if it lives and grows, it must assail the national life.

The imputed "COURAGE" of the chivalry involves an abuse of language, or rather of thought. To praise them for a courage common to criminals, prizefighters, gladiators, and beasts, were no praise. It is only the courage which attacks the rights of others. There is a courage of beasts and a courage of men. There are, who praise for mere animal courage, a race that has carried on a sixty years' war of tyrants, atheists, cowards, panders, misers, and pimps, upon the rights, the chastity, the honour, the intellect, and the souls of a subject race. There are, who call the hearty fighting for such a system, "courage," we don't. There is no true courage without moral sanctions. Courage is not the willingness to incur danger for the sake of committing a crime, or inflicting an injury.

Confederate "BONDS" may also turn out to be a contradiction in terms. The men who forged a constitution for Kansas, and passed off armed desperadoes, imported for the feat, as voters,—who violated the Ballot Box, and sent in false returns, —who violated the Missouri compact, made for "consideration,"—who conspired to assassinate Lincoln,—who seized the national property, and used it against the nation,—who repudiated money obligations, and repudiated the constitution,—who recommended the legalising of the forgery of notes,—these men are now headed by the arch repudiator Jeff. Davis, who considers it "unconstitutional," to pay certain State debts, who charged the English Government with repudiation, and talked of "*The Times*," as a "pensioned press," and "hired advocate," and charged the "London Change" with hiring it to denounce him.*

The word of Jeff. Davis is no doubt as good as his "Bond," and we presume the "London Change" relies upon that, or on. Southern "nationality," for payment. It seems to us that there is not very good security either for the will or the Deed,—for the "Principle" or the Interest.

§

SERVILE WAR has been unsparingly denounced by men who do not object to war on principle. But if any war can be justified, it appears to us that a servile war, undertaken with probability of success, is *a fortiori*, justifiable.

* See pamphlet hereon, by the Hon. Mr. Walker. Ridgway, 1863.

War is Sacrament or Murder, and they who instigate the doing of the one, are only worse than those who prevent the taking of the other. Peace at any price denies the first, and war at any price affirms the last. To risk life, either the yielding or the taking of it, for any cause that is not holy,—that is not dearer and more sacred than life, is a crime and a bad calculation. To refuse the sacrifice of individual life, when the conditions of a great perpetual national life are to be achieved, is not the teaching of prudence, of nature, of Humanity, of Statesmanship, or of God.

Those who deny the rights of the individual, and the rights of the Nation, affirm anarchy, Murder, and Secesh. Those who deny to the Negro the Sacrament of Battle, when his manhood and his nationality are in question, are either less or worse than men.

The right of the Negro to fight for his freedom and nation, is denied by none but anarchists, peace-at-any-price-men, and Secessionists. Nevertheless, the rights of freedom, nationality, and order, must be denied or affirmed together.

We leave to others the great crime of *discussing* an institution, which our very instinct teaches us to abhor. There are some things not to be argued about, but to be destroyed. Who that believes in God, can disbelieve in man? The fool hath said in his heart, there is neither People nor God, and in Politics, according to Carlyle, the fool is the only absolutely fatal personage.

A servile war has probably been *prevented* by Lincoln's proclamation, which is calculated to produce, not an insurrection, but a stampede, to be followed by the substitution of free for slave labour, and a re-organisation of the whole industrial system of the South. That, we say, is the probable result of the Proclamation, and it presents ample scope for meditation. We say, however, and on this stand fast, that in *this war for equality of races*, the slave of all men, ought to take a part. He has the most legitimate interest, and the most valid warrant. He must get his freedom, peacefully if he can, but get his freedom. This will not involve servile war, unless the Slaveholder will have it so.

There are *black Yankees* yonder, and what will the slave naturally do, believing that the North will receive him, and protect him as soon as he can reach it? Will he tarry in the South to plunder, to kill, to ravish, to destroy,—in the South where he has been, is being, and will be burnt alive, flogged to death, or riddled with bird shot? We should think not! This contraband will take the liberty to smuggle himself. This chattel will cut and run. The *servile war is nonsense.* When Black meets White, it will be, not as Slave against Master, but as man to man. Meanwhile, the question is, whether a man running for his life, may use his instincts of defence, and if not, why not?

But further, we say to those who fear a servile war,—"you have settled that war is sometimes "just and necessary, you have settled even that a "war of treason and treachery against a reasonable "majority, may be just and necessary. Let us "understand the difference between a white war, "and a black war. Is a war against Slavery, "worse than a war *for* Slavery? If you assert "this, your quarrel is not so much with a servile "war, as with your own servile nature, and with "the God who made the black man's soul in the "likeness of God. The black man has a right to "his freedom. The white man, you cannot deny, "has refused him that freedom, refuses it, and will "refuse it,—nay in oaths, and blasphemy, and "blood, has assumed before the world that that "system shall continue for ever a corner stone of "the Slave Republic, even as Christ is the corner "stone of the Christian faith." A servile war is horrible, you say. We answer there has been Battle for 80 years in the South, but it has been *battle all on one side*, battle on the shrinking flesh and degraded intellect of the African race, who now are nearly as many as their oppressors. That battle has been horrible too, and alas, there are "who can bear to look on torture, but who dare "not look on war." The White would not be taken unawares by the Black,—as the Black has always been by the White,—and overwhelmed by midnight massacre. There would exist between them the conditions of open war. Of what are these people afraid,—which is the worse, the sharp short war of battle, or the long prolonged the real servile war, on all means and appliances that might bring to the Negro's soul, education, self respect, honour, religion? Neither argument nor action can be detained for those who are too slow or too low to appreciate the vast cumulative, and destructive, and deteriorating results, of three generations of unresisted oppression on the rights of a subject race.

Place then in the scales, a servile war, and *servility itself.* Servility, that ignoble coward war on the souls, virtue, intellect, shortened lives, and miserable bodies, of now three generations, and which, in mere blood, to take your lower ground, has cost more than fifty pitched battles. Place, we say, these in the alternative, and there can be no question which, on any reasonable aspect, is the better or the least bad. Otherwise it would appear that the objection is, not to war in the abstract or in the concrete, not to *any* war against Slaves, not to a war by a minority against a majority, but simply and only to a war by Slaves for freedom! If the sword of the South were no sharper than the wits of their advocates, the war, like the argument, would be remarkably one-sided. For all these arguments against a servile war amount to this,—that the slave has not the inherent essential rights of a man,—that his master has better right to do him wrong than he has to oppose wrong,—in other words, that wrong is right and right wrong.

The hour of the Slave's redemption is now, and they who would defer his hopes would destroy them. He has the greatest stake and the greatest right in this contest. If Jefferson Davis has made of the South a nation, who first made the Slaves a people, with rights, energies, passions, interests, *will*,—all that is comprised in the word "*Soul.*" We say it is the supreme hour,—the passion-hour of the Slave's redemption. Let not prudes and doctrinnaires entangle us in vain words, which holy human nature, in the straightforward and magnanimous rush of its instinct, denies. If it be glorious for the South to fight for freedom to enslave the Black, it is more glorious for the Black to fight for freedom,—nay, if he do not fight, let him be accursed!

We say then to the Slave, "if the Stampede will "not do, and the South, after all the sevenfold "plagues and warning of Battle will not let ye go, "then we say,—*go*, and if the Red Sea itself even "of a servile war cover your enemies,—*go*. On "one condition only ye can rightly stay. If the "Southern lie is true, that ye be *beasts* and *not men*, "then submit, renounce your 'right of insurrec-"tion,' temporise, till the hour has passed for action, "let your wives be victims of lust for ever, your "children be slaves for ever, and yourselves de-"scend to dishonoured graves,—but if not,—if ye "be Men, Husbands, Fathers, Christians,—ARISE! "AND IN THE NAME OF GOD, AND *your* NATION,— "STRIKE!"

§

Necessity and common sense have established the maxim, that a man must stand by the certain consequences of his own act.

Certain men in the South have for eighty years been mixing fire and gunpowder, and belabouring gun-cotton. The result threatens. They go screeching through creation,—what? "Their folly? Their suicide? The wrong done to Society? Their repentance?" No! Slavery is too devilish a thing to produce candour. They proclaim, rather, the

Satanic nature of the Gunpowder. The infamous revolutionary spirit, so dangerous to Society, of the gun-cotton. And they make of the world the idiotic demand, that they shall be guaranteed in their vested rights of mixing the powder, and beating the cotton, and that the world shall see to it that no explosion come!—Depend upon it the world has something else to do than to constitute itself an insurance office for the special behalf and interest of its chiefest criminals.

But change the names from powder to man, and what have you then?

If there be anything in right, or in morals, he who holds Slaves, steals their freedom, and is a scoundrel. He—not the Slave. He must degrade them, get, as thoroughly as he can, the manhood out of them, for *that* it is that is so apt to explode. He is again, and throughout, a scoundrel. He,—not his chattel. He must at the last be prepared to shoot them down when they seek their own,—their freedom,—themselves. He is a murderer, or if they succeed, as of course they must at last, if *he* falls, he is a suicide, and that is all. What else can the man be, who wars against God, nature, freedom, and manhood? It is only the fool turned idiot, and the idiot committing suicide. The world is then well rid of them, their blasphemous theories, their thousand-fold body aud soul murders. They believe neither in the People nor God, but in the Devil only, and his "Iliads." The laws of God and nature will not be altered for murderers, but murderers will be altered by them. "Let them perish" is not an imprecation, but a necessity set from eternity in the very nature of God, of whose likeness they would make a Slave!

Let us then at least get *this* rubbish about a "servile war" gone. Well may the Pythoness of the North exclaim in the Capitol:—

> "When we are at war with the Devil, we are not particularly sorry to hear of an insurrection in Hell."

What do these Southern advocates want altered? The law to suit the system, or the system to suit the law. Would they have mankind debased to suit Slavery, or Slavery abolished to suit man. They cannot have both. Let them say which. They who want Slavery without its natural result, want a thing to be and not to be at the same time. Once for all,—to put the world askew, because Slaveholders and their advocates don't like its constitution and laws, is a concession that will be made neither to the monstrous practical folly of Slaveholders, nor to the credulity of their advocates. Any fool,—any animated atom, or speck of life-dust, may break a commandment. The archfiend could not set at nought—Law. If they violate Law, so much the worse for them. They must now stand aside, when God, in his own time, has brought round their violence and treason to work for order and for freedom.

Away with these drivellers about a servile war, they know neither what is war nor what is peace. Against the Slaveholder is the manhood of the Slave. Behind the manhood of the Slave, constituting it, stablishing it, fighting for it, is—God.

§

It is, perhaps, not to be wondered at, that in a

country that has six to one of its manhood unrepresented, the favoured few should cherish sundry little prejudices against the many elsewhere. A fellow feeling makes us wondrous kind. And it will perhaps be necessary for the many to conquer their rights here, before the few will be convinced of the value of the rights of manhood, either here, or there, or of the national loss resulting from their denial.

However, let us now catalogue the "notions" imported, for the use chiefly of the English middle classes, by speculative politicians down South. We cannot, for their sakes, much regret that the lot is depreciated full 50 per cent. Indeed it is curious that in the third year of the young "nation," its loans, and its arguments, should not be worth one half their original values, respectively, and that its territory also should have been cut in two by the forces of the "vanquished" North.

The argument for "STATE SOVEREIGNTY," which assumes a *provision for national suicide* in the parent constitution, and which by its own *raison d'être* necessarily adopts such a provision for itself,—for "RIGHT of secession," because a country refuses its territory as the theatre for the extension and perpetuation of a gigantic national *crime*,—for "NATIONALITY," on the acknowledged basis of an acknowledged offence *against individuals and nations*, against economics, morality, religion, and God,—for "Freedom," on the part of six millions, that they may perpetuate Slavery on four millions, —for "CONSTITUTIONAL RIGHTS," of a minority, that has ruled the majority for 80 years, and, at the first hostile election, *appeals from the constitu-*

tion to arms,—for "STATE RIGHTS," that six States may impose on twenty-eight the deadly wrong and propagandism of an institution always destructive and oppressive, and that cannot support itself without *assailing the rights of other* "*States*,"—for a separate and "peculiar INSTITUTION," that inflicts a *community of suffering* on every righteous interest, and on every uncompromised individual, within the baleful circle of that institution's action or influence,—for a "LABOUR SYSTEM," which shortens the lives of its victims, turns its own labourers into chattels, and degrades the principle, and would *deny the rights of labour* all over the world.

The argument that a false nation, born of treason, with Blasphemy for its sponsors; reducing oppression and lust to a science for forcing labour, and feeding the labour market; producing equality of races by licentiousness, while denying it to right; which degrades "white trash" to fight for it, and breeds black chattels to work for it; whose territory is divided into halves by Northern arms, and penetrated everywhere by Northern rivers or mountains; whose race is divided into nearly equal and hostile sections; whose governing class is a close corporation of 190,000, with the essential ultimate interests of the whole population against them;—The argument that this would be "nation," with no real grievances to escape, and no substantial advantages to fight for, has the right, the power, or the possibility, to permanently establish itself in separation from and defiance of the country of which it forms a part,—six millions out of thirty-one,—with whom it has a language, race, institutions, boundary, and nominal religion, in common, —that it can defy the re-uniting influences of intimate neighbourhood, and the supremacy of free systems of thought, politics, labour, and communication, throughout a conterminous territory of 2000 miles,—that it could prevent the ultimate entire reconstruction of its own unnatural labour system by those influences,—that it can offer any guarantees of stability, good neighbourhood, peace, or even commercial interchange, with other nations, —that it can be for one moment accepted by Americans as a "republic," or by the world as a nation having any rights that rest not on wrongs, any position that is tenable, any character that is not evil, any law of existence that does not deny higher laws of existence, of the individual within, and of the nation from which it would wrench itself, or the "equal right of nationality" of any one State which now joins it in revolt;—That this argument, for the existence, right, constitution, or recognition, of such a community,—an argument that is a jumble of self evident contradictions, of assumptions against fact, precedent, policy, law, right, government, and nature,—*an argument against argument, appealing to religion by blasphemy, to right by wrong, for nationality against nationality, by an oligarchy for a republic;*—that such an argument could have been put forth seriously, or received believingly, argues so confused an intellect, and so depraved a heart, such an amount of unbelief, folly, impolicy, or complicity with wrong, as should alarm human nature for itself, and rally the better part of all nations around the "army of execution" from the north, and around those institutions that are the Despair of partial interests, and evil influences, all over the world.

> " What if a million mole-hills were to league
> Their meannesses together, with due pomp,
> And to some mountain say, 'In the name of God!
> Whither dost thou aspire?' Does any deem
> That great imperial creature would descend
> To the mud-made world below, and parley there
> At its own footstool, and lay down its crown
> Because its height was so intolerable?"

BOOK II.

AMERICAN UNITY AND NATIONALITY.

CHAPTER I.

MATERIAL BASES OF UNITY.

GEOGRAPHY, STRATEGY, CLIMATE, MOUNTAINS AND RIVERS, CANALS, COMMERCE, BANKS, REVENUE, RAIL, TELEGRAPH, COIN, AND POSTAL SERVICE.

CHAPTER II.

UNITY OF IDEAS AND INTERESTS.

RACE, LANGUAGE, LITERATURE, RELIGION, BOUNDARY, AND INSTITUTION.

CHAPTER III.

THE MORAL FORCES.

UNITY OF PRINCIPLE AND PURPOSE.

CHAPTER I.

THE MATERIAL UNITY OF AMERICA.

GEOGRAPHY, STRATEGY, CLIMATE, MOUNTAINS AND RIVERS, CANALS, COMMERCE, BANKS, REVENUE, RAIL, TELEGRAPH, COIN, AND POSTAL SERVICE.

"*Every portion* of our country finds the most commanding motives for carefully guarding and preserving the union of the whole. The North * * * The South * * * The East * * * The West, must of necessity owe the secure enjoyment of *indispensable outlets* to the weight, influence, and future maritime strength of the Atlantic side of the Union, directed by an *indissoluble community of interest as one nation.* Any other tenure by which the West can hold that essential advantage, whether derived from its own separate strength, or from an apostate and unnatural connection with any foreign power, must be intrinsically precarious."

Washington, Farewell Address.

"*These outlets*, East, West, and South, *are indispensable;* which of the three may be best is no proper question, all are better than either, and all of right belong to that people and their successors for ever. True to themselves, they will not ask where the line of separation shall be ; they will vow rather that there shall be no such line. Physically speaking *we cannot separate.*"

Abraham Lincoln, Message, 1862.

"The *geographical position* of the country contributed to increase the facilities which the American legislators derived from the manners and customs of the inhabitants; and it is to this circumstance that the adoption and maintenance of the Federal system is mainly attributable."—*De Tocqueville*, p. 257-8, v. 1.

"The peculiar structure of the *Alleghany ridge*, beginning in New Hampshire, running across the New England States, through Pennsylvania and West Virginia, stopping in the northern part of Georgia. * * * Now all the world over, men that live in mountainous regions have been men for liberty, and from the first hour to this, the majority of the population of *Western Virginia*, which is in this mountainous region, the majority of the population of *Western Tennessee, of Western Carolina, and of North Georgia, have been true to the Union.*"—*H. Ward Beecher.*

"It (North America) contains every variety (within the temperate zone) of climate and produce, a greater extent of mines,—coal, iron, gold, silver, and quicksilver than all Europe. *A vast system of navigable streams, exceeding in cheap water communication all Europe.* The shore-line of its rivers is 122,784 miles, employing *an interior steam tonnage exceeding that of all the world, and the cost of canals of equal capacity, would have been more than TEN BILLIONS of DOLLARS,* and would have been subject to tolls and lockage. Its hydraulic power, timber, and raw material exceed those of all Europe. It has constructed *more miles of telegraph and rail than all the world.*"—Condensed from "Letter on American Resources," by the *Hon. Robert J. Walker.*

"That after cheap food, the next great desideratum is cheap transit, so that everything may be procured from the localities where, from natural facilities, it can be obtained with the least labour.

"That railways worked with quick trains cannot convey the *quantity*.

"I say that the *cost of transit by rail is absolutely destructive of the great traffic of a continental country;*—that what Dr. Lardner says is literally true—"that goods generally cannot bear the cost of railway transit," and consequently, as shown in America, that where there is not water transit, the great mass of goods are not moved at all, and all trade in them is prevented. If it were not for the water-line from the Upper Mississippi Valley to the Atlantic, not one barrel of flour would be shipped out of one hundred that are at present brought down.

"In the United States, the difference of the cost of the two modes is well known, and the effects of it clearly shown. On the Erie Canal, a through traffic of about 300,000 tons a month is conveyed, during the seven months that it is open, at a *charge* (not *cost*) of ½*d.* per ton per mile; and on the parallel railway the through traffic, during the five months that the canal is closed by frost, is under 10,000 tons a month. The report of the state engineer of New York, for 1853, is full of the most important information on this subject."—*Sir A. Cotton,* late chief engineer of Madras, in "Letter to the Society of Arts."

⁂ The above bears partly upon the material unity of America, and partly on its material resources. It shows the extent, cheapness, durability, and indestructibility of its water carriage. But the water system is mostly connected, directly or indirectly, with the Mississippi, which is the chief factor of the material unity of America. Sir A. Cotton's authority is very high, and his letter was written to urge the needs of Irrigation and improved river navigation in India.

CONTENTS.

Opinions of Washington, Lincoln, Jefferson, De Tocqueville, Napoleon I., Beecher. — The material problem of the South. —Nature against the South.—Special and extraordinary Geographical Unity of America.—Proved by Precedent, Authority, and War.—All countries own this Law of Material Unity.—The only unalterable conditions and influences.—Italy, Switzerland, Ireland, Russia, Turkey, Poland, &c.—Mountain and Water systems, and Climate.—Three leading positions as to American Unity.—The Mississippi, 27,000 miles of navigable water.—The only certain outlet.—America will not strangle herself.—*A fortiori*.—South, North, East, West, and Centre; moral, political and commercial aspects.—Future Capital.—Naval and Military Strategy.—Immense interior and coast navigation and tonnage.—Rail and Telegraph, Post and Revenue.—West of Rocky Mountains.—Canada and Mexico.—The task before the South.—Summary.

"There is on the globe one single spot, the possessor of which is our natural and inevitable enemy. It is *New Orleans*."

"The occlusion of the *Mississippi* is a state of things in which we cannot exist. * * * The use of the Mississippi is so indispensable that we cannot hesitate one moment to *hazard our existence* for its maintenance. Whatever power, other than ourselves, holds the country *West of the Mississippi*, becomes our natural enemy."—*Thos. Jefferson*, 1802, 1803.

"The *Times* is a great power, the greatest perhaps in the world, except the *Mississippi*."—*Lincoln to Times' correspondent*.

"So long as he held it (*New Orleans*) he had in his hands the future greatness of the United States, and would never have ceded it, were he not desirous of creating a counterpoise to the maritime strength of England."—*Napoleon I.*

La Galissonière pleaded that, considering the want of maritime strength, *Canada* and *Louisiana* were the bulwarks of France against English ambition.—*Memoire on French Colonies*, 1750.

"New Orleans is the key to Mexico."—*Spanish Ambassador*, 1766.

The Problem, and the dream of the South is,

how to dissever the Gulf and Border States from the North, and to connect them with the great western valley of the Mississippi, and the ancient and mighty realm of Mexico.* It is the business of the present chapter to show that *nature* has beforehand rendered this scheme visionary and impossible. The fiat of her perpetual and indestructible influences rendered a United Slave Empire as impossible as it is infamous. Those who deny the pertinence of this mode of reasoning, or its special applicability to America in consequence of the special and extraordinary geographical unity of that continent, will not deceive many others, even if they succeed in deceiving themselves, for any man who can look at a map, and has studied history, will admit the importance of the argument.

The geographical unity of America is proved by Precedent, Authority, and War. Historical analogies everywhere prove the force of geographical unity. Authorities prove it. The course and strategy of the present war prove it. The policy of the first French settlers was shaped by it. The

* This idea is as old as 1706, when Col. Burr organized the expedition for which he was afterwards tried. President Jefferson, writing to La Fayette, said of Burr, "His conspiracy "has been one of the most flagitious of which history will ever "furnish an example. He meant to separate the Western "States from us, to add Mexico to them, place himself at their "head, establish what he would deem an energetic government, "and then provide an example, and an instrument, for the sub-"version of our freedom. The man who could expect to effect "this with American materials must be fit for Bedlam."

Burr's first enterprise was to have been to seize New Orleans, the Gate of the Mississippi, "which he supposed would powerfully bridle the upper country."

possessors of New Orleans, Port Hudson, or Vicksburg, must either grasp the great natural artery, and cut the spinal cord of the aggregate national life, or hold it for the nation against all comers.

The special and extraordinary material unity of the American continent, is one of the most remarkable and influential facts in the whole world.

Other countries—all countries, feel the irresistible power of this natural Law.

The energies of civilization, and the genius of war, can only act through existing material conditions. Of these, the mightiest, and the only ones that remain, are those great geographical features that present unalterable conditions of attack and defence, and a certain unceasing influence in an uniform direction.

As Italy was kept in pieces, very much by her extreme length and narrowness, her open coasts, and midland mountain ranges, — as the natural fortresses of Switzerland for ages kept despotism at bay,—as the nearness of Ireland to England has retained her to the British sceptre,—as the great material disturbing force of this continent, for two centuries, has been the natural effort of Russia to seek her outlets at the Sound and the Bosphorus, and to communicate with Europe through Poland, which has, on her side, no great natural military frontier,—as in all these instances, time and space, represented by geographical facilities or obstacles, have constituted a Principle, have become immutable material guarantees for uniform efforts in a certain direction, and have thus produced, and must ever produce, certain great results,—so in America, where the natural features are on a vaster scale, and *material unity more marked than in any other country of the world*, we are bound to inquire, when considering the issues of the present struggle, on which side are these marked advantages, and against whom are these material obstacles? For whom declare these permanent influences, so apt to prevail in the end, and which are before and after every conflict, and always the same?

It has constantly been observed by philosophers, that the mountain ranges, beginning with the Pyrenees, and under the names of the Alps, the Balkans, the Caucasus, the Himalayas, traversing Europe and Asia from West to East, are amongst the mightiest agencies the world has known, hoarding certain influences on the one side, and damming them back on the other, until, in the course of Providence, and the increase of population, &c., the fresh and strong energies of northern barbarian nature have been let loose upon the effête and crumbling civilisations of the South,—upon systems refined into weakness, or enervated by vice, to destroy that which deserved destruction, or to share in that which had been thus prepared for their use.

But this is only one of the material agencies that help to constitute and guarantee the unity of nations.

The natural material Unity of a Nation is

constituted by its water and mountain systems, and its climate, and supplemented by its rails and telegraphs, and services of Post and Revenue.

The first thing which a Statesman or a Soldier, who has to keep, take, or make a Nation, does, is to look at the map. Let us imitate this example.

Three leading positions are to be noted, as affecting the geographical and strategical unity of America.

1st.—The Mississippi, and general river system which connects the North and North-west and the South, and bisects "Secesh," is the only indestructible means of conveyance. It is moreover the cheapest, and although artificial roads rival it in foreign trade, the North and North-west cannot allow any possible enemy to possess it.

2nd.—While the great river connects North and North-west with South, the rails, lakes, and canals from North-west to North-east take the produce of the West Eastwards and Europewards, and must continue to do so, and indissolubly unite the whole North, in bonds of intercourse, interest, and habit, —socially, commercially, and politically. They render the attempt to disunite one section of the North from the other, a hopeless task, and connect the West with the East, as thoroughly as the Mississippi connects both with the South. The rail and water systems of the North do not counteract the influence of the Mississippi, but they all work together for one political, strategical, commercial, and social, unity of the Continent.

3rd.—The mountain ranges do not, as throughout Europe and Asia, sever North from South; they rather connect them.

§

Although all State maxims and analogies, drawn from the history of empire in the past, combine as it seems to us, to show that separation is for the United States without the range of the possible, yet the American question can scarcely be discussed in deference to them, inasmuch as the history of mankind furnishes no precedent, nor the whole geography of the world a parallel, to the material and moral conditions under which this American contest must be decided.

The Mississippi represents, nay it *is*, the spinal cord, and arterial system, of the Body of the American Nation. Where is there a river like the Father of waters, connecting with the ocean 27,000 miles of navigation? Yet its mere mileage and volume are as nothing compared with the peculiarity of its position as regards the territory, the strategy, the commerce, and the nationality, of America. It may, without undue emphasis, be affirmed, that next to the characteristics of the race itself, the Mississippi is the mightiest element in this question. It may almost be said to control the future of America, whether in peace or war. It constitutes its physical unity, and makes disunion a synonym for eternal war and hampered commerce, whilst in every year of real union it will make war more disastrous and impossible.

It forms a colossal moving road, wide and interminable, traversing the entire length of a vast continent, connecting its extremities, and the cities built upon its banks; and hour by hour, as commerce lives and millions grow along its banks, its freedom becomes a more and more essential condition and appanage of the American Nation. Towards its outlet, it is for hundreds of miles thinly peopled. It is permanently conditioned at its mouth, for a comparatively enervated race, by a tropical sun and a prodigal soil. Now, the river is with the hardy North, and gives it easy transit as against the forced marches of the enemy; and always as population and freedom of movement increase in the South, unrestricted water-way will become more and more essential, and its advocates more numerous.

The Mississippi can never constitute the boundary between nations. Indians, France and Spain, have held it, but the limitation has each time failed. In 1803 it was in *Ohio* and *Kentucky* that violent commotions arose when the treaty right of deposit at New Orleans was suspended, for even then, every American understood the significance of their mighty river. As it stretches northward a thousand miles, the same political, commercial, and social necessity culminates; the freedom of the river becomes ever more essential, and the relative numbers and strength of those who would impede it become more insignificant; till it at last divides in twain and holds in its mighty embrace the most probable seat of the future empire of the people.

A situation unparalleled in the unity of its material and geographical conditions; in fertility and in climate; in its moral conditions; and in the spirit, energy, enterprise, freedom, intelligence, and common enthusiasm of the race, now beating down and out of their Republic and constitution the only element of weakness which the thirty-four Empire States have detected after eighty years.

This mighty North-west and Centre is growing faster than North and South together. It has freer and more natural conditions of human life, energy, enterprise, and expansion, and more essential antagonism to the oligarchic South. But there is *one thing that will always be fatal to it or to Secession.* While the gunboats of the Empire can always be made free of the Canadian inland seas, it possesses no water outlet which is always open and cannot be destroyed, except the Mississippi; for Canals are destructible, and the Gulf of St. Lawrence is in half frozen latitudes. The North-west and Centre CANNOT let the river go, nor do the possible guarantees exist, nor can they ever be invented, whereby an alien South could secure to them a free navigation.

The Mississippi is the gate of the North-west and Centre,—they will keep the keys. It is the door of their house,—they will protect its threshold. It is their thoroughfare,—they will have no toll-keepers and no obstructions. It is their moving road,—they will have no shooting from behind the hedge, no batteries to rake from shore to shore, for 600 miles. The Mississippi takes them to their best customers in peace, and it floats through the empire a navy equal to 100,000 fighting men. It bisects the Slave empire in the South and West, just as her tributaries invade its central territory, and as mountain ranges bisect, and offer opportunities against it, from the Potomac to South Tennessee.

The North-west, East, and Centre must be conquered, and dead, and buried, before the mouths of the river will be surrendered to any other keeping. The world cannot expect America to strangle herself.

Were the South an empire full fledged to-morrow, it would still be war, latent or patent, still war, irrepressible, eternal, and exterminating,—till the nation reunite, or till human nature be changed, the mountains of the border land and central South collapse, or the river flow back to its source. It were better and more peaceful even to let war capitalize the loss, and make a full end.

There exist, it is true, no adequate precedents for the Mississippi, and the political effect of its position, but as far as precedents go, they enforce the "a fortiori" as applied to her.

The Danube flows not to the ocean, but it was a prime object of Russia, as against Austria, to close its mouth against large vessels. The Rhine is but a gutter without an outlet. The nearest parallel, showing the force of geographical position, is found in the history and necessities of Russia, and her yearning to possess her outlets, and to get the keys of her house, at the Sound and the Bosphorus. It was this geographical necessity that dictated to Peter the terms of his Testament, and that pointed the road to Constantinople; but what have been the necessities of non-commercial, autocratic Russia, and her means of enforcing them, compared with the needs and the power of America towards a similar end?

The Mississippi unites a vast threefold territory. Some may conceive it possible for the South-west, and the South-east, to neutralise the stream. A situation of uneasiness, and in which one side, the West, would have to the Atlantic, in case of quarrel, no cheap and indestructible access, being barred by Panama. But no equal bargain, or any bargain at all, is possible for the North-west and central States. They *must have* a direct water-way for through and *intermediate* traffic to and from the South and the ocean,—for a disability there would act as a prohibition on Commerce, and as paralysis in war.

But the rivers that in Disunion would roll down war, are destined rather to distribute plenty, and to cause to grow rich as friends, instead of striking as enemies. By any hostility of which they can be made the instrument, no human soul or interest save about 190,000 head of slaveholders, in the shape of cotton-growing autocrats, can really benefit.

It results then, we say, from a complete view of the *whole* Geographical question, in its moral, political, and commercial aspects, that, be America slave or free, she CANNOT be divided.

Moreover, all the tendencies and future of the North lean still more decisively than the present situation against the supposition that this highway of empire can be tampered with. Amongst these is the ideal of the future, favoured by many, that the capital of America be somewhere at the confluence of the Ohio and Mississippi, the natural centre of her Unity. Will America have her seat of Empire and centre of civilization, subject to a state of siege, or to periodical wars to raise it? and can any power exist, or continue to exist in America, whose interest, or within whose power it might be, to beleaguer that capital *a thousand miles off?* Ye diplomatists and strategists of Europe, say,—has not America reason here?

§

But let us more directly consider the bearing of the science of military and naval strategy upon this question, and realise the fatal difficulties of the Southern position, even were its moral and commercial aspects ignored. We have seen that in self defence, the North, North-west, and Centre cannot let the Mississippi go, and that they would always have means to prevent such a catastrophe. Let us now see what a weapon the interior and coast line navigation would become—has become—in their hands, as against a Southern rebellion.

We shall see in the sequel, that the whole coast line of the United States, including bays, sounds, and rivers, up to the head of tide-water, is 33,663 miles, of which 5,120 is maritine front. There are therefore upwards of 28,000 miles of navigable water between the maritine front and the head of tide-water. The shore line of their rivers *above* tide-water is 122,784 miles. Of this stupendous water mileage, more than one-half is navigable by steam, employing an interior steam tonnage exceeding that of all the internal steam tonnage of the rest of the world. They have also more deep, capacious, and safe harbours, accessible at all tides, than all Europe, with more than twenty capable of receiving the Great Eastern.*

Through all the interior territory, rivers flow into the Mississippi and Ohio, and Federal gunboats interpenetrate. Upwards of seventy rivers running from the North pierce the South. The coasts of the South also will always be exposed, for it can create no equal navy.

Again, her *mountain ranges* extend from north of the Potomac along North Carolina, to and through the southern boundary of Tennessee, even to the state of Mississippi. Hence the reason why the South carried the war to the frontiers. Here is an open strategy either way for North or South if they be twain,—strongholds and weapons of affront, and mutual offence indestructible and ever ready for use. Thus do the mountains, as well as the rivers, war against disunion. Thus no halfway house or compromise of territory is possible. The South must have Washington or nothing. The mountain ranges from Carolina to Washington will either be the outposts of the capital overawing the South, or the outposts of Richmond, threatening or commanding the North. The mountains connect with the North, and so far sever from "the South," almost all but the first tier of States next

* This calculation is on the authority of the Hon. Robert J. Walker, late Secretary of the Treasury of the United States.

to the ocean, and for the mere Gulf States no man cares.

We say then Strategy forbids disunion, or would cancel it if effected, and consider what a mighty thing strategy is. The great water and land features of Continents, a chief element in all struggles for empire, remain from eternity to eternity, as it were, in comparison with man's transient pursuits, and direct or circumscribe, age after age, the movements of armies and of fleets. It is a coincidence often remarked that battles are constantly repeated over the same positions, and it is in fact only when great commanders arise,—one in an era or a century, capable of understanding nature, and impressing her into the service, that this everlasting influence comes adequately out in war, and teaches what the Creator meant politically by His outer world. Thus do the labours of great men, and the progress of the race, fill up the predestined outline of the future. Thus does the history of mankind, translate the hieroglyphics of God!

The three great rules of military science, which it of course applies according to actual geography, are in substance as follows;—

1st. Concentrate. Beat minorities by majorities.

2nd. Operate by the shortest lines, and, by gaining time, thus again concentrate.

3rd. Move on, and destroy the enemies' communications and supplies.

Now mark the conditions under which these maxims have to be applied to the present contest.

Supposing the South to be a separate power, not lying helplessly at the feet of the North, but a real independent people, we have seen that it could at any time, and in any quarrel, blockade the inner country, at a distance of a thousand miles, and strangle much of its commerce, impose duties, levy tolls, occasion breaking of bulk, necessitate land transit, and intercept vessels of war.

What would result from this? On the one side, — that of Northern unity, we see the strongest inducement that could be offered to a nation, namely, the avoidance of a standing and imminent menace to commercial life, and political honour. And that same side is also endowed by nature with an unchangeable vantage ground and system of natural means, in alliance with superior numbers, wealth, intelligence, and appliances, to prevent or to remove this peril, and to turn back its point against the South, with deadly effect.

For what would the Mississippi say evermore to the North. It would cry aloud, "Here are rich "slopes and open pastures, and I am the way to "them. I will bear you rapidly and safely through "some 10,000 miles of water way that penetrates "and interpenetrates the South. I am your stra-"tegy. I will concentrate your masses on the "fractions of the foe. I will give you the shortest, "because the easiest and swiftest lines. I will "open behind, or on the flank, of every Southern "army, communications by which you may cut "theirs off."

Whether the future of America be peace or war, the eighty or ninety thousand miles of internal steam navigation, will be one of its mightiest facts.

Were the South for a time successful, here are

for the North perpetual guarantees of re-union, and irresistible inducements to war against that side which would-be Statesmen and Generals, without a suspicion of the irony of their position, attempt in argument to maintain.

America has more miles of rail and telegraph than all the world, and iron roads, of course, may compete with water roads, but each have their place, and each their advantages and disadvantages. Most of the through traffic to Europe, and much of mediate traffic elsewhere, will of course go by way of New York, and through canals to other centres, which claim also financial and business facilities, but more than enough remains, and must always remain, to warrant all we have said of the great river, and its tributaries. They afford cheap transit always, cannot be worn out, removed, and broken up like iron in war, and are always essential.

With reference to the territory west of the Rocky Mountains, the natural features do not at first sight point so decisively to their incorporation with the political unity of America,* but a territory bounded on one side by the sea, and stretching for twenty degrees alongside an immense continent, both inhabited by a race of intense activity, and with the same language and institutions, cannot, according

* The Hon. Malcolm Cameron is reported to have stated at the London Tavern, on the 21st January, 1863.

"Which (Rocky) mountains have hitherto been deemed a serious obstacle to communication from East to West, but a thorough survey has now proved the existence of passes which are but gentle heights and rolling knolls clothed with verdure on the flanks, and offering no real obstacle to the traveller from the East, who seeks by that route to reach the gold regions."

to all experience, remain unabsorbed by the influences of peace, or unsubdued by the energies of war.

The future, and probably peaceful absorption of Canada, and the annexation of Mexico, are sufficiently obvious, according to all the probabilities of statesmanship. There is no substantive barrier either way, and southwards Panama is the natural boundary, and the Black Yankees are the natural settlers. But these questions are discussed elsewhere, and are not *as yet* distinctly put in issue by the present conflict.

§

In reference to *Banks*, *Coin*, *Commerce*, *Revenue regulations*, *weights and measures*, *and Postal service*, the effect of their being conducted on a national system is, with the exception of the first, too obvious to require comment in a book of this description.

The effect, however, of Chase's *national banking system* is misunderstood by many well-wishers of America, and is misrepresented by all her enemies who understand it. It is properly treated of in the chapter on "Reconstruction." We here refer the reader to Chase's first annual report of Dec. 1861, and to the subsequent ones. He asserts that Government had constitutional powers to regulate commerce, coin, and credit circulation, which last then depended on the laws of thirty-four States, and on some 1600 Banks, whose circulation commonly was in inverse ratio of solvency. He has substituted a circulation secured by national bonds, but based upon private means and credit, thus *binding most of the* 1642 *banks, and their interests, connection, stock, and note holders, and customers, to the Union.* The "State" bank system furnished Secession mainly with funds. Those banks are now generally insolvent, and with the present system the rebellion could scarcely have occurred.

Whatever may be otherwise thought of Chase's finance, *this* cannot be doubted,—that it is an immense accession to the cause of national unity, and it settles a question debated since 1780, when Hamilton and Knox, Jefferson and Randolph were divided in opinion as to its constitutionality.

§

We say then, that the teaching of geography confirms all other teachings, that America, whatever else she be, will be for ever one. Of all countries in the world, she more than any other country, must be one,—for reasons commercial, social, and political, and cannot be otherwise. If any man thinks otherwise, he has only to remodel military science; to alter mountain ranges; to turn back the Mississippi, or open Niagara, and guarantee perpetual free passage through frozen latitudes northward; to quench for ever one of the intensest and most powerful nationalities; to reverse motives of self interest; and to extinguish the greed of commercial gain and genius of commercial enterprise. He has only to do these little things, and a few other trifles like them, and the Slave empire may flourish in the stead of the North, to the destruction of free institutions. For if Slavedom flourish, it *must* expand. Then the mightiest fabric of human Government,—the vastest empire,—the best and widest education system,—the most orderly and peaceful and progressive nation,—the home and refuge of all the world, where all races, however languishing elsewhere, suddenly spring under new conditions into life, enterprise, and a career,—the nation which alone has complete religious and political freedom, where man is man, without let, hindrance, partiality, or handicapping,—all this will be scattered, broken, destroyed, and reversed. Rival states, diplomacies, policies, standing armies, frontier fortresses, tariffs, and interests, will take the place of that glorious political fabric which the future is impatient to consummate and crown.

Thank God, however, all this is but the Statecraft of fools,—the dream of the weak and the wicked, and these misbegotten twins of the South, with the treason they have spawned between them, will soon be consigned, after a pause of conflict, for America, but as one short dismal day,—to the places whence they came.

CHAPTER II.

UNITY OF IDEAS AND INTERESTS.

THE CONSTITUTION AND GENIUS OF THE AMERICAN NATION.
POPULAR, "STATE," AND NATIONAL SOVEREIGNTIES.
LABOUR. FREEDOM. LAW.
BALANCES OF THE CONSTITUTION.
PROPAGANDISM OF FREEDOM.
EQUALITY OF CONDITIONS.
POWER OF ASSOCIATION.

"No race of Kings have ever presented above one man of common sense in twenty generations. * * * If all the evils which can arise from *the republican form of our Government*, from this day to the day of judgment, could be put into a scale against what this country (France) suffers from its monarchical form in a week, or England in a month—the latter would preponderate."

Jefferson, 1787.

"Communities have existed aristocratic from their earliest origin, and which became more democratic in each succeeding age.

"But a people having taken its rise in civilisation and democracy, which *should gradually establish an inequality of conditions* until it arrived at inviolable privileges and exclusive castes would be a novelty in the world; and nothing intimates that America is likely to furnish so singular an example."—*De Tocqueville*, p. 433, v. 1.

"The Union is an accident * * but the *republican form of Government* seems to me the natural state of the Americans, which nothing but continued action of hostile causes always acting in the same direction could change into a monarchy."

"Although the Anglo-Americans have several religious sects, they all regard religion in the same manner. *They are unanimous upon the general principles which ought to rule Society.* From Maine to the Floridas, from the Missouri to the Atlantic Ocean the people is held to be the legitimate source of all power. The same notions are entertained respecting liberty and equality, the liberty of the press, the right of association, the jury, and the responsibility of the agents of Government. We find the same uniformity in the moral and philosophical principles which regulate the daily action of life and govern their conduct. They are not only united together by these common opinions, but they are separated from all other nations by a common feeling of pride * * and are not very remote from believing themselves to belong to a distinct race of mankind."—*De Tocqueville*, v. 2, p. 424: p. 383, v. 2.

"The *temporal Interests* of all the several parts of the *Union* are intimately connected, and the same assertion holds true of those *opinions and sentiments* which may be termed the immaterial interests of men."—*De Tocqueville*, p. 382, v. 2.

"The observer who examines the present condition (1836) of the United States upon this principle (that Society means a *similarity of opinions, thoughts, and impressions*), will readily discover, that although the citizens are divided into twenty-four distinct Sovereignties, *they nevertheless constitute a single People;* and he may perhaps be led to think that the state of the Anglo-American Union is more truly a state of Society than that of certain nations of Europe which live under the same legislation and the same prince."

De Tocqueville, p. 383, v. 2.

"*Associations* ought, in democratic nations, to stand in lieu of those powerful private individuals whom the equality of conditions has swept away.

"As soon as several of the inhabitants of the United States have taken up an opinion which they wish to promote, they look out for mutual assistance; and as soon as they have found each other out they combine. From that moment they are no longer isolated men, but *a power seen from afar*, whose actions serve for an example and whose language is listened to."—*De Tocqueville*, p. 226, v. 3.

"The colonists from Maine to Carolina; the adventurous companions of Smith; the Puritan felons that freighted the fleet of Winthrop; the Quaker outlaws that fled from jails with a Newgate prisoner as their Sovereign;—all had faith in God, and in the Soul." * * "The American mind in the largest sense eclectic, struggled for Universality while it asserted Freedom."—*Bancroft.*

"But the Confederate States of America had been long accustomed to form a portion of *one empire* before they had won their independence. * * * They amended their laws, and saved their country."—*De Tocqueville*, pp. 236, 238, 248, v. 1.

"The citizens of each State shall be entitled to all privileges and immunities of citizens in the several States."—*Art.* IV. *Sect.* 1, *American Constitution.*

"Their constitution rests upon a novel theory which may be considered a great invention of political science. In all confederacies formed before the American constitution of 1789 the Allied States reserved to themselves the right of ordaining and enforcing the laws of the Union. The American States agreed that the *Federal Government* should not only dictate the laws but *execute* its own enactments. This alteration produced the most momentous consequences."—*De Tocqueville*, p. 235, v. 1.

CONTENTS.

GENIUS of the nation,—Intensity—Self-reliance.—Loyalty.—Devotion to Principles of Equality.—Willingness to change.—Power of association.—Constitution unique.—THE NATION THE CONSTITUTION.—Committee of the whole nation.—Instances.—Conservatism of universal suffrage.—The *Balance* of the Constitution.—The state and nation preserve authority.—Individual and state preserve freedom.—The main chance.—Freedom and nationality.—Centralisation and Independence.—Nationality and faction.—Effect of intelligence on centralisation.—BASIS OF FEDERAL SUCCESS INDESTRUCTIBLE.—Balance of Interests.—State Organisation *versus* Despotism.—Freedom *versus* Oligarchy.—Thirty Millions of Kings.—Freedom and Law.—Independence and Union.—Opinions before armies or "State" influence. — Fundamental Principles. — Order, Equality, and Union *versus* "Secesh."—Propagandism of North.—MASTER PASSIONS OF NORTH.—Dignity of Labour.—National Independence and Loyalty. — Conservatism of Free Labour.—PROPAGANDISM OF FREEDOM.—Interlacing Boundary.—Aggression of Slavery; moral, commercial, and political. Universal uniform class, *versus* oligarchy. — Slavery *versus* equality.—Industry, genius, conservatism, and morality of America.—Slaveholding peace fatal.—Slavery and the Caucus.—Party discipline. — Conservatism *versus* centralisation. —Popular initiative.—Counterpoise to centralisation.—THE REAL GOVERNMENT.—Special circumstances and conservatism of American Democracy.—Democratic nations may always save themselves.—Equal conditioned Democracy destroys oligarchy.

"One of the circumstances which most powerfully contribute to support the Federal Government in America, is that the States have not only similar interests, a common origin, and a common tongue, but that they are also arrived at the *same stage of civilisation*. I do not know of any European nation, however small, which does not present less uniformity in its different provinces than the American people. Maine and Georgia, at the opposite extremities of a great empire, are in the natural possession of more real inducements to form a confederation, than Normandy and Brittany, which are only separated by a bridge."—*De Tocqueville*, pp. 257-8, v. 1.

THE circumstances that promote the Individuality, or the political, social, and intellectual

Unity of a nation, are a oneness of Race, Language, Literature, Religion, Boundary, and Institution. Out of these, or some of them, is nationality created, and, in proportion to *their* completeness, is *its* intensity and strength.

The Genius of the nation is before and after the constitution. Nevertheless, as the intention of the founders and of the People of America was embodied in the Constitution, and as the Constitution has had and has its effect upon the Genius of the nation, and is now, save as to Slavery, its tolerably accurate expression and embodiment, we shall discuss the three leading aspects of the Constitution, namely, its Legislative, administrative, and judicial *Unity;* its *peculiar Democratic provisions* and influence; and its *special Balance* between the rights and functions of the Individual, of the State, and of the Nation.

The net result of all this, namely, National Unity, is proved by fact and authority. By the opinions of representative men. By the text of resolutions unanimously adopted. By the text of the Constitution, and by the existence, attributes, and action of the nation.

Of these, the first two, the opinions and resolutions, we must refer to their more appropriate place hereafter, in the Book on the History of the making of the Nation. The second and third, namely, the direct and necessary result of the actual Constitution, and the character and specialities of the Nation as it exists, we discuss in the present chapter.

We have shown that the strength and value of

the spirit of nationality,—in other words, of the national Unity,—depends upon the strength and value of each component part, and on its capacity to combine and work together with the others. The man must be free, educated, loyal. The "Sovereign State" must be organised,—its rights admitted and its sphere defined: and the Constitution must give full legitimate play to the energies, freedom, rights, and will, of the Individuals, and of the Secondary Institutions or States, and yet be precise enough and strong enough to maintain legality and order.

In fact, STRENGTH and ADJUSTMENT, Unity and Power, are the two ideas that go to make up that of a great and complete nation.

We find accordingly, that the American Constitution has five leading characteristics, corresponding also with the Genius of the nation, adjusted thereto, and, in fact, growing thereout. It has, in the first place, the principles of *Popular* Sovereignty, *State* Sovereignty, and *National* Sovereignty, each complete, better defined, and better combined, than in any other nation.

To *combine* them in a practical constitutional Balance, two things are required; First, absolute respect for the law as long as it is Law; and, Second, a definite, manageable, and assured mode of alteration, when any part of such Constitution shall have become ill adjusted to the changing forces or altered character of the nation. These two elements of conservatism and progress, the Genius and Constitution of the American nation, combine in a remarkable degree. Americans stand by their laws, because they made and can unmake them. They stand by the Constitution as it is, knowing that no imaginable power can bind it upon them against their will.

This power of amendment constitutes the fourth peculiarity of the Constitution.

The Guarantee of the Republican form of Government is the fifth characteristic.

These constitutional and national peculiarities of America, as a federated Republic, sprang from the political Genius of the nation, and its truth to nature, and to the necessities of the situation.

The Genius of the American nation has five leading characteristics.

The Intensity of its nationality, and the rapidity and completeness with which it absorbs other races.

Its contempt for other countries and Governments, and reliance on itself.

Its devotion to the principle of equality of conditions.

Its obedience to the actual law, and readiness to change both law and constitution, when necessary.

Its extraordinary Powers of Association.

All these tend almost equally against Disunion, Secession, Slavery, and Despotism.

§

The first Principle of the American Constitution to which we have referred as springing from the Genius of the nation, and coinciding therewith, is the Principle of Popular Sovereignty. "The People of the United States are the independent and equal source of all its powers."

"He that will understand," says Bancroft, "the political

character of New England in the 18th century, must study the constitution of its towns, congregations, schools, and militia. *All New England was an aggregate of organized democracies.* Nearly all were descended from English emigrants of the time of Charles I. and II. They were, therefore, of *homogeneous origin.* They were frugal and industrious, and there was not enough of Slavery to affect their character."

"The plain meeting-house was everywhere the central point; near it stood the public school; the farms were freeholds and without quit rents. In every hand was the Bible. Every home was a house of prayer. In every village all had been taught, many had comprehended a methodical theory of the Divine purpose of the creation, and of the destiny of man."

"New York had been settled under large patents of lands to individuals; New England under grants to towns; and the institution of towns was its glory and its strength. The inhabited part of Massachusetts was recognised as divided into little territories, each of which, for its internal purposes, constituted a separate integral government, free from supervision, having power to choose annually its own officers; to hold meetings of all freemen at its own pleasure; to discuss in those meetings any subject of general interest; to see that *every able-bodied man within its precincts was duly enrolled in the militia,* and always provided with arms, ready for immediate use; to elect and to instruct its representatives; to raise and appropriate money, for the support of the ministry, of schools, of highways, of the poor, and for defraying other necessary expenses within the town."

It was the resolution of the Colonists to maintain entire liberty, both in Church and State, that drew from Wentworth the exclamation, "*The very genius of that nation* of People leads them always to oppose, both civilly and ecclesiastically, all that ever authority ordains for them."

"It was incessantly deplored by royalists of later days, that the *law which confirmed these liberties* had received the unconscious sanction of William the Third, and *the most extensive interpretation in practice.* Boston even, on more than one occasion, ventured in town-meeting to appoint its own agent to present a remonstrance to the Board of Trade. New Hampshire, Connecticut, Rhode Island, and Maine, which was a part of Massachusetts, had similar regulations. But the complete development of the institution (Democracy) was to be found in Connecticut and the Massachusetts Bay. There each township was also substantially a territorial parish; the town was the religious congregation; the independent church was established by law; the minister was elected by the people, who annually made grants for his support."

"Massachusetts was divided into little complete democracies in Church and in State. Calvinism addressed all and was Democracy. It rested on the chosen and made of the elect *every man a king and a priest* between God and the People."*

Second, there is the Principle of STATE SOVEREIGNTY and municipal right: "The People or the States, retain all powers not conferred by them on the general Government." And by Article X. amendment to the Constitution, it is provided that—

"The powers not delegated to the United States by the Constitution, nor prohibited by it to the States, are reserved to the States respectively, or to the People."

Third, the Principle of NATIONAL SOVEREIGNTY. The national compact is set forth in a written constitution; and special powers thus conferred were submitted to State conventions, and sanctioned by the direct consent of the People.

"All former confederate Governments," says De Tocqueville, "presided over communities, but that of the Union rules over individuals. Hence the term of federal government is clearly no longer applicable to a state of things which must be styled, an incomplete *national government*. The absence of this new species of confederation has been the cause which has brought all unions to civil war, to subjection, or to a stagnant apathy."

* The above is condensed from Bancroft's account of the old thirteen Colonies, but is in his own words.—See pp. 168, 169, 170, v. 1. American Revolution.

The direct, natural, and intended result of the actual constitution was national. The result of a supreme Executive, Legislative, and Judiciary, could not be other than national.

"All *legislative* Powers herein granted shall be vested in a congress of the United States," &c. Art. I., Sec. 1, American Constitution.

"The *executive* Power shall be vested in a President of the United States." Art. II., Sec. 1. "The President shall be Commander-in-Chief of the Army and Navy of the U. S. and of the Militia of the several States, &c. He shall have power, by and with the advice and consent of the Senate, *to make treaties.*" Art. II., Sec. 2.

"The *judicial* Power of the U. S. shall be vested in one supreme Court." Art. III. Sec. 1. "The judicial Power shall extend to all cases in Law and Equity, arising under this constitution, the laws of the U. S., and treaties made, or which shall be made, under their authority; to all cases affecting ambassadors, &c.; to all cases of Admiralty and maritime jurisdiction; to controversies between two or more States; between a State and citizens of another State; between citizens of different States," &c. Art. III., Sec. 2.

The Principle of national Sovereignty is also proved by the national character of the laws of Taxation and Commerce, and Trade; of national credit or debt; of coin, and weights and measures; of post offices and post roads; of patents and copyrights; of laws respecting piracies on the seas; respecting war, and army, and navy, &c.; and of provision for amendments of constitution, and adoption of state debts. It is also proved by the guarantee of the Republican form of Government, by the supremacy of the Constitution and the oath to it, by the purchase of territory by national funds, and the cession of territory. By the originating of revenue Bills in the People's House; the payment of members by the U. S. treasury; the election of President by the majority; the proportion of representatives to population, and the necessary rules of Congress, assuming it to be a representative body, one and indivisible.*

Fourth; there is a definite plan for altering and AMENDING the Constitution. (Article V.)

Fifth; a distinct guarantee to each State, by the whole power of the United States, of the REPUBLICAN form of Government, &c. "The United States shall guarantee to every State in this Union a Republican form of Government, and shall protect each of them against Invasion; and on application of the Legislature, or of the Executive, (where the Legislature cannot be convened) against domestic violence." (Article IV. Section IV.)

But there is a further Principle, that in speaking of the nationality of America, we must especially remember, namely, that where the Freedom and Equality of the Individual is thus reasonably provided for, the fact of neighbourhood, the habits of society, and the power of combined action, and the clashing policy and hostile interests of foreign Powers, will always insure a development of the forces of nationality in proportion to the homogeneity of the parts within, and the antagonism that threatens their unity from without.

* For those who want a technical and complete account of the proofs of nationality from the Constitution, we know no more satisfactory summary than "Rawlins' American Disunion."—Hardwicke, London, 1862. It appears as reliable and accurate as Spence's is unreliable and inaccurate and one-sided, and it would be difficult to express a more favourable opinion in stronger language.

Once ensure Freedom, and create a nation, and any other provisions against nationality are contradictions in terms of the essential forces of the situation. Once create the national life, and let it protect the individual life, and enact the reasonable individual will, and no other possible enactment against that life or nation can prevail against it. It would be cast out as abnormal, or reconciled as natural and true.

There are also many other subsidiary guarantees of freedom and equality of conditions, and therefore of Unity of Ideas and Interests, which are part and parcel of the Genius and Constitution of America, or of one or other of them. They have been catalogued by Hinton (p. 313, v. 2) as follow:—

> "A separation of the Legislative, Executive, and Judicial authorities, more complete than in England; the degree of control, possessed by the People by frequent elections, either directly or indirectly, over all those authorities, and public functionaries; rotation in office; the prohibition of orders of nobility; the substitution of a temporary President for an hereditary King; the abolition of the right of primogeniture; the absence generally of exclusive privileges; the absence of a national church and tithes; equality of all denominations of Christians; the admission (and practice) of its being a public duty to educate the whole community; and the frequent reference of great affairs to the people in convention."

These Principles, guarantees, and conditions, are in strict accord with the origin and objects of the founders of the nation.

§

Volumes might be written, and have been written, to elucidate verbal specialities in the American Constitution, but as the fundamental Principles and primary elements of *all Government* are those of relative and balanced right of the Individual, of associations of Individuals, and of the Government, and as the present revolt arises out of contrary interpretations of State rights, and from the invasion by the Southern principles of Slavery and oligarchy, of the rights of State, of Man, and of Nation, we prefer at once to consider the real question,—namely, "whether the rebellion is contrary to, or in harmony with, the Genius and Constitution of the American nation," and whether the Nation will not now use the Constitution to cast out these hostile principles and to reassert those of Freedom, Order, and Nationality. By the answers to this question will the rebellion stand or fall.

A constitution should consecrate and assert the principles of national Life. It should permit the conservative and progressive forces of nationality to adjust and to enact themselves.

It is our business to show that, in this respect, the American Genius and Constitution completely coincide. That as regards progress, the People are the source whence all power issues, and the tribunal to which it is responsible. That they have the initiative in amendments and alterations. That as regards conservatism, the people are law-abiding and property-owning, and that the organization of the States and of Government, are adapted to exercise and maintain municipal rights, and national interests.

The American Constitution is indeed, in this respect, unique in History, and political science is incomplete till its results shall be worked out.

The man who attempts to argue American questions, from analogies of any other Government or Federation in the past or present, reckons without his host, and argues against his facts.

It would of course be as reasonable to augur the same political results from the constitution of England as it is, and as it would be, were every county of ours a separate Sovereign State, with Parliament, Senate, and militia, separately organised and led, and had every man here a direct stake in the welfare, and a voice in the destiny of his country. Where a constitution is used by the few, as an instrument for exploiting the many, or in any country where the great question of equality of conditions is unsettled, a rent in the constitution is a serious thing indeed,—quite a case of the "Throne and the altar" on the one side, and of revolution (or process of ejectment with the recovery of damages for mesne profits fraudulently appropriated) on the other. On the one side, it would take an impossible conservative reaction; on the other, a thirty years agitation to recover lost ground.

But in America the NATION IS THE CONSTITUTION, and there, if anything goes amiss with the constitution, *the nation resolves itself into a Committee of the whole nation*, and settles the matter. They did this in 1787,—they have been occupied since then with the old-world question of equality of conditions, intruded upon their industrial, social, and political systems by slavery; but they are already preparing to celebrate the settlement of that question, by a re-adjustment of the Constitution to the national life.

The political Genius of the American people

seems likely, therefore, to avoid the three dangers of national life,—Apathy, immobility, and revolution.

At the last Presidential election the People determined to return Lincoln. The law, that, not the people, but men chosen by them, should elect the President, stood in their way. By a mere volition the people broke to pieces this part of the constitution, and made a previous compact with the electors. It was an act of audacious conservatism, achieved by a Democracy. They broke the constitution and saved the Union.

Again, it has been feared *in England*, that the Federation will be welded by war into a Despotism,—that centralisation will endanger freedom. But already,—before the idea is much ventilated here, it has been discussed, not so much with a view to a possible Despotism, as to strengthen and increase the popular initiative. One alteration proposed is the removal of the proviso for the three-fourth proposal, and the four-fifth ratification of alterations in the Constitution, and the substitution therefor of some clause that shall be less cumbrous, and yet not revolutionary.

§

In America every man has a vote and a revolver, and belongs also to a State with complete organisation. Opinion will not support his use of the revolver against the country, because in four years, at farthest, he can use his vote more effectually. The right of insurrection never comes till the right of voting is denied; and whenever the universal rights of the men who compose the "States" are assailed by Despotism, then, and not till then, will the State organisation be used by the Nation against the central Government.

In America every individual has a stake in the country, and a voice in State, and national affairs.

There, thirty-four "Sovereign States," possess, each an organisation, ready to express or to enforce opinion, whether as regards the individual, or the central Government.

There the Government rules (not as in other confederacies over separate States, but) over each individual.

In America there is not merely the Individual and the Government, but a State organisation, which will guard equally against encroachments of the Government upon Freedom, and of other States upon national rights, or upon its own.

The question, therefore, respecting Individual or State action, is, whether, if the central Government became Despotic, the 34 organised States would not successfully combine with individual votes and influence against it; and on the other hand, whether the Individual, and the Government, would not always join, as they now have joined, to suppress any anti-national and fractional effort of certain States? Whether nationality would not always be too strong for treason, and "State rights" too strong for Despotism?

We have already said, "Give us the assurance of the *Freedom*, Equality of Conditions, and *nationality* of America, and we leave it to others to amuse themselves with inconsequential theories, unsubstantial questions, and airy nothings, about "the Constitution." Even the questions, how, and by what agency the South is to be subdued, or whether or no it may gain temporary victories, form temporary alliances, or even occupy Washington, are subordinate to the larger questions of Freedom, Equality, and Nationality, and if these remain, the Constitution can only be changed for the better.

We believe that the Constitution and the Geographical Unity of America, and those opinions, customs, manners, and sentiments, that are before and after and stronger, than law, so settle the main chance in America, that nothing human or infernal can unsettle it; and that the power does not exist, that could destroy American Nationality, or its social and political equality of conditions.

We believe that the force and depth of that Nationality is so evident *there*, that no American, no Southerner even, ever yet dreamt of *its* permanent division. Notwithstanding the increased centralisation and administrative unity which followed the English war, yet for many years before the present contest became imminent, theorists speculated on some future derangement of the balance of power, between "State Sovereignty," and the central Executive, apprehending the gradual increase of the former; and it was De Tocqueville who said, "I repeat my assertion, that the present tendency (1836) of American Society appears to me to become more and more Democratic."

This tendency, represented in the North by the so-called Democratic party, and combined with a special class interest, geographically and politically defined, threatened the integrity of the Union, the morality of the Nation, and the efficiency of its Executive.

But the action of this sectional democratic force, taken precisely in the only way that could have *compelled* the North to resist, insulted the morality, defied the Nationality, strengthened the Executive, and has called forth such a force of opinion in favour of centralisation and national authority, and has been forming such habits of respect for and submission thereto,—as to more than redress the balance, and still further to nationalise the Government. This has been done to such an extent that ages must pass before the effect can be undone.

The war, then, on both sides, lessens for the time, the power of the "States," and begets habits of submission and centralisation, which will outlive the war.

§

We have now to discuss whether any possible event can compel or induce the Sovereign People either to surrender their nationality to Southern faction or their independence to domestic Despotism.

1st.—Would they surrender their Nationality?

Supposing that the South allied itself with foreigners, and so appeared to achieve its Independence, would that ultimately endanger the Nationality? We say, on the contrary, it would arouse the Nation in tenfold strength against the treason that would use foreign dictation, to thrust that one inconsistent, irreconcilable, anti-national interest, upon the Nation. And we ask what possible power exists that could finally undo the habits of a hundred years' Union,—the effects of oneness of Race, Language, Boundary, Institution, and Religion? What Interest then could oppose successfully, the natural tendency to reunite? What influence could counteract those other influences?

The material unity would remain. The social unity would return. The Constitution, laws, customs, habits of thought, ambition, and prestige of race, contempt of old world traditions and influences, the mutual dependence of North and South, for shipping and harbours, for produce and consumption, for freight and transit,—of the North-west for communion with Europe,—of North, West, and South and East—of all, for the use of their one great natural moving road, the Mississippi—all would combine to reunite America: nor folly, nor sin, alone, can have invented the delusion of the severance of such a country, and both together can hardly account for the hallucination.

But, 2ndly,—Is it supposable that under any circumstances, the Sovereign States would yield to a centralised Despotism?

We answer, to Unity, for military purposes, they will; but to Despotism, never. To a so-called Despotism, that should not destroy Equality, such submission would seem to some possible, but with Equality and Nationality remaining, and with such counteracting elements of power as the Sovereign States, organised and equipped, and with common anti-Despotic interests, Despotism, as distinguished from Unity, is impossible; for it could not exist without assailing some interest or principle common to the Nation, and then the People and the States, would take the opportunity and would combine to destroy it.

"If at all times," says De Tocqueville (p. 282, v. 4), "*education* enables men to defend their independence, this is most especially true in *democratic* ages. Men require much intelligence, knowledge, and art, to organise and maintain *secondary* powers, * * and to create * * such free associations, as may be in a condition to struggle against tyranny without destroying public order."

"Hence the concentration of power, and the subjection of individuals, will increase amongst *democratic* nations, not only in the same proportion as their *equality*, but in the same proportion as their *ignorance*."

We need only add to this, that the North makes "ignorance" impossible, while the South makes knowledge criminal.

*The basis of Lincoln's policy, and of Federal success, as against the Slave power, is absolutely indestructible.**

It rests upon the Balance of power, which two out of the three elements of the political system would always be interested in maintaining against the oppressions of the third.

Of the three forms of power in America, the Individual, the "Sovereign State," and the Nation, there would always, as far as can be foreseen, remain, between two of them, a general unity of interest and natural alliance on the side of the national interests and will. The "Individual" would advocate

* Save on a wilder hypothesis of national demoralisation than need be noticed.

and uphold freedom. The "State" would present an *organisation* always able, ready, and willing to oppose a Despotism that should menace State interests. The Individual, and the national Government, would always be desirous of restricting undue "State" powers. Between these forces any sectional immoral Slave State interest must, soon or late, be ground to pieces. If the demands of a State be popular, the universal vote will enact them. If they be excessive, the jealousy of other States, the will of the Individual, and of the nation, will combine against them.

These conservative interests, and energies, have not failed even against a combination of (Slave) States, coinciding with a certain geographical line, and compelled by interest and policy to hold together against the Union.

It is, and always must be, to the interest of the American citizen, and within his power, to use the "State" for two purposes—1st, to maintain national Unity, and (except Slavery) the Constitution substantially as it is;—2nd, to resist any attempt at centralised Despotism.

§

THIRTY MILLIONS OF KINGS rule America. Each knows right well that his Sovereignty depends on the common respect for the Law, and that the respect of the world for the power and the principles of Democracy, and the national institutions, depends upon the Union.

Opinion is omnipotent in America. It upholds, first, the Sovereignty of the People, and then the

Union. It rules the Government through the Press and Conventions, and we refuse to believe that any American, South or North, in his wildest or most deluded moments, ever believed or wished that America could, or ought to, be divided.

In America, the "State," which constitutes such a novel item in political combinations, is, after all, but a weapon to be used by opinion.

An Union with those false "Democrats," who would exact "State rights" against the national Sovereignty, and force, against opinion, has always been sought as the necessary basis of the policy of the Slave States and factions.

Thus for thirty years they attempted to debauch, and for three, have attempted to defy, opinion.

The situation always was, an Union of the compacted slave South, with any States, or persons, having a quarrel with the national Government. Such was the natural policy of a system that degraded and lessened the productive power of the individual, and so injuring both him and the Nation, could not but look to an ultimate struggle with both.

But against the combination that always really involved sectional failure or national division, the Free soil or abolition party, appealed naturally, necessarily, and successfully, to the general opinion of the country.

The major question in America always is, first, what is opinion, and afterwards, what are the armaments, or have been the Battles.

The dignity of Labour, arising from the Equality, and freedom of the Individual; *the Union, and na-*

tional Independence, and submission to the *authority* of the Law, these are the master passions of America, and quite as applicable to the parallel, and quite as appreciable by the inhabitants of the South, as of the North.

It is notorious that since open war began 700,000 negroes have left their owners. For 80 years the effort to retain them, was in reality, a chronic civil war waged by fugitive slave laws, and laws of death for the second teaching of slaves to read. It was a war against all intellect or intelligence,—a war against all news of Slave insurrections,—a war of Lynch law upon propagandists, missionaries, or free speakers,—a war by armies of overseers, and blood hounds,—by manacles, the lash, the gibbet, and the stake.

Before the overt war, the Slave was retained in his place, with only partial insurrections, (which the South has not succeeded in keeping entirely from the outer world)—because, though they might rise, they had no place to run to. All this is changed. There are cities of refuge for the Black, round a frontier of 2000 miles. The North has gone from connivance, to neutrality, and from neutrality, to propagandism, and help. The gun-boats of the Republic will haunt every river, and every shore, and instead of missionaries to hang, and negroes to burn, there is the armed Puritan race of the North, four times outnumbering Secesh, who, from the fatal hour when the South made Slavery a national question, have resolved that it is a national danger to be avoided, and a public foe to be destroyed.

The South tried Propagandism, and were beaten

by their own weapons. At the stage when this system began to assert its power without the range of the individual state, and to encroach on the universal right, whether of State or individual, which the sovereignty of the Republic was bound to protect at that stage,—then the chronic civil war became open national war, the private demoralisation of the South, became a public nuisance, and the conservatism of the North, became armed resistance, by virtue of a National necessity. The *casus belli* was that the North would not constitute itself and *the whole continent* a slave empire.

The mere existence of North and South, side by side, as hostile or neutral communities, the one republican, free, progressive, and intelligent, the other oligarchic, slave, retrograde, and ignorant, would suffice, alone, in a few years, not only to prevent the extension of slavery, but to dissolve the fabric of imposture and of violence as it stands,—unless we settle it now in the teeth of progress, that monopoly is the natural state of trade, —that slavery is the natural and chosen state of man,—and in the face of modern conclusions on self-government, that oligarchic rule, is, after all, the best guarantee for the progress and perfection of the individual.

That Despotic Governments cannot safely permit the neighbourhood of free people, and that the first will destroy the last, or the last absorb the first, is the teaching of every philosopher, orator, and statesman, since the world began. And yet we have the statesmen of oligarchic England, and of all Despotic, priest-ridden, and corporation-ridden countries, recommending, and pretending to believe in, the co-existence side by side, of two opposite systems of politics and industry,— with a continuous, and even an interlacing boundary, of thousands of miles,—with the same spoken and written language, and a similar institutional *form* of Government!

Border States in contact with free institutions and peoples, imbibing their education and habits of thought by force of self-interest, will learn to curse the influence of the despotic the ignorant South, and will transmit to its population their own ideas, and thus destroy the bases of the slave state, or remove the unnatural despotic element, and naturally reunite the South with the great free republic. The slave empire will destroy itself, or the population will work itself free by means of outer agencies and influences, and thus preserve themselves by casting out the institution.

The Propagandism of freedom is omnipotent, for it avails itself of all agencies, and works success even by its opponents.

§

In rapturous mood, on all other occasions, the advocates of slavery are accustomed to extol the "diffusive power of opinion,"—the "penetrative force of thought,"—the "generative and regenerating energies of ideas;" and they marshal these, with immense jubilation at the forefixed and sure result, against stone walls, rifled cannon, priests, edicts, excommunications, and armies. It is a pet phrase with those liberal writers, that the bayonets *will* think, and all the literateurs of the world are accustomed to give, in imagination, any odds, on the universal battle of moral, against physical force.

Moreover, all this is affirmed with respect to old countries, where every vantage is against the right, where *cordons sanitaires* have been for ages drawn round the traditions of mis-government, to keep and conserve the pestilence, in intensest virus, for retrograde propagandism.

But when these same men come to talk of America, all their judgments seem reversed, and all their ideas confounded. *There*, it is the *evil* opinions that are to go from conquering to conquer. Why? it would apparently be cruelty to inquire. America has hitherto been supposed to be a country of entire and absolute personal freedom before the Law; there, opinion, as the "*Times*" well said, pulsates through the millions like an electric current. It is the country of mad experiments, lightning trains, steam printing-presses, mass meetings of citizens by the acre, caucases, universal suffrages, conventions, and unequalled systems of communication, natural, artificial, and universal. There, is unrivalled skill in mechanism. There, intelligence is universal, as are also habits of ready speech and action. If these differentiæ do not account for the astounding conclusion, that this Slave oligarchy, of all things in the world, (which rested on a slave industry, and a mass of degraded whites, their victims, and their tools, and on the accident that England paid them a monopoly price) is safe from the spread of intelligence, and of universal self-interest—then the reason must be sought in the narrowness, or pronounced and isolated character of its boundary, in the just nature of its institutions, and in the conciliatory character of its leaders! But mountains and rivers pierce its territory through and through, the frontier counts its miles by the thousand; the institution is that of Slavery, and its necessary concomitants, ignorance, vice, degradation, and despotism. Death for teaching slaves to read,—the blood-hounds for those who run,—an industry such as is suited to low intelligence, and a policy which ever vibrates between *industrial exhaustion*, *territorial expansion*, *and political aggression.*

These are the national, territorial, and political conditions, of propagandism in America.

Everywhere, and always, Slavery first perpetrates oppression, and then commits suicide. The aggression of American Slavery, we have shown to be threefold, — moral, commercial, and political; and it rests on three monopolies,—of the Slave's life and work,—of the Englishman's staple, and of the mean White's sword and life. Slavery rests and must rest upon something and somebody else, out of whom it takes the life or the life's work,—and the vampires of the press who aid it, are only one remove better. The one assaults the peace of the world, the other assails its common sense. But the public opinion of the world is beyond their reach. Soiled reputations may reform, but rotten institutions must die, for the world demands its own. Soon or late, and rather soon than late, the mean White and the Slave, will labour honestly and freely,—the Englishman will pay a free trade price,—and as the result of these inevitable movements, the Slave oligarchy, if it be not first subdued, will perish amidst the derision and the contempt of the world.

§

The oligarchic rule of the South, its contempt for labour, and its grasp at supremacy, are essential conspiracy and inevitable war against free institutions.

Nature is the true propagandist, and nature has freer sway in America than elsewhere. From the mighty North-West and North, will issue irresistible *influences*, if not invincible legions. Through the North-West, we are told, that "for days and days together, for hundreds aud hundreds of miles, the traveller passes through States larger than European Kingdoms. Everywhere, railways and towns, growing up, and the wild soil of the prairie turned without effort into the richest corn producing country, and pasture for the world."

The ideas and feelings of these countries, which are growing at a rate to dwarf both North and South together, are in diametrical opposition to Slavery, and to oligarchic rule. Not only is there no aristocratic class, no dominant sect, but this universal uniform class are opposed to any artificial agencies, except those that protect the citizen, as he advances with nature and God towards the future. We repeat, *the dignity of labour*, *the freedom of the individual*, *and the authority of the law*, together with a full appreciation of the means by which these can be retained, *are the master passions of the North*, ingrained into the genius of the nation, by the circumstances of its origin and independence, the boundless expanse of territory, its history, institutions, principles, antipathies, and aspirations. What then will happen, now that the North is no longer restrained by compromises and pruderies, and that the South has shattered by war the bonds of the slave constitution? Why, the 190,000 slave-holders may command, organise, and administrate never so well, but the material of their armies, the instrument of their executive, the victims of their domestic policy, will discover that their interests lie apart from their masters, and are as essentially diverse therefrom, as are those of the Slaves. The masters, will, in fact, find themselves commanders without the faithful, organisers with nobody to organise, and administrators with nothing to administrate. The common Whites and Slaves will find out that they may be friends, and that they ought to combine against those who live upon their disunion, and WITH their own natural allies in the North. The first class will be no longer able to keep the second degraded, that it may keep the third at work. The second class will see that it has been abased in character, means, and life, that a slender faction which has laid the world under contribution, may grow rich. The third has constantly been in insurrection, constantly attempting escape, and is now invited to go *en masse*, and carry with it the base of the whole Southern "national" structure, or to stay and revolutionize it into a real nation.

The Slave empire assaults the political equality, the industrial well-being, the genius, constitution, and morality, of the American Nation. It cannot expand, either in territory or influence. It cannot retain its Slaves, nor resist the Propagandism of the North.

The results of Slavery are economic, moral, and political. It lowers the producing power of the man. It degrades his moral and intellectual capacity, tending to make the one revolutionary, and the other aimless, and everything that degrades the individual of necessity weakens the State. It also creates an aristocracy, bound to defend it, and to propagate it. It is localised to a certain climate, and so involves local combination. It compels antagonism with the general body politic, because it necessitates the defence of local against general interests. It secures a natural alliance with the State Sovereignty party throughout the Union, which it thus divides geographically and politically. Well might De Tocqueville say,—"If ever America undergoes great revo-"lutions, they will be brought about by the pre-"sence of the black race; they will owe their "origin, not to the equality, but to the inequality "of conditions."*

Slavery, thus allied with the spirit and interests of aristocracy on the one hand, and the interests of a spurious but powerful Democracy on the other, could not fail, during peace, to form a combination of tremendous power. It was, however, always certain, that the oppressive nature of their

* Pp. 227-8, v. 3.

system would bring them at last into openly hostile relations with the spirit of nationality, and with the material and moral interests of the majority.*

During peace, the Democrats had not to choose between Slavery and the Union, nor the Aristocrats between Peace and the chance of confiscation by war. Mighty as are the evils of Slavery, they had been a thousand times more deadly and infernal, could they have combined the forms and restraints of peace, with essential war upon mankind.

§

They who dream that opinion will enact State Sovereignty, as against national Sovereignty, forget those changes, that, as long ago as 1836, caused De Tocqueville to pronounce the American Government rather an "incomplete national," than a Federal one. They forget that since then, more than a third has been added to the age and consolidation of that nationality.

They who drivel about parties coming to the rescue of Secession, forget that Secession attacks the three fundamental principles of American

* With regard also to the influence of *Literature* on nationality, the census is "the great evangel." It must be thoroughly studied, by any one who would thoroughly understand the forces of the Propagandism of Freedom in America, or the "Unity of its Ideas and Interests." See, for instance, table 37, census of 1860, showing the annual number of copies of newspapers and periodicals in (Slave) Maryland to be 20,721,472, in (Free) Massachusetts, 102,000,760. Maryland possessed only 57 organs of opinions, *all political, that is, in favour of Slavery*, not a religious, literary, or scientific journal in the State!

politics and life,—order, and equality, and the Union. It attacks order, for order comes of Law, and Secession goes to anarchy. It attacks equality in a double sense, for it wars with the national authority in the name of Slavery. Secession, is, in fact, of the essence of the worst form of aristocracy. It puts itself above the law, and does battle for the interests of the few. "But," says De Tocqueville, "an Aristocratic Nation, which in "a contest with a Democratic People, does not "succeed in ruining the latter at the outset of the "war, always runs a great risk of being con- "quered by it;"* and, further, "as soon as there "is a regular war, the party which represents the "State is always certain to conquer."

The splendid political genius of the Americans, each of them educated, and each with a voice and stake in the commonweal, may be trusted to foresee political dangers, and to thwart political plots of the sections. The danger that a Statesman would foresee, the Nation will provide against, for they are all discussed, estimated, and understood.

If any man believes that opinion and Public will, beginning thirty years ago a small minority, gradually leavening the lump, and at last constituting itself the Government, and deliberately engaging in war for a Principle, will give either *occasion* or *power* to any "State Sovereignty" principle, to interfere with and reverse constitutional action, and deliberate, sustained and heroic resolve,—on him rests, heavily enough, the onus of proof.

* P. 240, v. 4.

American opinion, while it is the greatest power, is also (except as influenced by Slavery) the most sensitive, just, and intelligent, expression of power in the world.

The great antagonistic institutions of America have been unquestionably Slavery and the Convention or Caucus. They are the opposite terms and instruments in this great controversy.

The mechanism of the Caucus, is the perfection of party discipline. It ascertains what is the most urgent and popular expression of the opinion of each party, and who is its most popular candidate, and gives, as far as practicable, to the opinion and the man thus arrived at and selected, the united suffrage of the party. It is evident that the Caucus system has these results;—at each recurring period, an idea, or a measure, must be enunciated, clear enough and important enough to be the battle cry of a party; the next great national requirement is in fact proclaimed and declared, and then pressed upon the President, who is to be elected as its apostle and executor. The process clears the national mind, expresses the national will, and points out the man who is to enact it.

In other countries public opinion expresses itself without this extreme discipline, and besides, it is there usually controlled by other organisations of Despotism or Oligarchy,—of Church, of State, of Corporation, and it is only in a paroxysm or a crisis, a famine or a war, or after long and weary agitation, that the national will prevails, and the next step can be taken.

The vast numbers of electors in America, and

the vast distances between them, rendered this invention in political warfare, a necessity.

Thus the Caucus gives the uttermost force of expression, (within the bounds of the Constitution) to the popular will. It settles *beforehand* the terms on which the chief magistrate,—the very centre and arm of centralisation itself,—shall seek the suffrages of the People, and it binds him in honour and in interest to carry out the "Platform" and the policy of those who elected him. Nor can this influence be altogether confined to questions actually decided by the party conventions, each of which has a policy settled in principle, if not in detail, for every important contingency likely to arise.

The Caucus is the People's Initiative. It is before and after every President. It gives him his cause and his position beforehand; during office it discusses and settles his competency; and it rewards or degrades him by re-election or by extinction.

As the most powerful and sensitive development and assertion of the principle of association, it promotes the development of opinion, by teaching men to look to its coming power. It is always discounting futurity, and helping to realise it.

It defines the position of the Nation on every question; it prepares against, as well as for opinions, and to an extent, protects the country against sudden gusts of feeling, or unforeseen tempests of passion. By party discipline the Nation may thus pronounce itself whilst the executive prepares to act, and so by revealing a coming reaction, may steady and temper action.

It is, for the same reason, the best antagonist and counterpoise for excessive centralisation, for it is the shadow of the future thrown back upon the present; showing to power its limitations,—or its doom.

In the supreme matter of Slavery, it has acted as the compensatory movement of the executive; at the height and climax of executive power, it shows to him who is the depositary of all its forces, a force that already undermines and reverses, or ratifies and confirms his action, and prepares to enable him to repeat it.

The Caucus, we repeat, prepares, develops, tempers, expresses, and enacts, the national will. It is an outlet and safety valve for dangerous passion; a check against the mighty energies of administrative centralisation, when they are opposed to the people; while it gives to the executive, or takes away from it, the hopes and the substance of the imminent future.

We share none of the fears respecting the exercise of this mighty power. If the President's term is too short or too long,—causing him to yield too much or too little to the popular element, the American nation is most interested in setting it right, and is most likely to know how to do it."

"For myself," said De Tocqueville, "who now look back from "this extreme limit of my task, * * * I cling with a firmer "hold to the belief, that for democratic nations to be virtuous "and prosperous, they require but to will it. Many maintain "that nations are never their own masters. Such principles "are false and cowardly, and can never produce aught but "feeble men and pusillanimous nations."

It is in vain to allege against this popular initiative that the People cannot be expected to shorten their own arm, or lessen or adjust their own power. This might be true in other countries, where the people rush into power as an unknown delirium, or where the constitution contains no provision for the readjustment of right or the reassumption of privileges once surrendered.

If the political prescience, the material stake, the universal education, the habit of power, and association, and thought, and forethought, of the American people, cannot save the American nation from suicide, the predicament is certainly *not* to be remedied by placing power in the hands of the few, or retracing through the ages the weary inane cycles of the errors and crimes of the hundred, the twenty, the ten, the seven, the three, or the one,—of republics without the People,—of aristocracies where the worst ruled,—or of monarchies where one good king would be succeeded on an average by fourteen bad ones.

The Republic has nearly *steered itself* through the most tremendous moral and material crisis that ever occurred. The Pilot that weathered the storm is the Pilot to retain the helm. At some point the appeal to the people *must* come, and in a country of universal suffrage, it is idle to think of evading it, or of either saving, or destroying the country by procuration.

The intelligence, energy, and freedom, of American citizens, soon work every system of means to the utmost. You cannot have American institutions, without free and full political discussion, and that must create great parties, which will inevitably introduce discipline and organisation into their contentions, and find that a mob of voters has no chance against an army of partizans, disciplined by the Caucus, and with "Platform," and candidate, selected and agreed upon beforehand.

In any future contest, then, respecting terms of peace or war, or forms of Government, the public opinion of the majority will decide.

It were well for partisans of the South to remember, that a majority of the most equal-conditioned population in the world, are not likely to favour a policy that would jeopardise their national independence, or an aristocracy that depends for its existence upon the extension of a system of unequal conditions, both in social and political life. We repeat the words of De Tocqueville,

"They will not endure aristocracy. *All men and all powers seeking to cope with this irresistible passion (for equality), will be overthrown and destroyed by it.*"

CHAPTER III.

THE MORAL FORCES OF AMERICA.

UNITY OF PRINCIPLE AND PURPOSE.

"NATION IS A MORAL ESSENCE."—*Burke.*

" If they cannot settle this question (Slavery) for themselves they can no longer claim a national character."—*Times,* Oct. 22, 1863.

" The angel of MARTYRDOM and the angel of VICTORY are brothers; but the one looks up from Earth, and the other looks down from Heaven, and it is only, when, from epoch to epoch, their eyes meet between Heaven and Earth, that creation is embellished with a new life, and a People arises, Evangelist or Prophet, from the Cradle or the Tomb."—*Mazzini.*

EXTRACTS FROM SECESSION ORDINANCES OF SOUTH CAROLINA, ALABAMA, TEXAS, & VIRGINIA.

* * " The non-slaveholding States. Those States have assumed the right of deciding upon the propriety of our *domestic Institutions.*"

" The election of Abraham Lincoln, &c. by a sectional party, avowedly hostile to the *Domestic Institutions,* &c., is a political wrong," &c.

" The power of the Federal Government is sought to be made a weapon with which to strike down the interests and property of the people of Texas, and her sister *slaveholding States,*" &c.

" The Federal Government having perverted said powers, not only to the injury of the people of Virginia, but to the oppression of the *Southern slaveholding States.*"

EXTRACT FROM BUCHANAN'S MESSAGE.

" This does not proceed solely from the claim * * to exclude Slavery from the Territories, nor from efforts to defeat the execution of the Fugitive Slave Law."

" All for which the Southern States have contended *is to be let alone.*"

" Never in the palmiest days of the anti-slavery agitation in this country, even when they were upon the eve of victory, was there one-half the amount of anti-slavery sentiment in England that had existed for the last ten years in the United States of America. He would take senator for senator, writer for writer, man for man, woman for woman, labour for labour, penny for penny, shilling for shilling, pound for pound—and he could prove the truth of what he had stated. The chairman had referred to the hustling of Wilberforce at Liverpool in the early days of the anti-slavery agitation, but where, he asked, would they find the martyrs? Men and women in America had made themselves of no reputation; had taken the spoiling of their goods joyfully; had been cast out of Church and State; had had their trade ruined; their characters libelled; even had their lives taken; and never faltered."

George Thompson, 1863.

CONTENTS.

"The permanent renunciation of sound principles and natural laws, must in due time bring ruin. No great career can be before the Southern States, bound together solely by the tie of having a working class of negro bondsmen. Assuredly it will be the Northern Federation, based on the principle of freedom, with a policy untainted with crime, with a free working class of white men, that will be the one to go on and prosper, and become the leader of the New World."—*Saturday Review*, March, 1861.

"The doctrines of popular liberty, within the short space of two centuries, have infused themselves into the life blood of every rising State from Labrador to Chili."

"I have dwelt longer on the character of the early Puritans of New England, for they are the parents of one-third the whole white Population of the United States."—*Bancroft*.

THERE are but two grand generic lies that the Devil himself can tell to man or nation.

The one is, "Thou shalt die, obey as thou mayest the laws of human nature and of God."

The other is, "Thou shalt *not* die, have thou therefore thine own will and way."

The one has encouraged the South in its struggle against constitutional liberty and negro rights, and has said to evil, not only "Thou shalt not surely die," but, "Thou shalt surely live."

The other has said to the North, struggling for its own rights, and the heritage of all future ages, "Curse God and die,—Life is a lottery,—Destiny a riddle, and results are not consequences."

In applying the principles of morality to the question of nationality, it is essential to remember this distinction between the making and the unmaking of a nation.

Whilst morality has always sustained, and will always sustain a nation that already exists with adequate material elements of Power, it by no means follows, it were mere fanaticism to affirm, that morality can create a Nation without them, or furnish them at once to order.

If, therefore, we prove the morality of the North, its faithfulness as a whole, and as a Government, to the national ideal and destiny, there remains no room for suspecting a flaw in the nationality and vital force; whilst to prove the nationality of the South is a very different question, for admitting (which Heaven forbid) its morality—its nationality may be yet a thousand years off, or the elements of it may not exist even in futurity itself.

For the evil principle, South,—intense faith and desperate action.—For the good principle, North,—feeble faith and languid action. That was once the situation.

To strengthen the faith of the North in the good, or weaken that of the South in the bad, was the way —and the only way—to the end. Of two parties, one having a strong faith and a bad cause, and the other a weak faith and a good cause,—what better can be said, than, "Let them fight on,—the one till it be purified and triumph, the other till it surrender or be destroyed."

Faith and morality, together, are the cement of society, and the very chrism of nationality. To suppose that a lower faith can overcome a higher, or an immoral nation a moral one, is to suppose that which human nature, history, and common sense, reject as monstrous and impossible.

Slavery is consistent, logical, desperate.

Democracy also must avail itself of all the natural forces of the situation. It has discovered that it cannot fight Slavery with Slavery, nor Aristocracy with a bastard Democracy. It still had to discover that it can fight a race better led and disciplined than itself, only by a loftier faith, and a more concentrated purpose, and a reason of State absolutely one.

The key to all the bewilderment and bedevilment of America is, that she represents a great and pure principle,—the principle of Government by and for the all, and that she has not been great enough and pure enough thoroughly to work out the principle in practice.

We, in England, must confess to an analogous error. Many of our organs of opinion, and public men have been dazed by the facts,—the outside facts of the day. They note the marches of armies, and ignore those of principles; and the most wonderful march in the war,—perhaps in any war,—the march of ideas from "Non-extension," in 1860, to "Abolition, and Negro Regiments," in 1862, is not appreciated as a sign of the life, virtue, and power of the American Democracy.

America will now hold those principles fast, and hold them high, through whatsoever ordeal the task may take her.

§

But America, in the matter of Slavery, must be tried by her Peers, if the trial is to result in aught but an ideal verdict. She must be judged by the difficulties of her position, and in comparison with *other nations* who affect to judge her, and with the faction that attempts to dismember her. Those who would taunt the North with compromise must remember, in the first place, the immense difficulties that beset the infant Republic. Their army had only been saved from starvation by forced levies, their commissariat had been without money or credit, and Congress scrip worthless.*

Secondly, mark the apparent harmlessness and great advantage of Slave labour in the first rough work of the Settler's life.

Next, mark the difference between the will of the nation and the act of the Executive. Also the majority of votes required to pass an act, and the immense and prolonged efforts made habitually, even by the English nation, before it can force on the Executive a new and just course of action or policy.

Fourthly, the North had an uphill fight for Principle, against the South, for livelihood and institutions.

Fifthly, the majority in power and value has been

* Had they forgone the Union to extirpate Slavery, was not England ready to ally itself with the South, in influences or in arms, and so to uphold Slavery, and to force it back upon them?

steadily gravitating northwards, and bringing constitutional solution nearer and nearer at a rapid rate.

Sixthly, an effective party in the nation was always anti-Slavery, and kept up a never-ending series of efforts, which were, in fact, a prolonged constitutional battle against Slavery. In proof of these assertions, it is only necessary to remember the leading facts of the historical development of the struggle.

It is impossible to study intelligently the contest in America without perceiving that it is an attempt on the part of the South to snatch by violence the power that has for forty years been receding from it.—An attempt to set aside the laws of human nature and of God, in economics and civilization.

There may be some, but there are not many, who can look on the origin, history, genius, and struggles of America, and declare that her broad-based representation cannot make her strong or stable,—that her love of freedom cannot make her progressive,—or that her thirty years of war, latent or patent, secret or open, against Slavery, will not result in a purer freedom. That in the only land where the People are entirely identified with the Government, the People will despair of the Republic,—that the individual and the State have not, in America, rights adjusted and balanced, and that with these advantages,—with the individual man-power all complete, and the State working therewith in harmony, America is not fit for the world-race, or able to win in it against the Slave-baptized bantling of the South, or the handicapped nations and outworn political creeds of the old world.

The American anti-Slavery movement had in it all the elements of a great and successful moral revolution.

It begun, or rather recommenced, about thirty years ago, in contempt, and dishonour, and martyrdom. It advanced in numbers, influence, and organisation. It became more and more aggressive. It was shown to be as right in Statesmanship and economics, as it was in morality. New elements of power constantly gathered round what seemed at first but a naked germ of Principle. It became the ruling power. It carried its President. It committed the Nation to a struggle against the evil principle. It has rapidly educated the nation into the right position, and at last to secure the triumph of the right, and the present and future of the country, it sends out its army of execution against those who persist in the alternative of their own destruction, or their country's ruin.

Dastards and imbeciles,—men of compromise and duplicity, there are in plenty, but, on the whole, the movement has been marked by an earnestness, a spiritual power, a persistence, an unanimity, and *a success*, unequalled in the whole history of the world.

The American Democracy was trained for peaceful progress,—the South,—to plot, to rule, and to fight. The North is learning to fight, and the history of America will doubtless be the history of the triumph of the innate and indestructible vitality of popular institutions, over the most deadly, and insidious, and violent form of aristocratic influence.

There are more men, there is more faith,—better battle, and better blood in America now on the trail of slavery, than ever yet was poured out in oblation upon earth, or cried upon the God of battles. The sword of the spirit of that great People will go from conquering to conquer. The momentum of right thought, conviction, feeling, will, cannot but increase. The "war of execution" will prevail.

The only deadly unpardonable sin of Peoples is the failing to revolt successfully against injustice.

America *has* revolted against the Slave power. The war is an anti-Slavery war. The South fought it first against morality, then against the Constitution, and now it fights against the Nation armed. Unless this war be a fiction, entire as it is glorious,—unless the struggle of 40 years against Slavery, in Pulpit, Press, Platform, Senate, be a delusion,—the emancipation proclamation a phantasy,—the hanging in front of God, of the pirate, a sacrifice to Beelzebub,—the receiving of negro ambassadors, an insult to the Black—the stampede of 700,000 negroes, a popular error,—the famine down South a pretence,—and the Blockade an ocular illusion,—unless all these be fictions, phantasies, and fables, then we say America is in earnest against Slavery, and that for America, the laws of human nature, and of God, are contending.

The result is always beforehand awarded to those who can work, fight, and wait, for the right.

The remaining questions are merely those of detail and of time. The American quarrel is so good and so earnest that bad generalship cannot ruin it.

§

Where, as in the case of the South, a Nation, if it be made, must be made out of the fragments or ruins of another, we are called to witness the grand and rare spectacle of the death and execution,—of the birth-agonies and genesis of nations. The extremest penalty which Heaven itself can visit on deep seated, long prolonged, and colossal crime, on the one side, and the very crown and climax of intense or sustained heroism and virtue, on the other. We see the greatest crime, and the greatest punishment,—the highest virtue and the greatest reward.

A new Nation, means that a new race has been separated from the world, that it has been isolated from without, and knit together within, that institutions are ready, a great cause proclaimed, and that a new and spiritual life animates the whole.

In a word, there exist certain circumstances, ideas, and interests, which, in the one case, have made the failing Nation so weak, and low, and infamous, that the life cannot be sustained in it; and, in the other, have made the rising Nation so strong, and true, and valuable, that the grand and holy aggregate life can no longer be withheld from the world.

The question challenged then comes to this,—what, in the sight of God and the People, are the crimes, the weaknesses, and the suicidal courses, of America, that she should die the death, and undergo the sentence of denationalisation; what are the virtues, the energies, the coherence, the lasting bonds, of the South, that the voice should go out to her through Creation, "Well done, good "and faithful servant, thou hast been faithful over "a few things, be thou ruler over many!"

It is to this,—if they be either reasoners, diplomatists, or Christians,—that *they* dare us, who say that the South is being built up "a nation."

But the last heresy, and the worst, is that which doubts of nations. There be heretics that doubt of man; heretics that doubt of God; but the heresy that doubts the progress of a nation that has shown such moral heroism, such decision for the truth, such disdain of the easy and profitable path of infamy, as America has shown, *doubts, not that nation alone, but man, God, and the People, all at once.* He doubts,—the imbecile, and that at bottom comes to this, he has no sound theory of political causation upon which to believe *anything.*

It is a heresy of ignorance and fear. A heresy that ignores the moral of History, the progress of the race, the momentum of ideas, the logic of revolutions. It is a mistake that none can make who will learn the facts, or who are moved to action for the good and the true, for they who do the work know of the doctrine of the People. The Heresy we denounce is the most tremendous indictment of the moral Government of the universe that could be framed. It impugns all the facts and Government of the past, and would leave man without a motive, and the future without reliable issue.

In the rear of the camp of Lincoln, as of that of Cromwell, and of Washington, prowl the ghouls of party and the harlots of reaction, demoralising opinion, and retarding success. *The doubters and the moderates*, that have their uses in ordinary times, but are the worst enemies of the People in a crisis.

For us, we stand, as the world must stand, upon the future of the great democracy of America; based as it is upon the rock of universal suffrage, and having now for thirty years, been in open and declared constitutional warfare against the only great wrong that cries out against that country,—a wrong that England forced her to receive, and that the aristocracy of slavedom, till 1860, forced her to keep.

But *History alone* can properly exhibit the moral attitude of the American nation, and the patience, practical ability, moderation, and determination brought to bear upon the successful solution of this question. Slavery was bad enough for the Slave, but the dangers to the national character from vices of compromise, political intrigue, and oligarchy, were worse. From these vices agitation and war have delivered the nation.

The present is not the first struggle for principle, but the last. Secession and civil war only complete the trials which the Star Chamber and the pillory inflicted on the same race. Davis is but a parody of Wentworth, of Laud, and of the Stuarts. Lincoln, and Chase, and Butler, and Fremont, take up the work of Cromwell, and the theory that Religion alone is a match for blood, is carried out in New England by *her* Puritans against the Cavaliers of the South. We recognise the same race, the same parties, and the same cause.

"The King and Council," says Bancroft, speaking of the year 1635, "already feared the consequences that might come from the unbridled spirits of the Americans. The severe censures in the Star Chamber, the greatness of the fines which avarice rivaled bigotry in imposing; the rigorous proceedings with regard to ceremonies, the suspending and silencing of multitudes of ministers, still continued; and men were '*enforced by heaps to desert their native country.*' The injured party even learned to despise the mercy of their oppressors. 'The mutilated defenders of liberty again defied the vengeance of the Star Chamber; came back with undiminished resolution to the place of their honourable infamy, and manfully presented the stumps of their ears to be grubbed out by the hangman's knife.' Rising superior to fear, they derided the power, which, vainly desirous of producing passive obedience, only displayed its own feebleness by *inflicting punishments without attaining its end.* The dungeon, the pillory, and the scaffold, were but stages in the progress of civil liberty towards its triumph." And so rapid was the progress of these principles in the New World, that the same writer shews us, quoting Winthrop, how within a few years (in 1643), the United Colonies of New England were "made all as one." "Protection against Dutch and French, security against savages, the liberties of the Gospel in purity and peace, these were the motives of the Confederacy, which left a hope that a new and a better UNION would spring from the root."

Bancroft also makes the following remarks on the character and conduct of the Colonists.

"Church membership was the only qualification required for the office of Commissioners, of which there were two from each colony." "It had been as unnatural for a right New England man to live without an able ministry as for a smith to work his iron without a fire." "The State was a model of Christ's kingdom upon earth." "New England was a religious plantation, not a plantation for trade." "He that made religion as twelve and the world as thirteen, had not the spirit of a true New England man." "Of divorce I have found no example." "Cruelty to animals was a civil offence." "As Ireland will not brook venemous beasts, so will not that land vile livers." "One might dwell there from year to year and not see a drunkard, or hear an oath, or meet a beggar." The consequence was universal health. The average duration of life, as compared with Europe, was doubled. I have dwelt longer on the character of the early Puritans of *New England, for they are the parents of one-third the whole white population of the United States.* Each family has multiplied on the average to one thousand souls. To New York and Ohio, where they contribute half the population, they have carried the Puritan system of free schools, and their example is spreading it through the civilised world."

"The fanatic for Calvinism was a fanatic for liberty; for in the moral warfare for freedom his creed was a part of his army and his most faithful ally in Battle. Puritanism constituted, not the Christian clergy, but the Christian people, the intepreter of the Divine will. The voice of the majority was the voice of God; and the issue of Puritanism was therefore popular Sovereignty."

Such was the character,—such the purposes of the men, whose doctrines of popular liberty, according to this same writer, "*have infused themselves into the life blood of every rising state from Labrador to Chili.*"

Strangely enough "The philosophy of Slavery" lately maintained that a free system of Labour and of politics could not be adapted to the whole of the Western Continent,—had not in it the element of Catholicity, and accordingly, had it been possible, New England and her Puritanism was to have been left "out in the cold," and the Union reformed without her. But the highest glory of the Puritan race is that their principles are of universal application,—that they are the only principles of universal application, and that they have leavened the whole lump and body politic of the Republic.

But wherefore need we argue this matter? Does not the Old World resound with the conflict of opinion on the battle set by America against Slavery,—*Black* and *White?* Does not the New World shake with the tramp of the legions of Freedom? From the hour when her final war of Independence was over, and her nationality vindicated by Sea and Land, she turned her attention to internal foes. The same great historic qualities,—the character that deserved, the patience that organised, and the determination that achieved victory, are working throughout her story. *Now* the united and universal support of the Emancipation war, is unconquerable, insurmountable proof enough of the "moral Forces,"—of the "unity of Principle and purpose," of the American nation.

That there can be no unity without truth,—no nationality without strength and morality in the Individuals, and adequate social and political cohesion between them,—this is but a truism. That national morality superadded to the material basis of power ensures nationality, is equally a truism. It is also notorious that the American nation went into this fight advisedly and with their eyes open, first against extension of Slavery,—for its destruction, and then for its destruction directly. Witnesses to their devotion come from all sides—South, North, and neutral. "There are numbers of young men," says a neutral paper,* "of education and wealth, serving as private soldiers in the American army,—serving from pure patriotism and devotion to that which they deem a righteous cause,—fighting and dying with perfect patience and willingness, and mixed up and confounded all the while with the lowest of the low and the vilest of the vile."

The Secession Ordinances and Buchanan's message prove that the sin of the North was that it "*would not let Slavery alone.*" For thirty years it has been marshalling its moral forces against Slavery, until at last it wields against it the material forces also.

Wherefore then do we hesitate? What element of nationality does America lack? We say this war is her crown and consummation. It is the completing of the edifice. It is the last step in advance, of the most advanced nation. Individual Freedom had been fought out before America. America was to develop the creative energy that results in the "*collective reason.*" The *collective morality* is now also equally vindicated, and when this shall have been made more complete through suffering, then indeed shall the State emerge from the baptism of blood, "like the fabled spirit of beauty and love, out of the foam of the ever-troubled ocean."

John Brown died not in vain. His blood was the seed of Victory. The Statesmen indeed of the Betrayal,—of the compromise era, may have to die

* "Daily Telegraph," March 17th, 1863, by its Special Correspondent, neither Puritan by nature, nor ascetic by habit.

out, or to go out, before Victory can come. But for America there has been, and is, the martyrdom, and there will be the Victory.

No one of the positions taken up by America on this question has she abandoned. Shall *she* be abandoned?

"Shall I bring to the birth and not cause to bring forth," saith the Lord God?

And shall the million-fold man-power of America, be brought thus far through the birth-agonies of deliverance from Slavery, and not complete its entrance into the world of freedom, morality, and nationality?

God said to America, "Canst thou destroy "Slavery? Art thou worthy and able to take now "*the next essential step in thy national existence and* "*progress?* If so, come up and be first among the "nations; if not, descend and grovel amongst the "lowest!"

That was the great appeal to American Principle. Let those who can, consider what manner of men are they, who knowing how America has responded, can yet say to Slavedom,—"Eat the "fruit of wrong, and drink its sweets, bring forth "thy corner-stone with shouting,—Thou shalt not "surely Die,—*Jeff. Davis* has made of thee a "nation!"

We say of Slavedom, "Let it vanish in the gulf "of political perdition that yawns for it." Let America, and free institutions, live for ever!

BOOK III.

HISTORY.

CHAPTER I.

1607—1777.

UNION AND NATIONALITY.

ORIGIN, CONSOLIDATION, AND PROGRESS OF THE NATION.

CHAPTER II.

1777—1833.

DISUNION AND DENATIONALIZATION.

THE ERA OF COMPROMISE.

CHAPTER III.

1833—1860—.

B A T T L E.

DECLINE OF SLAVE POWER.

CHAPTER IV.

1860—.

VICTORY.

OLIGARCHY CAST OUT.

"The contest began in America. The *American* question therefore was, shall the continued colonisation of North America be made under the auspices of *English Protestantism and popular liberty*, or shall the tottering legitimacy of France, in connection with Roman Catholic Christianity, win for itself new empire in that hemisphere? The question of the *European Continent* was, shall a Protestant revolutionary kingdom like Prussia be permitted to rise up and grow strong within its heart? Considered in its Unity, as interesting *mankind*, the question was, shall the *Reformation* developed to the fulness of Free inquiry, *succeed in its protest against the middle ages?*

"Frederick beat down the dominion of the aristocracy of the middle ages by a military monarchy.

"The Providence which rules the world had elected Washington to guide the fiery coursers of revolution along untried paths, *and to check them firmly at the goal*."—*Bancroft's Revolution*, Vol. I. p. 359.

"Soon after the Reformation, a few people came over into this new world for conscience sake. This apparently trivial incident may *transfer the great seat of empire into America*."—*John Adams*.

"William Smith, the semi-republican historian of New York (1757), urged a law for an *American Union*, with an *American Parliament*." "The defects of the first plan will be supplied by experience. The *British Constitution* ought to be the model, and from our knowledge of its faults, the American one may rise with more health and soundness in its first contexture, than Great Britain will ever enjoy." — *Bancroft's Revolution*, Vol. 1, pp. 246, 305.

HISTORY.

CHAPTER I.

1607——1777—87.

UNION AND NATIONALITY.

ORIGIN, CONSTITUTION, AND PROGRESS OF THE NATION.

"But a new Principle was forcing itself into power. Successions of increasing culture, and heroes of the world of thought, had conquered for mankind the idea of the *freedom* of the Individual. *The creative energy that resides in the* COLLECTIVE REASON *was next to be revealed.* From this the State was to emerge, like the fabled spirit of beauty and love, out of the foam of the ever-troubled ocean."

"This is the praise of Wm. Penn, that in an age * * * * when Russell stood for the liberties of his order, and not for mere enfranchisements; when Harrington, and Shaftesbury, and Locke, thought Government should rest on Property,—Penn did not despair of HUMANITY, and though all History and Experience denied the Sovereignty of the People, dared to cherish the noble idea of man's capacity of *self Government.* * * * Penn believed that God is in every conscience, his light in every soul, and therefore stretching out his arms, he built 'A FREE COLONY FOR ALL MANKIND.' * * * The pure enthusiast, a voluntary exile, was come to the banks of the Delaware, to institute 'THE HOLY EXPERIMENT.'"

"Wm. Penn, in 1697, had proposed an annual congress of all the provinces on the Continent of America. * * Franklin revived the great idea, and breathed into it enduring life. * * Franklin (1775) had already projected a plan (for a Confederacy) and had brought the heads of it with him. * * * Having for his motto, '*join or die,*' he sketched the outline of a CONFEDERACY which should truly represent the whole American People."

"But in the mind of FRANKLIN the love for UNION attained still more majestic proportions, and comprehended the great country back of the Appalachian mountains. He directed attention to the vast convenience of *Inland Navigation* by the lakes and great rivers. Thus did the *Freedom* of the American colonies, their *UNION*, and their *extension* through the West, become the three great objects of the remaining years of Franklin."—*Bancroft.*

R 2

"On the one hand an *increasing production* of means of power and prosperity in Society; on the other, a *more equal distribution* among individuals, of the power and prosperity provided.

"Is this all? Have we exhausted the natural and common meaning of the word *Civilization?* * * * *

"Another development * * * of individual life, of man himself, of his faculties, sentiments, ideas.

"Two facts, then, are comprised in this great fact * * the progress of Society and of HUMANITY. * * * *

"If we examine the nature of the grand crises of civilization * * * It has always been of individual or social development; always facts which have changed the internal man, his faith, his manners,—or his external condition, his situation in his relation with his fellows."—GUIZOT *on Civilization.*

"Vast regions of America! EQUALITY keeps them from both luxury and want, and preserves to them purity and simplicity with Freedom. Europe will find there the *perfection of her political societies,* and the surest support of her well-being."—*Turgot,* 1750 (*afterwards a minister of France*).

"They sailed for the wilderness far away from Popery and Prelacy, from the traditions of the Church, from hereditary power, from all dominion but the Bible, and what arose from natural reason and the principles of EQUALITY. * * * Against a feudal aristocracy, the plebeian reformer summoned the spotless nobility of the elect fore-ordained from the beginning of the world. Calvinism acknowledged no patent of nobility but that of the elect with its seals of eternity. Calvinism addressed all but rested only on the chosen. It dissented from Dissent, invited every man to read the Bible, and made itself clear to the common mind by teaching as a divine revelation the UNITY of the race and the natural EQUALITY of man. It sought new truth, and stood up against the middle age and its power of Church and State, hating them with a fierce and unquenchable hatred."—*Bancroft.*

"She will give to the People of her Colonies her own form of Government * * * and great Peoples will arise even in the forests whither she (England) sent them to inhabit."—*Montesquieu,* 1748.

"The seeds of many a noble State have here been sown in climates kept desolate by the wild manners of the ancient inhabitants, and an *asylum is secured in that solitary world for Liberty and Science,*"—*David Hume.*

CONTENTS.

"By the side of the principle of the freedom of the individual, and the freedom of the separate States, the noblest work of human intellect was consummated in a FEDERATIVE UNION. And that union put away every motive to its destruction, by ensuring to each successive generation *the right to better its condition*, according to the increasing intelligence of the living people."—*Bancroft*.

THE future and the past belong to one organic whole of History, in which Providence develops its designs; and Destiny itself, is but the last inevitable step in a syllogism, of which the premises are in the facts and the philosophy of the past.

The history of that portion of mankind, called the American nation, gathers up, thus far, the results of its Democratic and Puritanic Principles and origin,—of its unique constitution, which gives citizen rights to all, and introduces into politics (with an effect before unknown) the third element of the "Sovereign State,"—of its geographical unity, and of its intense nationality, and contrasts these magnificent elements of power and prosperity with the results of its one blot and contradiction. We are now at a point where all these elements of greatness contend, quite successfully, with the one element of evil, which, by denying freedom and associative power to the individual, denies greatness and permanence to States.

The History of the making of the American nation has to do, in the first place, with the Original COLONISTS, and the *Physical, Moral, and Intellectual* characteristics and status which they brought with them, and transmitted to their descendants. Secondly, with the position, peculiarities, extent, and resources of the CONTINENT, upon which they settled. Thirdly, with the form of Government and CONSTITUTION which they adopted.

The intention here is, not to write the History of America, but to concentrate as in a focus such facts concerning the general Ideas, Principles, Interests, and Parties, as have, from its beginning even until now, had to do with those two principles of Freedom and Equality, which, *as opposed* to Slavery and Oligarchy, have been and are "the making of the American nation."

§

1st, then, as to the RACE; the Ideas, and Principles of the Colonists.

And here the most remarkable fact is, the *nature of those prevailing influences*, by which the intensest nationality in the world has been formed and assimilated, out of all that the world had of diverse, and contrary,—ethnical, moral, intellectual, and physical. All principles have contended there for the mastery, and we see which are the strongest.

"It was," says Bancroft, "the peculiar fortune of the United States, that they were severally colonised by men, in origin, religion, faith, and purposes, as various as the climes which are included within their limits."* They came from England, Holland, France, Spain, Sweden, Finland. From China, even, they come! "Gathered from every corner of Europe, spread over the surface of America, of all religions and tongues." It was, in 1754, admitted, even by Franklin, and in 1767, argued by French diplomatists, that they were as little likely to unite among themselves, as to remain united with England.†

Nevertheless, the English race and principles were dominant, and gave unity and homogeneity to the new national type. "Time and humanity, the principles of English liberty, the impulses of European philosophy, and the policy of France, were (in 1768) all assisting to emancipate America."‡

For instance, in Virginia, our first colony, settled in 1607, "of the first one hundred and five emigrants there were but twelve labourers, and with not a house standing, there were forty-eight gentlemen to four carpenters." The next arrival "were dissolute gallants, packed off to

* Bancroft's "United States," v. i. p. 255.
† Durand to Choiseul.
‡ Bancroft's "Revolution," v. iii. p. 190.

escape worse destinies at home, broken tradesmen, gentlemen impoverished in spirit and in fortune, rakes and libertines,—men more fitted to corrupt than to found a commonwealth. Amidst the horrors of famine, a band of thirty escaped to become pirates, and of four hundred and ninety persons, in six months, indolence, vice, and famine reduced the number to sixty."—*Bancroft's United States*, v. i. pp. 140-1. 154-6. 248.

But they were Englishmen, and this colony soon got possession of its own affairs, was the first State in the world to establish universal suffrage, secured freedom of trade, independence of religious societies, and exemption from foreign taxation, and were, in fact, the foremost to throw off the "old dominion," and to be on with the new.

"We were a free People," said Penn, in 1674, with the sublime simplicity of the Statesman and the Christian, "we were a free People by the creation of God, by the redemption of Christ, and by the careful provision of our never to be forgotten honourable ancestors."

The words of De Tocqueville on the character of the Colonists have been already quoted, but the reader will pardon their repetition here.

"The Americans (De Tocqueville, p. 66, v. 3) are *a very old and a very enlightened People,* who have fallen upon a new and unbounded country, where they may extend themselves at pleasure, and which they may fertilize without difficulty. This state of things is without a parallel in the history of the world."

"The two or three main ideas, which constitute the basis of the social theory of the United States, were first combined in the Northern British Colonies, the States of New England. *They now extend their influence over the whole American world.*

"These settlers all belonged to the more independent classes of their native country. The call which summoned them from the comforts of their homes was purely intellectual; and in facing the inevitable sufferings of exile, their object was the triumph of an idea. Puritanism was not merely a religious doctrine, but it corresponded in many points with the most absolute democratic and republican theories. It is impossible to read the opening paragraph (of Morton's "New England's Memorial," Boston, 1826) without an involuntary feeling of religious awe; it breathes *the very savour of Gospel antiquity.* In England, the stronghold of Puritanism was in the MIDDLE CLASSES, and it was from the *middle classes that the majority of the emigrants came.* A DEMOCRACY *more perfect than any which antiquity had dreamt of, started in full size and panoply, from the midst of an ancient feudal society.*

"The general PRINCIPLES which are the groundwork of modern constitutions—Principles which were imperfectly known in Europe, and not completely triumphant even in Great Britain in the 17th century, were *all recognised and determined by the laws of New England:* the intervention of the People in public affairs, the free voting of taxes, the responsibility of authorities, personal liberty, and trial by Jury, were all positively established without discussion. The principles of representative government, and the external forms of political liberty, were more fully acted upon in the North than in the South, but they existed everywhere."

The same facts are also given by Bancroft:—

"The settlement of New England was a result of the Reformation; not of the contest between the new opinions and the authority of Rome, but of implacable differences between *Protestant Dissenters and the Established Anglican Church.*

"The enfranchisement of the mind from religious despotism led directly to inquiries into the nature of civil government; and *the doctrines of popular liberty,* which sheltered their infancy in the wilderness of the newly discovered continent, within the short space of two centuries *have infused themselves into the life-blood of every rising State from Labrador to Chili,* establishing outposts at the mouth of the Oregon and in Liberia, and making a proselyte of enlightened France, have disturbed all the ancient governments of Europe, and awakened the public mind to resistless action from the shores of Portugal to the palaces of the Czars.

"Had New England been colonized immediately on the discovery of the American continent, the old English institutions would have been planted under the powerful influence of the *Roman Catholic religion;* had the settlement been made under

Elizabeth, it would have been before activity of mind in religion had conducted to a corresponding activity of mind in politics.

"*The Pilgrims were Englishmen, Protestants, exiles for religion; men disciplined by misfortune, cultivated by opportunities of extensive observation,* equal in rank as in rights, and bound by no code but that which was imposed by religion, or might be created by the public will."—*Bancroft's United States, p.* 286-7, vol. i.

§

2ndly; The nationality of America has been constituted by the *Position* (relative and positive), *Peculiarities, Extent, and Resources, of the American* Continent. There was (1.) *Distance* from England, rendering oppression (under the existing circumstances) impossible. (2.) Distance between the Colonists, developing individual self-reliance. (3.) Infinite scope for *expansion.* (4.) The special and unique *material Unity* of the territorial configuration. These influences have already received express notice, or will appear throughout the history.

§

3rdly; The American Constitution. It was (1.) good in itself. (2.) It was suited to the People. (3.) It was suited to the future expansion. (4.) It was balanced within itself. (5.) It was subject to amendment.

(1.) The American Constitution was the English, without the aftergrowths of feudality upon it, and with a race to work it, free and equal, and unburthened by privileged individuals or corporate bodies. In fact the Race, the Position, and the Constitution worked *together* for the making of the nation. The progress of America from Colonies to Independence meant essentially this:—They appealed in everything, and rested upon the Constitution of Great Britain. That Constitution rested ultimately,—and save so far as it was but a compromise and evasion of its own essential principles,—upon the fundamental rights and necessities of human nature. The circumstances of America freed the young nation from the limitations which restrained the development of those rights in England. Consequently in appealing to the *principles* of the English Constitution, America appealed to and adopted the *practice* of the purest and simplest theories of the rights of man.

We prefer here to take the account given by Penn himself of the British Constitution.* It shows not only what that was, but also what it was understood to be by one of the healthiest minds, and at a period immediately succeeding our most stirring and glorious epoch. It shows further, what it was *meant to be* in America.

"Englishmen," he said, in a tract published in England, in 1674, "have birth-rights. The first of these consists of an OWNERSHIP and undisturbed possession, so that what they have is rightly their own, and nobody else's, and such possession and ownership relates both to title and security of estate, and liberty of person from the violence of arbitrary power. This was the situation of our ancestors in ancient BRITISH times. They who governed afterwards, the SAXONS, made no alteration in this law, but confirmed it. The NORMANS, who came next, did the same. William, at his coronation, made a solemn covenant to maintain the good, approved, and ancient laws of the kingdom, and to inhibit all spoil and unjust judgment. The same covenant was adopted by his successors, and confirmed by MAGNA CHARTA.

---

* Penn's Works, vol. i. pp. 672-701. London, 1726. The treatise from which we have abridged this statement evinces extraordinary research. It appears almost to exhaust the authorities on the subject, from Cæsar and Tacitus to Penn's own time.

"The second birth-right of Englishmen consists in the VOTING of every law that is made, whereby that ownership in liberty and property may be maintained." This also was the case, as proved by quotations from laws and an appeal to history, in British, Saxon, and Norman times.

"The third birthright of Englishmen consists in having an influence upon and a great *share in the JUDICATORY power*, so that they are not to be condemned but by the votes of freemen. This practice, though not perhaps British, obtained very early in Saxon times. It was among the laws of Ethelred that in every hundred there should be a court, where twelve ancient freemen, together with the lord of the hundred, should be sworn that they would not condemn the innocent or acquit the guilty. The same law continued to be the law of the land under different kings, till it was violated by John; when Magna Charta *restored it.* Magna Charta, however, was not the nativity, but the restorer of ancient English privileges. It was no grant of new rights, but only a restoration of the old.

"Religion, under any modification of Church government, was *no part of the old English constitution.* The civil affairs of all Governments may be peaceably transacted under the different Liveries or trims of religion.

"Near three hundred years before Austin set his foot on English ground, the inhabitants had a free Government. This came not in with him, neither did it come in with Luther; nor was it to go out with Calvin."

This Constitution, then, respected the natural rights and forces of human nature. It was *good per se.*

"Any Government," said Penn, "is free to the People under it, whatever be the frame, where the laws rule and the People are a party to those laws: and more than this is Tyranny, Oligarchy, and Confusion."

(2.) The Constitution was *suited to the People*, for it represented their Genius, wants, and necessities. It was the English Constitution, treated by the

Americans according to the principle of "natural selection."

(3.) It was suited to the actual territorial conditions, admitting of easy expansion. It was probably the only possible machine for preparing America for one nation and Government.

(4.) It was before all things a "*balanced*," a working Constitution. It developed Freedom and Law, Force and Self-restraint, and checked the one by the other. It set the Individual and the Government to guard against encroachments of "State" power, and the "State" and the national Government to repress Individual excesses or anarchy. And it suggested to the Individual that he could, on occasion, successfully use the armed and organised nuclei of the various Sovereign States to resist oppression. The peculiar constitutional Balance between the "secondary Institutions" or Sovereign States of America, and the nation, was the necessary result of the Union under the actual circumstances between the Independent States. The progress of that union towards, and to, nationality, was and is the natural and inevitable result of the development of the Situation.

Lastly, the American Constitution was armed with a distinct clause and proviso for *amendment*. The effect of this was two-fold. First, it ranged the forces of Conservatism and Progress round some proposed alteration,—not against the collective authority of the nation; and, Secondly, it thus provided for the natural and expected progress of the People.

§

This history must be viewed as a whole, for it has character, tendency, and determinate issues. It is the mightiest Drama the world has seen, and its moral foreshadows the world's future. Three acts are played out; the fourth has well begun; and the fifth must follow.

The first was the era of national Consolidation.

The second was the era of Compromise and decline.

The third was the era of Battle against traitors and slave-drivers. It began in 1832, and is now.

The fourth is the era of Secession and also of Victory.

The fifth must be the era of political Reconstruction. The *constitution* must be purged of Slavery, the labour system freed, and the territory completed.

The second, or "compromise" era, from 1777 to 1833, was but a parenthesis in American history. The system of means that prepared the present war began distinctly in 1777. The system of means that prepared the triumph of the party of freedom and completed nationality, began in the dawn of English history itself, and distinctly amongst American parties in 1832.

During the first era, (of "national consolidation,") the enemies were from without. Indians, Dutch, French, English. Nationality conquered these outward foes, as it always must. This period extends from 1641 to 1782.

The next era was that of slave growth and compromise, but America met and withstood her only real danger. 1833 found her assured of victory and nationality, for it found her in essential War with the internal treachery and weakness of Slavery.

1863 was to inaugurate the completion of that nationality, for it inaugurated the completion of the freedom of the individual, and of the destruction of that interest which necessarily combined certain States against the Union.

Indeed, the whole History shows us seven stages of a gradual and consistent progress towards the completion and perfect reconcilement of the three ideas of *Freedom*, *Equality*, and *Authority*, together with special guarantees in the constitution and genius of the people, for their lasting union. For there has been added to the American nationality, a new and extraordinary feature of strength, never before realised amongst nations.

1st.—It shows us the will to be free expressed and sustained by separate appeals, each calm and temperate, to the British Nation and King,—and then by war.

2nd.—The Patriotism, Intelligence, and Political Genius, that learnt, from the exhaustions of war, to draw the Nation nearer together, to take a calm and comprehensive view of the whole Situation, and to concentrate the administration, and nationalise the Government by the peaceful revolution of 1787.

3rd.—The determined and ever existing hostility against the remaining national danger,—Slavery, which denied Freedom, Authority, and Union, the three pillars of the Nation. This hostility went near to destroy Slavery at the outset, and recoiled for a time before the extraordinary expansion of the Slave interest, only to recommence, in 1832, a contest of life and death.

4th.—The gradual close of the national opinion and will, around this social and political treason, and the deadly grip of the national power upon the traitors.

5th.—The Loyalty and resolution of the national party, in face of constant defeat in the field, and against Generals and Statesmen, their former leaders.

6th.—Submission to that executive Unity, essential in war, in spite of a seditious press, and seditious leaders in their midst, preaching a false freedom, which would have led straight to irrevocable defeat.

7th.—The approaching reconstruction of the Union, and final settlement and complete reconciliation of Freedom, Equality, and Authority, by the emancipation edict, and by revision of the Constitution giving fresh guarantees to each.

For when the American Nation has conquered the rebellion, there can be little reason to fear its competency to bring the words of the constitution up to a level with the great fact of the age, and the victorious will of the People.

§

Thus we see that the American Nation, from its birth until now, has answered the strain of every crisis, and arisen more powerful from every struggle.

When the question was, whether to emigrate or

to submit, they emigrated, and from nearest the heart of England, was taken the infant Nationality.

When the question was one of self preservation against Indians or Dutch, the necessary league was formed, and the enemy quelled.

When the English King would make war on them, they appealed earnestly to the English People, and humbly to the King for their English rights.

When the "Swiss of the Commons,"—the Chamberlains,—and Bishops,—and Pensioners, and Hacks of Parliament, had voted down the splendid efforts of Chatham and Burke for their freedom,—this people, governed, according to the evidence of Dr. Franklin, "at the expense only of a *little pen, ink, and paper*," and led by a thread, having, before 1763, a respect and *affection* for Great Britain, its laws, customs, manners, and fashions,—accepted the situation,—drew closer their league, and conquered Independence.*

When Peace revived faction, and danger called for still closer union, they transformed the league into a Nation.

When Slavery became a power, they fought it

* We cannot resist here introducing the following. Apart from the personal interest, it shows the sudden growth, and intensity, and sternness, of the new national feeling.

"Mr. Strahan, "*Philadelphia.*

"You are a member of Parliament, and one of that majority which has doomed *my country* to destruction. You have begun to burn our towns and murder *our People.* Look upon your hands!—They are stained with the blood of your relations. You and I were long friends; you are now my enemy, and I am yours.—*B. Franklin.*"

successfully at each stage, by the appropriate weapon.

When the South fought for States, they met it as well as the constitution would allow.

When it fought for Territory by armed ruffianism, they met it by Squatter Sovereignty, John Brown, and colonisation.

When the South had lost the majority of States, and the command of Territory; when it played the last card but one, and tried to propagate Slavery by the Unit,—by the Individual Slaveholder, according to the decision of Southern Judges in the Dred Scott case; when it determined that as States and Territory would not come to Slavery, it should go to them,—the North answered the ruse with LINCOLN.

When the South bombarded Sumter, it answered the salute with war.

After due notice and warning, that the constitution would be rent by military necessities, Lincoln, who had sworn to the constitution as it was, accepted the situation, and emancipated the Slaves.

And now America is casting out its sectional oligarchy, its slave faction, its complicities and inconsistencies, and standing up before the world, free of national sin, complete and unimpeachable.

Soon will this cycle of American questions also be complete. Democracy will have put its last enemy under its foot, and we shall ask, what fresh experiment there remains to be tried upon this great people?

And that last enemy is oligarchy. Slavery is but one of its phases. The revolt affirmed the will of the few against that of the many,—affirmed caste against authority,—affirmed a determination of the few to inflict a mistake in economics, a crime in morals, and a disease in Statesmanship, upon a protesting Nation.

Oligarchy fails, because American Democracy is too strong and pure for it. For the same reason, the People's Union will be restored and will endure.

1864 is the supplement of 1787. With Slavery in the Constitution, Destiny could offer to the American Nation but one alternative,—RECONSTRUCTION, or RUIN.

§

But it was clear how completely the colonists were 'masters of the situation,' either as against domestic or foreign tyrants, when they could always say as Franklin did in 1766;

'I will freely spend nineteen shillings in the pound to defend my right of giving or refusing the other shilling; and, after all, if I cannot defend that right, I can retire cheerfully with my little family *into the boundless woods of America, which are sure to afford freedom and subsistence to any man who can bait a hook, or pull a trigger.*' "*The log cabins having been planted, and hopes of self-government called into existence,* it was beyond the power of the British king to remove the one or the other."*

What indeed, was this but the principle and power of Squatter Sovereignty anticipated: a principle, of itself sufficient in a democratic country, to destroy, in due course, every vestige of oligarchy.

The words of Chatham (in 1766) contained the whole *rationale* of American freedom, whether

* Bancroft's "Revolution," vol. iii. pp. 5, 456.

against British 'prerogative' then, or 'Southern privilege' since. After declaring, in one of his stupendous orations on the American question, that he 'rejoiced that the Americans had resisted,' he proceeded to say,—"I draw my ideas of freedom from the *vital powers* of the British Constitution. I can acknowledge no veneration for any procedure, law, or ordinance that is repugnant to *reason,* and the first elements of our Constitution; and I shall never bend with the pliant suppleness of some who have *cried aloud for freedom, only to have an occasion of renouncing or destroying it.*"

And John Adams, in the same year, expressed the unalterable fact,—"The Patricians may sigh and groan and fret, and sometimes stamp and foam and curse, but all in vain. *The decree has gone forth and it cannot be recalled, that a more equal liberty* than has prevailed in other parts of the earth must be established in America."* In the same year, also, Jefferson, using the same expression as Chatham, "was persuaded that the whole code must be reviewed and adapted to the republican form of Government with a single eye to *Reason.*"† As Bancroft tells us, "the Republic came *unsought,* because Society contained the elements of no other organization;" and it is plainer now than it was in 1763; that "Society there will be organized again; but not till after the recognition of the *rights of the Individual;*—that UNITY will once more be restored, but not through the canon and *feudal* law; *for the new Catholic element was the* PEOPLE."‡

Indeed, History, Philososphy, and present Facts, combine to show that nothing but the intense artificial Unity of the Slave interest, could have so long maintained the principles of Oligarchy and

* J. Adams' Works, vol. ix. p. 287.

† Jefferson's Works, vol. i. p. 42. Autobiography.

‡ Bancroft's "Revolution," vol. ii. p. 4.

feudality in America, against the rights of the individual, the national Unity, and the Sovereignty of the People.

Such are the ideas, principles, and conclusions, which the outline sketch we now proceed to give,—not of the History, but of the "making" of the American nation, is intended to illustrate.

§

The various New England Settlements, of the years 1606-7, and thereafter, and the great events of 1643, 1754, 1765, 1776-7, 1787, 1833, 1860, and 1863, are the stages whereby descendants of fugitives and adventurers from all countries, settling upon the "edge and outside of the world," have become the most impassioned nationality, the freest Government, the most orderly and powerful community, in the world.

In 1638, nine years only after its patent, the people of Massachusetts threatened "to Confederate themselves under a new Government, which will be of dangerous example unto other plantations."

In 1641, the spirit of order and freedom dictated the first code of New England. "The body of Massachusetts liberties," consisted of one hundred laws. Slaves were to be treated with *Christian usage*. Strangers fleeing from tyranny were to be succoured. There were to be no monopolies. Deeds of conveyance were to be recorded. Worship was to be free, and the word of God decisive on defects in Laws.

1643 saw the first advance towards nationality. A loose alliance, suggested by claims and encroachments of Dutch and Indians, and formed between Massachusetts, Connecticut, New Plymouth, and New Haven, for mutual defence, and the *truth and liberties of the Gospel*, was called the "United Colonies of New England," and lasted about forty years, till James II. withdrew their charter. In 1675 their first army, two thousand strong, was called out to resist the Indians. This confederation provided for the mutual extradition of criminals and runaway servants.*

In 1701 appeared the first distinct tendency towards Independence, when the New York Assembly declared taxation without consent in general assembly, to be a "violation of the People's property."†

In 1753, the French completed their scheme of uniting their Canadian possessions and the St. Lawrence,‡ by a chain of forts along the Ohio and Mississippi, with their possessions on the mouths of the latter river. The object was to confine the English Colonists to the East of the Alleghanies, for the English grants had many of them been from the Atlantic sea-board, westward to the Pacific! §

In 1754, the British Government recommended

* See Pitkin's "Political History," vol. i. p. 51. This necessary provision was the germ of the Fugitive Slave Law.

† Smith's "New York," p. 116.

‡ This appears to be the first effort to realise the territorial Unity of America.

§ Hinton, vol. i. p. 237.

these Colonists to form an Union amongst themselves, and with the Indians, against the French. Accordingly a Congress of Commissioners met in that year in Albany, to confer with the Five Nations, and representing New Hampshire, Massachusetts, Rhode Island, Connecticut, New York, Pennsylvania, and Maryland. But the scheme of confederation was dissented from by the Connecticut delegates, because it gave too much power to the British Crown, and was rejected by the British, because it gave too little. Massachusetts also vehemently protested against *Imperial* taxation on any pretext. The nation was already weaning.

§

But to the complete and proper understanding of the future Nation, it is necessary to understand the particular qualities, progress, and tendencies, which the separate States were now, at this further stage, prepared to contribute to the coming Union.

The following is condensed, but almost entirely in his own words, from Bancroft's account of the "old thirteen Colonies," in the year 1754.

"GEORGIA. Industry was disheartened by the entail of freeholds, and the prevalence of pestilent vapours during many months. The people entrenched itself in the representative body, and, imitating older colonies, gained vigour in its infancy to restrain every form of delegated authority.

"SOUTH CAROLINA. Prospered. Slaves were supplied on credit. Its fiery people had increased their power by every method of encroachment on the executive, and every claim to legislative self-direction. They were yeomen, owing the king small quit-rents which could never be rigorously exacted.

"NORTH CAROLINA. The race was hardy, and rapidly increasing. Their independence was protected by great distances. If the royal Governor insisted on introducing the King's prerogative, the legislature did not scruple to leave the whole expense of Government unprovided for. Did he attempt to establish the Anglican Church, they chose their own pastor. Did he seek to collect the King's quit-rents, they postponed indefinitely the adjustment of the rent-roll. In the Carolinas, and Virginia, and every Royal Government, the freeholders elected one branch of the Legislature, and the Council formed the other.

"Virginia. The Governor lived in England, and would not hazard his sinecure by controversy. The Council therefore, bŷ the weight of personal character, gained great influence. The extent of parishes hindered unity of worship, and English priests were often ill-educated and licentious. The People were sportsmen and hospitable. The spirit of Individual freedom paralysed royal influence. Industry was the parent of Republicanism. The horse was their pride, and the race-course their delight. The English policy promoted the slave trade with a view rather to weaken any germ of resistance by a balance of races.

"Maryland, Pennsylvania, and Delaware, were proprietary.

"The King had no officers, but in Customs and Admiralty Courts. His name could not set bounds to popular influence.

Maryland. The Assembly scarcely had occasion to impose taxes, except for the wages of its members. The Act of 1702 established the Anglican Church. 'Ruffians, fugitives from justice, men of intemperance and lust,' nestled themselves in the parishes, and Baltimore, the lewd landlord, was patron. The King had no right of revising laws, and the People shared power through the Assembly.

"Pennsylvania. Thomas and Richard Penn were proprietors. The People were already (1754) masters. The Lieutenant-Governor had a negative on the Legislation, but depended on the Assembly for annual support. The Council had a right of revision. The Sheriffs, Coroners, Judges, the loan office of paper money, were under popular control. Franklin was the soul of the Legislature. Its able press developed the principles of civil right. It encouraged science, and possessed a library and academy. There was no established church. There were no oaths or tests, and the Quakers, who swayed legislation and opinion, were against war, prelacy, and forms.

"NEW JERSEY. Royal. Its Governor 'had to please the King's ministers and a touchy people,' to 'luff for one, and bear away for the other.'

"NEW YORK. Proprietary; settled under patents of land to *Individuals;* New England, under grants to *Towns*, which were its glory and strength. Its position invited it to foster American union. It had the most convenient harbours in the Atlantic, and river communication to the interior. It held the keys of Canada and the Lakes. The Statesmen of New York clung without wavering to faith in a United American empire. Nowhere was the collision between Royal Governor and the Assembly so violent and inveterate. (The former always at a disadvantage from natural causes.) Money power gave to the *Legislature* considerable *Executive* authority also. The province was chiefly peopled by Calvinists, who united against the royal authority which favoured the English Church. Half the population being of foreign ancestry, they resented English restrictions on trade, and evaded them. The large landholders were jealous of British authority and impositions, and lawyers joined with the merchants and proprietors.

"MASSACHUSETTS. Divided into little complete integral Governments, democracies in Church and State, which had received the unconscious sanction of William III.

"NEW HAMPSHIRE, CONNECTICUT, RHODE ISLAND, possessed the same character. All New England was an aggregate of organised Democracies. But the complete development of the Institution (Democracy) was to be found in *Connecticut*, and the *Massachusetts Bay*. There each township was also substantially a territorial parish; the township was the religious congregation; the Independent Church was established by law, and the minister was elected by the People, who made an annual grant for his support. There, too, the system of free schools was carried to great perfection.

The general influence of the Teutonic, English, and Gallic races on the American nation, is thus summarised and contrasted by the same writer (pp. 522-3. v. i. American Revolution).

"In America, the *Teutonic race*, with its strong tendency to *Individuality and Freedom*, was become the master, from the Gulf of Mexico to the Poles, and the *English language*, which but a century and a half before, had for its entire world a part only of two narrow islands on the outer verge of Europe, was now to spread more widely than any that had ever given expression to human thought.

"Nothing representing the new activity of thought in modern *France*, went to America. Nothing had leave to go there but what was old and worn out. The Government thought only to transmit to its American Empire the exhausted polity of the Middle Ages; the castes of Feudal Europe, its monarchy, its hierarchy, its nobility, and dependent peasantry; while commerce was enfeebled by protection, stifled under the weight of inconvenient regulations, and fettered by exclusive grants * * the *English* emigrants retained what they called European privileges, but left behind them in the parent country, European inequalities, the monarch, and nobility, and prelacy."

The English had singled out Washington for distinguished service, and had taught the Americans organisation and discipline, removed the French out of their way, and prepared the animus of an alliance between America and France against herself. Arms and the man were thus prepared, the occasion alone was wanting, and that the oppression denounced by Chatham and Burke soon furnished. Great Britain thus created for America all the elements of her Independence.

§

In 1765, Virginia began the opposition that gave to America a nucleus and a precedent of resistance to the Stamp Act, and ultimately caused the rebellion and Independence. Patrick Henry proposed, and the House of Burgesses passed, five resolutions,* of which are the following:—

Resolved,—" That the first adventurers and settlers of his Majesty's colony and dominion, brought with them and transmitted to their posterity, and all other his Majesty's subjects *since inhabiting*, all the privileges, franchises, and immunities, that have at any time been held by the People of Great Britain."

Resolved,—" That by two royal charters, granted by King James I., the colonists aforesaid are declared entitled to all the privileges, liberties, and immunities, of denizens and natural-born subjects, to all intents and purposes as if they had been abiding and born within the realm of England."

In May, 1774, the Virginian Convention recommended a *General Congress* to support American rights. In September, 1774, at the Congress at Philadelphia, at which Georgia alone of the thirteen colonies was unrepresented, Peyton Randolph, of Virginia, being president, these other resolutions were passed unanimously:—

" That the *inhabitants* of the English colonies in North America, *by the immutable laws of nature, the principles of the English constitution*, and the several charters and compacts, have the following rights:—

" First, That they are entitled to life, liberty, and property," &c.

" Second, That our ancestors, who first settled these colonies, were, at the time of their emigration from the mother country, entitled to all the rights, liberties, and immunities of free and natural-born subjects within the realm of England."

" Third, That by such emigration they by no means forfeited, surrendered, or lost, any of those rights, but they were,

* Wirt's Life of Henry.

and their descendants now are, entitled to the exercise and enjoyment of all such of them as their local and other circumstances enable them to exercise and enjoy."

"Fourth, That the foundation of English liberty, and of all free Governments, is a right in the people to *participate in their legislative council.*"

Then follows the declaration, that, as they cannot be represented in the British Parliament, they are entitled to legislate in the provinces, "in all "cases of *taxation and internal policy*, subject only "to the negative of their Sovereign." And the further right, by the *common law of England*, to be "tried by their peers of the vicinity,"—to the benefit of *English Statutes* that apply, &c.,—and to the right to assemble and petition.

Article 10, further declares,—

"It is indispensably necessary to good Government, and rendered essential by the English Constitution, that the constituent branches of the Legislature be independent of each other; therefore that the exercise of legislative power, in several colonies, by a council appointed during pleasure of the Crown, is unconstitutional, dangerous, and destructive of the freedom of American legislature."

Then follow recitals of acts, "which demonstrate a system formed to enslave America."*

This Congress also repudiated Slavery, and declared as one of its articles of association, that "they would neither be concerned in it themselves, "nor hire their vessels nor sell their commodities "or manufactures, to those who were concerned "in it."

In 1775, the great Chatham declared in the House of Peers respecting America,—

* Journals of Congress, v. i. pp. 28—30. Pitkin, v. i. 285—8. Allen, v. i. p. 210.

"When her inherent constitutional rights are invaded,—those rights which she has an equitable claim to enjoy *by the fundamental laws of the English Constitution, and which are engrafted thereon by the unalterable laws of nature,* then I own myself an American, and feeling myself such, shall, to the verge of my life, vindicate those rights against all men who strive to trample upon and oppose them."

In July, 1776, "The Declaration" stated:—

"We hold these truths to be self-evident: that all men are created free and equal; that they are endowed by their Creator with certain inalienable rights; that among these are life, liberty, and the pursuit of happiness. That to secure these rights, Governments are instituted among men, deriving their just powers from the consent of the governed."

Nevertheless, it must be stated, that article four of the Confederation of 1777, "The better to "secure intercourse," provided that, "the *free* in-"habitants of each State shall be entitled to all "privileges of *free* citizens in the several States."

But even South Carolina was not sure enough of the meaning of this, and in 1778 moved Congress to alter this clause to "free *white* inhabitants."

With this exception, all so far was right in the mighty counsels of the young republic, to secure freedom, to guard against anarchy, or to lay the eternal foundations of a great People.

§

The following short questions and answers on Franklin's examination before the English House of Commons, February, 1776, show at once the constitutional rights of Americans; the infringement of them; their just exasperation, their previous loyalty; the fatuity of imposing the Stamp Act; the immense force of the colonists on their own ground; and how natural, necessary, and inevitable, was their Independence.

It was just after this time that Franklin complained of having rendered himself suspected by Americans and Englishmen for his impartiality "having been born and bred in one of the countries, and lived long, and made many agreeable connections of friendship in the other."

"*Q.* How many white men do you suppose there are in North America?

A. About three hundred thousand, from sixteen to thirty years of age.

Q. What was the temper of America towards Great Britain before the year 1763?

A. The best in the world. They submitted willingly to the Government of the Crown, and paid, in their Courts, obedience to Acts of Parliament. They cost you nothing to keep them in subjection. They were governed by this country at the expence only of a little pen, ink, and paper. They were led by a thread. They considered the Parliament as the great bulwark of their liberties.

Q. In what proportion hath population increased in America?

A. I think the inhabitants of all the provinces together, taken at a medium, double in 25 years."

Amongst the reasons for alienation he named;—

"The restraint lately laid on their trade, by which the bringing of foreign gold and silver into the Colonies was prevented; the prohibition of making paper money among themselves, and then demanding a new and heavy tax by stamps, taking away, at the same time, trials by juries, and refusing to receive and hear their humble petitions."

In answer to questions about protection afforded by England:—

* * "Territories in Canada and Nova Scotia, to which the Crown laid claim. The contest in Ohio began about your right of trading in the Indian country, a right you had by the Treaty of Utrecht, which the French infringed. * * It was not till after Braddock's defeat that the colonies were attacked."

Further as to rights, and grievances;—

"The petition of right expressly says, it (taxation) is to be by *common consent in Parliament;* and the people of America have no representatives in Parliament to make a part of that common consent. * * They understand it thus: they are entitled to all the privileges and liberties of Englishmen.

"Suppose a military force sent into America, they will find nobody in arms: what are they to do? They cannot force a man to take stamps who chooses to do without them. They will not find a rebellion: they may indeed make one.

"I believe the number of Americans employed in the wars was greater than that of the regulars."

And the examination ended thus;—

"*Q.* What used to be the pride of the Americans?

A. To indulge in the fashions and manufactures of Great Britain.

Q. What is now their pride?

A. To wear their old clothes over again till they can make new ones."

See also Franklin's "Rules for reducing a great Empire to a small one," &c., "by a Modern Simpleton." And "A Prussian Edict assuming Claims over Britain.—*Dantzick, Sept.* 5, 1773."

§

The Ideas, circumstances, opinions, Genius, origin, constitution, race, territory, and distance; the quarrels with French and Indians, and the drill and organisation against both; the political science, morality, and character of the Colonists;

the mistakes of the English Government; the ignorance of the Colonial ministers at the time,—one of whom (the Duke of Newcastle) remained minister for British America for twenty-four years, from 1724, and used to address letters to the Island of New England, and could not tell but what Jamaica was in the Mediterranean,*—these, and all things else, tended to the inevitable issue. Amongst these causes is very remarkable, the period of confusion which followed the reformation of Church and State in England, the attainder of Strafford, and the impeachment of Laud, the great enemy of Massachusetts, a year or two after that State had threatened Independence, *and the twenty years of contest that followed in England, which secured twenty years of peace and consolidation to New England.*

The Puritans at home did more than they meant. The execution of the felons Strafford and Charles,—the first a statesman, the last an intriguer and a liar, a liar and an intriguer,—were the great central transactions, as Cromwell was the great central figure, humanly speaking, in the fate of the democracies of the two worlds.

"The American Colonies remember the years of Cromwell's power, as the period when British Sovereignty was for them free from rapacity, intolerance, and oppression. The People of New England were ever sure that Cromwell would listen to their requests, and would take an interest in all the little details of their condition. He left them Independence; perhaps he gave them advantageous contracts; he favoured their

---

* Bancroft, quoting J. G. Adams and Walpole, p. 19, vol. i. American Revolution.

trade. He may be called the benefactor of the English in America."*

The question of taxation and representation was the vehicle, so to speak, of the quarrel and its settlement.

"The strength of the people in America consisted in the exclusive right of the *Assemblies* to levy and appropriate Colonial Taxes. The Governors were paid by annual grants, and the amount varied according to merits."†

Taxation without representation, would have been Despotism. Taxation with representation, was impossible. The people of England at home were unrepresented, and a fair system of representation for the Colonists had been a fatal precedent against the oligarchy that ruled England. Moreover, *had a fair system been established it would have soon begun to draw the centre of political gravity away from England, and, soon or late, would have wholly displaced it.*

Thus all things fought against the continuance of English rule on the American Continent, and necessity and nature worked together at the making of the new nation.

§

The English war, or rather the un-English war of George III., found America a confederacy and left it a nation. The constitution was the result of a general conviction that the country must go backwards to anarchy, or forwards to a more complete and centered government. For want of this, evil had accumulated upon evil, and the confede-

* Bancroft, United States, vol. i. p. 483.

† Bancroft's "American Revolution," vol. i. p. 20.

racy was denounced as incompetent to protect commerce, revenue, or trade, whether at home or abroad, till at last the general public mind concurred in a change, long desired by Washington, and other distinguished patriots.

A great deal of acumen has been expended on the question, whether the ancestors of the American People intended to constitute a nation, and not merely a congeries of States. In the presence of the fact of that nation, and of the arbitrament, other than that of argument, to which the question of nationality has been submitted, we might leave this debate to antiquarians, or regard it as an immaterial issue.

That the intention was to make a nation is proved by *Writings of the representative men* of the age ;—by *distinct Expressions* in the "resolutions," and in the Constitution ;—and by the *necessary Effect* of that document.

One of the first resolutions was, "that a *national* Government ought to be established," and the word *national* occurs twelve times in the subsequent resolutions.

The Declaration opens with a reference to occasions when "it becomes necessary for *one people* to dissolve the political bonds which have connected them with another."

And under the first head, (opinions of leading men) we find dated June, 1783, the Address of Washington to the Governors of States, concluding ;—"These are the pillars on which the glorious "fabric of our independency and *national* character "must be supported."

Also his inaugural Address in the year 1789, in which he declares that "every step by which they "have advanced to the character of an *independent* "*nation* seems to have been distinguished by some "token of providential agency," and his Farewell speaks of "the name of American, which belongs to you in your *national* capacity."

President Adams, in his inaugural in 1797, referred to the result of the revolution in the "Establishment of *national* independence."

In the "proceedings in Congress," 13th Sept. 1788, we find the following:—

"Whereas, the Convention assembled in Philadelphia, pursuant to the resolution of Congress, 21st February, 1787, did, on the 17th September in the same year, report to the United States in Congress assembled, a Constitution *for the People* of the United States, whereupon Congress * * * did resolve unanimously, 'That the said report, with the resolution and letter accompanying the same, be transmitted to the several legislatures, in order to be submitted to a Convention of delegates, *chosen in each State by the People thereof*, in conformity to the resolves of the Convention made and provided in that case.' "—Hickey's *Constitution*, 190.

In the letter to Congress to accompany the Constitution, and officially signed by Washington, it is said:—

"In all our deliberations on this subject we kept steadily in view that which appears to us the greatest interest of every true American; the consolidation of the Union,—in which is involved our prosperity, felicity, safety; perhaps our *national* existence."—Elliott's *Debates*, 249.

Hamilton also insists that

"State power, as a separate legislative authority, must be annihilated, otherwise the States will be not only able, but will be constantly tempted, to exert their own authority against the authority of the *nation*."

Eloquence of United States, 1. 24.

And Madison declared that—

"Should all the States adopt it (the Constitution), it will be then a Government established by the thirteen States of America, not through the intervention of the legislatures, but by the *People* at large."—*Eloquence of United States*, 1. 137.

De Tocqueville, at a later period, thus comments on the intentions of the founders:—

"I have shown in the proper place that the object of the Federal Constitution was not to form a league, but to create a *national* Government. The Americans of the United States form A SOLE AND UNDIVIDED PEOPLE in all the cases which are specified by that Constitution."

But "nationality" soon gets the better of "exceptions," and a national Government, with supreme, judicial, legislative, and executive departments, now took the place of the alliance, or confederation.

The Constitution began "We, the People." The Confederation was between "States."

All the ratifications of the Constitution commenced, "We, the delegates of the People," and end, "in the name of our constituents, the People." The object was expressed by Washington, as in the extract on the preceding page.

The delegates from South Carolina and Virginia, introduced a resolution,—"That we now proceed to form a national Government." The New England delegates were then State rights men, and the South was for a national Government. The former were voted down, and the subject of a Confederacy never came up again.

The first draft of the preamble contained the words, "We, the people of the United States, for the purpose of forming a nation."

Amendment 9, of the constitution, proposed in 1789, declared that "the enumeration in the constitution of certain rights, shall not be construed to deny or disparage others retained by *the People*," and amendment 10,—"The powers not delegated to the United States by the constitution, nor prohibited by it to the States, are reserved to the States respectively, or *to the People*." Article 2 of the Confederation had retained the same, not to the People, but "*to each State*."

The ratification of the articles of Confederation in 1778, thus provides against unconstitutional opposition of separate States:—

"And we do further *solemnly plight and engage the faith of our respective constituents, that they shall abide by the determination of the United States in Congress* assembled, on all questions which by the said confederation are submitted to them, and that the Union shall be perpetual."

Art. VI. of the Constitution declares;—

"This Constitution, &c., shall be the supreme law of the land; and the judges in every State shall be bound thereby, *anything in the constitution or laws of any State to the contrary notwithstanding*. The senators and representatives before mentioned, and the *members of the several State legislatures*, and all executive and judicial officers, both of the United States *and of the several States*, shall be bound by oath or affirmation to support this Constitution."

But it is useless to quote separate articles to prove that, although individual and municipal rights were guarded, the Government was intended to be *national*. The whole constitution expressed this, and it was the demand and expression of the age and crisis, which had no other meaning.

§

The formative energy of the Principle of American nationality has encountered no serious check from without. But the essential contradictions of the Slave system, radiating from the germ of a false Principle within, have at last worked outwards and out in Secession, till, in 1862, the inherent antagonism of Slavery to the Principles of national life was recognised by the resolution of the New York mass meeting, "that Slavery is treason,—that it or the "nation must die,—that the national Government "must be wrested from the hands of the Slave "Barons, and immediate emancipation be pro- "claimed."

Slavery has been the "fate" of the drama of American politics and of English capital and labour. Mechanical inventions armed it with portentous strength. It has dragged the North and South against their wills to battle ; and in England, its 30 million spindles revolved the fate of 100 millions of capital, and four hundred thousand workmen without work, and £250,000 weekly wages lost. It assails the common weal politically, inasmuch as it depresses *a nation* beneath the status of citizens, and deprives them of their full rights, dignities, or suffrages, and, in return, elevates 190,000 to the position of slave barons, above and against the law. In economics, the result of substituting slave for free labour is equally obvious.

Nationality and Slavery thus contend to the death. Nationality can only triumph with the complete elimination of the hostile element.

The history of the making of the American nation is the history of the development of the Principle of Union by Democratic and free Institutions, and notably of their prolonged and final struggle against their last and greatest foe,—of their faithfulness which has marshalled them to their inevitable victory, and the wrong that has led Slavery to its forefixed doom.

Massachusetts had abolished Slavery. Pennsylvania (1780) adopted a gradual system of emancipation. Also Connecticut, Rhode Island, and New Hampshire. In New York, Delaware, Maryland, New Jersey, and Virginia, further importation was prohibited. In New York, and Virginia, gradual Emancipation Bills failed to pass. In Maryland and Virginia all restriction on emancipation was removed, and many of the most distinguished citizens were for entire emancipation. Virginia and Maryland were hostile to slavery, and South Carolina and Georgia were its advocates.*

In 1774 the first general Congress resolved against the Slave trade.

In 1785 an Abolition Society was organised at New York.

Till 1804, even South Carolina passed acts prohibiting the Slave Trade.

In 1784 a majority of six States to three, and sixteen members to seven, was for abolishing slavery after 1800 in the whole of the territories.

* Holmes' "Parties and their Principles, p. 33."

This proposition was "that after the year 1800, "there shall be neither slavery nor involuntary "servitude in any of the said *States*, otherwise "than in punishment of crimes," &c. The majority voting for freedom, in this first great party struggle, were Foster, Blanchard, Garry, Partridge, Ellery, Howell, Sherman, Wadsworth, Dewitt, Paine, Dick, Miffin, Montgomery, Hand, Jefferson, and Williamson. This majority was not, according to the rules, sufficient to pass the proposal, which was, however, adopted by the "ordinance of 1787," as to that part of the territory North-west of the Ohio.*

* From this period to the "Dred Scott" case, the facts, relating to Divisions in Congress, &c. are almost entirely on the authority of Arthur Holmes' Political Manual.

HISTORY.

CHAPTER II.

1777-87 to 1833.

DISUNION, OR DE-NATIONALIZATION.

THE ERA OF COMPROMISE.

"The real question is,—Are our Slaves to be presented with FREEDOM or with a DAGGER?"—*Jefferson*, 1820.

"The cunning minister neither sees, nor is concerned to see, any further than his personal interests and the support of his administration require. If such a man overcomes, triumphs, and is flattered by his mercenary train, it often amounts to no more than this, that he got into distress by one series of faults, and out of it by another. That scheme of the reason of state which lies open before a wise minister contains all the great principles of Government, and all the great interests of his country: so that as he prepares some events, he prepares against others, whether they be likely to happen during his administration, or in some future time."—*Bolingbroke.*

"The knave is a fool with a circumbendibus."—*Coleridge.*

"The general idea of the men of that day, was that somehow or other, in the order of Providence, the institution would be evanescent and pass away."—*Stephens*, Confederate Vice-President, 21st March, 1861.

"The principles of the amendment were agreed on,—that is to say, the freedom of all born after a certain day, and deportation at a proper age. But it was found that *the public mind would not yet bear the proposition*; nor will it bear it even at this day. Yet the day is not distant when it must bear and adopt it, or worse will follow. Nothing is more certainly written in the book of fate than that *these people are to be free*. It is still in our power to direct the process of emancipation and deportation peaceably. * * * If, on the contrary, it is left to force itself on, human nature must shudder at the prospect held up."—*Jefferson*, 1821. His Works, v. i. p. 48. Autobiography.

"If something is not done, and soon done, we shall be the murderers of our own children."—*Ibid.* 1797.

"I tremble for my country when I reflect that God is just."—*Ibid.*

"It can never be too often repeated that the time for fixing every essential right on a legal basis is while our rulers are honest, and ourselves united. *From the conclusion of this war we shall be going down hill.* It will not then be necessary to resort every moment to the people for support. They will be forgotten, therefore, and their rights disregarded. They will forget themselves, but in the sole faculty of making money, and will never think of uniting to effect a due respect for their rights. The shackles, therefore, which shall not be knocked off at the conclusion of this war, *will remain on us long, or will be made heavier and heavier till our rights shall revive or expire in a convulsion.*"—*Jefferson's Works*, v. 8. p. 402.

"If the South succeeds in establishing its independence, it will be nothing more than *the same Slave Power*, shorn of half its strength."

"Puritanism * * born fanaticism * * *this pestilence* * * a merciful Providence surely never designed that its power should be perpetual in any one country. *Eternal punishments are only inflicted in the eternal world.*

"And in this matter let me add that about which I may speak with the confidence of one who is familiar with the subject by a lifetime experience and observation. The relations subsisting in America between *the Africans and the inhabitants of European blood can never be materially changed by the consent of the latter*; which consent would be essential to a *gradual* enfranchisement of the slaves. *Slavery*, under the circumstances there existing, *can only be eradicated by violence*, sudden and overwhelming."—"*The South Vindicated*," pp. 128, 400, 408-9.

CONTENTS.

" ALL men free and equal," was the war-cry that defied the King, upon whose idiot brow had descended the tremendous inheritance of the Britannic crown,—" except the Blacks," was the continental aside whereby the adhesion of all the States was ratified, the Yankee " secret article," which in strict accordance with old world diplomacy and traditions, expressed one of the essential conditions between the "high contracting parties."

Georgia and South Carolina were admitted on their own terms as to Slavery. In 1783 the treaty of peace with Great Britain stipulated for the safety of "*negroes and other property*" of American inhabitants. The necessity of Union superseded all other questions.* Slavery was regarded as a fact, as an element in the body politic, and so in 1787, 51 years before Slavery was abolished in the British West Indies, it was recognised in the American Constitution, though not legitimatised, being considered a matter for municipal regulation.

But for this "damned spot" all had been well. America appealed to nature, and God, and the fundamental rights of man, and triumphed, and it was a triumph not to be repented of by either side. Up to this time, the two factors of nations, freedom and centralisation, had both been cared for, but then came a conflict between, and next a fatal compromise of those principles on which alone a Nation can be built up.

Henceforward for 80 years, this great Schism of Freedom divides American history in twain. It constitutes in fact two histories,—the history of infinite material prosperity, and of a fatal moral dereliction. The history of an attempt to get over a "moral difficulty," and to complete a nation-

* We find a striking parallel to this, in the partition of Poland. "The principal motive was to avoid a general war that was to explode. Everything well weighed, the partition was the only way left *to avoid new troubles*, and to make everybody happy."—*Frederick II. Œuv. posth.*

ality, while denying the principle of Freedom, its main element. The history of a mistake in morals, economics, and statesmanship, substituting an aristocracy of colour for one of worth, lowering the value of four millions of citizens, degrading the character and manhood of free whites, dividing the Union by a geographical line North and South, and binding over the whole slaveholding population and interest, to carry war into the heart of the Union, or to threaten all its elements of national life and value with deterioration and decay.

Inexorable northern will might have found the way to extirpate the disease in its infancy. Although the inducements to compromise were immense, the protests against Slavery were earnest and iterated, nor were they only protests. Nevertheless the American Nation started with an anomaly in its life, belying the declaration made in the agony of deliverance. It ran up the black infernal flag of human piracy side by side with the standard of human freedom, and so this mighty People went on its grand and sorrowful and foolish way towards that Niagara of retribution,—that irrepressible moral conflict, which it could not hope to escape, unless it could whip,—not only "Creation,"—but the Creator.

The Lie has rotted in the American soul and Nation ever since. The gangrene has spread. The wedge crashes towards the heart. The national debt of White to Black has compounded its interest for eighty years, and it must be paid off. They feared Division, and their expedients to prevent it have brought it to pass. The question *was* whether this great Lie against man,—citizen,—State,—Nation,—God, should come into the Constitution and Territories. The question *is*, whether the Nation shall come avowedly into the Lie, or pnrge it thoroughly out with fire and blood. None can doubt that that question is being right well answered, or that the power and will to answer it exists with the North.

Instead of a Nation manifestly one and indivisible in its truth and consistency, and probably retaining, or soon reclaiming, those erring States which were as obnoxious to Great Britain, and more needing protection and association. and which indeed without fugitive slave laws, &c., would long since have become assimilated,—instead of this, America has had to consider how much of the right consists with Union, and to wait till the Slave power, swollen with compromise and insolence, assailed with slavery the national integrity, and would have made of the North itself a Slave. Those who might have strangled the infant sin, have nursed it till the giant wrestles with the Nation for life,—and because there was not a Danton to dare, *there may yet be wanted an "incorruptible" to exterminate.*

§

The tendency of States to Nationality, and of the nation to Democracy, had, with this one exceptional element, steadily increased from the beginning of American history. This two-fold tendency was well represented by Jefferson and Hamilton. The one sought unity rather by organization, the other sought strength by individual development, "trusting the People" for their future. Jefferson would develop public education, —he thought those the best taxes which fell chiefly on the rich,—that the best republic, in which every citizen has an equal share in the management,—those the best governments which the people reduce to the condition of agents.

American Democracy has followed generally the instruction of Jefferson, and the revolt of American Oligarchy will force the nation to complete the Unity which the conservatism of Hamilton planned.

The danger which, at that period, threatened the nation's strength, has to be encountered now from the South. It was threefold:—It was "the coincidence, said Jefferson, in 1820, of a *marked principle, moral and political*, with a *geographical line*."

1st. A geographical line,—that drawn by the climate of the South.

2nd. A moral principle,—Slavery.

3rd. A political principle,—Oligarchy.

Earlier, he had indicated the forces which he then believed, and which we now believe, will overthrow all enemies of the nation, viz., *Republican Principles*, the *great extent* of the territory, and the principle of *State Government*. He declared (1811) that "the Republicans are the nation,"* and that the Government owed its permanence to the great extent of the country, "and the smaller portion, comparatively, that can ever be convulsed

* Jefferson's Works, vol. v. p. 577, 593.

at one time by local passion." "But," said he, "the true barriers of our liberty are *State Governments*, and the wisest conservative power ever contrived by man, is that of which our revolution and present Government (1811) found us possessed."

Nevertheless, the threefold strength of the South fights now its inevitable fight. Oligarchy,—(and Slavery, its extreme outcome) surviving by *Compromise*, and also through the *failure in the South* of Jefferson's schemes of thorough and universal *Education*, which is the conservatism of Democracy,—Oligarchy still wields much of the force of the Hierarchical principle. In 1774 this existed there in entails and primogeniture, monopoly of offices and concentration of wealth,—in fact, in politics, in society, and in religion. The war did not continue long enough then to subdue this Oligarchy to the necessities of national Unity, or to the principles of Equality so decidedly developed in the North in 1801 and 1802, when Maryland introduced universal suffrage, Ohio made judges removable at fixed periods, and voluntary contributions for religion were adopted in the South even earlier than in the North.

But the danger was seen and pointed out. John Adams, in 1775, declared that "*an alteration of the Southern Constitutions*, which must certainly take place if this war continues, will gradually bring all the continent nearer and nearer to each other in all respects." And in 1776, Jefferson considered four Bills, of which he was the mover and draftsman, as forming a system, *by which every fibre would be eradicated of ancient and future aristocracy*, and a foundation laid for a Government truly republican.

He uttered then a warning and a prophecy, which we have already quoted, and the fulfilment of which accounts for the present war. The nation was left unmade for fear of a "convulsion." *It has now to be remade by means of it.*

§

The root of the evil was in the principle of Oligarchy as developed and localised in the interest of Slavery. This principle expressed itself in the following items of the Constitution.

Article 1st (Section 2), in apportioning representatives and direct taxation, adds "to the whole number of *free persons*, excluding Indians not taxed, three-fifths of *all other persons.*"

Section 9, "The migration, or importation of such persons (meaning Slaves) as any of the States now existing shall think proper to admit, shall not be prohibited by the Congress prior to 1808, but a tax may be imposed on such importation."

Article 4 (Section 2) provides for the delivering up of any "person held to service or labour in one State, under the laws thereof, escaping into another."

Faithlessness to Principle has confounded the meaning of words, the truth of things, the balance of parties, and the statesmanship of the founders of the Constitution.

A "free" individual meant a free *white* individual. "Slave rights" soon got to mean the right of States to hold Slaves at the risk of the Union; and so for several generations the negro was lost to the State as a citizen, and his labour has supported the slaveholder in rebellion.

State rights, and negro wrongs, thus meant the necessity of combining with all the disaffected everywhere against the freedom and political value of the negro, and the supreme authority of the Union.

The "rights" of man, State, and nation, thus meant one thing South, and another North, till this conflict of opinion was found to be, and called "irrepressible."

Between New York merchants with Southern principles, compromise politicians, and "Southern" Presidents, on the one side, and Southern slave barons on the other, (as between Judas and Beelzebub) it would, thirty years ago, have puzzled even the King of the Belgians to choose.

Freedom and national unity were universally inculcated. Slavery was left to municipal action, and expected to die out; but it soon became a national question, affecting, first, the competence of the individual State, and then the unity, and power, and peace of the country.

The States were sovereign in a municipal capacity.

The Union was sovereign in a national capacity.

The question *was* whether Slavery was a municipal matter, or no,—as though a law of the Infinite could be municipal only. That question ceased for ever, save in the brain of doctrinnaires and fools, when Slavery *made war on the nation*, and settled its nationality so.

§

In 1790, seven States were free, and six slave, and the Free States contained 1,786,499 souls, and the Slave States 1,852,506. But so powerfully did population gravitate towards freedom, that in 1860 these balanced populations had become, in Free States, 18,950,759, and in the Slave, 12,433,409. In 1790, the debates showed the Carolinas and Georgia to be what is now called "the South," and even Virginian and Maryland representatives seemed hostile to Slavery. Emancipation, though doubtless difficult then, became more difficult every year.

In 1791-2, Vermont and Kentucky were admitted, the one slave, the other free.

In 1793, the first fugitive Slave law was enacted. It was thought quite unimportant, and many free States passed "personal liberty Bills," which rendered it a dead letter. Thus free municipality met the doctrine that "Slavery was a municipal matter."

In 1793 the Cotton gin invented by a Northerner, a Massachusetts man, and spinning jennies and carding machines, about the same time in England, gave an immense stimulus to the Cotton trade. In 1791, the first mill was erected in the United States; in 1794, the crop was 4,000,000 lbs.; and in 1806, Liverpool received from the United States 47 per cent. of all imported there.*

* British Quarterly, p. 359. 1849.

From 1804 to 1806, repeated attempts of the Sections were made in Congress to admit Slavery into the North-West territory, and they were defeated.

In the 8th Congress also, that body was invited to prohibit Slavery in the territory of Louisiana, and to check African Slavery, but at the intercession of South Carolina the matter was allowed to rest.

In 1804 was held the first republican caucus.

Jersey became a free State. The seventh and last freed State of the old Confederacy.

In 1808, the African Slave Trade was abolished.

In 1812, Louisiana was admitted, with Slavery, which had been legalised there, under both Spanish and French rule. This was a momentous event.

Also in this year the Declaration of War against England was voted by 79 members, of whom 62 resided *South* of the Delaware, and by 19 senators, of whom 14 resided South.

In 1814, a movement to give to separate States more freedom of action and independence, was made by Massachusetts, Rhode Island, and Connecticut, and called the Hartford Convention, but soon fell through. Slavery appears not to have been mixed up with this movement, and the event tends to show that the nation was consolidating fast, and that no project of disunion could be urged that was not dictated and maintained by the industrial and political necessities of the mighty Slave-holding interest.

In 1817, the Colonisation Society was organised.

In 1816-17-18, Indiana, Mississippi, and Illinois were admitted. Two free, to one slave.

In 1819, the Slave Trade was prohibited under penalty of Death; but the Slave labour system now gave unity and a fixed aim to the whole South, and the battle has raged ever since.

§

The "Missouri Compromise" itself was not a compromise in the sense of a gratuitous abandonment of principle,—it was the result of a severe and prolonged conflict,—a part of the great battle for nationality and freedom.

In February, 1819, came on the discussion of what is called the MISSOURI COMPROMISE. When the Bill to admit Missouri was submitted, a double amendment was proposed. 1st, to prohibit further introduction of Slavery therein;—2ndly, that slaves born therein after admission of the State should be free after 25 years of age. The 1st clause gained a *majority* of 87 votes against 76; the 2nd clause, 82 against 78. The Bill thus amended passed by 98 to 56; but *the Senate struck it out*, [there being, by the 1810 census, 182 representatives to 50 senators.] Upon this discussion Pennsylvania, Delaware, New York, Ohio, New Jersey, and Indiana, agitated, and emphatically declared against Slavery, both in popular assemblies, and in the State legislatures.

In the next Congress (16th) the Bill with prohibition clause, again passed the House, 91 to 82, a greater majority than before; but the *Senate again* (now 54, to 213 representatives) struck out the prohibition clause as to Missouri, and the restriction on Slavery in all other territory North of 36° 30′ was afterwards carried, 134 to 42.

In characterising the American *people* on this vote, it must be remembered that the Senate is renewed every six years, and the representatives every two years, also that the Senate is a fixed quantity, two for each State, and does not vary with population. In reference also to future territorial questions, it must be noted that the whole Missouri Debate is a proof that *no right* existed by the Constitution to introduce Slavery.

In 1820, therefore, when President Monroe submitted to his Cabinet two questions,—the first, "Has Congress the constitutional power to prohibit Slavery in a territory?" the unanimous answer was "Yes."

The second related to the Missouri Compromise. Whether the prohibition of Slavery contained therein, and using the term "for ever," meant forever while such other territory should remain "territory," or "for ever" in the plain sense of the word, so as to prohibit Slavery in States erected thereout? Adams thought for ever meant for ever. The others thought it meant a mere territorial for ever. This point was not publicly mooted, and Calhoun suggested the dodge of phrasing the inquiry in general terms,—"Was the proviso constitutional?" To this all could say "Yes," and in writing, each reserving his own meaning. The writing was deposited in the archives of the State, whence they have since disappeared. Thus Monroe had signed the Missouri proviso in a different sense from that of Congress. Therefore the South gained Missouri by *false pretences*, and the majority of representation was against that "Compromise."

In 1826, the "Panama Mission," *for mutual defence against European aggressions*, was supported in the House, after long discussions, 133 to 61. Delegates from Columbia, Peru, Central America, and Mexico, had constituted this Congress.

In 1820, on Missouri presenting her Constitution, *keeping out free negroes*, the North considered the prohibition clause defiant and insulting, and at first refused to admit,—even with that clause expunged,—by a division of 146 against 6.

§

The Tariff was not, except with factions, and fractions, and "politicians," an item of "compromise," nor was Free Trade then an axiom in economics. Taxation must be direct or indirect, and the South was not likely to vote for direct taxation of its own chattels, even in the proportion of three-fifths. Indirect taxation only reaches consumers, and the very servant girls of the North consume more taxable articles than the whole naked and barbarous South.

As a writer of that day remarked, "it *was* Democratic in all the South to protect domestic manufactures, and force regulations of trade on the people of the East; but now it is democratic with many, and not in the South only, to stand violently opposed to domestic manufactures."

Up to 1812 the revenue system had afforded incidental protection to American industry, and in 1816 Clay supported the first protection Tariff Bill, and was seconded by Calhoun and Lowndes of South Carolina, on the ground of its advantages to the Cotton growing interest,* but was opposed by Webster, and most of the members of the Eastern States. In 1817 this Tariff was amended, increasing the duties and adding fresh articles to the list, and such was the unanimity, that on the Woollen and Cotton Goods Act, continuing duties for seven years, there were but three dissenting voices† in the Senate, and sixteen in the House.

In 1819 there was a general call for relief from bad state of trade, and a Bill for Protection of Manufacturers passed the Representatives, 88 to 69, and was defeated by the Senate, 22 to 21. In 1824 a Bill passed both houses by a slight majority, 107 and 25, against 102 and 22. According to Nile's Register, the agricultural vote carried this Bill, representing 95 votes from grain-growing States, against 57 votes from planting States. In 1828, the Tariff was readjusted, and passed, 109 and 26 to 91 and 21. In 1829-30 a Bill further promoting Protection of Manufacturers, and of Revenue from Frauds was passed. In 1831-2 was passed, 132 to 65, and 32 to 16, a Bill diminishing the rate per cent. on imports, which it was hoped would propitiate the South. But for ten years South Carolina had waged a vindictive war against the Tariff. On the Bank, Tariff, and Improvements Bills, she had been (in 1790-1 and 1816) first in advocating the

* Holmes' "Parties and their Principles," p. 78. † Ibid. p. 82.

sovereign power of Congress. But in 1828, her representatives had threatened resignation, and she now became the advocate of State rights.

Since then South Carolinian policy has been to tax all imports, except such sorts as the North manufactured, and this from jealousy of free-trade labour. Otherwise there has been no sectional advocacy of direct taxation, or chiefly in the North-Western or grain countries, the *strongest Union countries.* Louisiana has been more protected than any other section, by tax on sugar, which is mostly consumed in the North. The South, in fact, taxed the Union. It may be said to have paid nothing. Having monopolised the Government, it has artificially contrived the Tariff to relieve itself, and has consumed of national funds, in office monopolies, and expenditure on its own sections, more, according to free populations, than its entire tax. Carolinian policy has been intensely protective as to itself and ultra free trade as to the North.

But not only this. The South has taxed *the whole cotton world.* No instance ever existed of a pure Slave Power that did not live and feed on others. The West Indies leant on England. The South, on a complication of monopolies and protections.

> "Jove fixed it certain that whatever day
> Makes man a Slave, takes half his worth away."

Millions on millions, for 40 years, has the South taxed the whole Cotton-buying world, to support a bad system of culture, and an infamous system of Government. One million a year, since 1815, for the Slave squadron. Ten millions a year, lately, before the war, for monopoly price of Cotton, and millions every year since 1846. Again, through buying of the barbarous South, our yearly imports have exceeded exports thereto by millions, and thus our transactions have been deranged, our circulation injured, and our specie withdrawn.

We may add that Mr. Buchanan, inaugurated in 1857, held "property in man, and Tariff duties, and protection to manufacturers."

In 1827, Georgia had resolved to submit only to State construction of the Federal compact, and in November, 1832, the day after the passing of the Tariff Act, a convention met in South Carolina and declared void the Tariff Act, void any act of Congress authorizing force, and void the obligations of that State to the general Government, from the date of any such Act. The State Legislature also *ordered* 10,000 *stand of small arms to be procured, and the requisite military munitions.* By a policy of strength and conciliation this question was put to rest.

The spectre of secession was quelled for the time by President Jackson, who was empowered to coerce Carolina, and the "Enforcement Bill" passed the Senate, 32 to 1, and the House, 150 to 35.* Massachusetts, New York, Connecticut, Delaware, Tennessee, Indiana, Missouri, North Carolina, and Alabama, and even Georgia, denounced nullifica-

* Jackson afterwards declared that had Calhoun and his fellow conspirators persisted, he would have hanged them "as a terror to traitors to all time, and that posterity would have declared it the best act of his life."

tion. Virginia acted the part of conciliator. Jackson issued his famous constitutional proclamation, declaring the Constitution and the laws made under it to be the supreme law of the land,—State laws or Constitutions, notwithstanding. In 1833, Clay's Compromise Tariff passed.

We have now the decisive authority of Mr. Cobden, who travelled in America in 1859, that "there was then no party formed, no public agitation, no discussion whatever upon the subject of free trade and protection." *

Henceforward Slavery absorbed and involved all other questions, and the battle was desperate. Cotton monopolies had empowered, and Slavery had envenomed the South, and free progress and principle empowered and confirmed the North.

At risk of national freedom and life, by losses through a barbarous system of cultivation, by the suppression of the Slaves nationality; at the risk of starvation and commotions in England, and of the destruction of the American Union, the South has been upheld until now. Yet it *complains* of protection, and its advocates would have the world believe that the North had compromised its anti-slavery opinions for the sake of a Tariff!

In fact, in 1861, the South itself adopted a tariff similar in scale to that of the United States Bill of 1857.

The North did not expunge Slavery from the Constitution because all parties believed it to be evanescent. The coming decennial period, ending 1830, proved that human nature was against

* Speech at Rochdale, Nov. 1863.

Slavery, and inaugurated that final term of struggle, wherein the South, by unity and desperation, would fain have retrieved the victory in the battle that Freedom and the North had set against it.

HISTORY.

CHAPTER III.

1833—1860.

BATTLE.

DECLINE OF SLAVE POWER.

"The immediate peril arises from the fact, that the incessant and violent agitation of the Slavery Question throughout the North, for the last quarter of a century, has at length produced its malign influence on the slaves, and inspired them with vague notions of freedom."—*Buchanan's Message, Dec.* 1860.

"We assert that fourteen of the States have deliberately refused for years past to fulfil their constitutional obligations, and we refer to their own Statutes ("Personal liberty Bills," rendering inoperative the Fugitive Slave Law) for the proof."
Declaration of Causes of Secession, South Carolina.

"You may destroy the Oak as effectually by girdling it as by cutting it down.

"It cannot be doubted that an administration of the Government based upon this policy (of having for its prime object the repression of Slavery as a permanent administrative policy, with a view to its ultimate extinction,) could operate far more effectually in bringing about the extinction of Slavery in the South, through official influence and patronage, than by any more direct mode of attack."—*The Hon. John Bell, of Tennessee.*

"We are told by the leading spirits of the South Carolina Convention, that, neither the election of Mr. Lincoln, nor the non-execution of the Fugitive Slave Law, nor both combined, constitute their grievances. They declare that *the real cause of their discontent dates as far back as* 1833."—*Governor Hicks,* to the people of Maryland.

BATTLE.

"The question meant everywhere, '*Is there anything of nobleness in you, O nation, or is there nothing?*' Are there, in this nation, enough of heroic men to venture forward, and to battle for God's truth *versus* the devil's falsehood, at the peril of life and more? Men who prefer death, and all else, to living under falsehood,—*who, once for all, will not live under falsehood;* but having drawn the sword against it (the time being come for that rare and important step), throw away the scabbard, and can say in pious clearness, with their whole soul: 'Come on, then! Life under falsehood is not good for me; and we will try it out now. Let it be to the death between us then!' Once risen into this divine whiteheat of temper, were it only for a season, and not again, the nation is *thenceforth considerable through all its remaining history.* What immensities of dross and crypto-poisonous matter will it not burn out of itself in that high temperature in the course of a few years! Witness Cromwell and his Puritans—making England habitable even under the Charles-Second terms for a couple of centuries more. Nations are benefited, I believe, for ages, by being thrown once into divine whiteheat in this manner. And no nation that has not had such divine paroxysms at any time is apt to come to much."

"He who wants that (Loyalty to the Maker of this universe), what else has he, or can he have? If you do not, you man or you nation, love the truth enough, but try to make a chapman bargain with truth, instead of giving yourself wholly, soul and body, and life to her, *truth will not live with you,* truth will depart from you; and only logic, 'wit' (for example, London wit), sophistry, vertù, the æsthetic arts, and perhaps (for a short while) book keeping by double entry will abide with you. You will follow falsity, and think it truth, you unfortunate man or nation. You will right surely, you for one, stumble to the devil; and are every day and hour, little as you imagine it, making progress thither."

"He that will prefer dilettantism in this world for his outfit, shall have it; but all the gods will depart from him; and manful veracity, earnestness of purpose, devout depth of soul, shall no more be his."

"Nations did not so understand it, but *the question of questions* for them, at that time decisive of their history *for half a thousand years to come, was, Will you obey the heavenly voice, or will you not?*"—*Carlyle.*

CONTENTS.

Power and Population.—Collision guaranteed.—Decennial redistribution of Representatives.—Gravitation of power to free States.—Three parties; North, South, and Compromise.—Squatter Sovereignty for the North.—Future Policy of South.—Three Points.—Penal laws against Abolition, Slave Trade, Territorial Slavery, and Secession.—Terrorism, armed Emigration, and the Slave trade, versus Political Economy and Democracy.—A POLICY OF DESPAIR.—Slavery attempts murder, and commits Suicide.—The North has rallied victoriously after every aggression—Anti-Slavery efforts since the beginning of the Union.—In 1833, Anti-Slavery Society formed and numerous auxiliaries.—Meetings, pamphlets, and agitations.—$50,000 for an abolitionist.—Penal repression demanded.—In 1836, Anti-Slavery petitions were neither printed nor referred to.—In 1836, 27,000 petitions.—Next Session 110,000.—In 1845, the restriction was removed.—In 1840, ABOLITION CANDIDATE for President and Vice.—In 1836-7, Texas recognised.—In 1839 Florida war really against fugitive Slaves.—Cost 20 million dollars.—Van Buren defeated by 234 to 60, 1844.—Texan Compromise in 1848.—New Mexico and Upper California annexed.—The war had been a Slaveholders' war, and cost 130 million dollars.—The WILMOT PROVISO, prohibiting Slaves in all Mexican conquests was adhered to by free-soil party, weakening the Democrats.—1840 the House passed the Wilmot proviso, 110 to 89; but Senate rejected it.—Real Government had long been by Convention.—In 1840, the "liberty party" was organised, and its vote less than 7000.—In 1844, 60,000.—In 1848, as the "free soil party," it was 290,000.—In 1844, Slavery was prohibited in Oregon, by amendment of 85 to 56; but failed to pass the Senate.—In 1848, it was prohibited, 129 to 71, and passed Senate after long struggle.—The Slave party began to deny right of legislation on Slavery in Territories.—1849, Speaker, and Wilmot proviso, 62 ballots.—COMPROMISES OF 1850.—Presidential campaign of 1862.—The Whig platform accepted the Compromises as "final."—The Democrats resolved that Congress had no power over Slavery, and that Abolitionists were dangerous.—The Free Democracy Principles were Free soil, Free land, no extension of Slavery, &c. 157,000 votes.—The compromise Whigs died of Fugitive Slave Law.—The Slave Democrats triumphed. — 1853, of the Louisiana purchase Louisiana, Missouri, and Arkansas were slave, and Iowa and Minnesota free.—1854, The Kansas-Nebraski Bill repealing the Missouri Compromise, (prohibiting Slavery elsewhere North of 36° 30′,) now passed.—Mr. Chase's amendments.—1856, Kansas, free or slave.—Missouri Desperadoes at the poll.—Importance of Kansas.—Speeches of Wade and Upham against Whigs and Compromise.—Kansas Free State Constitution passed the House and failed in Senate.—Brooke expelled.—National Republican Convention at Philadelphia.—Union and Anti-Slavery.—Charged on Pierce the Kansas outrage; and threatened the guilty.—Democratic platform at Cincinnati.—State rights.—Limited federal power.—Fugitive Slave Law and Squatter sovereignty.—Democrats nominally triumphed, but Free party had multiplied eight-fold since 1852.—1857, Buchanan sent the Kansas Slave Constitution to Congress, though it had been rejected by the majority.—Dred Scott Case; momentous results.—Free soil party gains strength.—South prepares for next election by clearing off all free negroes.—Resumé thus far.

Given, a Constitution recognizing Slavery, and also re-apportioning representative Power to Population every 10 years,—and political economy and human nature, which happen to be on the side of Freedom, will guarantee an early collision between Slavery and the Representative power. Slavery must be all or nothing, and it cannot be all in a free country.

The great facts of the gravitation of population towards the free States, and of decennial re-distribution of representatives according to population,—facts above and before almost all others in the constitution and democratic polity of the United

States, must be deeply pondered by those who would charge its populations generally with lukewarmness as to freedom, or with a conservatism that prefered the constitution to justice, for in this free population-power and right, the doom of Slavery was assured, even before its birth.

Population meant power. Power would certainly enact the interests of Population. Population and power were gravitating Northwards and Westwards. The interests of North and West were anti-Slavery.

These facts dictated the political logic of parties, and mapped out beforehand the inevitable battle-fields. The Senate-power,—two votes for each State, was stationary. The representative-power was advancing, receding, stationary, or progressive, according to population. The ratio being, in 1790, one in 33 thousand; in 1830, one in 47,700. The electoral votes for President and Vice-President ranged also from 3 to 35 per State, according to Population. Given, then, this number-power of the American constitution, and the Slave-power of the South, and from the nature of men and of things, there must spring three parties, and policies,—the national or anti-Slavery party, with its power naturally augmenting—the Southern or pro-Slavery party, and a third which worshipped the Union, and thought to save it by compromise.

Up to 1830, Slavery maintained an unequal fight for States; but the census of that year revealed a fact, which in connection with the law apportioning representatives to population, bad the

Slave Power do or die. Henceforward Slavery absorbed and involved all other questions.

The census of 1830, showed decisively the North and the North-West increasing, and the South decreasing. In other words, it showed that power was travelling Northwards and Freedomwards with the population.

It showed that even should the South succeed in acquiring nominal "Slave States," they would speedily be filled up by a Population that would send representatives to vote against Slavery. In fact "Squatter Sovereignty" was already arrayed with the North.

§

Henceforward the policy of the South was *crystalline, radical, and absolute.* Penal laws against abolitionists.—More Slave States.—Expansion of Slavery through "Territory."—Re-opening of Slave trade, to use the political and economic elements of new States in the struggle that approached. These failing, there remained Secession. Without these, soon, and with them, late, the South, sterile, doomed, beaten, outnumbered, outvoted, would not only be infamous,—but weak.

Political economy having declared against the South,—and that mighty democratic-conservative provision for re-distribution of representatives to population, having also declared against it,—it remained to see what fear could do,—whether by terrorism, insult, conspiracy, and threats of secession, American democracy would compromise its character and its future, in order to avoid or to postpone a struggle. Whether America would become an accomplice in overturning itself by denying the laws of God and of nature, or whether there were righteous men enough to save the nation.

The only question was, whether America would be kind enough to get up a *pose plastique* of suicide, because the South wished for "company in hanging."

The Policy of the South was a POLICY OF DESPAIR, but such as it was, it was as logical as necessity, and as unavoidable as fate.

1. To league with the party of compromise, with sectional, corrupt, and anti-national parties, in the North, with the party of the waverers, the most numerous in all countries.

2. To occupy by armed emigration and violence, the new ground of future States,—to introduce Slavery, and commit them to it by interest, by menace, or by the force of a *fait accompli*,—gaining thus the *Senatorial vote, the representative power, and also the electoral power*.

3. To reintroduce the Slave Trade, in order to accommodate the mean Whites with "free trade in niggers," to cultivate and people the new States, and utilise them, politically and industrially, for Slavery.

Since 1818, when the Missouri question drew on, and old party lines became extinct, and the question of Slavery supreme, the far-reaching statecraft of the South saw its policy, and adhered to it with subtlety, tenacity and desperation. It has fought a losing battle against the progress of Population, and the interests of free Societies, but it has fought with the discipline, organisation, and *unity*, common to all oligarchies.

Thus was fought out,—by the space of 80 years the great fight between Despotism and Democracy, —the former boasting the most favourable conditions under which it has ever defied attack or assaulted its hereditary foe. Despotism has had three or four millions of Slaves for its industrial support,—four or five millions of white trash, degraded, desperate, bound up body and soul with it, to fight its battles, and it has had statesmen and generals, and a body corporate of 190,000 slaveholders, to prepare, organise, and arm the mass. Despotism nevertheless fails.

Democracy has had an unfair field, a disastrous start, and certainly no favour, and it is winning because it *is* a Democracy, because (we are not using the term according to the slang of the parties) the individual man-power of the nation, has had room to expand, and scope enough to act. The world has never seen tried a mightier issue,—mightier for the future than the past. The genius of democracy has at last tried *conclusions* with its enemies, and so American democracy, refusing to perish with Slavery, has become its executioner.

§

The history of the next 30 years is, in fact, one word. Slavery attempts murder and commits suicide. From the great constitutional repulse in the attempt at nullification, dates the *conspiracy* of the South. From the hour when Slavery attained a certain growth, it dictated to the Slave States proper, one solitary and inextricable issue,—Dominate or Die. Destroy the nation or yourselves. Fight you for "Empire," and force the nation to fight, not for "Independence," but for *existence.* In this issue the whole Slave South was gradually enveloped, but the nation was too strong for it.

Nullification failed. The other form of secession was tried, and the history of the attempt involves three results.

1st. States at first too bad to abandon Slavery, and too good to abandon the Union, were, in the year 1860, by the weakness of a false position, involved in the crime and the penalties of Secession. They have been used on both sides, and have been the chief battle-fields.

2nd. In the republic of the People we find this law. Every political aggression of the South, however apparently successful and *final*,—was followed, step by step, in the struggle, by a victorious rally against it.

3rd. The logic of the South "to do or die," meeting the logic of the North, and challenging the omnipotence of the moral force of free institutions based upon the universal People,—fails before it. The Principles of Aristocracy and Democracy contend. That is all. And the right, which is God, succeeds.

The People is too truly the People. The real Democracy is too pure a Democracy. The universal *is* the universal. The few, the oligarchy, the Slaveocracy, is in America not enough entrenched behind corporate class interests, and high political and social vantage ground, and so *there* we shall find that the final universal issue is also the specific one.

From the origin of the Federal Government, petitions had been presented against the Slave Trade and Slavery.

In 1833, the National Anti-Slavery Society was formed, and numerous auxiliaries. Public meetings in the North denounced Slavery, and Public meetings in the South denounced abolitionists as enemies of the Union. Abolition meetings were broken up, and the speakers mobbed. The Legislature of Georgia offered $5000 for the delivery there of William Lloyd Garrison, the editor of a paper started to advocate immediate emancipation. A war of Anti-Slavery documents began. The Governor of Alabama, made a requisition upon the Governor of New York, for the delivery of the publisher of the New York "Emancipator," and $50,000 were offered by a vigilance committee in Louisiana, for the delivery of Arthur Tappan, a New York abolitionist.

Pro-Slavery meetings were held in the North, but the "Richmond Whig" declared "all to be sounding brass and tinkling cymbal," without penal enactment against abolitionists, who, according to the "Southern Patriot," were "at war with "every moral duty, and suggestion of Humanity."

A meeting in South Carolina resolved for disunion with liberty and property, if the murderous designs of the abolitionists were not restrained by penal laws from *interfering with their slave population.* A resolution soon after passed Congress, 129 to 74, against interference with Slavery in the district of Columbia. Northern Whigs cast this vote.

In May, 1836, it was resolved, by large majorities, that Anti-Slavery petitions should be neither printed nor referred, and that no action be had thereon.

Mr. Adams refused to vote, and demanded to enter his protest, and, day by day, amidst a tempest of abuse, persevered in presenting petitions. In 1836, there were only 37,000 petitions. Next session there were 110,000. One motion against petitions was met by 300,000 petitioners, and Northern legislatures denounced the restriction, which was not however rescinded till 1845. Five times,—in 1836, 1837, 1837, 1838, and 1840, resolutions against reception of these petitions were passed, by majorities *declining* from 51 and 58, to 6, till, in 1845, the North triumphed, and they were admitted.

An attempt to prohibit conveyance of abolitionist papers by public mails, was also made and failed.

In 1838, the great Abolition Society was formed, for *immediate emancipation.*

In 1839, *the abolitionist party first started candidates of their own for President, and Vice.*

In 1836 Michigan entered free, and in 1836 and 1845, Arkansas and Florida, both slave.

In 1836-7, the independence of Texas was recognised. It had rebelled against Mexico in 1835. The legislature of that republic had abolished Slavery in 1824. The South proposed to annex Texas in order to re-establish it.

In 1837 began the "Patriot War" for a reform in the Canadian government.

In 1839, the war with Florida occupied much attention, requiring large appropriations, and in 1840 it was almost universally denounced. It cost 20 million dollars, was really aimed at fugitive slaves, and injured its promoters. Van Buren was denounced as "a Northern man with Southern principles," and his rival elected President by 234 to 60.

In 1841, Harrison's inaugural "depreciated agitation against Slavery, and expressed *a devout confidence in the Christian religion.*" Also, a petition for dissolution of the Union was rejected, 106 to 40.

In 1842, the ratio of representatives to population was altered to one in 70,680.

In 1844, the South insisted on the admittance of TEXAS, and it was accomplished, her independence having been maintained for eight years, but Slavery was prohibited "in such State or "States as should be formed out of said *territory* "*north of the Missouri compromise line.*" The division in the House on third reading was 120 to 98. The Bill, however, was not passed in the Senate till it had been amended.

The Oregon Bill was now introduced, and an amendment by Mr. Winthrop, of Massachusetts, prohibiting Slavery, carried by 85 to 56, but the bill failed in the *Senate.* Northern Democrats would make no issue against Slavery, and joined the South as to Texas and Oregon. Their candidate pledged himself "The whole of Oregon or none, with or without, war with England."

In 1845, Polk, the new Slave Democratic President, violated the constitution by ordering troops into Mexico (Texas), and thus levying war, also making false and hypocritical charges against Mexico.

Mr. Wilmot, of Pennsylvania, moved the "WILMOT PROVISO," prohibiting Slavery from all territory that might be *acquired from Mexico.* It was carried, but the House adjourned, and the bill failed to pass. In the next session the Wilmot Proviso passed, 110 to 89, but was rejected in the *Senate*, 31 to 21.

In 1846, Iowa was admitted, free. Since then Wisconsin, Minnesota, Oregon, and Kansas.

In 1848, New Mexico and Upper California were ceded to the United States, who paid Mexico 15 million dollars. The war cost 130 millions of dollars, and was a slaveholders' war.

After the treaty, the American Secretary of State wrote to the American Chargé in Mexico, that the war had been in self-defence against the abolition policy of Great Britain, so dangerous to the Slave States and to the Union.

§

The Free-soil party, adhering to the Wilmot Proviso, now divided and weakened the democratic party, and objected to a Slaveholding President.

The real Government had long been by convention, which nominated candidates for Presidents, and discussed and settled the policy to which he should be pledged.

In 1840, the "Liberty party" perfected its organisation, but the vote was less than 7,000. In 1844 it was more than 60,000. In 1848 it was organised as the " Free-soil party," and the vote was more than 290,000. Its convention at Buffalo "declared that Congress could not make a slave. "That Government ought to free itself from "Slavery, wherever it could constitutionally, and "that *no more Slave States* should be admitted."

In 1848, the progress of the Free-soil party was demonstrated by the fact, that the Slave party, in discussing a Government for OREGON, did not agitate for the introduction of Slavery there, but simply denied the right or power of Congress to legislate on that interest in the territories. The *Senate pro-Slavery Bill* passed, 33 to 22. However, Slavery was prohibited in the Oregon territory, by 129 against 71, and the Bill passed after a protracted struggle with the Senate.

In 1849, in the election of Speaker, a fight was made over his acceptance of the Wilmot Proviso, and 62 ballots were had thereupon without resulting in a choice.

In 1850, California was admitted, and chose free institutions.

In 1850, on the organisation of the territory acquired of MEXICO, the difficulty was,—Slavery. The attempt now to exclude the South from territory acquired from Mexico, was cited by Calhoun as a proof of the danger of the Union, and the destruction of the equilibrium by Anti-Slavery zeal.

The real issues in the great controversy of the republic were now apparent, though the leaders regarded the "Compromises of 1850" as a final adjustment. Henceforth Freedom and Slavery contend in their own names, and the experience of all ages has repeated itself, that institutions tend to be all slave or all free.

"THE COMPROMISES OF 1850," were the final effort of the statecraft of America to ignore the rights of man, and the laws of human nature.

The "Omnibus Bill," of 1850, which embodied these compromises, proposed, amongst other things, to dispense with the Wilmot proviso, to provide for the return of fugitive slaves, and to continue Slavery in the district of Columbia. Successive amendments reduced and destroyed all these provisoes. But they were afterwards passed in separate acts.

The Governor of Texas notified Government of his determination to extend the jurisdiction and authority of Texas into that part of New Mexico east of Rio Grande. The Texan Boundary Bill was passed. Also bills for the organisation of the territory of New Mexico, &c.

The South, through Clay, conceded "SQUATTER SOVEREIGNTY," in return for a new, stringent, and traitorous FUGITIVE SLAVE BILL, which passed the Senate, 27 to 12,—the House, 109 to 75. Also the Bill for Abolition of Slave Trade in Columbia, to which Mr. Seward moved an amendment, abolishing Slavery.

§

Thus far as to the "Compromises of 1850," and of the Representatives and the Senate. The People met their treason with the roar and the bound of a Lion.

The presidential campaign of 1852 presented three platforms.

The Whig Platform accepted the Compromise Acts of the 31st Congress, "as final in principle and substance, and deprecated all further agitation," &c.

The Democrats resolved that Congress had no power to control domestic institutions. That Abolitionists were dangerous to the happiness of the People, and the permanence of the Union, &c.

Whigs and Democrats were in fact one. Both rallied round Slavery and Fugitive Slave Laws, as the pillars of the constitution.

The FREE DEMOCRACY met in national convention, and nominated their candidates for President and Vice. Their Principles were FREE SOIL, FREE LAND, NO EXTENSION OF SLAVERY, &c. Their candidate polled 157,000.

The Whig party was defeated. It died of an attempt to swallow the Fugitive Slave Law, which a powerful section of Northern Whigs would not accept, being opposed generally to the extension of Slavery.

The Slave Democrats triumphed, but the power of the Free Democrats, and the divided state of the Whigs, clearly fore-shadowed a re-construction of parties.

In 1853, the Slave democrat, President Pierce, declared the rights of the South constitutional, and hoped that "no sectional, ambitious, or fanatical excitement might again threaten our institutions."

Further,—notwithstanding the Slave Question, "the "devotion of distinguished citizens to the Union had "given renewed vigour, and restored a sense of re-"pose and security," &c.

Of the tier of States facing the Mississippi on the west, Louisiana, Missouri, and Arkansas, were slave; Iowa and Minnesota, free. The Bill for organising the vast region called Nebraska, was now brought on. Neither friend nor foe had intimated that the Compromises of 1850 would void the Missouri line. Nebraska was North of it. But on the 15th December, 1853, Senator Dodge, of Iowa, having submitted a Bill for its organisation, it was so *amended as to supersede the Missouri line*, declaring it annulled by the Compromises.

The reason for this was specious. The "Compromises," included the organisation of territorial Governments for Utah and New Mexico, formed out of Mexican territory, but had negatived in relation to them the Wilmot Anti-Slavery Proviso; and it was said that as those Compromises, "rested on the "great principles of self-government, the people "should be allowed to decide questions of domestic "Institutions for themselves."

The excitement through the North was intense; but the amendment was sustained against Mr. Chase's Motion, by 30 against 13, and afterwards the following was substituted, 35 to 10:—

"Which (the Missouri restriction) being incon-"sistent with the principles of non-intervention by "Congress with Slavery in the states and territories, "as recognised by the Legislation of 1850, is hereby "declared imperative and void," the intent being to leave Slavery to the regulation of the People, &c.

This was the famous KANSAS-NEBRASKA Bill of 1854, which repealed the Missouri Compromise.

"KANSAS, free or slave," was the question of 1855-7. The Kansas question was more important even than the Missouri question of 1819, for it involved it. The South marshalled all its ruffianism to the conflict, and accordingly we are told* that 5000 Missouri desperadoes invaded Kansas, and that of 8501 souls and 2905 voters upwards of 6000 polled, of which 4908 were illegal! The result was what was called the "Bogus Legislature."

It is well known also that neither the Federal troops, nor Federal President interfered, whilst the invaders enacted, that any one, resident or not, might vote, who should on the election day pay one Dollar, and swear to the Fugitive Slave Law.

The importance of Kansas cannot be overstated. As a Slave State it would stand out with Slave-holding Missouri, side by side, far into the free North. As a free State it would, with free Iowa and Illinois, almost surround Missouri. The Kansas-Nebraska Bill was the tocsin of the Union and Anti-Slavery party. Senate Wade, of Ohio, declared:—

"The humiliation of the North is complete and overwhelming. No Southern enemy can wish her deeper degradation. I have all my life belonged to the great National Whig party, and have never failed to support the regular candidates, slaveholding or non-slaveholding. The South has made up the issue,—put the North at defiance, and declared sectional war

* "American Slavery and Colour," W. Chambers, London, 1858.

for the mastery. I accept the issue. *Slavery must now become general, or it must cease to be at all.* All further compromises are at an end."

Also Mr. Upham, of Massachusetts:—

"Let those engagements (the Missouri Compromise, &c.) be violated, *from that hour the North is an unit*, and the race of dough faces disappears for ever. You have united the Free States by this untimely, unprovoked, and astounding proposal, in one unbroken, universal, and uncompromising resistance of the Slave power everywhere. What has been pledged to freedom shall be free for ever."

The famous protest of three thousand eight hundred ministers of religion sent to the National Legislature against the pro-Slavery measures and compromises, from 1850 to 1854, now shows the advent upon the stage of a power which never appears except ultimately to conquer. It was the infamous Mason, who, on this occasion, complained that ministers of the Gospel were, of all others, the most encroaching, and moved that the Petition be not received!

In 1856, the Kansas Committee was voted to investigate frauds and violence in the elections; 101 from Free States voted for it, 76 from Slave States against. The Committee reported violence on the Ballot-box, organised invasions of voters from *Missouri*, and void elections, &c.

The Kansas Free State Constitution, framed at Topeka, was reported by them regular, and the Bill for admission under it passed the House, 99 to 97, after a close and prolonged battle; but it *failed in the Senate*, only 16 Senators would vote for it.

The excitement was universal and intense. On

the 22nd May, 1856, Preston S. Brooks struck down Mr. Charles Sumner in the Senate, and was expelled.

§

In 1856, in anticipation of the presidential campaign, many withheld support from either of the two great Slave parties, Whigs and Democrats, in disgust at the excesses of the Slave party.

The Anti-Nebraska, Fusion, or Republican party, gained strength; and, in 1856, the NATIONAL REPUBLICAN Convention met at Philadelphia. Delegates were present from all Free States, and several Slave.

It declared the primary object of the Government to be to secure "the right to life, liberty, and the pursuit of happiness." It denied the right of Congress, of territorial legislature, or of any individual or association, to give existence to Slavery in any territory. It asserted the right and duty of Congress to prohibit in the territory "those twin relics of barbarism—*Polygamy and Slavery.*" That the Constitution was ordained to form a more perfect Union. That Kansas should be immediately admitted with its present free Constitution. It invited men of all parties to concur.

The National Republican platform also distinctly and categorically charged upon President Pierce, and his administration, all the Kansas outrages, murders, robberies, and arsons,—declared them to have been done with their knowledge, sanction, and procurement; *and for this high crime against the Constitution, the Union, and Humanity, arraigned that Administration, the President, his advisers, agents, supporters, apologists, and accomplices,* either before or after the fact, *before the country and the world,* and declared it their fixed purpose to bring the actual perpetrators to sure and sudden punishment."

This was one of the most tremendous political indictments ever framed, and one of the best established.

The DEMOCRATIC PLATFORM at Cincinnati resolved "that the American Democracy placed their "trust in the intelligence, patriotism, and discriminating (between White and Black?) justice of the "American people. That Federal Government was "of limited power. That Congress had no power "over State institutions, that abolitionists were "dangerous, that Fugitive Slave Law must be "maintained, Anti-Slavery agitation put down, "squatter sovereignty maintained, partisan legislation and monopolies discouraged, the Monroe "doctrine and free trade upheld, and ascendancy "in the Gulf of Mexico secured," &c.

The Democrats nominally triumphed, gaining 174 electoral votes against 114 to the Republicans; and 1,834,337 of the popular vote against 1,341,812 to the Republicans. The votes were almost entirely North and South. *The votes of the Free Soil party had multiplied eight times since* 1852.

Pierce had ascended the Presidential Chair with great popularity, and now his own friends would not renominate him.

§

In 1857, President Buchanan, the Slave Democrat, soon showed that he approved not only "Squatter," but mob-sovereignty also. The vote on the fundamental law of Kansas as to Slave-holding was taken unfairly and illegally, and the free soilers abstained from voting. Slave-holding had been at first illegally adopted, by 6143 to 569, and afterwards rejected, by a *majority* of 10,226. Nevertheless Buchanan, the "popular Sovereignty" slave President, sent this minority Constitution to Congress, and recommended its passage!!

Buchanan's message declares,—"Everywhere "throughout the Union they (supporters of the "Kansas-Nebraska Act) publicly pledged their "faith and their honour, that they would cheer-"fully submit the question of Slavery to the de-"cision of the *bonâ fide* People of Kansas, without "any restriction or qualification whatever!"

The Slave Constitution for Kansas passed the *Senate*, 33 to 25. In the House, the Crittenden Compromise, submitting the Constitution to the People, passed, 120 to 112, and afterwards the Senate, agreeing to a similar proposal.

After exciting and stormy debates in both Houses the Lecompton Slave Constitution was again, under the name of the English Bill, submitted to the People of Kansas. If they rejected it, they were to remain excluded until their ratio of representation should be complete.

They rejected it by a *majority* of 9513.

§

The same year the "DRED SCOTT" case came on.*

* To understand this case, and the "platforms" of the time,

Judge Daniel affirmed, that "no other Property is placed by the Constitution upon the same high ground" as the property in slaves. Judge Taney affirmed, there was "no distinction between property in a slave and other property."

The case, in fact, *involved the whole principle and question of Slavery*, for if Slavery attached to the *man*, and not to the place, then by taking the slave into free States, free States become slave States. If, on the other hand, Slavery attaches to the place, and the slave cannot remain such in a free State, then, without frontiers or complicity, fugitive Slave laws and slaves would be soon ended.

The *Lecompton Constitution*, (recommended by Buchanan), Article 7, Section 1, ordains that "the "right of property is before and higher than any "constitutional sanction, and the right of the "owner of a slave to such slave, and its increase, "is the same, and as inviolable, as the right of the "owner of any property whatever."

Buchanan's message, December, 1858, affirmed property in man, and that, whatever is held as property in any of the States, may be equally so held in the Territories, was a "well-established position." It also recommended a protection tariff for manufacturers.

and Mr. Lincoln's subsequent remarks thereon, it must be understood that American judges are not bound to follow "cases" in point, but may reverse preceding judgments, if they consider them "against the Constitution." See also De Tocqueville, p. 141, V. 1:—"Whenever a law, which the judge "holds to be unconstitutional, is argued in a tribunal of the "United States, he may refuse to admit it as a rule. This "power gives rise to *immense political influence*."

Strong indications were now manifest of the re-opening of the Slave Trade in some of the Southern States, which the Government lacked ability or disposition to restrain.

All events, parties, and principles, were gravitating towards a decision for Freedom or Slavery. The Chief Justice had held, in the Dred Scott case, that "neither persons imported as slaves, nor their descendants, whether free or not," were intended as part of "the People." "If anything was settled that was."

In a message to the Senate, with the Kansas Lecompton (Slave) Constitution, February 1858, Buchanan declared:—"It has been solemnly ad-"judged by the highest Judicial tribunal that "Slavery exists in Kansas by virtue of the Con-"stitution of the United States. Kansas is, there-"fore, at this moment, as much a Slave State as "Georgia or South Carolina."

The endeavours of parties to hush up the Slavery question were fruitless, and the final issue approached.

The Slave Democrats, from affirming power of Congress to legislate for Territories, passed to Squatter sovereignty, and thence to *mob* sovereignty, thereby practically affirming the right to establish Slavery in Territories, *against* territorial legislation.

Pending the Presidential Election, the South began *to set its House in order*. They passed laws expelling all free negroes. In 1859, the presentment of a South Carolinian grand jury was, that *free* negroes were a nuisance, and it recommended a law to relieve the community of them. They were given till January 1860 to leave, and after that, if found down South, were to be seized, and hired out, or sold, and half the value paid to the School Fund!

The up boats on the Mississippi were crowded. All Whites travelling from the North or Europe were spied upon. Discussion forbidden. Suspected abolitionists were set upon by the White trash, and thrashed, or served with a coat of tar, or worse. In fact, the reign of terror and of vigilance committees was fairly inaugurated. The Sops of the South had failed. The North could be neither bribed nor drugged. The ascendancy of the free soil party, and the population-power and influence of the free North, was palpably increasing, and so, while it could, the South held its carnival of license, threats, duels, and violence,—North, South, East, and West.

Upon the whole history of the Slavery question to this date, we observe—

1st. That the votes and sentiments of the majority,—of the People, were anti-Slavery.

2nd. That the votes of the Senate were almost uniformly pro-Slavery.

3rd. That hence, we may infer that in America the instructed Democracy has some reason to consider itself better instructed on these subjects, than its betters.

4th. That Virginia, South Carolina, and other "Slave States," began their career as portions ot the American nation by claiming for *all Inhabitants* of the English colonies, according to "the im-"mutable laws of human nature, and the principles "of the English constitution,—Life, Liberty, and "Property," &c.

5th. That in claiming for the Slaves a three-fifth vote, they affirmed their own Hypocrisy in questioning his manhood.

6th. That the early acts of the country affirmed the right of *Congress* to abolish Slavery in future *States*, see, for instance, the resolution by six States against three, and sixteen members against seven, reported to Congress, 19th April, 1784.

7th. That later, the South denied this, and affirmed the right of Congress to legislate for the *Territories* only.

8th. That then they denied this also, and took their stand successively upon Popular, and "*Squatter*," *and mob Sovereignty.*

9th. That they denied Popular Sovereignty on the first demand for its application in Kansas, and this, notwithstanding "they had publicly pledged their faith and honour to the contrary."

10th. That they affirmed the *national* indelible character of Slavery,—that it was part of the Constitution.

11th. That they further attempted extensively to fraudulently condemn Free Blacks as Slaves.

12th. That in attempting to make Slavery national, they in fact declared war on its behalf against the Nation.

13th. That they began by admitting the *national* right to abolish slavery in future States. Even the

South admitted this. The Select Committee, in 1784, to consider the Government of the whole Western territories, from 31° north latitude to the northern boundary of the United States, contemplated the creation of 17 States. This Committee consisted of Jefferson of *Virginia*, Chase of Maryland, and Howell of Rhode Island, and recommended that Slavery should cease in said States after 1800, South Carolina being the only *Southern* State that was not divided on that point.

14th. That as the evil effects of Slavery became greater and wider, the South attempted to lessen and narrow the remedies; till when those effects became national, the South asserted that Slavery was identified with the Nation and the Constitution, and that the Nation had no right to expunge it from the Constitution.

There remained now but one chance more for the South. To force the Nation to acquire new Territories and States towards the torrid zone. To prostitute the authority of the Union Southwards to Slaveholders' uses. Or, failing that, to destroy the Union, and establish a vast Slave Empire.

HISTORY.

CHAPTER IV.

1860—.

VICTORY.

OLIGARCHY CAST OUT.

"This thirst for an *African Slave trade* has been the chief motive that has influenced the Secessionists, and which has made a *compromise almost impossible.*

"In the Southern States social position almost entirely rests upon the possession of slaves.

"Hitherto, the northern States, in conjunction with the *breeding States,* have been able to keep in check this longing for an influx of cheap slaves. *The Whites have grown restless under this yoke, and now their determination is to open up a trade in slaves with Africa, and thus reduce the price of negroes.*"—*Saturday Review,* March 2, 1861.

"I would rather have the small-pox, yellow fever, and cholera, all together in my camp than a man without principle. It is a mistake, sir, that our people make, when they think that bullies are the best fighters, or that they are the fit men to oppose these Southerners. Give me men of good principles—God-fearing men,—men who respect themselves, and with a dozen of them I will oppose any hundred such men as these Buford ruffians."—*John Brown,* "of Kansas."

"With one son dead by his side, and another shot through, he felt the pulse of his dying son with one hand, and held his rifle with the other, and commanded his men with the utmost composure, encouraging them to be firm, and to sell their lives as dear as they could."—*Henry D. Thoreau,* on John Brown.

"Harper's Ferry is the turning point in the Slaves' History."

"This infernal march—this tramp of men, possessed by him whose name is legion, over all human and divine law and life, has suddenly been made to halt."—*Gilbert Haven.*

"The South were brave enough, but they saw afar off. They saw the tremendous power that was entering into that charmed circle; they knew its inevitable victory."—*Wendell Phillips.*

"*The unity of government, which constitutes you one people,* is also now dear to you. It is justly so; for it *is a main pillar in the edifice of your real independence, the support of your tranquillity at home, your peace abroad, of your safety, of your prosperity, of that very liberty which you so highly prize.* It is of *infinite moment that you should properly estimate the immense value of your national union* to your collective and individual happiness; that you should cherish a cordial, habitual, and immovable attachment to it, accustoming yourselves to think and speak of it as of the *palladium of your political safety and prosperity;* watching for its preservation with jealous anxiety; discountenancing whatever may suggest even a suspicion that it can, in any event, be abandoned; and indignantly frowning upon the first dawning of every attempt to alienate any portion of our country from the rest, or to enfeeble the sacred ties which now link together the various parts.

"The name of *American,* which belongs to you in your national capacity, must always exalt the just pride of patriotism, more than any appellation derived from local discriminations. With slight shades of difference, you have the same religion, manners, habits, and political principles. *Every portion* of our country finds the most commanding motives for carefully guarding and preserving the union of the whole.

"While, then, every part of our country thus feels an immediate and particular interest in union, *all the parts* combined can not fail to find, in the united mass of means and efforts, greater strength, greater resources, proportionably greater security from external danger, a less frequent interruption of their peace by foreign nations; and, what is of inestimable value, they must derive from union an exemption from those broils and wars between themselves, which so frequently afflict neighbouring countries, not tied together by the same government, which their own rivalships alone would be sufficient to produce, but which opposite foreign alliances, attachments, and intrigues would stimulate and embitter. Hence, likewise, they will avoid the necessity of *those overgrown military establishments,* which, under any form of government, are inauspicious to liberty, and which are to be regarded as particularly hostile to republican liberty; in this sense it is that your union ought to be considered as the main prop of your liberty.

"Will it not be their wisdom to rely for the preservation of these advantages *on the Union by which they were procured?*

"To the efficacy and permanency of your Union, a government for the whole is indispensable. No alliance, however strict, between the parts, can be an adequate substitute; they must inevitably experience the infractions and interruptions which all alliances, in all time, have experienced.

"*The basis of our political systems is the right of the people to make and to alter their constitutions of government; but the constitution which at any time exists, till changed by an explicit and authentic act of the whole people, is sacredly obligatory upon all. The very idea of the power and the right of the people to establish government, pre-supposes the duty of every individual to obey the established government.*"—From WASHINGTON'S FAREWELL.

CONTENTS.

"That the Black Republican party claims *to abolish the inter-State Slave trade.* That it *repels* all further admission of *new Slave States. It opposes protection to Slavery on the high seas.* It has nearly abolitionised two of the Border Slave States—Maryland and Missouri, and is making similar inroads constantly upon Virginia and Kentucky. It has extended fanaticism into our own Borders."—*See Mobile Secession Declaration, Dec.* 1860.

"That the Slave trade must be re-opened to prevent the formation of a *dangerous class* without direct interest in Slavery."—*See message of Governor Adams of South Carolina two years before Secession.*

"That the new dogma, that the Constitution of its own force carries Slavery in any or all the Territories of the United States, is a dangerous political heresy," &c.

"That the normal condition of *all the Territory* of the United States is that of freedom, &c. and we deny the authority of Congress, of a territorial Legislature, or of any Individuals, to give legal existence to Slavery in any Territory of the United States."

From 7th and 8th clauses of the Lincoln platform, Chicago, 1860.

"Resolved,—That we, Democrats, will sustain the War * * till Victory shall crown our efforts, and peace, founded upon the Union, shall be restored. We therefore urge our fellow Democrats to sustain the Government as it exists, and to support the Candidates who express these views."—*War Democrat Convention, New York, Nov.* 1, 1864.

"That Slavery must be always and everywhere hostile to the principle of Republican Government. National safety demands *its utter extirpation.*"—*See Republican platform,* 1864.

The LINCOLN PLATFORM was the non-extension of Slavery into the territories; the territories meant the Future of America; the exclusion of Slavery therefrom, involved the holding of the Union for Freedom. The alternatives were the destruction of Slavery in the Union, the use of the Union to conquer fresh Slave States in the far South, or the erection *out* of the Union, from the Potomac to Panama, of a vast Slave Empire.

And now comes the beginning of the end. We proceed to quote the "platforms" upon which the two great parties appealed to Americans. The Division of the Democratic party into "Slave" and "Squatter" Democrats, was the occasion of the triumph of Lincoln. To understand the reason of his triumph, or the present strength and future prospects of the Free-soil party, it is necessary to understand the principles upon which the Democrats split, and also the proportionate strength of each division.

In April, 1860, the first of TWO DEMOCRATIC CONVENTIONS assembled at Charleston, comprising representatives of all free States, except California and Oregon.

Sixteen Delegates voted for Squatter Sovereignty, and 17 for a complete Slave code, to be enforced by the Federal Government. After debate the Northern section proposed, as their utmost compromise, the following;—

"Inasmuch as differences of opinion exist in the Democratic party as to the nature and extent of the powers of a territorial legislature, and as to the powers and duties of Congress under the Constitution of the United States over the institution of Slavery within the territories:

"Resolved, That the Democratic party will abide by the decisions of the Supreme Court of the United States, on the questions of constitutional law.

"Resolved, That it is the duty of the United States to afford ample and complete protection to all its citizens, whether at home or abroad, and whether native or foreign."

This compromise did not go far enough for the South, and was rejected, 17 to 16. They demanded the "majority platform," which

"Resolved, That the platform adopted at Cincinnati be affirmed with the following explanatory resolutions.

"That the Democracy of the United States hold these cardinal principles on the subject of Slavery in the territories:—

"1st. That Congress has no power to abolish Slavery in the territories.

"2nd. That the territorial legislature has no power to abolish Slavery *in ANY territory, nor to prohibit the introduction of slaves therein*, nor any power to exclude Slavery therefrom, nor any power to destroy or impair the right of property in slaves by any legislation whatever.

"Resolved, That it is the duty of the Federal Government to protect, when necessary, the rights of persons and property *on the high seas*, in the territories, or wherever else the constitutional authority extends."

This INFERNAL PLATFORM, coercing the State legislatures, and reversing the old pretences about State rights, and with the Slave trade and Federal war against English or other champions of the "right of search," pretty distinctly enunciated, was none too bad,—nay, was logically and strictly necessary to the maintenance of the Slave power. Aught less bad had been illogical. But this was *too bad* for the Democratic party to unite upon.

In the ballot for President at this Convention, Douglas, the Squatter (moderate Slave) Democrat, received 166 votes against 88, *not* reaching the necessary two-thirds majority. The Convention adjourned to re-assemble on the 18th of June, at Baltimore, hoping that by that time the party might be re-united.

But the split remained, through which Lincoln was to enter into power. As usual before any great anti-slavery movement, it was solemnly resolved that slavery should be put at rest for ever, and the national Democratic platform maintaining the contradiction, that "Federal powers" were to be strictly construed and restricted as against slavery, and that "State powers" were almost to be construed *away* on behalf of the same interest, went to the country upon the issue, determined to "resist all attempts at renewing in Congress or out of it, the agitation of the slavery question, under whatever shape or colour." It maintained also the compromise measures and the Fugitive Slave Laws.

Stephen A. Douglas represented the Squatter Sovereignty Democrats, and John C. Breckenridge represented the Democrats, who were for the ultra Slave measures, and for Cuban annexation.

John Bell of Tennessee, was the "Constitutional Union" candidate. That party met at Baltimore in May. It deprecated any discussion of Slavery, and maintained that Congress had nothing to do with it!

Abraham Lincoln was the Republican candidate. That party met at Chicago in May. The

REPUBLICAN PLATFORM declared adherence to the principles enunciated in the Declaration and Constitution: "That all men are created equal, "and are endowed by their Creator with certain "inalienable rights. That amongst these are life, "liberty, and the pursuit of happiness." That the nation owes its prosperity "to the Union." It acknowledged the principle of "State rights." It denounced the invasion of Kansas, and the measureless subserviency of the then Democratic administration to sectional interests. It rebuked the Government for corruption, extravagance, and mal-administration. It declared the normal condition of the territories to be freedom, and demanded that Kansas be immediately admitted free. Furthermore it branded the recent attempted reopening of the African Slave trade as a crime against humanity, and a burning shame to the country and age, and called upon Congress to suppress it. The text of the clauses referring to Slavery in the territories is as follows:—

7th Clause,—"That the new dogma, that the Constitution of its own force, carries Slavery in any or all of the territories of the United States is a dangerous political heresy, at variance with the political provisions of that instrument itself, with contemporaneous exposition, and with legislative and judicial precedent; is revolutionary in its tendency and subversive of the peace and harmony of the country."

8th. "That the normal condition of all the territory of the United States is that of freedom: that as our republican fathers, when they had abolished Slavery in all our national territory, ordained that no person should be deprived of life, liberty, or property, without due process of law, it is our duty, by legislation, when such legislation is necessary, to maintain the provisions of the Constitution against all attempts to violate it:

and we deny the authority of Congress, of a territorial legislature, or of any individuals, to give legal existence to Slavery in any territory of the United States."

§

Mr. Lincoln was elected on the 6th of November. An analysis of the election returns proves two things,—the union of the North, and the disunion of the South. We first give the figures.

On the Republican Ballot for candidates, the votes had been:—For Lincoln, 354; Seward, 110½; Dayton, 1; M'Clean, ½.

On the Election, the statement by the Electoral College was as follows:—

	Total Votes.	Lincoln.	Brecken-ridge. Slave Democrat	Bell. Union.	Douglas. Squatter Democrat.
Free States . .	183	180	—	—	3
Slave States . .	120	—	72	39	9

Strength of Lincoln's Position.

The Popular Vote was:—

	Republican. Lincoln.	Squatter Democrat. Douglas.	Slave Democrat. Brecken-ridge.	Union. Bell.
Free States . .	1,831,180	1,202,451	277,082	74,658
Slave States . .	26,430	163,525	540,871	515,973
	1,857,610	1,365,976	817,953	590,631

Touching the union of the North, and the strength of Lincoln's position, it is thus shown, that the

North plumped for Lincoln. That his majority in the preliminary ballot over the next candidate was more than *three to one*. That his majority in the votes of the Electoral College was more than *two and a half to one* over the Slave Democrat, the next candidate. That his majority on the popular vote over the Slave Democrat was 1,009,657, or more than *two to one.*

The disunion and weakness of the South also appears by the same figures.

The "Slave Democrat" only commanded 17 votes against 16 in the Democratic Convention.

He polled only 72 Southern votes against 48 in the Electoral College.

He polled, on the popular vote, 518,023 less than the Compromise Slave Democrat candidate.

Against the whole Union vote, North and South, he polled 817,953, to 3,814,217,—less than one-fourth.

Against the Union candidates he polled 817,953 to 1,956,607—not one half, without reckoning votes for Lincoln.

And yet this ultra Slave faction, *a minority in a minority*, passed, in South Carolina, a SECESSION CONVENTION BILL *four days after* the election of Mr. Lincoln. The Hon. R. B. Rhett then denounced Mr. Lincoln as "*a black republican president and a mulatto*," and declared the North would soon begin to starve, and would crush the Abolitionist party in the dust. That they would then make a tremendous effort to reconstruct the Confederacy, and say,—"There has been a mistake,—

make friends,—what do you want?—stick it in the Constitution."

But in a good portion of the South Western, and nearly all the frontier Slave States, the editors recommended moderation and caution; and public opinion in the South, after the first surprise, was decidedly against Disunion. Southern conservatives suggested "conferences," "statements," "conditions." *South Carolina formed an army nucleus.* Extraordinary conventions were appointed in each State, to consider and advise in case no compromise should be adopted by Congress before the 4th March.

§

At this crisis, on the 3rd December, 1860, came Buchanan's annual message, a complete Slave manifesto,—cowardly, meaningless, throwing all blame on the North, recommending it to concede the Slave Code,—a weak endeavour to serve the Union at the cost of all that rendered it valuable. But Buchanan was almost the last of the "Doughfaces."

The message states, that "the long continued "and intemperate interference of the Northern "people with the question of Slavery in the "Southern States has at length produced its natural "effects. This does not proceed solely from the "claim to exclude Slavery from the territories, nor "from the efforts of different States to defeat the "execution of the Fugitive Slave Law. The im- "mediate peril arises, not so much from these "causes as from the fact, that the *incessant and*

" *violent agitation of the Slavery question* throughout " the North for the *last quarter of a century*, has " at length produced its malign influence on the " slaves, and inspired them with *vague notions of* " *freedom* * * * *apprehensions of servile insurrec-* " *tion* * * * *homes and firesides habitually and* " *hopelessly insecure.* This agitation has been con- " tinued by the public *press*, by the proceedings of " *State and county conventions*, and by *abolition* " *sermons and lectures.* The time of Congress has " been occupied in *violent speeches on this never-* " *ending subject*, and appeals in pamphlets and " other forms, endorsed by distinguished names, " have been sent forth from this central point, and " *spread broadcast over the Union.*"

" How easy would it be for the American people " to settle the Slavery question for ever, and to " restore peace and harmony to this distracted " country!"

" All that is necessary, and all for which the " Slave States have contended, is to be let alone, " and permitted to manage their domestic institu- " tions in their own way. For this (Slavery) the " people of the North are not more responsible, " and have no more right to interfere, than with " similar institutions in Russia or Brazil. Congress " * * * I believe never will pass any act to ex- " clude Slavery from the territories."

This was in December. In June, Douglas had publicly declared, that " those who enlist under " the Secession banner now will be expected to " take up arms against the constituted authorities " in certain contingencies." The crisis was understood, and Buchanan took care *not* to provide for it.

Then came the Crittenden Compromise proposal, to carry the Missouri line through to the Pacific, and which would have gained 900,000 square miles to the Free States, and 280,000 to the Slave.

On January 30, 1861, Texas was admitted, Free.

Buchanan's second, and extraordinary message, appeared on the 9th January, 1861, urging to preserve the Union, and suggesting all sorts of compromises. Debates followed, extending even to the Monday morning of the 4th of March, when the 36th Congress ended.

This arch-traitor, Buchanan, declared that "a "State has no right to secede, but that the Govern- "ment has no right to prevent its secession!" His staff of traitors; the Vice-President, Breckenridge; the Finance Minister, Cobb; his Secretary of War, Floyd; and his Secretary of the Interior, Thompson, are since in the rebel army.

§

On the 4th February the convention of seceded States met at Montgomery, Alabama, and on the 9th the Provisional Constitution was published. The preamble speaks only for South Carolina, Georgia, Florida, Alabama, Mississippi, and Louisiana. North Carolina was attempting adjustment and compromise.

Article 2, which was a blind to the European world, and a bribe and a threat to the Border States, revealed what was considered the critical point of the rebellion, namely, the adhesion of the

Border States. It declared that Congress ought to have power to prohibit the introduction of slaves from any State not a member of this Confederacy. It was notorious that the powerful Slave breeding oligarchy of the Border States found mere *agricultural* Slavery unprofitable. South Carolina, wanting to make Charleston the New York of the South, and to carry on a "free trade" in negroes, and especially to become more independent, was in danger of finding herself surrounded by States with hostile interests. The leader of Secesh was soon in danger of becoming its victim.

South Carolina contemptuously refused to attend the Peace Conference of Virginia, at which twenty-two States were represented, and to which Georgia was willing to adhere. This Conference met in January.

On the 9th February Davis and Stephens were elected President, and Vice, and by the 12th all the departments were organised.

From that hour all the choice the South had, was, in fact, by what death it (that is its Slavery) should die. The Free Population power was every year encroaching, out-voting, out-numbering, and out-fighting it. Since 1790, of twenty-one new States, twelve were free, and nine slave.

On the other hand, simultaneously with the election of Lincoln, in addition to the United Slave votes of the South, New York chose ten, New Jersey three, and Illinois five, anti-republican members for the next House, besides seven from Pennsylvania, seven from Ohio, four from Indiana, one from Oregon, an all but unanimous pro-Slavery delegation from Missouri, and several probably from Connecticut and California. *A neutral, or pro-Slavery House seemed inevitable*, — a conflict between the North and its representatives seemed probable, but the South had withdrawn many of its delegates, and the result was, for the first time, a clear republican majority in either House, and that *Slavery, and not Freedom, came into collision with the armed power of the Government.*

§

It remains now to notice three sets of documents.

THE SECESSION ORDINANCES.

THE SECESSION CONSTITUTION.

LINCOLN'S MESSAGE.

And first, as to the ordinances of Secession.*

Six States, namely, South Carolina, Georgia, Florida, Alabama, Mississippi, and Louisiana, first adopted the new Constitution and chose Jefferson Davis, President.

Five States,—Virginia, North Carolina, Tennessee, Arkansas, and Texas, joined afterwards.

The MOBILE Declaration of Causes, made December 15th, 1860, was the earliest, and most remarkable of the Secession documents, and the best witness to the energy and determination and success of the Abolition party. It declared that ;—

"Anti-slavery fanaticism has lifted to the chief magistracy, a man pledged to carry on a relentless war of oppression upon the rights and equality of fifteen States." That the black repub-

* For the facts of this Chapter, we are indebted chiefly to the works of Putnam and Victor on the Rebellion.

lican party claims "*to abolish the inter-State slave trade*, and thus cut off the Northern slave States from their profits of *production*, and the Southern of their resources of supply of *labour*." That "*it repels all further admission of* NEW SLAVE STATES. It opposes protection to slavery on the high seas. It has * * *nearly abolitionised two of the Border slave States—Maryland and Missouri;* and it is making similar inroads constantly upon *Virginia and Kentucky. It has extended fanaticism into our own borders.* It has published its plans for the abolition of slavery everywhere. * * * To rescue slaves, to establish presses, to use vote and ballot, to detach non-slaveholders from slaveholders in slave States, to encourage anti slavery emigrants in the South and West, &c. It assails us from the pulpit, press, and school room. It divides all sects and religions, as well as parties. It has already a majority of the States under its domination; has infected the Federal, as well as the State judiciary; will ere long have a *majority of the House of Representatives* of the Congress of the United States; will soon have by the new census, *a majority of the Senate;* and before it obtains the Senate, will certainly obtain the chief executive power of the United States. It has announced its purpose of total abolition everywhere."

The Secession Ordinance of SOUTH CAROLINA, passed December 20th, 1860, declared that the 4th Article of the orginal Constitution (respecting the delivery up of "persons held to service"), "was so material to the compact, that without it "that compact would not have been made. The "States of Maine, New Hampshire, Vermont, "Massachusetts, Connecticut, Rhode Island, New "York, Pennsylvania, Illinois, Indiana, Michigan, "Wisconsin, Iowa, have enacted laws ("personal "liberty Bills") which either nullify the acts of "Congress, or render useless any attempts to ex-"ecute them. In many of these States the fugitive "is discharged from the service of labour claimed, "and in none of them has the State Government "complied with the stipulation made in the Con- "stitution." * * * "We affirm that these ends, for "which this Government was instituted, *have been "defeated, &c., by the action of the non-slaveholding "States.*" Then follows a denunciation of the twenty-five years' agitation against Slavery, and of President Lincoln, elected, "because he has declared "that Government cannot endure permanently "half slave and free, and that the public mind "must rest in the belief, that Slavery is in the "course of ultimate extinction."

The FLORIDA Convention, on the 7th January, declared that "all hope of preserving the Union "upon terms consistent with the safety and honour "of the slaveholding States has been finally dissi- "pated by the recent indications of the strength of "the anti-Slavery element," &c.

The ALABAMA ordinance, January 11th, began, —"Whereas the Election of Abraham Lincoln and "Hannibal Hamlin to the offices of President and "Vice-President, by a sectional party, *avowedly "hostile to the domestic institutions*," &c.

The LOUISIANA ordinance, January 26th, states,—"Whereas it is manifest that Abraham "Lincoln, if inaugurated as President of the United "States, *will keep the promises he has made to the "Abolitionists* of the North; that those promises, if "kept, *will inevitably lead to* the emancipation "and misfortune of the slaves of the South, *their "equality with the superior race*, and, before "long, to the irreparable ruin of this mighty

"Republic, the degradation of the American name, "and corruption of the American blood," &c.

The TEXAS ordinance, February 1st, states,— "Whereas * * * the power of the Federal Go- "vernment is sought to be made a weapon with "which to strike down the interests and property "of the people of Texas, and *her sister slaveholding* "*States*," &c.

The VIRGINIA ordinance, April 17th, recites, —"The Federal Government having perverted said "powers, not only to the injury of the people of "Virginia, but to the oppression of the Southern "*slaveholding States*," &c.

THE CONFEDERATE CONSTITUTION.

This Document, adopted March 11th, 1861, being founded on the American Constitution, it is only necessary to notice those clauses which differ from it on the main point.

Article I., Section 9, Clause 4, declares that "No "Bill of attainder or *ex post facto* law, or law "denying or impairing the right of property in "Negro Slaves, shall be passed."

Article IV., Section 11, Clause 1, "The citizens "of each State shall be entitled to all privileges "and immunities of citizens in the several States, "and shall have the right of transit and sojourn in "any State of this Confederacy with their slaves "and other property, and the right of property in "such slaves shall not be thereby impaired."

Section 111, Clause 3. "In all such territory "the institution of Negro Slavery, as it now exists "in the Confederate States, shall be recognised

" and protected by Congress, and by the territorial " Governments, and the inhabitants of the several " Confederate States and territories, shall have the " right to take to such territory, any slaves law-" fully held by them in any of the States or ter-" ritories of the Confederate States."

LINCOLN'S MESSAGE.

In reply to secession, President Lincoln issued an address, dignified, conciliatory, and *inexorable.* It appeared on the 4th March. It stated his intention to collect revenue, and protect the national property in all the States, not as a menace, but in order constitutionally to defend the Union.

As to Fugitive Slave laws, he would have all safeguards of liberty known in civilised jurisprudence, to be introduced, so that a free man may not in any case be surrendered as a slave. Touching Secession, he asks, " Can aliens make treaties, easier than friends can make laws?"

In contemplation of universal law, he declared the union perpetual, and that no State can, of its own mere motion, get out of the Union. " The " central idea of secession is anarchy." As to Slavery in the territories, " Congress decides by " the majority, and the minority must abide by the " result, or else there is no Government."

With regard to another point then profoundly agitated, namely, the decision involved in the Dred Scott case,* Mr. Lincoln proceeded temperately to

* It should be repeated here, that according to the American Constitution, "precedents" do not bind future cases, unless they follow the Constitution.

repudiate it as a precedent, and then to solemnly declare his intention to preserve the Union. "I "do not forget the position assumed by some that "constitutional questions are to be decided by the "Supreme Court, nor do I deny that such decisions "are *binding in any case upon the parties to a suit*, "as to the object of that suit, while they are also "entitled to very high respect and consideration, "in all parallel cases, by other departments of the "Government; and while it is obviously possible "that such decision be erroneous in any given "case, still the evil effect following it being limited "to that particular case, with the chance that it "may be overruled, and never become a precedent "for other cases, can better be borne than could "the evils of a different practice."

* * * * *

"You have no oath registered in Heaven to "destroy the Government, while I have the "solemn one to preserve, protect, and defend it. "I am loath to choose. We are not enemies but "friends. We must not be enemies. The mystic "chords of memory stretching from every battle-"field and patriotic grave, to every living heart "and hearthstone all over this broad land, will "yet swell the chorus of the Union when again "touched, as surely they will be, by the better "angels of our nature."

§

The last of the Doughfaces was clearly gone. Here was a "President," but neither a blusterer, a craven, nor an imbecile. *The South knew Lincoln.* Not an hour too soon had he come to torment them. They knew that if force would not serve their turn, *nothing would.* The character of Lincoln entered into the contest, as an element about which there could be no more doubt than about the rivers and mountains of America, or the fundamental Principles of its nationality. Slavery had evoked PURITANISM, its antagonist, its master, its destroyer. Lincoln's character was as certain a basis in the calculation as was the flow of the Mississippi, or the range of the Alleghanies. The South bade farewell to hope,—"and with hope, farewell, fear."

"Nigger on the Brain," was, indeed, not one of Lincoln's ailments. To a moral nature, untarnished as childhood, he has added a practical ability that has been victorious. The first inspired confidence, and presented a rallying point. The last, disciplined and led the force thus aroused. His anti-Slavery enthusiasm was not impracticable. He recognised in the Union, the best means for the destruction of Slavery, but a true conservative, right well he knew that the Union cannot be preserved if Slavery remain. He saw that if the country was to live these two parties must merge in one great national party. The anti-Slavery party must effect their objects by means of the Union, and the Union party must effect theirs by the destruction of Slavery. Both are for war against disunion. Both should logically be anti-Slavery, and both essentially conservative, and essentially democratic.

According to the allies of Despotism and class

interest in England, who cry out for the war to be arrested, one might almost wonder whether anybody ought to go to war for anything. According to the impulses of the other party, it was the duty of President Lincoln to have at once asserted emancipation, without studying and preparing the combinations necessary to assert it successfully. He will secure the objects advocated by the one, by means of the policy denounced by the other.

§

There were then the Slave party, and the Abolition party, and, at the first, a third party,—the Prudes, the doctrinnaires, the constitutionalists, the trimmers, the moderates, the formalists,—scribes, and Pharisees, hypocrites. A party always the most numerous at first, and which, after furnishing for a time to both parties, the fools, the tools, and the victims, always and everywhere slinks and sinks away before the logic of facts and the momentum of ideas and opinions, which would otherwise grind it to powder.

All possible attempts at compromise had been made by Patriots, Traitors, and Copperheads. But the only compromise that could give to the South a future, related to *Slavery in future Southern territories*, and that the North would not grant.

The South knew the issue. They must do or die, and the inexorable logic of their *institution* dictated to them their policy. Terror had long reigned there. On the authority of Mr. W. H. Russell, the *Times* correspondent, we know that, at New Orleans, "*charges of abolitionism appear in* "*the reports every morning*, and persons found "guilty, not of expressing opinions against Slavery, "but of stating their belief that the Northerners "will be successful, are sent to prison for six "months. The moral suasion of the lasso, tarring, "feathering, head shaving, ducking, and horse-"ponds, deportation on rails, and similar ethical "processes, are in favour. The North have not "arrived at such an elevated view of the necessities "of their position." There were at one time 70 murderers, pirates, burglarers, violators, and thieves, in a prison at New Orleans, which was said to be a Hell upon earth, and "Professor" Mitchell, the jailor of the workhouse reformatory there, was represented by the papers as having opened "a course "of instruction in the humane institutions for abo-"lition fanatics."

The South had denied the right of Petition, of speech, of carriage by mails of anti-Slavery documents. It denied the right of the majority, and of manhood, and of chastity, and its own deliberate engagements as to Slave boundaries. It denied the right of presidential election, and the national vote. The South sinned morally, socially, politically; against the Slaves, the mean whites, the Africans, the commerce and industry of England, the future of America, and the interests of the world. Its weapons were terrorism, dismemberment, conspiracy, and rebellion. It crowned all with the farce of prizes for prize negroes, and prize sermons in favour of African slavery.

It added to Avarice, Idleness; to Idleness, Lust; to Lust, Oppression; to Oppression, Cowardice; to

Cowardice, Lying; to Lying, Murder; and to Murder, Rebellion.*

There remained nothing but for the South to destroy, or be destroyed.

§

As one of the essential portions of the History of this contest of Oligarchy for dominion, we give a few more illustrations of the *force*, *fraud*, and *cruelties*, of the South, *perpetrated upon Southern Unionists.* We quote authorities, but, be it marked well, authorities are not needful. The South develops but the Logic of its Situation. Had it not done so, it would only have had to die a little earlier. It prefers dying later. In fact, as is the way with felons, cannot see the necessity of dying at all. And so it tears up its own "State" Constitutions, and maltreats or murders those of its own citizens and neighbours who would not join them. The knife-grinder got kicked, because he could not see his wrongs. "Union shrieking" SOUTHERNERS GET SHOT, HUNG, BURNT, AND SCALDED TO DEATH by the White and "free Democrats" of the South. Well they nursed Barbarism for eighty years, and now it is grown up. They liked it well enough for the Slave, and Destiny, in a certain stern wholesale way, always at last, brings home the argument. The object of all criminals is to argue with Destiny to a certain point, and then to leave it. But although the Devil may be defied, he *cannot* be cheated.

* The animal "courage" that fights for the right to breed human property, and to sell one's own flesh and blood into Slavery, is about the worst species of moral *cowardice.*

We quote from one whose neutrality might have pleased any but Slaveholders. He says:—

"I am a pro-Slavery man. There is not a single passage in the New Testament, nor a single act in the records of the Church during her early history, even for centuries, containing any direct, professed, or intended censure of slavery."

And first we take his evidence as to the force and cruelty of Disunionists.

"I have suffered deeply in person and estate, have avoided no responsibility, have endured evil treatment and imprisonment, and been compelled day by day to contemplate the near prospect of a brutal death upon the gallows,—all in behalf of the sacred cause (the Union) I have espoused.

"I was arrested, refused a trial and bail; was thrown into jail, where I found about one hundred and fifty men, representing all professions. We had not room for all to lie down at one time. The prisoners took rest by turns." The rebel soldiers washed their hands and faces in their drinking water. "Blackguard songs were sung for our benefit, and we were cursed day and night. The feeling was as a general thing, that any sort of treatment and fare was too good for a set of ——— Union shriekers and bridge-burners. * * Colonel Leadbetter, who, after serving fifteen years in the United States army, has become the champion of Southern rights," tied the knot for the hanging of Hensie and Fry. "*He ordered them to hang four days and nights, and the trains to pass slowly, so that the passengers could see and kick and strike with canes their dead bodies*,—which was actually done.

"One day they came with two carts, and took old Harmon, a methodist class-leader, and his son. The young man was hung first, and the father compelled to look on. Then being feeble and overpowered by his feelings, two of the ruffians took hold of him, one saying, 'Get up there, you old traitor.'"

"*Sketches of Secession*," *pp.* 8, 108, 311, *by W. E. Brownlow, Editor of the Knoxville Whig*, 1862.

On the question of cruelty we will select one other witness:—

"Mr. N——'s sentiments had become known, and refusing

to take the oath, they resolved to put him to death on the spot. He had a large family, who, with his wife, begged that his life might be spared. Among his foes the only point in dispute was as to the mode of his death. Some favoured shooting, some hanging; but the majority were in favour of scalding him to death. And there, *in the presence of his weeping and helpless family, these fiends deliberately heated water, with which they scalded to death their chained and defenceless victim.* The corpse was then suspended on a tree, with a label on the breast stating that whoever cut him down and buried him, would suffer the same fate."

"All attempts on the part of the slaves to obtain their liberty are resisted by the slaveholders by the infliction of appalling and barbarous cruelties. Thirty-two negroes were executed at Natchez, Mississippi, recently, because they expressed a determination to go to Lincoln; six were hanged in Hoxubee county, and one burned in the streets of Macon. The Southern papers state that the Hon. Mr. Orr of South Carolina, attempted to drive his slaves into the interior to prevent their escaping to the Yankees, and upon their refusal to go, he ordered them to be driven at the point of the bayonet and in the execution of the order, fifty were slain."—"*The Iron Furnace*," pp. 197, 278, by the Rev. J. H. Aughley, a refugee from Mississippi.

§

The CONSPIRACY of Southern Leaders against, as well as with, their own people, and their utter disregard of their own State constitutions, completes the evidence of the essential weakness of their cause, and of the hypocrisy of their claim to fight for "freedom and independence."

"As the entire Secession movement has been made over the heads of the people * * * it was expected by the Southern communities that, when the Permanent Constitution was to be ordained, the people would have a vote. * * * * *In not a single instance was the Constitution allowed to go before the people for their vote!* * * * * * *Thus, men chosen merely to* *consider the question of Union or Disunion—or, if the latter was decided upon, to agree upon an Ordinance of Secession, upon which the voters alone should be permitted to pass judgment—usurped dictatorial powers, remained in permanent session, passed Ordinances of Secession, inaugurated a new Government, and, finally, sealed their revolutionary proceedings by adopting the new Constitution—all without once allowing the popular voice any expression."—Victor's History of the Rebellion,* p. 22, V. 2.*

These assertions are well substantiated. Amongst other numerous facts, the following scene between Mr. (Vice-President) Stevens and the war Democrat Toombs, in the Hall of the House of Representatives of Georgia, Nov. 14th, 1860, is not a little suggestive:—

"The first question that presents itself is, Shall the people of the South secede from the Union in consequence of the election of Mr. Lincoln? I tell you frankly, candidly, and earnestly, that I do not think that they ought.

"Let a convention of the people of Georgia be called. *Let the Sovereignty of the People speak.* An honourable gentleman (Mr. T. R. R. Cobb) advised you to take this course—*not to wait to hear from the cross-roads and groceries.* You have no power to act. You must refer this question to the People, and you must wait to hear from the men at the cross-roads or the groceries; for the people in this country, whether at the cross-roads or the groceries, whether in cottages or palaces are all equal, and *they are the sovereigns* in this country. Sovereignty is not in the Legislature. We, the People, are the Sovereigns, You Legislators are but our servants.

Mr. Toombs (interrupting)—"*I am afraid of conventions.*"

Mr. Stephens—"I am not afraid of any convention legally chosen by the People."

Mr. Toombs—"I do not wish the People to be cheated."

Mr. Stephens—"I think the proposition of my honourable

* This work enters into full detail of the facts which demonstrate the above assertions.

friend had a considerable smack of unfairness, *not to say cheat.* He wished to have no convention, but for the Legislature to submit their vote to the People—'submission to abolition rule or resistance?'—now who in Georgia would vote submission to abolition rule?" (Laughter).

Mr. Tombs—"*The convention will.*"

Putnam, pp. 225-6, v. 1.

We add, from "Putnam's Rebellion Record,"* and from Victor's work, the following evidence of Southern Force, Fraud, Intimidation, and Cajolery, used in the matter of Secession in the *Border States*, and in those represented at the *Montgomery Congress*, collectively, and specifically in the States of *Virginia*, *Tennessee*, *Kentucky*, *Georgia*, *Louisiana*, *Texas*, *Alabama*, *&c.* In South Carolina, probably, no force was necessary, only the stupendous treachery of the "thief Floyd," and a headlong rush over its own State Constitution to Rebellion.

The movement was (Putnam, Vol. 1, p. 368) truly a "conspiracy," to give the minority a command over the majority. It avoids reference to the popular consent, screens its plans from public criticism by secret sessions, *and plies the machinery of passion to rush the people into the abyss of revolution.*

The Convention of the BORDER STATES, held in June, 1861, in its address to the American People, after considering how to protect their *interest* as slave states in a minority, &c., affords conclusive

* It should here be stated, that this Rebellion Record, compiled by Moore, and the similar work by Victor, are collections of Documents published on the instant of the events to which they relate, and afford therefore a better basis for history than perhaps has ever been furnished before.

evidence of two things: First, *that the People of the Border States were with the North.* Second, that *Southern Leaders attempted, and were expecting to coerce the Border States.* They declare:—

"We consider that our *interests would be irretrievably ruined by taking part in the conflict on the side where the strongest sympathies of our people are*, and that our sense of honour and of duty requires that we should not allow ourselves to be drawn or *driven* into a war in which other states, without consulting us, have deliberately chosen to involve themselves."—P. 352, Vol. 1, *Putnam.*

On the 21st June, 1861, the East Tennessee Union convention adopted a "declaration of grievances," in reference to the violence and fraud of the Secession agents. Amongst other grievances it states as follows:—

"That they *allowed no discussion,* or speeches, or papers; that they would have *no folded tickets;* that *disunionists had charge of the Polls;* that they proclaimed their determination to hold the State though in a minority; that there were *falsehoods as to action of Congress, as to battles never fought and victories never won,* as to the purposes of Lincoln," &c., &c.—*Putnam,* Vol. 2, 156-7-8.

Also Governor Pierpont's message of July to the Senate and House of Virginia, states that—

"At the election for members of the convention in February last, there was a majority of over sixty thousand votes given to the Union candidates; and the People, by an equal majority, determined that no act of that Convention should change the relations of that state to the Federal Government, unless ratified by the popular vote. Yet the delegates to that Convention passed the ordinance of secession, and attached the state to the Southern league; and to render the step irretrievable, and to *defeat the whole object of requiring a ratification of the people* to render such acts valid, they put them into effect immediately; and before the vote could be taken on the question of ratification, *transferred the whole military force of our state to the Confederacy*, and surrendered to him (Davis) military possession of our territory.

"When the chains had been thus fastened upon us we were called to vote upon the ordinance of secession," &c. &c.—Vol. 2. pp. 159-60. *Putnam.*

The VIRGINIAN convention was not called to dissolve the Union; yet, as soon as the Convention had secretly acted upon the subject without any promulgation of the ordinance, and while the People were yet ignorant of its existence, the executive officers of Virginia rushed, incontinently, into open war against the United States.

The Legislature of TENNESSEE, in secret session, passed an ordinance of secession. The Legislature had, two years before, sworn to the United States Constitution. The ordinance contained an arrangement for voting *afterwards.*—*Putnam*, pp. 305-204, Vol. 1.

The "Philadelphia Press" of July 18th, 1861, gives the following statement of a Philadelphian, who, after various arrests and attempts, had succeeded in leaving Richmond:—

"In *Alabama* and *Georgia* many men were forced against their will to enter the Confederate army—three alternatives being placed before them—'*to enlist, to go to jail, or to be hung.*'"—P. 333, Vol. 2. *Putnam.*

The following is from an address by John Jay, on the 4th July, 1861, declaring that the convention of LOUISIANA was elected by a *minority* of the people, and quoting the "Augusta Chronicle and Sentinel," a leading paper of GEORGIA, which openly complained that—

"*The result has been produced by wheedling, coaxing, and bullying, and all the arts of deception.* The whole movement for Secession, so far at least as Georgia is concerned, was *pushed through under circumstances of great excitement and frenzy by a fictitious majority.*" "The Georgian convention," continued that paper, "and the Confederate (Montgomery) Congress have gone forward in their work, as none can deny, *without explicit and direct authority from the People.* Sooner or later the People must be heard."

Mr. Jay then quotes Mr. Rhett—'The secession of South Carolina is not the event of a day. It has been gathering head for years.'

"Mr. Parker—'It has been gradually culminating for a long series of years.'

"Mr. Keitt—'I have been engaged in this movement ever since I entered political life.'

"Mr. Inglis—'Most of us have had this matter under consideration for the last twenty years.'"

"We can now," continues Mr. Jay, "trace step by step *the progress of the conspiracy*, and read the history of the last thirty years without an interpreter. *We can understand the motive of the Texan Rebellion, the war with Mexico, the persistent efforts to secure Cuba*, the philibustering expeditions to *Central America*, and the determination to re-open *the African Slave Trade.*"—*Putnam*, Vol. 1. pp. 378-96.

§

Senator Douglas' last words for the Union, were (1st May, 1861), these:—

"The Slavery question is a mere excuse. The election of Lincoln is a mere pretext. *The present secession movement is the result of an enormous conspiracy formed more than a year since*—formed by leaders in the Southern Confederacy.

"If the disunion candidate had carried the united South,

their scheme was, the Northern candidate successful, to seize the Capitol last spring, and by a united South and divided North, hold it. *That scheme was defeated in the defeat of the disunion candidate in several of the Southern States.* The conspiracy is now known. When the history of the two years from the Lecompton charter down to the Presidential election shall be written, it will be shown that the scheme was deliberately made to break off this Union."—P. 299, *Putnam*, v. 1.

Senator Rousseau, also, in the Kentucky Senate, May 21, 1861, confirmed Douglas as to this intentional division of the Democratic party. *Putnam*, v. 1, p. 331.

And Mr. W. H. Russell says:—

"The more stoutly Demagogy, immigrant preponderance, and the blasts of universal suffrage, bore down on the South, the more resolutely she held on her cable.

"The tide of immigration waxed stronger, and by degrees she saw the districts into which she claimed the right to introduce this capital (slaves) closed against her, and occupied by free labour.

"I am satisfied that there has been a deep-rooted design conceived in some men's minds thirty years ago, and extended gradually year after year to others, to break away from the Union at the very first opportunity. * * * The clause in the Constitution of the Confederate States which *prohibited the importation of negroes, was especially and energetically resisted by them*" (the South Carolinian planters).—*W. H. Russell, London Times*, May 28th, 1861.

Ex-Governor Thomas relates (Putnam, V. 2. p. 478,) how, in February, 1837, he attended a kind of secret meeting of sixty or seventy representatives of Slaveholding States, and how they discussed the resolution, "That they ought not again to take their seats until satisfactory resolutions on Slavery had been adopted."

On the system adopted for "Engineering" the rebellion, Brownlow also quotes the following:

"*Mobile Mercury*, April, 1859.

"Conferences have already been held by leading patriotic gentlemen of this city, of all parties, and the plans of Southern organization have been set on foot and almost matured, preparatory to action.

"The country is ripe for the movement, and if judiciously inaugurated, it will sweep over the land with a force that no opposition will be able to check."

On the 7th January, 1861, D. L. Yulee writes from *Washington*:—

"On the other side is a copy of resolutions adopted at a consultation of the Senators from the seceding States, at which Georgia, Alabama, Louisiana, Arkansas, Texas, Mississippi, and Florida, were represented. * * '*If we left here*, force loan and volunteer bills might be passed, which would put Mr. Lincoln in immediate condition for hostilities, whilst, *by remaining in our places until the 4th of March, * * we can disable the republicans*,' " &c.

"The substance of the whole affair is that a knot of senatorial traitors, fourteen in number, so late as January and February, 1861, sat in their seats, under an oath to support the Constitution, and to act as the confidential advisers of the President, and yet were plotting the overthrow of the Government.

"The St. Louis Republican asserts, "the rupture at Charleston and Baltimore is seen to have been a preconcerted part of the Disunion programme, *concocted in the secret lodges of the Disunion leagues*. * * That by a division of the Democrats in the North, and consequent election of Lincoln, the Disunionists hoped to fire the Southern heart to the work of the overthrowing of the Constitution and the Union."—*Brownlow*, pp. 172-5-6.

"Douglas overheard Mason say in the Senate, 'No matter what compromise the North offers, the South must find a way to defeat it.' In the Senate, had the Southern States remained, they would have had a majority of six, and in the House, of thirty-six over the Republican party."—*Ibid.* p. 277.

And the following letter is from W. S. Yancey to Jas. Slaughter, June 15th, 1858 :—

"The remedy of the South is in a diligent organization of her true men for the prompt resistance of her next oppression. No national party can save us; no sectional party can ever do it. But if we should do as our fathers did—*organize committees of safety all over the Cotton States* (and it is only in them that we can hope for an effective movement), we shall fire the Southern heart, instruct the Southern mind, give courage to each other, and at the proper moment, by one organized concerted action, WE CAN PRECIPITATE THE COTTON STATES INTO A REVOLUTION."—*Ibid.* p. 167.

We do not seek to demonstrate an actual Union majority in the South, after Sècession became a fact. But immediately before, at the Presidential election, the Southern Senatorial votes for the Union and Squatter Democrat candidates, were 39 and 9 against 72 for the Slave Democrat. Whilst the Popular vote South was 163,525 and 515,973, to 540,871 for the Slave Democrat,—a considerable majority against him.

"The *Richmond Examiner*," moreover, in an elaborate eulogy of the thief, Floyd, avows that "*the Southern Confederacy would not and could not be in existence at this hour but for the action of the late Secretary of War.*" It proceeds :—

"The plan invented by General Scott to stop secession was very able in all its details, and *nearly certain of general success.* The Southern States are full of arsenals and forts commanding their rivers and strategic points. He desired to transfer the army to these forts as speedily and as quietly as possible. The Southern States could not cut off communication between the Government and the fortresses, without a great fleet, which they cannot build for years, *or take them by land without an hundred thousand men.* Had Scott been able to have got these forts into the condition he desired, the Southern Confederacy would not now exist."—*Putnam*, V. 1. pp. 378-96.

It will be observed that the Senate,—the "Conservative" element, was the first to become demoralised, and that, although a considerable majority of the popular vote South was against the Slave Democrat, yet the logic of the situation—as it always must in a crisis, rapidly bore the multitude with it. In such crises those who are "not against" the wrong, will always very properly be appropriated by it. The time had come when the South must be either wholly Oligarchic and Slaveholding, or wholly Republican and free.

§

The following representative facts, amongst a multitude of others of a similar character, are stated and vouched in detail in Orville J. Victor's "History of the Rebellion."

Virginia may be said to have been annexed to Secession by the traitorous Governor, Letcher, and his co-conspirators. The votes under compulsion, and in secret session of convention, were 60 to 53. The election of delegates to the State convention had resulted in a large Union majority. Tennessee was transferred in spite of a tremendous Union majority.

Texas, also, was forcibly transferred.

Kentucky was more than two to one for Union.

In January, 1861, the Legislature refused to call a convention.

When Missouri was reorganised, the convention denounced the chief officers of State as conspirators.

As far north as near the Iowa line, notices to leave the State for ever were served upon Union men in April, 1861.

It was the complaint of the South that Mr. Lincoln still stood square on the Chicago platform, and that there was actually *not a slaveholder in the cabinet.* The South threatened Virginia with losing her $400,000,000 worth of negroes, and with becoming the battle-field and foraging ground for both parties. The Union, they said, was dead, and they might have a Protestant funeral or an Irish wake. The army of Lincoln would be gathered, said the "Raleigh Banner," from the sewers of the cities; Old Abe, said the "Richmond Whig," had been beastly drunk for thirty-six hours; and the "New Orleans Delta" repeated the lie on the authority of "a gentleman who had been taken into the presence of the august Baboon."

Vigilance Committees teemed throughout the South; meetings were suppressed, the White terror reigned, and in Texas, Georgia, Alabama, and Mississippi, a great many free debaters were hanging from the trees. "Even thought was not free;" a moderate allowance for Abolitionist remarks was thirty lashes, a coat of tar, and expulsion.

The leaders in this movement were the far-seeing and unscrupulous Southern statesmen. Many of their tools were of the same class and character as the Missouri desperadoes, who have been thus described:

"Tall, slim, athletic; yellow complexion, hairy faced, dirty flannel shirt—red, blue, or green; a leather belt, in which a dirty handled bowie knife is stuck; eye slightly whiskey red, teeth colour of walnut,—such is your border ruffian. His body might be composed of gutta percha, Johnny cake, and badly smoked bacon."

Virginia was still in doubt, but knowing she must "go to war with somebody," considered that the North would be most forbearing.

North Carolina was, in March, more loyal than Virginia. It was anywhere at a distance from the moral support of the North, that "debaters" for freedom were hung, and that force and fear, the determination of the mean Whites to have free trade in niggers, and the desperation of the leaders, succeeded in "running the States out."

Not one of the Gulf States first in rebellion submitted the ordinances of Secession to a fair vote of the people, and almost the entire proceedings of the convention were illegal according to their own constitutions.

And Mr. Brownlow informs us that:—

"When the storm arose in the South, and the current set in seemingly in favour of secession, vast numbers rushed into their ranks, actuated by the worst motives that ever governed the actions of as many bad men. The daring, improvident, indolent, thoughtless, bankrupts; the thousands indebted to Northern merchants, debauched members of the churches, apostate preachers, and the intemperate,—all the loose elements of society to whom no change could be productive of injury.

"It was a common thing to hear men of this class swearing that they intended to have their rights. Ask one of them what rights he had lost, and was so vehemently contending for, and the reply would be the right to carry his negroes into the Territories. *At the same time the man never owned a negro in his life, and never was related to any one who did own a negro;* nay, I have heard captains of rebel companies bluster in this way, *who could not get credit in a Secession store for a pair of shoes or a pound of coffee.*"

The poor Whites were agitating for cheap niggers, but would they not also, bye and bye, agitate for the preservation of Democratic forms of Government? It would not be so bad a stroke of business to kill two birds with one stone, and these ideas of a prurient Democracy must be put down, and, in case of war, these poor Whites would be used up. Accordingly the *conventions* appointed the *Congress*, and the *Congress* appointed the *executive!* Virginia would fain save her four millions of dollars annually got by breeding slaves. So much for the traders. The Slave States would fain save their slaves, valued from seven hundred millions to one thousand millions of dollars. So much for the men of wealth. Thus, the leading men "run the States out." "And why did they not go out according to form and rule?" Why! Because then most of them could not have gone out at all, and for this further reason,—these Democratic provisions,—this Democracy of the States and of their constitutions, WAS THE VERY THING THE OLIGARCHY OF THE SOUTH WANTED TO GET RID OF.

Free press and speech, which were guaranteed by almost every Southern constitution, would have neutralised the compromises in the national constitution; but Secession was a revolt against the rights of labour, and against the rights of man, and Slavery, however valuable to the South, *was valuable chiefly to the statesmen and leaders, as the sheet anchor of the oligarchic power and principle, as against their own populations.*

§

The whole programme of the South was thus categorically explained by the Richmond Examiner, of May 28, 1863.

> "The establishment of the Confederacy is *a distinct reaction, against the mistaken civilization of the age.* For Liberty, Equality, and Fraternity, we have deliberately substituted Slavery, Subordination, and Government. Reverently we feel that *our Confederacy is a God sent Missionary to the nations* with great truths to preach."

This same gospel according to Jeff. Davis, has also been interpreted, perhaps in somewhat too plain a way, by one of the current Historians of the Rebellion.

> " It was one of the secret purposes of the ruling class South, to disfranchise the non-property holders of the Confederacy.
>
> "The conventions acted out the principle of exclusive rule, by themselves appointing members of congress ; and congress acted on its exclusive authority by appointing the Executive officers of Government."*

Also the famous message of Governor Adams to the legislature of South Carolina, about two years before secession, recommended the re-opening of the slave trade to re-adjust the condition of poor men South ; and to prevent the formation of a *dangerous class of men* interested in free labour or Capital, and without direct interest in Slavery,—to make, in fact, every White a Shareholder in Slavery, with dividend and interest.

The alternative of the acceptance of this South-

* *Victor*, vol. ii. p. 520. " Remarks on Report of Virginian State Convention."

ern mission, was announced beforehand, by the Richmond Enquirer, of Oct. 16, 1863.

"Once more we say it is all or nothing. This Confederacy, or the Yankee nation, one or other, goes *down, down to perdition.* One or the other must forfeit its national existence, and lie at the mercy of its mortal enemy. * * They cannot make peace except through their utter exhaustion and absolute inability to strike another blow.

"We shut them out for ever, * * and without, as St. John says, 'are dogs.'"

The "Unanimity" of the South is illustrated and accounted for in Putnam's record as follows:—

"It is a notable fact, that *wherever the minute men have had an organisation,* those counties have voted by large majorities for immediate Secession. Those that they could not control by persuasion and coaxing, they dragooned and bullied by threats, jeers, and sneers. By this means thousands of good citizens were induced to vote the immediate secession Ticket through timidity. Besides, towns and cities have been flooded with sensation despatches and inflammatory rumours manufactured in Washington city for the especial occasion. To be candid, *there never has been as much lying and bullying practised in the same length of time since the destruction of Sodom and Gomorrah,* as has been in the recent state campaign."—*Rebellion Record,* vol. i. p. 12. *Putnam.*

Special instances of this system are given in Putman, pp. 247-283, vol. i. In one of them, according to a letter from Major Sprague, of San Antonio, Texas, April 24, 1861, the news received there from New Orleans was, that Lincoln had fled, Scott resigned, and joined the Confederates, and that fifty thousand men from the South surrounded Washington, &c. &c.; and General Harney, in his Proclamation, dated May 14, 1861, complains, that in his absence the General Assembly of Missouri had drawn up a "Military Bill," which was in fact *an indirect Secession ordinance, ignoring even the forms resorted to by other States.*

The result of the Rebellion was foretold by one of the chief Rebels, Vice President Stephens, January, 1861, in the Georgian State Convention.

"This step of Secession can never be recovered, and all the baleful and withering consequences that must follow will rest on the convention for all coming time. * * Who but he who shall have given his vote for this unwise and ill-timed measure shall be held to strict account for this suicidal act by the present generation, and probably *cursed by posterity for all coming time.*"

The South were dominated by the necessities and the logic of their cause. They succeeded in their plot, *and their plot will destroy them.* For a deeper and an universal logic fights for freedom.

§

The oligarchic character of the revolt is thus admirably described by a German newspaper:—

"The whole civilised world has an interest in this war. It is a war which the People of the United States, *conservative by the nature of their industrial and political habits,* could not longer put off; and it is a war which, under perhaps other names, many a nation of Europe will have to take up in its turn. It is with them as with us; the *feudalism of the middle ages* is arrayed in arms against the CITIZENSHIP *of the nineteenth century;* an exploded theory of society is lifting up its head against the triumphs of our thinking, industrial, and progressive century; *the poverty struck Don Quixotes of the Southern plantations give battle to the roaring windmills and smoking chimneys of the wealthy North.* It is the supercilious *noble* in arms against the spirit of the century in which the *Citizen* is supreme. In such an issue we can wish success only to the constitutional Government."—*Cologne Gazette,* May 5, 1861.

Wendell Phillips powerfully put the same thoughts, at New York, in April, 1861:—

"We imagined that the age of bullets was over; that the age of ideas had come.

"But this nation is made up of different ages,—a mixed mass of different centuries. The North *thinks*,—can appreciate argument,—it is the nineteenth century. The South *dreams*—it is the thirteenth and fourteenth century,—baron and serf—noble and slave. Jack Cade and Wat Tyler loom over the horizon, and the serf rising, calls for another Thierry to record his struggle. There the fagot still burns which the Doctors of the Sorbonne called, ages ago, 'the best light to guide the erring.' * * The cannon shots against Fort Sumter were the yell of pirates against the Declaration of Independence."—*Putnam*, p. 130, v. 1.

And as if in very echo of his words, L. W. Spratt, a man of mark, addressed to a Louisiana delegate to the Southern Congress at Montgomery, and published in the "Charleston Mercury," the 13th Feb. 1861, the following "Protest,"—*a protest of Despair*, from South Carolina:—

"The real contest is between the two forms of society. If the foreign Slave Trade had never been suppressed, slave society must have triumphed. It extended to the limits of New England. The large majority of our People are in legitimate connection with the institution. But when (free) labourers come in greater numbers from the North, * * *this town of Charleston*, at the very heart of slavery, *may become a fortress of Democratic power against it*, and here also the contest for existence may be waged between them (Democracy and Slavery).

"It thus appears that the contest is not ended with a dissolution of the Union. Our Slaves are still drawn off by higher prices to the West. Maryland, Virginia, Kentucky, possibly Tennessee and North Carolina, may lose their slaves, as New York, Pennsylvania, and New Jersey have. *Having achieved one Revolution to escape Democracy at the North, it must still achieve another to escape it at the South.*

"*You are commissioned to erect,* not only a Southern, but *a slave Republic. But if you shall not,*—if you shall exhibit care but for a Republic, respect but for a Democracy, you re-inaugurate the blunder of 1789; you will have no tests of faith; hireling labour will be free; *your Confederacy is again divided* into antagonistic Societies; *the irrepressible conflict is again commenced;* another revolution comes, but *whether in the order and propriety of this, is gravely to be doubted.*

"If the clause (prohibition of external slave trade) be carried into the permanent Government, *our whole movement is defeated.* It will abolitionise the Border States. Slavery cannot share a Government with Democracy. *It is to be feared this fatal action will be consummated.*"—*Putnam*, pp. 358-65, v. 2.

If the South is to live, this would be the logic of its life. Without contact with free labourers, says Spratt, "*the Slaves might be increased to forty millions*, without a corresponding increase among the Whites, *and yet no disaster!*" England and France "would pocket their philanthropy with their profit!" And if England and France should oppose this? Why, so much the worse for England and France, or for the South.

Right true is it, that in this contest, not only the North or the South, but rather the South or the Free Labour power and opinion *of the world*, must go *down, down, to perdition!*

§

The Documents here referred to are full and accurate. They relate for the most part to actors now living, and to recent, almost present events. They are vouched by references to time, place, and authorship. They could not have been falsified without exposure, for they themselves supply the means of detection. But the general tone of the

South—its rowdyism, violence, and desperation, in contrast with the waiting, hoping, astonished and determined aspect of the North, is sufficiently established, even for the most cautious, by Mr. Russell's Diary, and amongst others, by the following extracts:—

"At Goldsborough the enthusiasm of the Citizens not quite free from a taint of alcohol. A General drunk."—Vol. I. pp. 134-5.

"At Willmington the artist Moses," who accompanied him, "was pounced upon by a Vigilance Committee who were drunk, and who watched the post-office and railway station."—Vol. I. p. 137.

At Savannah "many would willingly stand aside if they could, and see the battle. Pressure put upon Irish and Germans which they cannot well resist, and the white population obliged by moral force draughting to go to the war."—P. 229.

"The South," said President Davis to him, "are perhaps the only people in the world where gentlemen go to a military academy who do not intend to follow the profession of arms." —P. 250.

"At Mobile a Vigilance Committee busy deporting abolitionists after certain preliminary processes."—P. 274.

"In New Orleans, as in New York, the opinion of the most wealthy and intelligent men in the community, so far as I can judge, regards *universal suffrage* as organised confiscation, legalised violence and corruption,—a mortal disease in the body Politic. *The Thugs of New Orleans*, a band of native-born Americans, at election times *were wont deliberately to shoot down Irish and German voters* occupying positions as leaders of their mobs. These Thugs were suppressed by an armed Vigilance Committee."—Vol. I. p. 364.

"The tone in which they (any of the real adherents of the South) alluded to the Northern people, indicated the clear conviction that trade, commerce, the pursuit of gain, manufacture, and the base mechanical arts, had so degraded the whole race, they would never attempt to strike a blow in fair fight for what they prized so highly in theory and in words.

I am persuaded that these feelings of contempt are extended to England, one evidence of our canker of peace is our abolition of duelling."—Vol. I. p. 93.

"An argument which can scarcely be alluded to, was used by them (Southern gentlemen) to show that seduction, &c. of white women in *Slave States* had not the excuse which might be adduced elsewhere."—Vol. I. p. 94.

Up the Mississippi from New Orleans, "if you are bold enough to be unconvinced (of justice of Slavery) and to say so, I advise you not to come within reach of a mass meeting of our citizens, who may be able to find a rope and a tree in the neighbourhood."—P. 385.

In Louisiana he asks a lad "whether he can read and write, and goes to Church, and has heard of our Saviour." The master, his host, interposes, and "says it is getting hot, and complained that such talk disturbed the minds of Slaves, and led them astray."—Vol. I. p. 197-8.

Near Baton Rouge a man buying chickens of Negroes; "Lucky he was not caught. If the citizens had been drunk they'd have hung him on the spot."—P. 418.

"If ever," said a master to slave, "you goes aboard them steamers to meddle with newspapers, I'm —— but I'll kill you."—P. 419.

"Cotton at 10 cents a pound gave a nugget in every boll. Land for a few dollars an acre, negroes cheap, but ruin awaiting them if they did not shut out the sounds and utterances from the North."—P. 423.

"Authorities confiscate all property of unpatriotic persons, and mob law supplants any remissness."—Vol. I. p. 424.

"Concession of belligerent rights created a thrill of exultation through South. Considered an admission of independence."—Vol. II. pp. 30-6.

"State rights meant protection to Slavery, extension of Slave territory, and free trade in Slave produce."

"In state of Mississippi, and other Southern states, law powerless, and brutal shootings and stabbings."—Vol. II. p. 44.

"One principle of this revolt, hostility to universal suffrage." —Vol. II. p. 45.

"Never did a people enter on a war so utterly destitute of any reason for waging it, or of the means of bringing it to a successful termination against internal enemies."—P. 57.

"The abrupt outburst of the North filling the South with astonishment and something like fear."—P. 113.

"Butler and Banks saved Baltimore in spite of Scott, and when McClellan talked of slaves as property, Butler used them for State purposes."—Pp. 140-185.

"I am satisfied by an actual inspection of the lists that the Northerners retain the same preponderance in officers who have received military education, as they possess in wealth and other means."—Vol. II. p. 328.

Under date of April 22, 1861, we find decided testimony of Mr. Russell to Lincoln's policy:—

"Had the administration been as strong in all respects as any United States Government ever could, or can hope to be in reference to such emergencies as the present, *it really could have done little except* precipitate a civil war, in which the Border States would have arranged themselves on the side of the Cotton States."

Also the "own" correspondent of the *Times*, under various dates in April and May, 1861, writes to the same effect, but in rather more outspoken terms, as follow:—

"Parties are more divided in TEXAS than in any other; complete anarchy seems to reign there."—April 10th.

"The general assembly of MISSOURI, 62 to 42, resolved It is inexpedient to take any steps for a national convention to propose any amendments to the Constitution as recommended by the State Convention."—*Times*, April 15th.

"In the Virginian Convention the sixth resolution expresses an earnest desire for the re-establisnment of the Union."—April 20th.

"A military government founded on treachery and conspiracy."

"I could have no doubt (this was written after the magnificent uprising in New York described as though it were the most earnest, thoughtful, and formidable gathering in all History) that Democrats and Republicans had alike mistaken that (the national) heart; that the South had indeed been deceived—lamentably, dreadfully deceived."—May 6th.

"Virginia has seceded, subject to approval by the People at an election to be held *under the guns of Jeff. Davis' troops.*" —14th May.

Jeff. Davis's message "does not tell the world that the plot was conceived long before the last election. That every one of the conspirators have been elevated without a single exception to a place of power, trust, and remuneration in the (Southern) Government."—8th May.

"The manner in which Virginia has been carried against its will into the Southern camp is of a piece with every step in this great conspiracy. *The Governors of Missouri, Kentucky, North Carolina, and Tennessee, are each trying to force his State into the Southern ranks.*"—*Ibid.*

§

We have thus at length developed the proofs of Southern "Force, Fraud, and Conspiracy," because they demonstrate that "Nationality" was only a pretence, and that the real moving causes were the spirit of Faction, and the interests of Slaveocracy.

But let us here appreciate more precisely *the Problem of the Situation*—the North—the South —Lincoln.

There are three kinds of force; material, mental, moral.

What was the problem of successful Secession?

"To carry certain States out of the Union,"—a decidedly *active* operation, it was necessary to have a preponderance of two out of three of those forces. In other words, to have greater material and organising power; or greater material power, and power of Principle; or greater organising power and loftier Principle.

And what was the *actual* Secession? It had

the material and moral elements against it, whilst it had no monopoly of talent and organisation. It was, in numbers, as ten to twenty millions. It attempted to seize States well within the temperate zone, and therefore fully exposed to a free labour propagandism; and also obnoxious to the strategic, commercial, social, and political influence of the mountain ranges, and of the vast water system of America. Moreover, it fought for that which was not a "Principle." It fought, *not* for Independence, pure and simple, but for Independence to maintain Slavery, and the Oligarchic system.

It could not rise to the full inspiration of "nationality" as a Principle. It played and intrigued thirty years too long, and went out at last, not on the principle of nationality, but on the pretence of "*State* rights." *It waited thirty years too long*, while Free Labour influences "demoralised" the Border States, and while, for the better half of its life, the *American* nationality, consolidated, intensified, and grew.

The compromises of the North, criminal as they were, were "God's trap to catch fools with." *Calhoun should have struck*, if he meant anything, or if there was anything to strike for. As it was, this predestined failure, "Secession," is led forth by Davis and Lee,—not so much to Intrigue and Battle, as to Execution.

The South was too soon or too late. It should have arisen before the great North-West grew,—while the Border States yet believed that Robbery was Property,—as soon as the great Jackson died,—when the Slave interest was already strong, and the true nation yet unmade. If it could *not* do this, it should have waited, and used the arms and resources of the North, to carve out for it in the real South a future.

And the North? Its thirty years of compromise-Presidents,—a brigade of Southern shoeblacks,—its political figurants, prostituting their "Democracy," forsooth, for Southern influence*;—its litterateurs, tilting with goose-quills against destiny;—its officials, thinking themselves the nation. And behind them all, the descendants and heirs of those "embattled farmers," who—

"Fired the shot heard round the world."

Is it not Aristotle who tells us of the real Democracy which farmers are best fitted to make? It is enough that Americans are one nation, and that the nation is a Democracy.

"I divide you," said Wendell Phillips, "into four sections. The first is the ordinary mass, rushing from mere enthusiasm to battle. Behind that class stands another. whose only idea in this controversy is Sovereignty and the flag. The seaboard, the wealth, the just converted hunkerism of the country, fill that class. Next to it stands the third element, the People; the cordwainers of Lynn, the farmers of Worcester, the dwellers of

---

* The Satirist describes the situation well:—

"Now don't go to say I'm the friend of oppression,
For I ollers hev strove (at least that's my impression)
To make cussed free with the rights of the North,"
Sez John C. Calhoun, sez he:—
"Yes," sez Davis o' miss,
"The perfection o' bliss,
Is in skinnin' thet same old coon," sez he.
"At the North we don't make no distinction o' color;
You can all take a lick at our shoes when you please."

Biglow Papers.

the prairie, Iowa and Wisconsin, Ohio and Maine—the broad surface of the People who have no leisure for technicalities, who never studied law, who never had time to read any further into the Constitution than the first two lines—'*establish justice and secure liberty.*' They have waited long enough; they have eaten dirt enough; they have apologized for bankrupt Statesmen enough; they have quieted their consciences enough; and now that they have got their hand on the neck of a rebellious aristocracy, *in the name of the People they mean to strangle it.*

"That I believe is the body of the People itself. Side by side with them stands a fourth class—small but active—the abolitionists, who thank God that he has let them see his salvation before they die."—New York, April, 1861. *Putnam*, p. 130. v. 1.

And Lincoln? It is the old story of the hour and the man. Passion blinding them, the South asserted the barren right to take Slaves into Free States, instead of into new territory only. They incensed and outraged the North, when they should have tried to use it.

The mistake was made. The South itself took Slavery from the category of State questions, and made it a national question, demanding its protection, not only against free citizens, but against foreign nations on the high seas. Certain Southern leaders even went so far as to boast of planning the Breckenridge party division, that Lincoln might be elected, and Secession follow.

"Slavery against the nation." That was the challenge—the merit of Lincoln is, that surely, if slowly,* he answered it with, "The nation against

* A great deal has been said about his slowness by gentlemen who have not compared dates. The uprising of the North and the call for 75,000 men was within three or four days of the bombardment of Fort Sumter.

Slavery." That when war gave him, as Commander-in-chief, the right to use negroes in battle, he used them on behalf of their own freedom, and the nation's. *That he has not compromised*, but kept clear the issues. He used opportunities which others would have abused. His *power* consisted in this, that his whole life was consistent with itself, and that his official acts were not too advanced for the nation,—that is, for success. The man who could wait till abolition became possible, aud when possible, could say, "I should deserve to be damned in time and eternity, if I receded from this,"—That is the man for the crisis.

But naturally and necessarily as these things have seemed to come to pass, there were agencies more than human in the conflict.

The hostile elements were brought face to face. The next step must be taken. The Pause was natural, for the next step would involve the destruction of the weaker.

The result now rested neither with North nor South, save as victim or instrument of the Principles which respectively had created them.

The North was the development and creation of the Principle of Freedom, resting on its material basis of Free Labour.

The South was the creature of the principle of Oligarchy, resting on *its* material basis of Slavery.

Each was the essential and deadly foe of the other. *Each must advance over its rival or perish.*

Slaveocracy must advance into the Territories, or lose the Balance of representative and

Senate power, and become (that horror of Mr. Mill) a minority, with votes that are useless.

Democracy and free labour would naturally and certainly occupy the Northern and Central States, and the Mississippi was within the natural Boundary of its empire.

And before all things *there was the organic and indestructible unity of the American nation.*

Two courses were open to the South. To grasp at a dominion marked out by nature for free enterprise, or to look to the future development of Slavery in more Southern and appropriate latitudes.

The first was urged upon it by passion and jealousy, and Democratic alliances, and by the ferocious self-assertion and Barbarism, natural to the "Institution."

It attempted the Impossible, and relinquished the possible. For had the South really constituted a separate "*nation*," the question of Northern vote power might for the time have been disregarded.

In the real South, where there is plain speech and no scruples, these things are better understood or more clearly expressed. Governor Call, of Florida, in a long and able letter dated, Feb. 1861, after complaining of the determination of the North to circumscribe Slavery, proceeds to declare that;—

"Even if the whole American Family should not advance, the Southern division will, with the institution of African Slavery, *advance from the banks of the Rio Grande to the line under the sun,* establishing in their march the waymarks of progress, the altars of the reformed religion, the temples of a higher civilisation, a purer liberty, and a better system of human government!"—*Putman,* v. 1. p. 422.

But the Southernmost territories were not destined for Slaves or Slave barons. For their useful colonization there wanted two things—the consolidation and purification of American Democracy, and the extermination or submission of the Slaveocracy. This contest will accomplish both. Obviously,—for we venture not on prophecies, which are impious and vain,—this alternative, which the maddened South have forced so far on the country, is, after all, in view of the majestic proportions of History, and of the true perspective of events, but a faint convulsion,—a short interregnum,—a trifling parenthesis, in that mighty future which Destiny and God are unrolling for the Anglo-American nation, and for the free negro; upon the double continent and home of the People. For the White American in the North; and for the free Black American there, or perhaps in the South, under the Equator,—the empire of the Sun, and more natural home of the race.

When Secession had become a Fact, the question between North and South changed its character, and it is important to distinguish.

Prior to Secession, the question was one of Oligarchy versus Democracy.

Now it is one of a pretended Nationality, against the American Nation.

The question of ascendency was soon done with. Oligarchy could not live under the American Constitution. It cannot resist American power. It did its possible, aided by the might of the Slave interest, and by traitors under every pretence and of every shade. The result was that step by step, as the party of Freedom rose in numbers, determination, and power, so, in all save resolve, did the South decline. That is the most emphatic moral of eighty years of American History.

Oligarchy is *out* of the nation, except exactly that fraction of it implicated in material servile interests. Those interests become, however, day by day more circumscribed; and they are but those of a faction.

The question henceforward is one of Nationality, and we shall show in the chapter headed RECONSTRUCTION, the wisdom, the strength, the conservative and re-creative energies that reside in a free Republic; as we have shown in the pamphlet called "THE FALSE NATION"* what chance *it* had in the home and Continent of the People.

"Re-construction" completes the "Making of the Nation," and its union, more perfect, and nobly planned, with Democracy.

"The False Nation," thus applied to the case of the South those inexorable laws of political science, according to which nations do live and die;—

"If the South stand against the North, it must stand either as an *Oligarchic* nation, or a *Republican* nation. The former is impossible, and the latter a contradiction in terms. A Republican nation it could not become without "casting out its oligarchy," and coalescing with the American Republic—one and indivisible, and with which (having then as a nation no single item of difference)

* Stanford, August, 1864.

it must necessarily assimilate. The process would consist in unmaking all the habits, manners, customs, associations, and principles of the ruling class, in order to get rid of everything that could distinguish the South from the rest of the American nation. As an *oligarchic* nation it cannot stand against the free North, for the North has long been, and is, the stronger in every element of power save that of organisation, and in that it is now equal."

Tested by *Numbers*, *Policy*, *or Principle*, we get a like result as the essence of the History we have recounted.

Votes of the Free Soil party, which in 1840 were 7000; were 60,000 in 1844; 290,000 in 1848; in 1852 (the great effort for compromise) 157,000; in 1856, 1,341,812; in 1860, 1,857,610.

The *Policy* of the South sought the three-fold power of Senate-vote, Representative-vote, and Electoral-vote. It lost them all.

The *Principles* of either side are as they were. But the natural results are working out. In 1833 the legislature of Georgia offered $5000, and the Governor of Alabama $50,000, for the delivery there of Abolitionists, and now the NATION IS ABOLITIONIST, and Sherman has delivered eighty thousand abolitionists into the capital of Georgia.

Soon after war removed Slavery from the category of a Domestic, State, or municipal affair, and submitted it to national jurisdiction, the national power was used against it.

It is simply that the Republican party has become the national party. The platforms of 1856 and 1860 maintained the principles of Jefferson and of the revolutionary fathers, and declared the determination to read the Constitution as they read it. The REPUBLICAN PLATFORM of 1864 declared that *Republicanism and Slavery cannot co-exist*, and demanded the destruction of the latter. This platform was accepted by Mr. Lincoln, and its chief plank is as follows:—

"Resolved,—That as *Slavery* was the cause, and now constitutes the strength of this rebellion, and it *must be always and everywhere hostile to the principle of Republican government*, justice and the national safety *demand its utter and complete extirpation from the soil of the Republic*, and we uphold and maintain the acts and proclamations by which the Government in its own defence has aimed a death-blow at this gigantic evil. We are in favour, furthermore, of such an amendment to the Constitution, to be made by the people in conformity with its provisions, as shall terminate and for ever prohibit the existence of slavery within the limits of the jurisdiction of the United States."

§

Our plan does not permit us to detail the process by which the Republic destroys its foe. We deal with Causes and Results—with the essential principles, and their ultimate triumph.

The Truth of the North is proved by *its essential Unity*, and by the fact that the logical development of its principles is identical with their triumph.

The falsehood of the South is proved by its pretence to war for "Independence," whilst retaining a nation of slaves. It is but proved again, when it revealed its *last* meanness in proposing to make slaves fight for them without giving them their freedom.

The "Times," Nov. 19th, 1864, described a meeting worthy of especial notice, attended by some of the wealthiest and weightiest men of New York—men who three years ago were against the coercion of States, and in favour of the maintenance of Slavery as it was, but who now profess to be an embodiment of the true Democracy.

These men, and amongst them conspicuously such conservatives and aristocrats as Major-General Dix, *demand more popular institutions still*, the direct vote of the People, and a return to the spirit of 1828-32 when presidents like Jackson were chosen, not for "availability" or compromise, but for genius and character.

The re-election of Mr. Lincoln as commander-in-chief of the armies and navies of the American nation, by a *majority* nearly half as large as the whole number of votes polled at the last election by the Slave Democrat, was the sign and seal of the united will of the People.

We say then, finally, that the *very act of Secession was in fact the "casting out of Oligarchy."* It was directly caused by the declaration of the vast majority against its purposes and power. Virtually it was an act of the North,—a sufferance of the South.

It is the *Republic* that triumphs, for the Republic is abolitionist, and the abolitionists are the Republic.

And what of the principle of Oligarchy? It has been the occasion of a movement that will destroy slavery, that has made freedom consistent with itself, and every individual of the Republic politically free and equal. That creates for the nation a true unity, by making of its men true units. That has removed for ever that great national danger, a clashing of State and national Sovereignties. Oligarchy unmade itself, and has been "the making of the American nation and Democracy."

America is one in History,—one in her graduated self-Government, local and general,—one in her water and mountain system,—one in Boundary,—one in the two-fold unity of *national* and *popular* Sovereignty,—of Industrial Freedom, and centralised Government,—one in Religion,—one in Will,—one in her Fusion of races,—one in Ideas, Interests, and Civilisation.

In that only item in respect of which she was *not* one,—this war will have completed her Unity.

Slavery introduced a barbarous code and system,—an alien and perverse element. The North has cast it out, and is closing in healthy granulations round the wound that war has lanced and opened.

The Union must have been restored,—by war or by peace. By war, with or without temporary Disunion; or by peace, through a Free Labour Propagandism.

Either way, Secession and Oligarchy go out, and the nation and Republicanism remain.

It was De Tocqueville's main position that *the Republican form of Government was more deeply rooted even than the Union.* That Republicanism was the natural state of the Americans, and that *their strongest passion was for equality.*

The game of Slavery being played *out*, now that we are come to the last move, let us review the seven stages of the contest:

Ist. England encourages the Slave trade in the Colonies, and the Fathers of the Republic anticipate and provide for the extinction of Slavery, but recognise it as a fact.*

2nd. England must have cotton. No Anglo-Indian Statesmen exist. The South gets a stupendous monopoly, *slightly* tempered, occasionally, by Indian cotton. Hence *a money power, a policy, and a sectional Slaveholding interest in the South.*

3rd. The South fights for States, and loses.

4th. Losing that, and with it the national executive and administrative power, its next move is to *extend and consolidate sectional power.* It seeks on the plea of popular sovereignty, to get it enacted that each territory or State may choose or refuse Slavery for itself, whether North or South of the compromise line,—it being understood by Slaveholders, that while a given region remained territory, the Slaves would be introduced, and once introduced, no State acts could well be passed or enforced to turn them out. On this issue John Brown and the free emigrants' societies beat them. The "Squatter sovereigns" go for freedom. The South is also beaten in California, and loses all hold on the Pacific.

* In the words of John Quincy Adams, as chairman of a Committee in 1844, in his report to Congress;—"The Declaration of Independence constituted *a sacred pledge in the name of God,* solemnly given by each State, to abolish slavery soon as practicable, and to substitute freedom in its place."

5th. The Dred Scott case is to remedy all failures, by giving masters power to take slaves *anywhere*. The Supreme Court rules, in effect, that negroes are not men.

6th. It is found that though Slavery be taken,—forced, into the territories, it does not pay, and will not live there. The temperate zone, and a propagandism of freedom, fight against it.

7th. The Dred Scott heresy being useless, and Squatter sovereignty a mockery,—there being yet territory enough for more than twenty new States, which would go for freedom, the South now,—the set time foretold by Calhoun having fully come,—with perfect logic, and as much statesmanship as *can* be used for evil, sets itself to force on the *last* alternative. There would be thirteen millions of negroes by A.D. 1900. Virginia, with its great breeding aristocracy, its vast stake in slave property, and its strategic lines of mountain and river—Virginia would be the outwork. Mexico would take the new Slave empire to the Pacific, denied it by California. Panama would command the commerce of both oceans, and might dictate alliances,—and from the Potomac to Panama, the most "enlightened" and resolute despotism, the strongest and intensest oligarchy of the world, with the torrid zone for its helper, and blacks from the thirteen millions* for its battalions, might try, for the last time, the question,—whether man has

* As we have seen, p. 370, *if contact with free labour could but be avoided*, the Slaves might be increased to forty millions without danger to the Whites.

rights, history a meaning, or the world a government!

It is true, there were a few things against the success of this project. The great river cuts it in twain, and between the river and Panama Napoleon placed his legions, nor could the South have prevailed against them. Yet the Slave empire, were it ever to exist, must *begin* at the Mississippi; for northwards, Slavery cannot live, and without Slavery, Oligarchy in America cannot continue. Against all the stupendous policy and unique determination of the South, let *this* be remembered,—that, apart from Slavery and Oligarchy, there existed no basis for a separate Southern nationality,—and that without Slavery, Oligarchy would soon fail in the Gulf States, though a phantom nationality were erected there to-morrow.

This war *for* Slavery,—that was "to rend God's moral Government from turret to foundation,"—has worked out remorselessly for the South the Logic of its suicide. The South turned from no foe. It rejected no weapon. It denied no conclusions. Drunk with blasphemies, it challenged every power, whether of Earth or Heaven, that could contend against it for the right. In its despair, it allied itself with the torch, the bowl, the dagger, and the plague,—till gibbets creaked with its reputation, and hemp was heavy with its honour.

Its work has been so thorough,—its lesson so well taught,—its moral so clear, that there will need for all time no further repetition or enforcement.

The mean whites contended that each man might "whop his own nigger." The negro has been drilled and disciplined to beat *him!* The Slaveholder intrigued for forty years, and has fought for four, to make his title sure to his property, —but alas riches have wings, and the chattel has cut and run! The Slave Barons would establish their "institution,"—and it is proposed to give to the subjects of it, Freedom and their master's Land! The leaders of the rebellion would have fame,—and are damned to it everlastingly.

The South fought against Destiny, Nature, and God. But America is worthy and able to enact the Law. The secret of its power was formulated by Aristotle even before the Christian era:—

"*If the Popular party exceed more in Quantity, than they are excelled in Quality, Democracy must prevail.*"

And again in the words of Fichte:—

"A regard for their own security compels all Free States to transform all around them into Free States like themselves; and thus for the sake of their own welfare *to extend the empire of culture over barbarism, of freedom over slavery.*"

And HE, who rolls rivers, orders climates, and laid the foundations of the continent, has, as far as we can trace his workings, caused all things, from the foolishness of the Stuarts, to the foolishness of Davis and Lee, to work together for the "Making of the People's Nation."

BOOK IV.

CHAPTER I.

RIGHT OF SECESSION.

CHAPTER II.

RECONSTRUCTION.

"*The States* have their status in the Union, and they *have no other legal status if they break from this.* They can only do so against law by revolution. The Union, and not themselves separately, procured their independence and their liberty, by conquest, or purchase. The Union gave each of them whatever independence and liberty it had. The Union is older than any of the States, and, in fact, it created them States. Originally some dependent colonies made the Union, and in turn the Union threw off their old dependence for them, and made them States. Such as they are, not one of them even had a State constitution independent of the Union."

LINCOLN, Message to Congress, July, 1861.

"*The proper Federal Union* is where two or more States, having their separate Governments for all domestic purposes, are united by a *central Government,* which regulates their mutual relations as members of a political community, but does not interfere with the functions of the several Governments, and their authority over the individuals which are their subjects, *unless in so far as those functions, and that authority may affect the Federal relation, &c.* * * * *There must be certain things* laid down, certain rights conferred, certain provisions made, *which cannot be altered without universal consent,* or a consent so general as to be deemed equivalent for all practical purposes to the consent of the whole."

BROUGHAM, on the United States Government.

"*The Congress,* whenever two-thirds of both Houses shall deem it necessary, *shall propose amendments to this constitution,* or, on the application of the Legislatures of two-thirds of the several States, *shall call a convention for proposing amendments,*" &c.—*Art. V. United States Constitution.*

"Nor shall any alteration at any time hereafter be made in any of them, *unless such alteration be agreed to in a Congress of the United States;* and be afterwards confirmed by the legislatures of every State."—*Art. XIII. of* CONFEDERATION.

"No convention of the People shall be called, unless by the concurrence of two-thirds of both branches of the whole representation.

"No part of this constitution shall be altered, unless a Bill to alter the same shall have been read three times in the House, three in the Senate, and agreed to by two-thirds of both branches; neither shall any alterations take place until the Bill so agreed to be published three months previous to a new election." &c.— *Constitution of* SOUTH CAROLINA. *See also similar provisoes in Constitutions of Georgia, Louisiana, &c.*

CHAPTER I.

'RIGHT' OF SECESSION.

CONTENTS.

"The South cannot submit to a President who is not their devoted servant. Unless every power in the Constitution is to be strained in order to promote the progress of Slavery, they will not remain in the Union; they will not wait to see whether they are injured, but resent the first check to their onward progress as an intolerable injury. This, then, is the result of the history of Slavery. It began as a tolerated, it has ended as an aggressive institution, and, *if it now threatens to dissolve the Union, it is not because it has anything to fear* for that which it possesses already, *but because it has received a check to its hopes of* FUTURE ACQUISITION."—*Times*, Jan. 7, 1861.

"The Monster of State Sovereignty."—*Washington.*

"The establishment of a constituted anarchy."—*Hegel.*

THE glory of all the American State Constitutions was, that in constituting and organising the power that had conquered Freedom, they enunciated the principles that should perpetuate it amongst their descendants. The infamy of Secession was, that while it destroyed order by rebellion, and freedom by Slavery, it dared also to do this in the sacred names of Freedom and Independence.

If the South was "in its right," the right must be either that of *revolution*, or of *amendment* and alteration under the Constitution.

The South saw this intuitively, and the broad basis of logic upon which the great fighting South went, was, in fact, a kind of bastard "right of revolution," professing to rest upon necessity and nature.—"Negroes are property, we have a right to protect property, and to extend it." The North denied that right. Hence the war.

There is no flaw in this logic, save in the major premiss, no fault in the building, but in the foundation. If negroes be chattels, the South is right, —if not, not.

But there is a third "basis of right," now discovered. It is not in the Constitution. It is not in the nature or necessity of things. It is a right to secede, supposed to subsist in certain States, notwithstanding no such right was reserved; notwithstanding the same States entered into a solemn covenant to "form a nation," the Union of which was to be "perpetual;" notwithstanding many clauses and undertakings in the Constitutions of these States, which are incompatible with Secession,—either the fact of it, or the mode in which it was attempted.

But we must not anticipate. It will not take long, even *selon les regles*, to hunt this vermin to its hole. The South stood upon its so-called "rights," upon its unity, and upon its force, and proclaimed before the world the necessary and natural inequality of the negro. As for this doctrine of Secession, we suppose some people believe in it, and it requires a short notice.

§

The national Constitution declares that it is constituted by the People the supreme law of the land;—that the Union is to be perpetual, &c.; and it provides a mode of amendment.

The State Constitutions attribute to the People the supreme power; and those of South Carolina, Georgia, Alabama, Missouri, Mississippi, Louisiana, Tennessee, and others, contain distinct regulations as to the mode of alteration of the Governments of those States.

Prima facie it follows, that neither the National, nor State Constitutions, were intended to be altered, save by the means and in the modes provided. It follows, also, that any argument for a violent or informal abrogation of the first, would apply with equal force to a violent and informal abrogation of the last. If "the States" can secede from the Nation, in any other way than by the defined amendment, then it follows, that the individuals or the townships which constitute the States, can also, in their turn, secede from the States. In other words, that the nation can constitutionally reconstitute the whole State organisation of the South.

Moreover, certain of the States' Constitutions asserted the right of *the People* to "alter, reform, or abolish" the form of Government, in certain cases stated. This right being asserted in the State Constitutions, and not asserted in the National Constitution, would so far apply rather against the former than the latter. But such right is, in fact, one of the fundamental rights of human nature, and is simply recognised as such by the form of amendment provided. And inasmuch as the American Constitution has for its constituents every individual in the nation, it follows, unless the contrary be distinctly proved, that the right to "alter, reform, and abolish it" does not belong to the States, *but to the Nation.* Nor can it exist at all, until, 1st, *the right of amendment has been denied;* and, 2nd, *the fact of despotism proved.* Then, and not before, could the "natural right" of revolution, accrue.

Secession is, in fact, anarchy. It has been well said, that if it means anything, it means a deed by which a State loses all advantages of the Union, without being released from any of its duties to it.

The State constitutions declared the People the source of all power, and the People of the United States had adopted a national Constitution, and assumed and declared a national character. The popular Sovereignty is, therefore, thenceforth pledged to the national Sovereignty and Constitution, which could not be assailed by the States, or even by the People, except through the recognised mode of amendment.

The second of the articles of confederation of 1778, retained to "each *State*" its sovereignty, &c.

This was the vital defect. The Convention of 1787 was assembled to cure it. During the debates *Madison* said,—

"Some contend that the States are sovereign, while in fact they are only political societies. There is a gradation of power in all societies, from the lowest corporation to the highest sovereign. The States never possessed the essential rights of

Sovereignty. The States at present are only great corporations, having the power of making by-laws, and these are effectual only if they are not contradictory to the general confederation."

And *Washington*, in his letter of the 17th Sept. 1787, declares,—

"It is obviously impracticable, in the Federal Government of these States, to secure all rights of independent sovereignty to each, and yet provide for the interest and safety of all."

The Statesmen of that age would allow no doubt or reservation upon that subject, directly or by inference. New York actually proposed to withdraw within a certain number of years, if the amendments proposed by the New York Convention were not adopted. Hamilton declared the reservation was inconsistent with the Constitution, and *would not be a ratification.* He wrote to Madison for his opinion. Madison wrote, that such an adoption with reservation would not make New York a member of the Union, and that she could not be received on that basis. "The Constitution requires an adoption *in toto* and for ever." "Influence is not Government," says Washington; and Madison, writing to Randolph from New York, April 8th, 1787, said—

"I hold it as a fundamental point, that the *individual independence of the States is utterly irreconcileable with the idea of an aggregate Sovereignty.* . . . Let the national Government have a negative in all cases whatsoever on the legislative acts of the States. . . . This, I conceive, to be essential, and the least possible abridgment of the State Sovereignties. Without such a defensive power, every positive power that can be given on paper will be unavailing."

Thus we see that the centralisation realised in the national Constitution fell far short of that recommended by the Statesmen of the period.

§

The original Seceding States were the seven Cotton States, South Carolina, Georgia, Alabama, Florida, Mississippi, Louisiana, Texas. Two months after, Virginia joined. North Carolina, Tennessee, and Arkansas, were thus dragged in, and afterwards, Kentucky and Missouri were impudently claimed.

"Right" of Secession involves four questions;—

1st. Had the seceding States an absolute covenant right to secede, *ex mero motu?*

2nd. If they had such right originally, has it lapsed?

3rd. If their right was not absolute, what were the conditions of its exercise?

4th. Have they observed them?

The replies to these questions can hardly be mistaken.

First. The *seceding States* had never an *absolute* right to *secede. Such* right was not even claimed or asserted by the States themselves, in their constitutions, as we shall show presently.

Secondly. If, technically, they had such a right, do eighty years of change, during which the States have become consolidated into a nation,—does this lapse of time, and entire change of circumstance, make no difference? If six or seven years forclose a debt, shall all that is meant by Unity and Nationality, throughout three generations, foreclose nothing?

Third, and Fourth. The conditions of rightful "*abolition, reform, or alteration*" (not secession), were six, as follow, and were so stated by the Constitutions, &c. of the States themselves.

(A.) Certain States *did* assert for the People, an absolute right to abolish a positively bad Government, *but*, with two exceptions, *those States were not the States lately in rebellion.*

(B.) Certain States asserted a right to reform, &c. *if the proper objects of Government* were *not* secured by the Government. Amongst these States are four of the seceding States. The answer is threefold; —First, that this right applies as much (or more) against the Governments of the States, in whose constitutions it is asserted, as against the national Government. Second, that the "proper objects" *were* secured by the North. Third, that the very secession ordinances, the declared intentions, and further, the raison d'être itself of the South, affirm a principle of Government, not only *not* "proper," but infamous and destructive.

(C.) A certain State,—North Carolina, ceded the territory, which afterwards became the State of Tennessee, *upon an openly immoral condition*,—upon condition of the unconditional perpetuation of Slavery. *That condition was void ab initio.*

(D.) Certain States undoubtedly joined the Union upon the implied *understanding* that their fair rights as Slaveholders should be respected. But to claim from a nation, "rights" that would destroy that nation is vain and contradictory. The question, therefore, is, "has the nation given these States a fair chance of gradually lessening, and ultimately extinguishing their interest in Slavery?" The answer to this and to them is, that their "rights" had not only a fair, but an unfair, chance,—that Slavery has grown more dangerous, inveterate, powerful, and desperate, year by year, and that now the question is—Slavery or the nation? Obviously, no nation ever would or could contract to commit suicide.

(E.) These rights were generally asserted on behalf of "*the People*," the community, or the majority, and the majority of the People in the South pronounced against Secession. Of the Southern votes alone, the Slave Democrat only polled 25,000 more than the Union candidate, without reckoning Lincoln's votes, or those of the squatter Democrat Douglas, the third Southern candidate. The actual secession, therefore, not only defies the national Sovereignty, but tramples on that very *popular* Sovereignty so boastfully relied on to prove this very "right of secession."

(F.) A certain delay of three months, and certain other delays, constitute part of the "State" regulations for reform or amendment. These were not complied with.

§

It is, indeed, abundantly easy to prove that Southern Secession violates every Law, Right, Principle, and necessity, upon which communities are based, or even social existence is possible.

The question is, "Had the South the right to secede for Slavery, and under the actual circumstances?"

The question of the abstract right of Secession

under some possible circumstances that have not existed, is a very nice question for "vindicators" of the South, provided they believe that the public can see no difference between the practical and the speculative,—between Statesmanship and Hair-splitting.

The most practical of all questions must be treated in a practical manner. There is a certain line of argument, not without weight, to show that the Sovereign States had the right, according to the original compact, to secede upon due occasion.

But it is maintained that they possessed that right, upon undue occasion, or without occasion, and the *claimants* have appealed to the moral sense of the world, and the world must judge what is, and is not, justifying cause and occasion.

It were to amuse or to insult the reader to argue that any States had the right, from mere whim, caprice, or phantasy, to dismember a nation, first solemnly formed, constituted, and compacted with all the moral and mental forces of the continent.

Besides, of two things, one. The separate constitutions were before or after the national Constitution, and they agree or they disagree with it. If before and disagreeing, then their ratification voids the disagreement. If after and disagreeing, then the national compact, being with the whole, and for national consideration, voids every subsequent private compact which any State might choose to make within itself. *The People that made the nation must be appealed to, before the nation can be unmade.*

But the essential and ultimate revolt,—revolt against God and man alike,—is the revolt against that ever-approaching union of Freedom and Law, towards which all civilisation and progress tend. A denial of, and a shrinking from, those political conclusions, which will now be *tried out* in America. Wherein all should become self-restrained, and all politically equal, where Conservatism should become Democratic, and Democracy Conservative. For the climax of all Histories, constitutions, laws, progresses, — the very meaning, politically, of God in the Race, is it not *the realisation of Truth*,—" Truth," so far, " made flesh," *in the myriad-folded national life?* The truth,—the political and social truth, not talked about, and seen from afar, but realised, enacted, and lived.

§

What then were the *actual circumstances* under which the right of Secession is maintained?

They were the claim of the South to extend Slavery into the territories, and by the Dred Scott law, into every Free State also.

Upon the denial of these "rights," the South seceded, and upon these questions the "right" of the South must stand or fall.

Let us now see how the text of the Southern Constitutions justifies the much urged "right of Secession."

And here we take all those States created up to 1833. And referring back to the preceding pages, we may say they have been written in vain, if it be not quite clear that without these claims of Slavery extension the Slave South could not continue to exist at all. This is quite sufficient to demonstrate the wrong of the South *ab initio.* Slavery could not exist except on the life of Freedom. It therefore made the attempt to appropriate and sequester the territory, or to destroy the Constitution of the Union. Failing that, it seceded. So far from possessing any right to attack thus the life of the North, it clearly had no right even to insist on retaining the cause of national weakness within its own borders.

MAINE. 1819. "They (*the people*) have an indefeasible right to institute Government, or to alter, reform, or *totally change* the same, *when their safety and happiness require it.*" Art. 1, Sec. 1.

The Governor * * shall be Commander in chief, * * * of the militia, except when called into the actual service of the *United States.*" Art 5, Sec. 7.

MASSACHUSETTS. 1779. * * "*Natural rights, and the blessings of life,* * * and whenever these great objects are not obtained, the *People* have a *right to alter the Government.*" Preamble to constitution.

NEW HAMPSHIRE. 1792. "Government, instituted for the common benefit, protection, and security of the whole, &c., whenever the ends of Government are prevented, or *public liberty manifestly endangered, and all other means of redress are ineffectual, the people* may, and of right ought to reform the old, or establish a new Government." Part. i. art. 10.

VERMONT. 1793. "That all men are born equally free, &c., *therefore* (prohibition of Slavery or Slave Trade) Ch. I. art. 1. Government for common benefit, &c. The community hath an indefeasible right to reform or alter Government." Ch. I. art. 7.

CONNECTICUT. 1818. "The People * * at all times an indefeasible right to alter their form of Government in such manner as they may think expedient." Art. 1, sec. 2.

PENNSYLVANIA. 1790. The same as Connecticut. Art. 9, sec. 2.

NEW YORK and NEW JERSEY. No reserved rights.

DELAWARE. 1831. "And they (the people) may for this end (happiness) as circumstances require, alter their constitution of Government." Constitution, first clause.

MARYLAND. 1812. Same as New Hampshire.

VIRGINIA. 1776. "*That all men by nature are equally free, &c.*, and have certain inherent rights of which they cannot by any compact deprive their posterity. Government instituted for common benefit, protection, and security of the People, &c., and when found inadequate or contrary to these purposes, *a* MAJORITY *of the community*, hath an indefeasible right to reform, alter, or abolish it, &c." Sec. 1 and 3. Bill of rights. "That no man or set of men are entitled to exclusive or separate privileges, &c. That no free Government can be preserved but by frequent recurrence to *fundamental principles*." Sec. 15.

1830. "No person Governor, unless a native citizen of the *United States*." Art. 4, Constitution.

NORTH CAROLINA. 1776. "All political power vested in and derived from the People only; no exclusive privileges." Sec. 1—3. *No right to alter national Government reserved.*

SOUTH CAROLINA. 1798. "The Governor shall be commander in chief of the army and navy of this State, and of the militia *except* when they shall be called into the actual *service of the United States*." Art. 2, sec. 6.

"All power is originally vested in the People, &c. Trial by Jury, and liberty of the press, shall be for ever inviolably preserved." Art. 9, sec. 1 and 6.

No right to alter national Government reserved. Also Art. 11 imposes (as do other constitutions), certain forms and delays on the discussion of any project for altering the constitution, and declares that such alteration shall not take place until the Bill so agreed to, be *published three months, &c.*

GEORGIA. 1798. "No Governor who shall not have been a *citizen of the United States* twelve years. Art. 2, sec. 3. Freedom of press and trial by Jury inviolate. Art. 4, sec. 5. No Slave Trade after 1798. Art. 4, sec. 11.

No right to alter national Government reserved.

Same punishment for killing or dismembering slave, as white. Art. 4, sec. 12.

KENTUCKY. 1799. "The Governor shall be a citizen of the United States." Art. 3, sec. 4.

He shall be Commander-in-Chief of the army and navy, and of the militia, except when they shall be called into the service of the United States. Sec. 8.

That all power is inherent in the people: for the advancement of these ends (peace, safety, and happiness), they (the people) have indefeasible right to alter, reform, or abolish their Government, in such manner as they may think proper. Art. 10, sec. 3.

TENNESSEE. 1796. " Governor shall be Commander-in-Chief of, &c. except when troops shall be called into the service of the United States." Art. 2, sec. 5.

Same right as Kentucky to " alter, reform, or abolish the Government," for the sake of "*peace, safety, and happiness.*" Art. 11, sec. 1.

That no citizen shall be compelled to bear arms provided he will pay an equivalent. Sec. 28.

OHIO. 1802. " All men equally free. To effect these ends (liberty and independence), they have complete power to alter, reform, or abolish Government, whenever they may deem it necessary." Art. 8, sec. 1. Slavery prohibited. Sec. 2.

INDIANA. 1816. Same right to " alter or reform." Art. 1, sec. 2.

LOUISIANA. 1812. Government formed " to secure rights of life, liberty, and property." Preamble: " No representative, *unless* a free white male *citizen of the United States.*" Art. 2, sec. 4.

Every free white male, citizen of the United States, &c. shall enjoy the rights of an elector. Governor shall be a citizen of the United States. Art. 3, sec. 4.

" *For ever disclaiming* all right to the waste or unappropriated lands in territory of New Orleans. The same shall *be and remain at sole disposition of the United States.*

MISSISSIPPI. 1817. Government formed " to secure rights of life, liberty, and property." That " general, great, and essential principles of liberty and free Government" be established, therefore:

" All political powers in the people.*** Indefeasible right to alter or abolish Government in such manner as they may think expedient." Art. 1, sec. 2. Trial by Jury inviolate. Sec. 28.

Representative, citizen of United States. Art. 3, sec. 7. Senator, citizen of United States. Art. 3, sec. 14.

Governor, commander-in-chief, &c. except when troops shall be called into the service of the United States. Art. 4, sec. 5. Waste or unappropriated lands in the State *for ever disclaimed*, and shall be and remain at the *sole disposition of the United States,** and that the river Mississippi*, and the navigable rivers and waters leading into the same, or into the Gulf of Mexico, *shall be common highways, and for ever free*, as well to the inhabitants of this State, as to other *citizens of the United States*, and this ordinance is *irrevocable* without the consent of the United States. Militia to be organised, &c. in manner *not incompatible with constitution and laws of the United States.*

ILLINOIS. 1818. "No slavery to be introduced. Art. 6, sec. 1. Government for peace, safety, and happiness of people. Art. 8, sec. 2.

ALABAMA. 1819. Government formed "to secure rights of life, liberty, and property." Preamble: "That principles of liberty and free government be established."—"People indefeasible right to alter, reform, or abolish government." Art. 1, sec. 2.

No representative, unless citizen of United States. Same as to electors. Art. 3, sec. 4 and 5. Governor, native citizen United States, and Commander in chief, &c. except when they shall be called into service of the U. S. Art. 4, sec. 4 and 6.

Militia to be organised and disciplined, not incompatibly with constitution of United States. Art. 4, sec. 1.

Waste lands, &c. at disposition of United States; *all navigable waters* within this State shall *for ever remain public highways, free to the citizens of the United States*, and this ordinance *irrevocable* without consent of United States.

MISSOURI. 1820. Same provisions as to altering Government when necessary to safety and happiness; as to electors, representatives, Governor, Commander-in-Chief; as to freedom of Mississippi, and navigable rivers leading into it. *State never to interfere with the primary disposal of the soil of the United States.* Laws to be passed securing humanity to slaves, and abstinence from injury to their life or limb.

This summary suggests the question, whether

the gentlemen who assert the right of Secession upon the State constitutions, have ever read them, and if they have, with what *intention* they make such assertions *respecting States that reserved no power of Secession*, or that reserved it only on the condition of insupportably bad government.

§

And going back from the STATE CONSTITUTIONS, to the RATIFICATIONS of the National Constitution; and from them to the NATIONAL CONSTITUTION; and from that to the RESOLUTIONS of Independence; and from them to the DECLARATION of Independence; and from that to the BRITISH CONSTITUTION; and from that to the rights of HUMAN NATURE, upon which all the philosophy of the Revolution was avowedly based,—what say all these? We take them in their order.

HUMAN NATURE declares, as the British Constitution, the Resolutions, and the Declaration, declare, that men are equal in their natural rights before God, and as towards their fellows.

The South herein gave them all the lie, and was itself essentially a liar from the beginning.

And the BRITISH CONSTITUTION, what says that? We have already seen what it says, and the customs and rights founded upon it are as Penn expounded them:—

"No man in England is born Slave to another, neither hath one right to inherit the sweat of the others brow, or reap the benefit of his labour but by consent.

"So sacred were the fundamental rights of the People reputed in the days of Henry III., that not to continue and confirm them, was to affront God, and to damn the souls of the King's progenitors and successors, and to depress the church and deprave the realm."

"And twice every year, the Bishops should pronounce the greater excommunication agaist the infringers of the great Charter, though it were but in word or counsel, for so saith the statute."

The South, that stood, forsooth, on its "rights," denied every basis or authority from which right can be deduced.

The British Constitution declares that no man in England shall be enslaved. The South enslaves a nation.

British usage declares the sacredness of freedom. The South sold all free niggers who did not promptly leave, and hangs "home made Yankees."

British birthrights declare that men shall be tried *by their peers* and by a jury. In the case of Welshmen the jury was of old half composed of Welshmen. The South rejects Negro evidence, and tries Negroes by Slaveholders.

And yet the South first based its existence as part of the American nation, upon necessity and nature, upon the "rights of British Colonists and subjects."

And what say the "Resolutions of Independence?"

They base their action and their right upon human nature, and the British Constitution.

They claimed for all "inhabitants." Are negroes "inhabitants"? Is their nature "human"?

And the "Declaration"

It says, "all men are free and equal." If negroes

are not "men," then Southerners are *beasts*, for their blood is in the veins of a large proportion of the four millions of Slaves.

And the CONSTITUTION? It was formed *by the people*, for a *more perfect Union*. And the South attempted, against the vote of its own majority, to destroy this Union!

And the RATIFICATIONS of the Constitution?

We have already seen that the ratification of New York would have been rejected as no ratification, had it been conditional.

§

The Constitution of 1787 was *the organic and fundamental law of the Commonwealth*. It was not a "compact," for there were *no parties* to it. There was but one party,—the People.

The Constitution was neither drawn up, nor promulgated, nor ratified, nor acceded to by "States" as such.

The conditions on which the Southern People ratified may be fairly shewn by quoting Mr. Nichol, the latest ultra Secesh advocate. He quotes (p. 308, v. 2.) the declarations of Maine, Michigan, Virginia, and New York for the right of Secession. Maine and Michigan asserted the right of the people to alter and abolish their Government "*when their safety and happiness, and the public good required it.*" And Virginia and New York, in ratifying, declare in the first case that the State, in the second that the People, could resume the powers of government "*whenever perverted to their injury and oppression*," or "whenever it shall become *necessary to their happiness*." And from these quotations Mr. Nichol thinks he proves *the absolute right* to thrust aside the Constitutional proviso for amendment, and to secede for the purpose of perpetuating and extending Slavery! He also asks "can inconsistency and falsehood go further" than for these States to join in forcing the Northern Government back on their sister States!!

For the same purpose he also quotes, (p. 311), the Virginia resolution of 1798, "almost identical" with the Kentucky resolution of 1797, and which declared "that in the case of a *deliberate, palpable, and dangerous exercise* of powers not granted by said compact, the States should "interfere for *arresting* the progress of the *evil*, and for maintaining, *within their respective limits, the authority, rights, and liberties, appertaining to them*."

And so, the right to *secure* safety, happiness, and public good; to *resist* injury and oppression, warrant a war to perpetuate fugitive Slave laws, and to force Slavery on the territories! To "*arrest the progress of the evil*," is synonymous with *extending Slavery*, and to "maintain *within their respective limits*, their authority, rights and liberty," means the same thing!

This is truly the *reductio ad absurdum* of State rights, and of Secesh, and it is, perhaps, as well that Mr. Nichol has lived forty years to set it forth.

Granting the validity of the "reservation," and waving all other objections, they one and all claimed it *upon a contingency that has not arisen*. That contingency was bad Government. The occasion of Secession was that the principles of Freedom, or good Government, were about to be completed and made universal.

The Declaration justified revolt by Despotism, and the very words in most cases, the exact sense, in all, of the intense national feeling against the inveterate tyranny of the English Oligarchy, were copied into the constitutions or ratifications, to perpetuate the remembrance of the rights of Freedom.

Democracy formulates its protest against oligarchy and prerogative, and, lo! the intensest Oligarchic despotism in the world, fits and forges the formulum into a protest against the completion of Freedom, and the establishment of Democracy.

Really, the only answer to this should be:—"Stop thief! stop thief!"

All goes to this, ARE NEGROES MEN? In the only Democracy the world ever saw,—Is a *nation* to be denied the primary rights of manhood?

§

We say then that Secession was not right, but wrong—because:—

1st. The terms of ratification by the Seceding States do not justify it.

2nd. The circumstances of the case condemn it.

3rd. Instincts of national preservation and life will prevent it.

4th. The South has had a fair chance of gradually ending Slavery, and has failed.

5th. The right to secede was reserved to the People, and the majority, and these voted against Secession.

6th, 7th, 8th, 9th, 10th, and 11th. Human nature, the British Constitution, the Resolutions, and the Declaration of Independence, and the Constitution, and the Ratifications, all condemn *Secession for Slavery.*

12th. Because national funds had been applied chiefly in the South.

13th. Because the State Constitutions contain irrevocable compacts with the United States, as to "Lands," "Soil," the Mississippi, &c.

14th. Because they, some of them, contain declarations that Slavery shall never be introduced; and the Dred Scott case, and the Slavery extension platforms, and Secession, &c., intend and declare the contrary.

15th. Because the Constitutions of the chief Secession States contain, as to alteration of national Government, *no reserved rights whatever!*

16th. Because the forms of alteration &c., were not complied with, and the right of amendment was not demanded.

17th. Because "the People" of 1787, are the *Nation* of 1860.

18th. Because many of the rights and privileges (press, speech, jury, &c.) guaranteed by State Constitutions to the People, have been negatived, denied, and reversed, by the necessary action of Slavery.

19. Because, as we have shown, the same interpretation of Southern Constitutions, that would justify the States in seceding from the Union, would justify the North in reconstituting the whole State organization of the South.

§

The question of the indebtedness of the South concerns the question of "right," and requires a little amplification. Brownlow (p. 234) thus puts it:—

"Ought the three rebellious States, Louisiana, Florida, and Texas, to be tolerated in their schemes of treason after costing the people of the other States *six hundred and eighteen millions of dollars?* Louisiana, purchased at $15,000,000; interest paid, $8,385,353. Florida, $5,000,000; interest paid, $1,430,000. Texas (boundary), $10,000,000; for indemnity, $10,000,000; for creditors, $7,750,000; Indian expenses, $5,000,000; navy and troops, $5,000,000; all other expenditures, $3,000,000. Mexican war, $217,175,575; soldiers' pensions, &c., $100,000,000. Florida war, $100,000,000; pensions, $7,000,000; to remove Indians, $5,000,000. For New Mexico, $15,000,000; to extinguish Indian titles, $100,000,000. Georgia, $3,082,000."

And Senator Doolittle, Dec. 1860, spoke to the same effect, as follows:—

"Your right of Secession involves the right of expulsion. Let us see how this doctrine would apply in time of war. * * * Any one of the New England States could have resolved itself out, and gone over to the enemy, * * and turned our own guns against us. But again, take it in time of peace. PENNSYLVANIA could cut off all the mail routes. So too with Illinois, we could not go to New York, except by leave of Illinois or Kentucky. How is it with FLORIDA, that has 50,000 whites? We purchased it to get rid of foreign jurisdiction—also to get possession of the Key and command the entrance to the Gulf. And now Florida attempts to resolve herself out, and take all these fortresses, which we have spent thousands of dollars to make, with all our own guns, and turn them against us. How is it with LOUISIANA? The Government of the United States upon principles of great national policy, purchased it from the Emperor of France at an expense of $15,000,000, to obtain possession of the great valley of the Mississippi, and above all things to hold the mouth of that river. How has it been with TEXAS? The result of her annexation brought the Mexican war, which cost us 40,000 lives and nearly $100,000,000."

To this may be added that the Mississippi is the highway for ten States, and touches on thirteen,—that the secession of Louisiana cut Texas off from the Union, and that Louisiana had cost 60 million francs and many years protection by the sugar duty of about seven millions of dollars annually: also the mails in the seven slave States, cost two millions of dollars annually above the receipts.

Mr. Everett also states nearly the same facts. But he adds that:

"A great part of the military establishment of the United States has been incurred in defending the SOUTH-WESTERN FRONTIER. If to all this expenditure, we add that of the forts, the navy yards, the court houses, the custom houses, &c. in these regions, *five hundred millions of dollars* of the public funds, of which at least five-sixths have been levied by indirect taxation from the North and North-west, have been expended in and for the GULF STATES in this century."

§

In England, where the matter is not relegated to the logic of Bayonets, and where public morality is not violated with impunity, such works as the British Copperhead press has produced, ought to forward immensely the cause of the North.

They evince a profound political and social immorality, resting the logic of Secession, ultimately, on the theorem that right is wrong, and wrong is right—that black is white, and white black. Their right of Secession rests upon the right of Slavery; the right of Slavery rests upon the wrongs of the Slaves.

They say, almost with the clearness and sequence of a syllogism—"We reserved a right of securing good Government, *therefore* we have the right to make a Slaveholder's war upon the nation."

Mr. Williams, writing (of course) from the meridian of Constantinople (whose Sultan was lately praised as moral, because he discharged his father's old ladies), and adopting his tone to the congenial meridian of Charleston, likens "Puritanism" to "eternal punishment," calls it a "Pestilence" (p. 409), and unconsciously justifies the North, by declaring that a gradual setting free of negroes is impossible, and that slaves must for ever remain so, unless the South be exterminated. (p. 128.)

The South is now going through a course of primary instruction as to the meaning of right and wrong, and as to their consequences. Also of the meaning of "freedom, safety, and happiness," and the way to secure these good things. It has often wished itself well back, with its peculiar Institution as it was, and bitterly rues the day when it appealed to the "fundamental rights of the people."

It throws a clear light on the real moral and political situation of the South, to have these gentlemen, with all the unction and odour of Southern sanctity about them, explaining to *Englishmen*, how Slavery and Slave necessities, are identical with "freedom, safety, and happiness;" and how the great country that has gone nigh unto wholesale destruction for the sake of peace, and compromise with Slavery, has at length violated the rights of the Slaveholders, by staying—almost "on the verge."

Clearly, NO conservatism would suit these

Southern devotees, BUT A CONSERVATISM OF DESTRUCTION AND DESPAIR.

They would perpetuate in America a "*constituted anarchy*" such as Hegel lamented in Germany, and declared that the world had never seen before. They assert the position he thus denounces:—

"The position that an empire is properly a unity, a totality, a state, while yet all the relations are determined so exclusively on the principle of private right, that the privilege of all the constituent parts of that empire to act for themselves, contrarily to the interest of the whole, is guaranteed by the most inviolable sanctions."

"A State," says Burke, "ought not to be considered as nothing better than a partnership agreement in a trade of pepper and coffee, calico and tobacco, or some other such low concern, *to be taken up for a little temporary interest, and to be dissolved by a fancy* of the parties. It is to be looked upon with other reverence, because it is not a partnership in things subservient only to gross animal instincts of a temporary and perishing nature. *It is a partnership in all science, a partnership in all art, a partnership in every virtue and in all perfection, a partnership not only between those who are living, but between those who are dead, and those who are to be born.*"

CHAPTER II.

RECONSTRUCTION.

"BEHOLD THE WORLD PHŒNIX, IN FIRE CONSUMMATION AND FIRE CREATION; WIDE ARE HER FANNING WINGS; LOUD IS HER DEATH-MELODY, OF BATTLE THUNDERS AND FALLING TOWNS; SKYWARD LASHES THE FUNERAL FLAME, ENVELOPING ALL THINGS; IT IS THE DEATH-BIRTH OF A WORLD."

"This nation under God shall have a new birth of Freedom, and Government of the People by the People and for the People shall not perish from the earth."—*Lincoln*.

"To realise these grades of national progress is the boundless impulse of the world-spirit,—the goal of its irresistible urging."
Hegel.

"They meant *to set up a standard maxim of free Society*, which should be familiar to all, and though never perfectly attained, constantly approximated, and thereby *constantly spreading and deepening its influences, and augmenting the happiness and value of life to all people of every colour, everywhere*."—*Lincoln*.

"The incurable defect of all former *Federal* Governments is, that they were Sovereignties over Sovereignties."—*Chancellor Kent*.

"FREE LABOUR has, at last, apprehended its rights, its interests, its powers, its destiny, and is organising itself to assume the Government of the Republic. It will meet you everywhere, in the Territories and out of them, wherever you may go to extend slavery. It has driven you back in California and Kansas. It will invade you soon in Delaware, Maryland, Virginia, Missouri, and Texas. It will meet you in Arizona, in Central America, and even in Cuba. You may, indeed, get a start under or near the Tropics, but it will be for a short time. Even there, you will found States for free labour to occupy. * * * The interests of the white race demand the ultimate emancipation of all men. The White man needs this continent to labour on. His head is clear, his arm is strong, and his necessities are fixed. He must and will have it."—*Seward*.

"We need no safeguard. *Not only the inevitable, but the best, power on this side of the ocean, is the unfettered average common sense of the masses.* * * You may sigh for a strong Government, anchored in the convictions of past centuries, and able to protect the minority against the majority, *able to defy the ignorance, the mistake, or the passion, as well as the high purpose of the present hour.* * * The fact remains, that *we are launched on the ocean of an unchained democracy, with no safety but in the instinctive love of right in the popular heart.* * * *Trust the people with the greatest questions*, and *you secure, not perfect, but the best possible institutions.* Now, my idea of American civilisation is, that it is a second part, a repetition of *that same sublime confidence in the public conscience and the public thought*, that made the groundwork of Grecian Democracy."—*Wendell Phillips*.

"The Home of Freedom disenthralled, regenerated, enlarged and perpetuated."—*Lincoln.*

"Behold now this vast City; *a City of refuge, the Mansion House of Liberty*, encompassed and surrounded with his protection.

The shop of war hath not there more anvils and hammers making, to fashion out the plates and instruments *of armed justice in defence of beleaguered truth*, than there be pens and heads there, sitting by their studious lamps, musing, *searching, revolving new notions and ideas wherewith to present*, as with their homage and their fealty, *the approaching reformation.* Others as fast reading, trying all things, assenting to the force of reason and convincement.

What could a man require more from a nation so pliant and so prone to seek after knowledge? *What wants there to such a towardly and pregnant soil, but wise and faithful labourers*, to make a knowing people, a nation of prophets, of sages, and of worthies? We reckon more than five months yet to harvest; there need not be five weeks, had we but eyes to lift up, the fields are white already. Where there is much desire to learn, there of necessity will be much arguing, much writing, many opinions; for opinion in good men is but knowledge in the making. * * * * *

I doubt not, if some great and worthy stranger should come among us, wise to discern the mould and temper of a people, and how to govern it, observing *the high hopes and aims, the diligent alacrity of our extended thoughts and reasonings in the pursuance of Truth and Freedom*, but that he would cry out as Pyrrhus did, admiring the Roman docility and courage, if such were my Epirots, I would not despair *the greatest design that could be attempted to make a church or kingdom happy.* Yet these are the men cried out against for schismatics and sectaries, as if, while the temple of the Lord was building, some cutting, some squaring the marble, others hewing the cedars, there should be a sort of irrational men who could not consider there must be many schisms and many dissections made in the quarry and in the timber, ere the house of God can be built. And when every stone is laid artfully together, it cannot be united into a continuity, it can but be contiguous, in this world: neither can every piece of the building be of one form.

Nay, rather *the perfection consists in this, that out of many moderate varieties and brotherly dissimilitudes that are not vastly disproportional, arises the goodly and the graceful symmetry that commends the whole pile and structure.* No marvel, then, though some men, and some good men too, perhaps, but young in goodness, as Joshua then was, envy them. *They fret, and out of their own weakness are in agony, lest these divisions and subdivisions will undo us.* The adversary again applauds, and waits the hour; 'When they have branched themselves out, saith he, small enough into parties and partitions, then will be our time.' *Fool! he sees not the firm roots out of which we all grow*, though into branches. And that we * * * shall laugh in the end at those malicious applauders of our differences, I have these reasons to persuade me."—*Milton.*

"ONE ONLY DESTROYS WHAT ONE REPLACES."—*Napoleon I.*
"THE NEW CATHOLIC ELEMENT WAS THE PEOPLE."—*Bancroft.*

"There is in every nation *a general Spirit upon which power itself is founded.* When power clashes against this spirit it clashes against itself, and is necessarily stopped."—*Montesquieu.*

"Every Government is composed of two distinct elements, its nature (structural identity) and its principles (passions)."—*Ibid.*

"*A Government can be a strong one only in the case where its principles are in harmony with its nature.*"

"When in a country so democratised (as was France) the principle of *equality* is not generally applied, it *must be introduced into all its laws before Liberty can be possible.*" "Where Feudality has been replaced by something else, *it has never revived.*"

"A Government of the present day must base its moral influence on a *Principle*, its physical strength on *organisation.*"

"To build on a rock means to establish a Government on Democratic Principles."—*Napoleon III.*

"The grand political problem is to invent the best combination of the powers of legislation and execution: one power would fix them to a centre, and another carry them off indefinitely; but the first and simple principle is EQUALITY AND THE POWER OF THE WHOLE."—*Otis*, 1764.

"True Democracy means the elevation of the masses. Labour is dignity, dignity is manhood, manhood is aristocracy. The time has come to lay broad and deep the foundations of the new Aristocracy."—*Johnson*, President United States.

"The true barriers of our Liberty are State Governments."
Jefferson.

"We can have no permanent peace with the South *but by Americanising it.*"—*North American Review*, 1865.

"It requires a strong hand *to destroy the despotism of Servitude through the agency of the despotism of Liberty,* and to save the country by the same means which otherwise would have subjugated it."—*Napoleon III.* Vol. I. p. 168, Life and Works.

THE Destiny of Oligarchy in America is determined on. Let it be accomplished.

Let us try to see now what is plain respecting that of the American nation.

The Principles that have conquered must culminate. They are called FEDERAL REPUB-

LICANISM. They mean political *Equality* between Individuals, a proper and orderly *Adjustment* of functions between the parts and the whole, and *Freedom* as between the Individual and the State.

Development produces association. Developed associated manhood produces Equality, and is Republicanism. Republicanism must make the Federation lasting, as Federation has made the Republic an Empire.

With Reconstruction comes Reconciliation. State Rights have not to be destroyed, but to be re-adjusted. Federal Republicanism has got to complete that reconciliation of Democracy with Centralisation, which is the sum of political questions. Federation, as the binding principle of a vast political framework, will with Freedom and Equality, secure just relations between Individuals, "State," and nation, and present at once the following problems and consequences.

1st. The fall of Oligarchy in the West, its completed Destruction by negro suffrage, or by white immigration Southwards if necessary; and the influence of American Democracy,—on the Peoples everywhere.

2nd. The Future of the Negro Race. It is an ethnical, a geographical, and a political question. Politically, negro suffrage will constitute a material guarantee of Equality, and a crucial test of its sincere and unqualified adoption, in the case of Labor, Poverty, and a Pariah race. Moreover, Central America, and the region from Panama to Texas, is now alive with events and movement. Panama commissions, railways, and schemes; the commerce of the Antilles; the throne of Mexico, and the *diminuendo* of French occupation; the Monroe doctrine, and the advance of the American frontier;—all these tend to make the future of these regions a pressing and a "burning" question. The negroes will be thirteen millions in A.D. 1900, and now whether the process of fusion of White and Black races, continues, or not, *there is the race, and the race is free*,—to remain, or to find a home and a country in a warmer zone; for since John Brown died for them, the banner and the nationality of America, is that of the negro,—sacred, bought with blood. The future of America will be his, and he may be destined to receive in that future, tenfold for all that he has suffered in the past.

3rd. And is there not another process that will go on? What do we behold in America? ALL NATIONALITIES FUSED AND FEDERATED. Not as a dream, but as an accomplished fact. An extension of the process would bring back to the world the olden times of one tongue, and one blood? The idea was Napoleon's, of an European federation,—in 1860, Garibaldi urged it, and we have heard of the "Federation of man," and of war-drums dumb in the future. Here, in America, is the beginning of it, wrought out, done, *concluded*. Whether it be the beginning of the end, let us leave for time to show. But if there be anything in the aspirations of all those best qualified to judge,—from John Adams to De Tocqueville, and from De Tocqueville to John Bright,—there will be, certainly, but one tongue, one People, one mode of Government,—from the ice-thrones of the Pole, to the flaming belt of the Equator.

§

When the profundity of the Statesmen of the South shall come at last to be more generally appreciated, and the veil of policy which obscured their measures, has been removed by a knowledge of the facts and essential logic of the situation,—then the world will take in at once the majesty of the Intellects of South Carolina, and their Despair,—Despair that there is yet ONE above them to baffle, and, again, *to use*, the grandest scheme of evil since the Fall. Then it will be seen that had that scheme prospered in the Union, the battle for States might have been revived with no disadvantage to the South,—that millions upon millions of "chattels," would hereafter have teemed upon its multiplying States,—that in a region past the Mississippi, and where the temperate zone would cease to fight against them,—that *there*, whether in the Union, or out of it, by votes, or by arms, Slave States might neutralise free,—that *there*, oligarchy might perpetuate, and more naturally organize an inferior race,—that *there*, even from Panama to the great river, a new world of slaves might recuperate the exhausted energies of the Gulf States,—command the chiefest thoroughfare of the world's commercial future,—menace or possess the great natural outlet of the products of the free North,—use the resources and products of the Antilles,—bestride the indispensable route of England to her children in the seas, and, from the throne of the Montezumas, seal up the half of the universe, from the influences of civilisation and freedom.

Then, also, the policy of a Titan elsewhere, will be comprehended, and the fact that whatever Napoleon may have meant about the North,—in occupying Mexico, *he* pierced the very heart of Southern Statesmanship, and occupied beforehand, *that*, without which the South could have neither a future, a capitol, or even an aim.

We do not imitate those who seek to penetrate the future. But Napoleon is in Mexico. With the Union divided, he can remain there,—against the resources of the Union he cannot. The postulate of his policy is the disunion of the nation.

It will also become clear, that the fatal weakness of the South was not in their conduct, but in their fate. The South simply *could not* win. They could not wait, for the propagandism of Freedom was rapidly penetrating them. They could not advance Southward at once, for the Slaves were not numerous enough, nor was their own policy matured; and the Abolitionists of 1833, John Brown of Kansas, Lincoln of Illinois, and all the noble army of martyrs since, have *precipitated* upon them a policy of territorial freedom.

§

Nevertheless, three steps, only, were wanted to this Avernus. The North, the *official* North, took two of them;—and then the nation stopped! "Man is Property. Property ought to be protected in the actual Territories. Property shall be protected on seas, on land, anywhere, especially *in Territories that may hereafter be acquired.*" The Chief Justice ruled that "man is property,—that property, of course, should be protected,—that"—

he would have ruled *anything*. But the Republicans got their President. The hour and the Man came together. *The South defied the flag.* Nationality and abolitionism were at last one, but, maugre both, the nation, which for seventy years had, in person, or by procuration, done the work of sin and the Devil, was near also taking the wages,—Death.

It may be said that the nation was not with compromise. We answer, it was not enough *against* it. They passed personal liberty bills, started Societies, &c.; but, nevertheless, Materialism and a mock Democracy took, till John Brown and Lincoln, joint possession with Slavery and Oligarchy, of the Government and the representative power. Disregard of Principle is the master sin of *all* nations. Generally, it comes through mere disregard or want of Statesmanship amongst Leaders or People, and in America, of all nations, that ought not so to have been.

"But," says Wendell Phillips, "put one Christian, like John Brown of Osawatomie, and he makes the whole crystallise into right and wrong, and marshal itself on the one side and the other." This was the statesmanship and the defence of John Brown;—

"This court acknowledges, too, as I suppose, the validity of the law of God. I see a book kissed, which I suppose to be the Bible, or at least the New Testament, which teaches me that all things whatsoever I would that men should do to me, I should do even so to them. It teaches me further, to remember them that are in bonds as bound with them. I endeavour to act up to that instruction. I say I am yet too young to understand that God is any respecter of persons. I believe that to have interfered as I have done,—as I have always freely admitted I have done,—I have done in behalf of HIS despised poor, no wrong but right."

And so the creed of John Brown has become the creed of the nation, and his blood and the abolitionist creed, would seem to have worked together that stupendous miracle, the RESURRECTION of a great nation. *They taught the White man how and what to destroy.—The Negro, in whom he might believe.*

§

Compared with all previous crises of a similar nature, the technical work of reconstruction ought to be clear, as the appointed means are simple.

The past ages and races of the world have simplified the work for the Americans to-day.

The three great political labours of the living nations of the world were:—1st, to destroy the idea of the right divine of rulers; 2nd, to establish against Privilege the right of representation; 3rd, to establish the Principle of the political competency of the masses.

Of these three, two were accomplished by the English race and Democracy, before they were transplanted to America,—there to carry out, at least a century earlier than had been possible in England, the third and last great principle.

Further, the American Constitution was a written one, and organised the national political life upon an acknowledged basis, many features of which might have been taken (as far as the circumstances were parallel) from the English "Declaration of Rights," incorporated in the instrument by which the Prince and Princess of Orange were called to the throne.

The "Principles of the English Constitution were, on the other hand" (says Macaulay, pp. 663-4, V. 2), "not formally and exactly set forth in a single written instrument, but they were to be found *scattered over our ancient and noble statutes;*" and stating what they were,* he adds, that although "the realm stood in no need of a new constitution," the convention had two great duties to perform. The first was *to clear the fundamental laws of the realm from ambiguity;* the second was to eradicate the idea of the divine right of prerogative.

Now, compared with this English, the easiest of all revolutions, what is the task of American politicians? Simply, "*to clear the fundamental laws from ambiguity.*" This done, and all except detail is done. As to the constitutionality, as well as to the momentous results, we may adopt the language of Macaulay, and apply it to the American crisis: "The whole English law was * * exactly the same after the revolution as before it. * * *It finally decided the great question whether the popular element * * should be suffered to develop itself freely and to become dominant.* The strife between the two principles had been long, fierce, and doubtful. It had lasted through four reigns. It had produced

* "That, without the consent of the representatives of the nation, no statute could be enacted, no tax imposed, no regular soldiery kept up; that no man could be imprisoned even for a day by the arbitrary will of the Sovereign; that no tool of power could plead the royal command as a justification for violating any legal right of the humblest subject; were held, both by Whigs and Tories, to be fundamental laws of the realm."—Macaulay's *England*, p. 664, v. 2.

seditions, impeachments, rebellions, battles, sieges, proscriptions, judicial massacres. Sometimes liberty, sometimes royalty had seemed on the point of perishing. *During many years one half of the energy of England had been employed in counteracting the other half.* The executive power and the legislative power *had so effectually impeded each other, that the State had been of no account in Europe.*"

The work of America is more difficult, because more radical aud rudimentary, than was that of England. But, in proportion as Oligarchy is more powerful and desperate than was Royalty, so will the political, social, and economic results of the new national unity be more conspicuous.

Granted, the success of the Principle of Democracy, and the question of Reconstruction is an exceedingly simple and decisive one, for Democracy supplies the objects, the means, and the form. The details, however, are somewhat elaborate.

The whole question consists of six Parts.

The first describes the Principles of the South. The second, the Policy of Lincoln. The third, the Principles of Reconstruction. The fourth, the National Resources, or Materials for Reconstruction. The fifth, certain items of Reconstruction. The sixth, certain probable Results.

PART I.

THE POLICY AND "PRINCIPLES" OF THE SOUTH.

The South seceded, because the North commanded a majority in both Houses, and could command the national policy. According to the Census of 1860, the eight North-western Free States progressed in population in ten years at the rate of sixty-seven per cent.—the average increase in the whole country being 35·53 only. And Ohio, alone, has more free white population than the whole six Slave States of South Carolina, Georgia, Alabama, Florida, Mississippi, and Louisiana. The South seceded because it became evident that the majority of the North would be used to defeat the one only means by which the South could regain its power in the Union,—namely, the creation of new Slave States out of future territory.

Although Mr. Lincoln's Inaugural declared, that the people must not "resign their Government into the hands of the Courts," yet the Supreme Court had ruled the admission of slavery into every State.

The real question in fact was, not shall it be lawful to admit slavery into existing States, but, *is it likely that* SUCH *States will be admitted into the Union, as will, from a more congenial population, climate, and soil, admit of the perpetuation of Slavery?*

As the territories in question were not ripe for annexation, as the Republican party was growing, and as Lincoln could neither be bribed nor bullied, the South seceded.

Let us establish this two-fold position by quotations on both sides.

Slavery and the Territories. The first was the cause of the strife. Both were to be the prizes of victory. "Slavery" meant, not only the bondage of the Black, but *the eternal subordination of the masses* as a political principle. "The Territories" were synonymous with the new—to be—completed Slave empire.

That "territories" were the main object of Secession has been proved by all the recent resolutions, and platforms, and conventions of that party. But that the veiled object of this policy of "Territories" regarded the immense future, which was by them to be opened up, has not been shown.

That Slavery, in its *generic* signification as Oligarchy,—as a political principle, regarding new territories as its own essential material basis,—that *this* was the alpha and omega of Southern policy, we now proceed to show by selections from every kind of evidence, not already adduced.

Oligarchy, and New Territories, were, we say, to constitute with the old Slave States, the POLICY AND POWER of the South.

LABOR-RIGHTS AND MAJORITIES
TO BE RESTRAINED.

"Governments," said one of the most authentic documents of the South, "are instituted for the protection of the rights of persons and property; and any system must be radically defective which does not give ample security to both. * * Capital belongs to the few; labour to the many. * * The political condition of the Northern States presents a striking illustration of the *evils incident to the preponderance of the element of labour*. * * This tendency to a conflict between labour and capital has already manifested itself in many forms, * * free schools, homestead bills, communism, disregard of religion and of matrimony, and more distinctly, in the form of *abolitionism*.

"No system of Government can afford *security to life, liberty, and property*, which rests on the basis of unlimited suffrage, and the election of officers of every department of the Government *by the direct vote of the people*. These, however, are the vital principles of the North, &c. In the Southern States *more conservative and rational principles still prevail. This is due mainly to the institution of slavery.* * * In the North, *every class and condition are entitled to vote.*

"*Slavery also constitutes an effectual barrier* against that tendency to antagonism between labour and capital which exists in the North. * * *Here, capital is the owner of labour*, and naturally seeks to enhance its rewards."—*Report of Committee appointed by* VIRGINIAN CONVENTION, to consider amendments to Virginian Constitution, Richmond, Nov. 19th, 1861. See Putnam, also Victor, V. 2, p. 519.

And the chief prophet of the new dispensation thus expounded and extolled his Gospel:—

"Whether Jefferson fully understood the great truth upon which that rock stood and stands may be doubted. The prevailing ideas entertained by him and *most of the leading statesmen at the time of the formation of the old constitution*, were, that the enslavement of the African was in violation of the laws of nature: that it was wrong in principle, socially, morally, and politically. This was an error. It was a sandy foundation, and the idea of a Government built upon it, when the storm came, and the wind blew, it fell.

"Our new Government is founded upon exactly the opposite principle; * * this great physical and moral truth. I cannot permit myself to doubt the *ultimate success of a full recognition of the principle throughout the civilised and enlightened world.* For his own purposes the Creator has made one race to differ from another, as He has made *one star to differ from another star in glory!* * * We are now the nucleus of a *growing power*, which, if we are true to ourselves, our destiny and high mission, will become *the controlling power on this continent.* To what extent accessions will go on in the process of time, or where it will end, the future will determine." — VICE PRESIDENT STEPHENS, *March*, 1861. Victor, V. 1, p. 30-1.

"The cause of all the trouble is the persistent war of the Abolitionists *upon more than two billions of property;* a war waged from pulpits, rostrums, and schools, *by press and People.*" —*Delaware Governor*, 1860.

"The one great evil is the overthrow of the Constitution. The Government is no longer the Government of a confederate republic, but of a *consolidated Democracy.* It is no longer a free Government, but a Despotism. Not only their fanaticism, but their erroneous views of the principles of free Government, render it doubtful whether, separated from the South, they can maintain a free Government among themselves. Brute numbers is with them the great element of free Government. *The very object of all free constitutions* in free popular Governments *is TO RESTRAIN THE MAJORITY.* * * * We prefer, however, our system of industry, by which *labour and capital are identified* in interest, and capital therefore protects labour, &c. *We ask you to join us in forming a confederacy of Slaveholding States.*"—*Address of* SOUTH CAROLINA CONVENTION, to People of Slaveholding States, *Dec.* 24, 1860. Putnam.

NEW SLAVE TERRITORY.

"I am a plain, blunt spoken man," said Wigfall of Texas, in the Senate, in 1861. "I usually say precisely what I mean, and I always mean precisely what I say. * * * We say that man has a right to property in man. We say that our slaves are our property. We say that it is the duty of every Government to protect its property *everywhere.* * * If you wish to settle this matter, declare that slaves are property, and like all other property, *entitled to be protected in every quarter of the globe*, on land and on sea. Say that to us, and then the difficulty is settled."

The following, from Seward, Douglas, and Adams, explains why the Oligarchy *must* seek new Slave States, SOUTHWARDS, in a more congenial region, or rend the Union:—

"What is the extent of the Territories that remain after the admission of Minnesota, Oregon, and of Kansas? One million, sixty-three thousand, five hundred square miles—an area twenty-four times that of the State of New York, the largest of the old and fully-developed States. *Twenty-four such*

States as this of New York are yet to be fully organised within the remaining territories of the United States. *How many slaves have been brought into it* during these twelve years in which the Supreme Court, the legislature, and the administration, have maintained, protected, and guaranteed Slavery there? Twenty-four African slaves! *One slave for every forty-four thousand square miles!* One slave for every one of the twenty-four States, which, &c., Sir, I confess that I have no fears of Slavery anywhere."—*Seward, in the Senate, January 31st,* 1860.

"Does not this fact prove the utter fallacy of the Government attempting to plant Slavery where the climate is adverse, and the People do not want it, and the utter folly of the other side bringing this country to the very verge of disunion, in order to prohibit Slavery where the very power of the Government *could not make it exist.* * * Do that (declare that Congress cannot legislate on the subject), and you will have peace; do that, and the Union will not perish; do that, and you do not extend Slavery one inch, nor circumscribe it one inch—you do not emancipate a slave, nor enslave a freeman." —*Douglas.*

Mr. C. F. Adams, one of the foremost statesmen, son and grandson of Presidents, during his exposition of this subject, in 1861, demanded:—

"Who excludes the slaveholders with their slaves? Have they not obtained an opinion from the Supreme Court which will in effect override any and every report of Congress against them? They can, if they choose, now go wherever they like on the public domain. *The law of political economy* regulates this matter much better than any specific statute. It guides this species of labour to the most suitable place, and that place is *not the Territory* of the United States. *New Mexico* has now twenty-two slaves on a surface of over two hundred thousand square miles, and of these only twelve are domiciled. New Mexico shows, then, all that ten years of protection has made her. I say then, in answer to a demand of a constitutional guarantee of protection to Slavery in New Mexico, that you are asking for what in substance you enjoy already, and what is good for nothing to you if you get it." * * * "We are told that the

Union must be dissolved if we refuse to put in the Constitution a pledge that we will protect Slavery in the States of Sonara, or Coahuila, or Chihuahua, or New Leon,—*when we get them!* Why, then, is it that harmony is not restored? You must make the protection and extension of Slavery in the territories now existing, "and *hereafter to be acquired*," a cardinal doctrine of our great charter. Are you going to fight because we cannot agree upon the mode of disposing of our neighbour's land? * * If the alternative of the salvation of the Union, be only that the people of the United States shall, before the Christian nations of the earth, plant in broad letters upon their Charter of Republican Government the dogma of *Slave propagandism,* over the remainder of the countries of the world, I will not consent."

§

Thus it is clear that the South seceded because the North commanded the majority, and would not agree to protect Slavery *in future Territories.* The reason is equally clear. The threefold power of wealth, numbers, and representation, in the Union, was against the South. Politically, unless it could look to multiply the Slave States, its rule in the Union was played out. It was useless to take Slavery into the northern, or middle States, for Slavery would not stay there or pay there. That game also was played out. But if the faith of the Union could be pledged to Slavery in future States "that might be acquired," the South would then only have to "acquire" them!

That secession was part of a predetermined plan of the leading spirits of the South, and, since 1812, *kept ready, on any given occasion, to supersede or supplant the alliance with the so-called Democrats, North,* is evident from the following:—

"You in the South and South West," said one to Calhoun, "are decidedly the *aristocratic* portion of the Union. You are so in holding persons in perpetuity in *slavery;* you are so in every domestic quality; in every habit of your lives; in habits, customs, intercourse, and manners; you neither work with your hands, head, nor any machinery, but live and have your being, not in accordance with the will of your Creator, but by the sweat of Slavery; and *yet you assume all the attributes, professions, and advantages, of Democracy.*"

Mr. Calhoun replied, "You lose sight of the politician, and the *sectional policy* of the people. I admit your conclusions in respect of us Southerners,—that we are essentially aristocratic. I cannot deny but we can and do yield much to Democracy; this is our sectional policy. We are, from necessity, thrown upon and solemnly wedded to that party, for the conservatism of our interests. It is through our affiliation with that party in the Middle and Western States, we control, under the Constitution, the governing of the United States. *But when we cease thus to control this nation through a disjoined Democracy,* or any material obstacle in that party, which shall tend to throw us out of that rule and control, *we shall then resort to the dissolution of the Union.* The compromises of the Constitution, under the circumstances, were sufficient for our fathers, but, under the altered conditions of the country from that period, leave to the South no resource but dissolution; *for no amendments* to the Constitution *could be reached through a convention of the people, and their three-fourths rule.*"—*John C. Calhoun, Dec.* 1812.—Putman, Vol. I., pp. 186-7.

(Conversation with Commodore Stewart, communicated by him, May 4th, 1861, to Mr. Childs of Philadelphia.)

There can be no mistake about Southern Statesmanship. It was projected by the logical necessities of a false position. It was, as Lincoln charged it, "to rule or ruin."

Well, whenever the three-fourths rule of *the People* should become too strong for the Oligarchy of the South, and their allies, the "disjoined Northern Democrats," the South was prepared to revolt; and why? Because, in a separate establishment, Slavery might be preserved *as the material basis of the labour system, and also as the basis of the rule of an exclusive class and race*,—as the material basis, and political guarantee of oligarchy, "in territories HEREAFTER TO BE ACQUIRED."

The proof is that, as we have already shown, the South went against the two opposites of these, namely, FREEDOM, and the RULE OF THE MAJORITY.

How, and with what Principles, Mr. Lincoln prepared to meet this two-fold conspiracy against the rights of labour, and political equality,—how, on behalf of the future, as well as of the present, he accepted this contest, we shall show presently. It is our duty first to trace his *policy*,—how he prepared the forces, that should carry out his principles. How he organised the Victory.

PART II.

POLICY OF LINCOLN.

Lincoln, one of the greatest masters of "how to do it," knew Principles and facts, and was neither too much before nor too much after his age.

Lincoln saw and grasped the great problem of the Battle-stage in this mighty epic,—this completing and reconciling of the Individual Freedom, and the national Unity.

The necessity of Unity involved what we will call the three great LABOURS OF LINCOLN. The Problem which Lincoln proposed to himself was, "How to commit the nation to an anti-Slavery "war, which should, by the inexorable logic of "the situation, carry on the moderates, the weak, "the interested, the abject, and the infamous, "to the national end,—freedom, and completed "nationality." How to purge and wean the Union from moral complicity with Slavery, and to unite the Border States and Democrats with the North.

This problem has been successfully solved. The North is an unit. Its administration is organised under trustworthy men. It has destroyed rebellion in the Field, and prepares to extirpate its causes from the soil and the constitution.

Lincoln's policy of preparation involved the achievement of a threefold unity of MORALS, of PRINCIPLES, and of NUMBERS.

He had to remove and overcome the *moral complicity* of the North with Slavery.

He had to gain over the adherents of "Sovereign *State Rights*" and of Property in man, to the principles of *national* Sovereignty, and Individual Freedom.

He had to win over the four millions of slaves, and to neutralise or to win the three millions in the Border States to the Union, by a policy which should *conciliate, enfranchise, and use the Blacks, without encountering the public opinion of the Whites, their masters.* And all this must be done without violating his oath to the constitution.

It was a situation of extraordinary difficulty, but Lincoln, by a policy of honesty, in itself one of the greatest powers of the age, has converted the difficulty into victory, and the danger into triumph.

His first and greatest difficulty is clearly seen, when we remember that, when vibrating on the edge of the crisis, the Northern States returned many anti-republican and compromise members, and that, had the Slave States sent and left their quotum, a considerable pro-Slavery majority might have assembled to uphold Slavery constitutionally, and to identify abolition with rebellion. Even in 1862, there were, of all parties present, 173 members, and 63 Secesh vacancies.

The question as to NUMBERS, stating the figures in round numbers, and giving the South every advantage, stood thus:—

The Free States population was 18,000,000; the Slave States, 10,000,000; and the Border Slave States, 3,000,000. As the Border States ranged themselves, the North would find itself, either as 21 to 10, or as 18 to 13; the gain or the loss of the Border States being equal to 6,000,000 on either side. It was necessary also to reduce the 10,000,000 of the Slave States to 6,000,000, and to add the 4,000,000 slaves to the 21,000,000 of Border States and North.

Putting the Border States and the Slaves together, with their respective four and three millions, we get an aggregate of seven millions, which, leaving one side to join the other, would constitute a difference amounting to the enormous item of fourteen millions, out of the grand total of thirty-one!

The basis of this policy throughout, was the natural alliance of State and Popular Sovereignty, or individual interest, with the national Sovereignty, Policy, and Will.

The interests of the Individuals, and of the

Government, were one; the interests of rebellion opposed, and were opposed by, both.

As much of this policy as was possible, Lincoln has accomplished. It consisted in rousing the principle of nationality in advance of that of abolitionism. He induced action which would destroy property in Slaves, instead of arousing jealousy for property, which might have overcome the love of Union.

The actual success of Lincoln is represented in the following figures:—

Total white population of Free States and Territories	. ·	19,117,911
Do.	Loyal Slave States .	2,698,841
		21,816,752
Do.	Eleven seceded States	5,581,630
		16,235,122

To the nearly 22 millions, add the 4 millions of slaves as they can be reached, and the odds appear five to one.

§

The work of Lincoln the President, differed materially from that of Lincoln the candidate. As candidate he had to show what he wanted to do. As President he had to do it. He had to combine parties, and to organise victory. It is by no means clear that he did not go the best way about it.

Nevertheless, thus did the English people argue about Lincoln:—

"A government exists by virtue of the authority "of its executive, and is approved of for the sake "of the advantages it confers upon mankind. A "nation that would entitle itself to the general "sympathy in a contest for existence, must have "identified itself therein, with some great and dis- "tinct principles; it must, in fact, fulfil the law of "its existence, and appeal, as a government, to "governments, on behalf of the principle of *autho- "rity*, or as a people, to the peoples, as a champion "of *right*,—otherwise it will be condemned as use- "less by the one, and forsaken as incompetent by "the other."

The United States unfortunately *appeared* to violate both of these considerations. They seemed to vacillate to the very verge of imbecility, while rebels organised an opposition, arranged their diplomacy, bore off their material, and armed their troops,—and they hesitated fourteen months to declare that the principle of human freedom was that for which they contended.

But this was not all. There appeared at the same time a contradictory, a counterfeit, and a hypocritical presentment; for they appeared willing to defend the principle of authority by the sacrifice of freedom, and they have appeared to call at last upon the principle of freedom, because without it, the Government was in danger.

These apparent discrepancies, in fact did exist, to a certain extent. But there also exists in England an appalling ignorance and carelessness as to the treachery of the South, as to the genius of the American people and constitution, as to the real anti-slavery force of really popular institutions, as to the history and meaning of their party contests, —and also a lurking disbelief in the human race itself, and its capabilities for self-government, and orderly progress. The old Governments of Europe neither trust nor believe in the people or God, but that so large a portion of educated English,—the same blood, the same tongue, and the same history, should so generally misappreciate the situation, or decry "the great experiment of the people," is the last moral monstrosity and wonder of the world and of the age.

That which would be impolicy in a despotic Government, or with an educated people, may have been the height of political wisdom in America. Such is the conservatism of a people universally educated, that it was the one point at first to put the South completely in the wrong before the nation, getting it committed, at whatever cost, to violence and oppression, without provocation and without excuse. No one susceptibility of freedom would the Government wound, while the South having wounded all but one,—the *ultima ratio* of the executive,—then struck at *that*. The authority of the people's government was in no danger, except from being exerted without ample warrant against the people, and, as the tide *had* turned, and the millions were going to submit no longer to the units, there wanted no "policy" but to avoid extravagances or reactions, and to await from all the loyal, the support of freedom, of authority, and of nationality.

As for danger from delay, or doubt of ultimate result, the *People* never doubted; the rebellion had got a certain head; to subdue it was a "big job," but it was to be overtaken and destroyed by the certain, comprehensive, and universal action of a people that understood well the value, the honesty, the moderation, and also the power of the Government under which they lived.

That Government moved with the momentum, and marched to the step of the million, and such a "million" never before existed, to appreciate the wisdom of the Government, and to uphold it with their conservative and self-sacrificing energies. Military events have been slow and chequered, as is the way especially with republics, and nations that are not always under arms, but the Government has kept pace with the march of opinion, and has not so advanced as to have to retire. The momentum of popular ideas, and the logic of the situation, have now plainly developed themselves, and although so-called Conservatives would still compromise the question of Slavery, *they* also demanded that the rebellion be crushed by the physical force it challenged. The Democrat or Conservative is thus not irreconcilable with the Abolitionist. The Democrat contends for order, the Abolitionist for freedom, but against the same foe.

We repeat, the great problem for Lincoln was, "how to free the Slaves without alienating the neutral and border Slave powers."

We know how far this has been done by Lincoln's actual policy. The contrary might have been done by any other. The problem was, and is, "*how to conquer the Slave power without lessening union or anti-slavery zeal,*"—to unite the material forces of the republic, without opposing them to the principles of morality, which constitute its spiritual forces.

PART III.

PRINCIPLES OF RECONSTRUCTION.

THE MAN.
THE STATE.
THE NATION.

So much for Southern principles and for Lincoln's Policy as to Numbers, the Border States, and the national Complicity with Slavery.

Reconstruction depends, primarily, upon the GENIUS OF THE NATION, and in subordination to that, upon the PRINCIPLES of the Constitution, THE NEW SITUATION, and the leading MEN.

The characteristics of the American *Genius* and *Nation*, have been already enlarged upon in the chapter so entitled. They are five. The Intensity of the nationality, and its assimilating power. Its self-reliance. Its devotion to the principles of equality of conditions. Its obedience to the law, and readiness to make necessary changes. Its power of association.

The leading characteristics of the American *Constitution* are also five. Popular, State, and National, Sovereignty. The three-fourths power of Amendment. The Republican Guarantee.

Except State *Sovereignty* and the Amendment, which are matters subject to modification, the characteristics of the national Genius and Constitution may be summed up in two words,—FEDERAL REPUBLICANISM. The component principles are

Equality, State Rights, and Nationality. They complement each other, and properly combined, constitute the perfection of Government.

The Situation is made up of the Resources of the country, and the character and energies of those who wield them. The Resources of the country consist of its great Men, and of its Races, Numbers, Territory, Education, Wealth, Armaments, etc.

Individuals, in an actual Democracy, in time of peace, would not be of paramount importance. But there is yet latent war in the South, and there are grave questions in Canada and Mexico.

§

The first of these three Principles which the Situation calls for, and which, as far as they are known, the Nation and the Men are ready and pledged to carry out, is Nationality.

NATIONALITY.

This is the sum of the forces, of the principles, and of the interests of America. Equality and Federation have made the nation, and *that is the living Organism* that will protect them. The whole history of the world pointed by its struggles and aspirations to the coming of this Federal Republic: the whole history of America, from the beginnings of representative freedom in the woods of Germany, the struggles of Puritanism and religious independence in England, and then in America—

the growth of the Federative Principle, and now, the completion of Equality—all these have prepared for the great Democratic empire which now completes its equipment.

The Principles which are the completion of political science, and the nation that is their embodiment and vindication, have now but to carry out in form that which has been thought and fought for through the ages, and so lately crowned with victory.

Nationality is the intensest and most powerful idea that rules in American hearts. If it was doubted in 1860 it is not doubted now. In all the quotations, and throughout, on the question of reconstruction, we must beg the reader to note especially two things; First, that *the national party are at one with the Genius and Constitution.* Second, *That their opponents are opposed to both.*

It was well said by Mr. Seward, one of the most tentative and cautious of Statesmen, by no means one of the "old men," and immensely underrated in England:—

> "I therefore declare my adherence to *the Union in its integrity, and with all its parts,* with my friends, with my party, with my State, with my country, or without either, as they may determine,—in every event, whether of peace or of war,—with every consequence of honour or dishonour, of life or of death."—*Seward, in Senate, Jan.* 1860.

This is the almost universal feeling of Americans: we are not going to prove it. If the result of the war does not prove it, nothing will.

But this principle of nationality, however intense, was neither consistent with itself, nor with the true Democratic Principle, and was therefore incomplete and assailable, as long as it was possible for the national suffrages to be used for the extension of Slavery into future territories; as long as four millions of citizens were not regarded as Americans, or as that distrust of the common people, which is the sin and the weakness of the old world, still finds excuse and toleration. Thus OLIGARCHY is again shown to be the master danger, and Oligarchy could never have been cast out by a Democracy that persisted in making Colour and Poverty an exception, or in conniving at a misapplication of the State Right Principle.

And in this respect, the past of America does not lead us to fear for her future.

America wars against Oligarchy, because;

1st. It assails its nationality, and as nationality is the all, the essence, the totality of a nation, that which assails it, assails that which is best and divinest in it, as well as its mere autonomy.

2nd. Because, in defending its nationality, it defends also its Independence.

3rd. Because the present and future *internal* interests of America are against Oligarchy,—for, if triumphant in the South, it would infect its territory and all its future. The interests of morality, of economics, of Democracy, of freedom, and also of the "States," demand the triumph of the principle of Equality.

4th. Because America is trustee and depositary before and on behalf of the world, of those great internal and political interests, which appear likely soon to change the whole face of the earth.

EQUALITY.

This principle was created by manhood development and association, and these two, having destroyed the opposite principle of Inequality, and prepared America for Equality, will, by mere force of self-interest, continue to associate to preserve the latter.

Inequality caused the War. In the same nation the two principles could not live. The war became a contest for Equality even to the extreme case of the negro. The nation has warred for Equality, and it won by Equality. Equality is the ruling essential power both in the nation and in Society, and notwithstanding temporary halts or indiscretions, it must work out its problems.

The two crevices in the panoply of American nationality, mistrust of the common People, and the outlawry of the Negroes, could not be more clearly defined than in the sublime language of the greatest orator America has produced. Wendell Phillips and Abraham Lincoln thus expound the principles of Equality.

"The last twenty years have been an insurrection of thought. We seem to be entering on a new phase of the great American struggle. It seems to me that we have *never accepted*, as Americans, *our own civilisation*. We have all the timidity of the old world when we think of the People; we shrink back, trying to save ourselves from *the inevitable might of the thoughts of the million*. The idea on the other side of the water seems to be, that man is created to be taken care of by somebody else. * * We need no safeguard. *Not only the inevitable, but the* *best, power this side of the ocean, is the unfettered average common sense of the masses.* With us law is nothing unless close behind it stands a warm living public opinion. You may frame them strong as language can make, but once change public feeling, and through them or over them, rides the real wish of the People.

"You may sigh for a strong Government, anchored in the convictions of past centuries, and able to protect the minority against the majority, *able to defy the ignorance, the mistake, or the passion, as well as the high purpose of the present hour.* You may prefer the unchanging terra firma of Despotism; but still the fact remains, that *we are launched on the ocean of an unchained democracy, with no safety but in* those laws that bind the ocean in its bed—*the instinctive love of right in the popular heart.* The divine sheet-anchor that the race gravitates towards right, and that the right is always safe and best. * * Daring to trust justice, the preliminary consideration is trusting the people. *Trust the people with the gravest questions,* and in the long run you educate the race; while in the process *you secure, not perfect, but the best possible institutions.* Now, my idea of American civilisation is, that it is a second part, a repetition of *that same sublime confidence in the public conscience and the public thought,* that made the groundwork of Grecian Democracy."

"I admit," said Lincoln,—in his campaign against Douglas, in Illinois, October, 1854, just after the passing of the Nebraska Bill,—"I admit that the emigrant to Kansas and Nebraska is competent to govern himself, but *I deny his right to govern any other person* WITHOUT *that person's consent.*"

"As I understand the *spirit of our institutions,*" said he, in May, 1859, "*it is designed to promote the elevation of men.* I am, therefore, hostile to anything that tends to their debasement. * * In respect to a fusion, I am in favour of it whenever it can be effected on *Republican principles,* but upon no other condition. A fusion upon any other platform would be as insane as unprincipled. * * *I shall oppose the lowering of the Republican standard even by a hair's breadth.*"

"The Principle of self Government, lies at the bottom of all my ideas of just Government."

And earlier, on October 15th, 1858, at Alton, Illinois:—

"They (the Fathers) did not mean to assert the obvious untruth, that all were then actually enjoying that equality. They meant simply to declare the *right*, so that the *enforcement* of it must follow as fast as circumstances should permit. *They meant to set up a standard maxim for free society, which should be familiar to all:* constantly looked to, constantly laboured for, and even, though never perfectly attained, constantly approximated, and thereby *constantly spreading and deepening its influence, and augmenting the happiness and value of life to all people, of every colour, everywhere.* * * * Irrespective of the moral aspect * * I am in favour of this (free territory) not merely for our own people who are born among us, but as an outlet for free white people everywhere, the world over, in which Hans, and Baptiste, and Patrick, and *all other men, from all parts of the world may find new homes, and better their condition in life.*"

But Lincoln could scarcely open his mouth, without, of the abundance of his heart, enlarging on these three things,—The universal equality of right, the universal welcome to men throughout the world, the banishing from America of that one exception, which was its blot and curse. In his pitched battle with Douglas, who pretended that Slavery should be left alone, he said:—

"There never was a *party* in the history of this country, and there probably never will be, of sufficient strength to disturb the general peace of the country. But does not this question make a disturbance outside of political circles? Does it not enter into the Churches and rend them asunder? * * The great Methodist Church, * * every Presbyterian General Assembly, * * the Unitarian Church, * * the great American Tract Society. Is it not this same mighty, deep-seated power * * in politics, in religion, in literature, in morals, in all the manifold relations of life? Is that irresistible power, which, for fifty years, has shaken the Government, and agitated the people, to be subdued by pretending that it is an exceedingly simple thing, and that we ought not to talk about it? Yet this is the policy that Douglas is advocating."

[We quote Lincoln's speeches throughout from Bartlett's authorised edition.]

And lastly, at Galesburgh, in 1858, he said:—

"I believe the entire records of the world, from the date of the Declaration of Independence, up to within three years ago, may be searched in vain for one single affirmation, from one single man, that the negro was not included in the Declaration of Independence."

STATE RIGHT.

This Principle, what it is not, and what it is, next requires our attention.

And the Fathers of the Constitution, were as clear as are the present rising leaders, on the questions between National and State Sovereignty. Washington's opinions are well known, and have been quoted. His farewell was the combined work of himself and Hamilton, and passed the critical *legal* inspection of Judge Jay. We add a few opinions to those already given:—

"In every free and deliberating Society, there must, from the nature of man, be opposite parties. * * But if on a temporary superiority of the one party, the other is to resort to a *scission* of the Union, no Federal Government can ever exist." —*Thomas Jefferson.*

"However *gross a heresy* it may be to maintain that a *party to a compact has a right to revoke* that compact, the doctrine has had respectable advocates. The possibility of such a question shows the necessity of laying the foundation of our national Government *deeper than in the mere sanction of delegated authority.* The fabric of American empire ought to rest on *the solid basis of the consent of the People.*"—*Hamilton,* in Federalist.

"Have they said, 'we the States?' Have they made a proposal of compact between States? If they had, this would be a confederation; *it is* otherwise, most clearly, *a consolidated Government*."—*Patrick Henry*, Virginian Convention, 1788.

"The great and fundamental defect of the Confederation of 1781, was, that it carried the decrees of the Federal Council to the States in their sovereign capacity. *The great and incurable defect of all former Governments*, such as the Amphictyonic, Achæan, and Lycian Confederacies, and the Germanic, Helvetic, Hanseatic, and Dutch Republics, *is*, *that they were sovereignties over sovereignties*. The first effort to relieve the people of the country from the state of degradation and ruin came from Virginia. The General Convention afterwards met at Philadelphia, in May, 1787. The plan was submitted to a Convention of delegates, *chosen by the people* at large in each State for assent and ratification. Such a measure was laying the foundations of the fabric of our national polity,—*where alone they ought to be laid*,—on the broad consent of *the People*."—*Chancellor Kent*. Commentaries, VI. p. 225.

"In the most elaborate expositions of the Constitution by its friends, its character as a permanent form of Government, as a fundamental law, as a supreme rule, *which no State was at liberty to disregard*, *to suspend*, *or to annul*, was constantly admitted and insisted upon."—1. *Story*, 225. "*There was no reservation of any right* on the part of any State to dissolve the connection, or to abrogate its assent, or *to suspend the operation of the Constitution as to itself*."—*Chief Justice Story*.

In 1830, Maddison, when appealed to by Clay as the author of the idea of nullification, denied the truth of any such construction; and Mr. Everett says:—

"It was repeatedly and emphatically declared by Mr. Maddison, that they (the resolutions of nullification) were *intended to claim*, *not for an individual State*, but *for the United States*, the right of remedying its abuses in constitutional ways," &c.

Mr. Pinckney declared, that "The separate independence and *individual Sovereignty of the several*

States were never thought of by the enlightened band of patriots who framed the Declaration of Independence."—*Elliott's Debates.*

"I hear," said WEBSTER (March 7th, 1850), "with distress and anguish, the word 'Secession.'!! And HENRY CLAY, in 1850, thus referred to Rhett, "If he pronounced a sentiment attributed to him, raising the standard of disunion and of resistance to the common Government, whatever he has been, if he follows up that declaration by corresponding overt acts, *he will be a traitor*, and I hope he will meet the fate of a traitor. If Kentucky to-morrow unfurls the banner of resistance *unjustly*, I never will fight under that banner. *I owe a paramount allegiance to the whole Union*—a subordinate one to my own State. * * I said that I thought there was *no right* on the part of one or more of the States *to secede* from this Union. * * Sir, we may search the pages of history, and *none so furious, so bloody, so implacable, so exterminating* * * *as will be that war* which shall follow that disastrous event, if that event ever happens, *of dissolution*."—*Benton's ab. Deb.* v. 16, p. 594.

The principles of National and State rights are not conflicting. They support one another. On this no man has spoken more ably or clearly than Mr. Lincoln.

His inaugural declared that:—

"Our States have neither more nor less power than that reserved to them in the Union by the Constitution,—no one of them ever having been a State *out* of the Union. The original ones passed into the Union even *before* they cast off their British colonial dependence; and the new ones came into the Union directly from a condition of dependence, excepting Texas.

"Much has been said about the '*sovereignty*' of the States; but the word even is not in the National Constitution; nor, as is believed, in any of the States Constitutions. What is a sovereignty? Would it be far wrong to define it 'a political

2 G 2

community without a political superior?' Tested by this, *no one of our States, except Texas, ever was a sovereignty,* and even Texas gave up the character on coming into the Union.

"This relative matter of *National power and State rights* is no other than the principle of GENERALITY and LOCALITY. Whatever concerns the whole should be confided to the whole; whatever concerns *only* the State, should be left exclusively to the State."

FEDERATION.

Thus the American Constitution laid the foundation of a perpetual Federative system for the first time in the world. The rebellion, which assails the rights of Nation, State, and Individual, and outrages the new principle they have set up, has been crushed by them. All previous confederacies that have gone down, have gone down for the want of the principle introduced into the American system. It was the especial admiration of De Tocqueville. *It avoided the fatal error of placing a Sovereignty under a Sovereignty.* It laid its foundations on the People. It denied to States the right of dissolution or secession. Herein, Kent and Story both point out what it is, what it ought to be. As to its sphere, the principle of Locality binds State action, leaving the principle of Generality to be vindicated by the People, upon whom the national Constitution reposes, and who are members alike of State and Nation. There wants no reconstruction here, nothing but "to execute the laws," and to see that Slavery, the only element that disturbs National and State relations, is—as the Fathers supposed it would be—*extinguished.*

The true, the special, the noble, and the indispensable use of the American State right theory is this—*not* to establish an organized anarchy of impossible conflicting Sovereignties, but *to give to every Individual in the Empire, immutable material guarantees of the Sovereignty of his Freedom under the Constitution, as against any possible Despotism.* This war has proved that the Individual will side with the Government against unconstitutional State Sovereignty. Human nature itself guarantees an union between the Individual and the State against any great abuses of centralised power.

§

As to these true principles of Democracy, the rights of majorities under the Constitution, loyalty to that Constitution,—the *spirit* and the *form* of Republican government, the conflicts between Labour and Capital, and the great principle of Equality, it is worth while to quote the dicta of Lincoln, the most representative man of the age—one of the most conservative also— on the following ;—

EQUALITY.

"What I do say is, *that no man is good enough to govern another man without the other's consent.* I say *this is the leading principle of American Republicanism.*"—Oct. 1854.

"That central idea in our political system at the beginning was, and until recently continued to be, *the equality of men.* Slavery and oppression must cease, or American liberty must perish. True Democracy makes no inquiry about the colour of the skin, &c."—*Lincoln,* Sept. 1858.

LOYALTY.

"There is scarcely one (of our regiments) from which there could not be selected a President, a Cabinet, a Congress, abundantly competent to administer the government itself. * * This is essentially *a people's contest.* On the side of the Union it is a struggle for maintaining in the world that form and substance of government, whose leading object is to *elevate the condition of men,—to lift artificial weights from all shoulders,*—to afford all an unfettered start, and a fair chance in the race of life."

"I am most happy to believe that the plain people understand and appreciate this. * * Not one *common soldier* or common sailor is known to have deserted his flag. To the last man, so far as is known, they have successfully resisted the traitorous efforts of those whose commands but an hour before they obeyed as absolute law."

MAJORITIES.

"If the minority will not acquiesce, the majority must, or the Government must cease. *A majority held in restraint* by constitutional checks and limitations, and always *changing easily* with deliberate changes of popular opinion and sentiments, *is the only true sovereignty of a free People.* Whoever rejects it does of necessity fly to anarchy or despotism."—*Inaugural.*

"Our popular Government has often been called an experiment. Two points in it our people have already settled;—the successful *establishing* and the successful *administering* of it. One still remains;—its successful *maintenance* against a formidable internal attempt to overthrow it. It is now for them to demonstrate to the world that * * when ballots have fairly and constitutionally decided, *there can be no successful appeal back to bullets,* * * teaching men that what they cannot take by an *election,* neither can they take by a war.

"* * After the rebellion, the Executive will be guided by the Constitution and the laws."

CAPITAL AND LABOUR.

"There is one point to which I ask a brief attention. It is

the effort to place CAPITAL on an equal footing with, if not above LABOUR, in the structure of Government. It is assumed that nobody labours unless somebody else, owning capital, somehow, by the use of it, induce him to labour. Now there is no such relation between capital and labour as assumed, *nor is there any such thing as a free man being fixed for life in the condition of a hired labourer.* Both these assumptions are false, and all inferences from them are groundless. LABOUR IS PRIOR TO, AND INDEPENDENT OF, CAPITAL. Capital is only the fruit of labour. *Labour is the superior of capital,* and deserves much the highest consideration. The prudent penniless beginner labours for wages awhile, saves a surplus, then labours on his own account another while, and at length there is another new beginner to help him."—Dec. 3rd, 1861.

REPUBLICAN FORM.

"The Constitution provides, and all the States have accepted the provision, that 'the United States shall guarantee to every State in this Union a Republican form of government.' But if a State may lawfully go out of the Union, having done so, it may also discard the Republican form of government; so that to prevent its going out is an indispensable means to the end of maintaining the *guarantee.*"

"* * No popular Government can long survive a marked precedent, that those who carry an election can only save the Government from inevitable destruction by giving up the main point upon which the people gave the election."—July 4th, 1861.

§

As far as the phase of the contest would then admit, all the principles for which the friends of freedom contend, and which have been specially affirmed by the Republicans, are specified in the platforms of 1856 and 1860.

Let us note here the *culminating force* of the Principles of the Party of Reconstruction.

The Platform adopted at Philadelphia, June 1856, by the National Republican Convention, demanded, as we have seen, the restoration of the Principles of Washington and *Jefferson*, of the Declaration, and of the inalienable rights of man.

It also denounced the Ostend manifesto (about Cuba); demanded the railroad to the Pacific; improvements of rivers and harbours, &c.

The Chicago Convention, of May, 1859, through its chairman, Mr. Wilmot, declared that "it was the mission of the Republican party *to restore to the Government the policy of the revolutionary Fathers:* to read the Constitution as they read it. Slavery was sectional—Freedom, national." &c.

This convention also re-affirmed the principles of the Declaration. Further, it demanded a complete Homestead Bill, a full welcome to foreigners, national improvements, and a railway to the Pacific.

And even the "War Democrat" convention, of November, 1864, at New York, adopted as a funmental condition for regaining the confidence of the country, the advocacy of the direct vote of every citizen for President and Vice-President.

REPUBLICAN ASCENDANCY.

And we have seen that the main plank of the platform of Mr. Lincoln's second term election, was a resolution, that, inasmuch as "*Slavery* must be always and everywhere hostile *to the principle of Republican Government, justice and principle demand its utter and complete extirpation from the soil of the Republic;*" and without Slavery, its material basis, how can Oligarchy stand against that which is *at once the Ideal, the Law, the Policy, the Custom, and the Passion of the Nation?*

§

Having examined the *Principles* of American Nationality, Democracy, and Federation, as interpreted by the opinions, intentions, and acts of the leading men and parties, let us see now, firstly, *what is this Nation* that has to be reconstructed,—that is to say, what are its RESOURCES, intellectual and material; and secondly, what are the main ITEMS OF RECONSTRUCTION; and thirdly, what, in our judgment, will be the most PROBABLE RESULT of the process?

PART IV.

THE NATIONAL RESOURCES.

MATERIALS OF RECONSTRUCTION.

The resources of the American nation is a subject so vast that the merest outline tries the attention and strains the imagination.

Yet now that those resources have been organised and developed to an extent which fifty years might not otherwise have equalled,—now that the great disturbing and retarding influence is being cast out,—now that Democracy re-commences, with fresh advantage, a career, that before had no parallel, we must at least count the elements of reconstruction, and see whither this royal nation of the people now doth tend.

The Resources of the American nation consist of its Great Men, its Races, its Climate, its Numbers, its Territory, its Individual Value, or education, its Wealth, its Armaments, &c.

First (for the great men are already known), its wealth of bloods. Its new national type assimilating all others, and tending to retain the good and refuse the bad qualities of all the races that flow into it.

RACES AND CLIMATE.

The greatest gift of God to the world is a new and noble race, and the American type, now that it has conquered the cavaliers, and has proved its breeding, may perhaps be thought worthy of attention. We call that of the reader to the following, from the *North British Review*:—

"Remarkable as are many of the phenomena presented to us in the New World, the most remarkable, as it seems to us, is the *extraordinary commingling* of diverse races. * * From every country in Europe settlers have reached the American shore, * * and are shaken together and amalgamated, till the original distinctions disappear, and a new national type is formed. * * Within a century we may expect to see * * an *ethnographically composite*, yet *socially homogeneous*, population, existing all over North America. The intermingled white blood of Europe will here and there be tinged with the native red blood of America. Nor does the strange commixture of population stop here. Not only Europe and America, but *Africa*, and, in a lesser degree, *Asia*, will be represented in the *new race* which is growing up in the New World. The *Chinese* settlers in California are the *vanguard* of a more numerous emigration, which will, ere long, take place from the crowded fields of China to the American shores of the Pacific."

The earth has been so organised as to prescribe and prophesy the actual order of Human History. This historic course of empire is westward along the north temperate zone.

"The general structure" (says Capt. Hunt, corps of Engineers U.S. army, in "Union Foundations, a fact in Science," Trübner, 1863) "of the North American continent is strikingly simple. The Sierra Madre and Rocky Mountain system extending 4000 miles north-westerly from the Isthmus to the Arctic ocean, is the grand axis of upheaval; a vast triangular plain resting on this great mountain barrier as a base, projects its vertex outward to the coast of Labrador. This magnificent continental plain, having an average elevation above the sea of between 600 and 700 feet, and nowhere in mass exceeding 2500 feet, unlike the vast, bleak, sterile and frozen table lands of Asia, has every orographical, climatic, and fertile requisite for playing a master part in the grand drama of human progress. The table lands of Bavaria and Spain are elevated much above even the summit lines of this great American expanse. There is a general ascent Southwards through the West-American valley. This upward slope tends to counteract the increase of heat, thus preserving a temperate climate even in Mexico.

"There are tropical races and temperate races, each thriving only in its own proper climate. The U.S. territory lies wholly in the north temperate or truly historic zone. North America directly confronts Europe, and in the grand order of historic progress belongs to the Caucasian race. The African is of all men most tropical. Caucasians will soon want all the temperate land of the Earth.

"We cannot but connect our negro problem with the still mysterious future of the Amazon valley. The true solution of the whole negro problem may perhaps be found in a destined African Empire of the Amazon, the Equatorial Empire of the future."

In view of these vast possibilities of race-adjustment in the future, we must remember that the plain of the Amazon out-measures one and a half Mississippi valleys, that its rain-fall exceeds that of the Gulf States, and that the climate is greatly mitigated by trade winds, whilst the abounding forests mark the fertile soil. Even the effête civilisation of China may be destined to be vitalised here. In 1848 Brazil contained three millions of slaves and half a million of free negroes, out of a population of about five millions and a half.

Yet while Humboldt's Isothermal lines show the temperature of New York to resemble that of Dublin, Berlin, (south of) and Sebastopol, that of New Orleans equals Cairo and north of Canton, and a line drawn between Guatemala and Panama cuts the north of mid Africa and Madras, thus affording ample heat for mixed African races north of Panama.

In these central American republics, there are about 100,000 Whites, 800,000 mixed races, 10,000 Blacks, and 1,109,000 Indians. These races range from 6 individuals to 41 per square mile, and average, according to Squier's estimate, only 13. But the census shows that the mere *increase* of Population in the Free States of America, from 1790 to 1860, was nearly 51 per square mile, whilst the Population of Germany and France, are about 148 and 176, respectively, to a like area. With such sparse settlements, such adaptation of climate, such facilities, inducements, and necessities, as will be brought to bear upon them, there is much to be said for the "manifest destiny" of the "Black Yankees" in Central America.

This question of race-mixture is now being tried out. If the African will mix with the White, the question settles itself thus. It seems probable that he will. But whether he will or not, the American History, Genius, Constitution, and Nationality are pledged to his political Equality.

The natural home of the Negro pure is under the vertical sun; the political tendency is to give him freedom and equality; that of Slavery *has* been to mix the qualities of the races with their bloods, and to fit the African for the temperate zone.

The physical geography of North America proclaims her Unity organic and indestructible, and shows that there can be no permanent conflict of races there. The history of the world would seem to devote that region to Caucasian immigration, but the political tendency, no less marked and clear, is to share political immunities with all other races the Caucasian can absorb.

The effect of the race-mixture of negroes with Americans depends absolutely on two things; 1st, *The proportions* of the one to the other; and, 2nd, their *Localisation:* the first again depends upon *the continuance or cessation of immigration*, and on *the ratio of natural increase:* as to the second, the negro race may of course be settled *as such* in Florida or elsewhere, or allowed to commingle. In the latter case, the causes that promote homogeneousness, namely, blood admixture, and the influence of climate, will both have full sway. The whole thing is no matter of doubt or chance, but as Mr. Draper explains, of mathematical demonstration.

"A national type pursues its way physically and intellectually through changes and developments answering to those of the individual. This orderly process may be disturbed exteriorly by emigration or interiorly.

* * * "By interior disturbance, particularly by *blood admixture*, with more rapidity may a national life be affected, the result plainly depending on the extent to which admixture has taken place. *This is a disturbance capable of mathematical computation.* If the blood admixture is only of limited amount and transient in its application, its effect will sensibly disappear in no very great period of time, though never, perhaps, in absolute reality. This accords with the observation of philosophical historians, who agree in the conclusion that a small tribe intermingling with a larger one will only disturb it in a temporary manner, and, after the course of a few years, the effect will cease to be perceptible. Nevertheless, the influence must really continue much longer than is outwardly apparent; and the result is the same as when, in a liquid, a drop of some other kind is placed, and additional quantities of the first fluid added. Though it might have been possible at first to detect the adulteration without trouble, it becomes every moment less and less possible to do so, and before long it cannot be done at all. But the drop is as much present at last as it was at first: it is merely masked; its properties overpowered.

"Considering in this manner the contamination of a numerous nation, a trifling amount of foreign blood admixture would appear to be indelible, and the disturbance, at any moment, capable of computation by the ascertained degree of dilution that has taken place. But it must not be forgotten that there is another agency at work, energetically tending to bring about homogeneousness: it is *the influence of external physical conditions.* The intrusive adulterating element possesses in itself no physiological inertia, but as quickly as may be is brought into correspondence with the new circumstances to which it is exposed, herein running in the same course as the element with which it had mingled had itself antecedently gone over.

"National homogeneousness is thus obviously secured by the operation of two distinct agencies: the first gradual but inevitable dilution: the second, motion to come into harmony with the external, natural state. The two conspire in their effects." —Pp. 14-15, v. 1. *Draper's Intellectual Development of Europe.*

The following extract from a speech at the Cooper Institute, New York, 1863, well puts the question, from the Republican point of view:—

"God, counselling with himself how to crown this people the greatest on the earth, said, 'Of what fibre shall I make them?' and he poured into their veins the *Saxon* blood, painting their eyes with the sky, and gilding their hair with the sun. Then he mingled with it the Celtic, quickened with mercury and touched with fire. Then he poured into it the sunny wines of the *South of Europe.* Then, after many other gifts, he added,—last, but *not least,*—a strange mysterious current that * * carries the blackness of darkness into men's faces," &c.

"*Three stupendous processes of intermingling* are going forward in this country. First, we are absorbing the *Irish* race. Second, we are absorbing the *German* race. Third, are we absorbing the *Negro* race? * * The black race in this country is losing its typical blackness. The race is taking to itself the blood of the aristocracy of the South. The negro is filling his veins from two fountains of life. A hundred years ago a mulatto was a curiosity: now the mulattoes are half a million.

"God said, 'How shall I prepare a continent to be the home of such a people?' And he ribbed it through the centre with mountain chains, that the *Swiss* and the *Swede* coming hither might renew their ancient fellowship with the eternal hills. He salted it on either side with two great seas, that the *maritime people of Europe,* coming hither, might find still fairer coasts for their ships. He laid his levelling palm upon it, that the *Hollander,* coming hither, might see the Zuyder Zee, touched by miracle of nature, blooming into an illimitable level of prairie grass. Last, but not least, he stretched its Southern slope into the tropical heats, that the *negro* also might find a home, where he and the eagle should look together at the sun." —*Theodore Tilton.*

With regard to the past mode of this mixing of the races, we should not be justified in omitting the following:—

"Licentiousness is one of the foul features of slavery everywhere; but it is especially prevalent and indiscriminate where *slave breeding is conducted as a business.* It grows directly out of the system, and is *inseparable* from it. The pecuniary inducement to general pollution must be very strong, since the larger the slave increase, the greater the master's gains, and *especially since the mixed bloods command a considerably higher price than the pure blacks.*"—Report of the British and Foreign Anti-Slavery Society.

POPULATION.

Perhaps the best illustration of the extraordinary increase in Population in America is given by Lincoln himself, when he says:—"There are already among us those who, if the United States be preserved, will live to see it contain *Two hundred and fifty millions!* The struggle of to-day is for the vast future also."

And here it must be remembered, that now, Labour and Capital will work *together*, in the progress of the nation, and will be aided by the new homestead law, high wages, extinction of slavery, increased confidence in national institutions, and augmented immigration. Population, if as dense as in England, would exceed *Twelve Hundred millions.* If as dense as Massachusetts, it would nearly reach half that number.

Of resources and capabilities in Territory, Education and labour,—the three other material bases of nationality (and of wealth, their common result), we here submit an analysis of a census summary, &c., by the Hon. Robert J. Walker,—1st as to

TERRITORY.

The area of the United States is 3,250,000 square miles; larger than all Europe, and sixty times as large as England.

Up to September 1860, 1,055,911,288 acres were unsold and unappropriated.

The United States territory is all within the temperate zone.

It fronts two oceans; contains every variety of product; a greater extent of mines—coal, iron, gold, silver, and quicksilver, than all Europe; a vast system of navigable streams, exceeding, in cheap water communication, all Europe. The shore line of its rivers is 122,784 miles, employing an interior steam tonnage exceeding the internal steam tonnage of all the world besides, and the cost of canals, of equal capacity, would have been more than ten thousand millions of dollars, and would have been subject to tolls and lockage.

It has more harbours, accessible at all tides, than all Europe. Its hydraulic power, timber, and raw material, exceed those of all Europe.

It has constructed more miles of telegraph and rails than all the world. It has more lighthouses than any other country, and *no light dues.*

The tonnage, at its present ratio of progression, would, in A.D. 1901, exceed that of all the world.

The imperial railway to the Pacific, will flood

the mighty districts which it penetrates, with population, labour, capital, and supplies.

It offers every variety (within the temperate zone) of climate, produce, stock, society; 160 acres free to every emigrant adult, *whose sons, at* 21, *are entitled to the same quantity*, and whose widow, children, or heirs, succeed thereto. It offers also *freedom, competence, hope, suffrage, and free schools.*

LABOUR, EDUCATION, WEALTH.

These three are indissolubly connected. "Labour is King." Slavery curses but a fraction of this vast dominion, and has now been prohibited by an organic law of the Constitution, probably agreed to by many more than the requisite three-fourths of the States. The *mines alone* exceed in value the public debt.

The average annual value of produce per man, woman, and child, in Massachusetts, in 1860, was $300. The average annual immigration, from December 1850 to December 1860, was 259,821,—take it at 260,000, and reckon their annual labour value at only $100, the immigration labour value of the first year produced $26,000,000,—the last $260,000,000, and the total, in ten years, $1,430,000,000 (fourteen hundred and thirty millions of dollars.)

This allows for no re-investment or increase in population.

But wealth there increases 126-45 per cent. in ten years. Compound this increase from immigration, the result is over three thousand millions of dollars in 1870, and seven thousand millions in 1880, *apart from any immigration after* 1860.

American resources rest on bases so natural and indestructible, that no probable events can essentially impair them.

The census (p. 195) shows the total value of real and personal estate to have been

In 1860	. . .	$16,159,616,068
„ 1850	. . .	7,135,780,228

An increase of 126-45 per cent. in the ten years.

The same rate of increase, for the four succeeding decades, would give, in 1900, $423,330,438,288 (more than four hundred thousand millions.)

Subtract one-fourth, and the result is that the whole national and war debt is less than three-fourths *of one per cent. of the increase of national wealth.*

The causes of these stupendous results are freedom, education, unlimited land, absence of unnatural restrictions, and a vast immigration.

Four States were added, from 1850 to 1860. Six more will be added, from 1860 to 1870. Five of the new territories were not valued at all in 1860, and nine of the free States and Territories had grown in value 411 per cent in the decade.

The Intensity and power of a free Labour propagandism, is best shown by consulting that oracle of Destiny,—the American Census.

§

EDUCATION is nothing less than the propagandism of free and just ideas.

50,000,000 acres of public land were appropriated for education up to 1860. During the last fiscal year 1,160,533 acres were entered under the Homestead Act.

The census analysis demonstrates that *South Carolina*, the apostle of Slavery and head of the great oligarchic rebellion, is *nearer to the lowest savage and barbarous condition than she is to the free State of Massachusetts.*

Also that one man's *labour* in free Massachusetts was worth more than two in Maryland, and four in *South Carolina.*

That the *circulation of newspapers*, &c., in Massachusetts, exceeded, in 1860, that of South Carolina by ninety-eight millions of copies. That the former State had 158,637 more *pupils at public schools* than the latter.

That, in 1860, Massachusetts had 222 newspapers and periodicals. Maryland 57, *all devoted to Slavery*,—not one to science, religion, or literature.

That in Massachusetts *profit on capital* was 35 per cent. In Maryland 17. That in the former State the annual value of *products* of labour, commerce, and navigation, *per capita*, was three times that in the latter, although the latter is more favoured by nature.

That the miles of railroads were, in 1860, 1340 in the former State, against 380 in the latter.

That the natural inevitable results of a change from Slavery to Freedom would soon add to the national wealth a sum, in comparison with which the debt is scarcely a flea-bite.

That the increase of Population is nearly threefold in Free States, as compared with Slave States.

That, in comparing these, it must be borne in mind that in *area*, Maryland exceeds Massachusetts 43 per cent. In climate it far exceeds it. In fertility, in mines of coal and iron, in harbours, and length of shore line. Also, that, in 1790, the two States contained about equal population.

But it must be noted that the great results achieved in Massachusetts are not those of free labour alone, but of universal free-schools, press, speech, and government.

These results, therefore, of their universality of Freedom and equality, are not alone witnesses for Freedom as against Slavery, *but for Democracy as against Oligarchy.*

"Including commerce, the value, *per capita*, of the products and earnings of Massachusetts exceeds not only those of any State in the Union, *but in the world.*"

"It is," says Walker,—after an elaborate analysis of the census, "a fact, that the Governments of the United States, State and Federal, since 1790, *have appropriated for* EDUCATION *more money than all the other Governments of the world* combined, during the same period. This is a stupendous fact, and one of the main causes of our wonderful progress and prosperity. We believe that knowledge is power, and have appropriated nearly $300,000,000, during the last 74 years, in aid of the grand experiment.

"Our *patent office* is a wonderful instance of this principle, showing on the part of our *industrious classes*, more valuable inventions and discoveries, annually, than are produced by the working men of all the rest of the world."—(P. 12., Letter V.)

In South Carolina more than three-fourths of the people can neither read nor write.

By census, table 37, the total copies of newspapers and periodicals, circulated in 1860, in the

United States, were 927,591,584, of which only 167,917,188 were in the Slave States.

* * "It is thus demonstrated by the official statistics of the census, from 1790 to 1860, that the total annual product of the Free States, *per capita*, exceeds that of the Slave States, largely more than two to one, and, including commerce, very nearly three to one. As regards *education* also we see, that the ratio in favour of the Free States is more than *four to one* in the year 1850, and, in the year 1860, more than *five to one*. In 1859 agricultural products of the Free States were $2,527,676,000 per annum, and of the Slave States only $862,234,000. The value of the lands of the Free States was $25·19 per acre,—of the Slave States $10·46 per acre. The product of the improved lands of the Free States was $28·68 per acre, and of the Slave States $11·55, whilst, *per capita*, the result was $131·48 to $70·56."

Thus we prove, not only what the North is, but what the South might be,—what it will add to the national value when it is replanted with freemen.

The increase of wealth is 126·45 per decade. If the wealth of the country were increased only *one-tenth* in the next ten years, *by the gradual disappearance of Slavery* (far below the results of the census), then, the wealth being now (1860) $16,159,616,068, such one-tenth additional increase would make the wealth in 1870, instead of $36,593,450,585, more than sixteen hundred millions greater; and, in 1880, instead of $82,865,868,849, three thousand six hundred millions more. The *additional* increase being more than the debt.

ARMAMENTS.

The question of armaments, is a question of

money and of science,—and, ultimately, of nationality. It is one of permanent interest.

The leaders of rebellion have used force, to make up for every want in every movement, since Slavery, as an organised interest, has existed. Their finance was sequestration. The national Government has not used force as a financial element, though in that, as in every other national struggle, force is a just and necessary instrument as against those who would profit by the national agony, but refuse to sustain the national life.

A Government pays, in the first place, in promises and paper. The only *substance* then received, is coin for interest. Finance, therefore, depends upon Faith. Faith, pure and simple, where interest is paid in paper,—or Faith, tempered with cash-paid interest. Faith in the Material Resources, and in the national willingness to pay. And the willingness depends, at last, upon the principle of nationality. The average unbelief in the convertibility of paper money, or the inconvenience felt in its use, or its redundancy, constitute the depreciation,—any laws about it notwithstanding.

A Government gets the means of buying, in one of two ways. By making and circulating paper money;—by raising loans, bearing interest, payable in coin. Of course, when lenders are obliged to take interest in paper, or obliged to Fund their advances, force comes in, and the financier proper goes out. Paper depreciates;—Loans command terms according to the condition of the market for the time being; Taxes may or may not be submitted to. The ultimate questions then about money resources are; First, How far will the nation submit to be taxed? and, Second, what amount of unbelief is felt in the ultimate payment,—or of inconvenience, in paper payments, or in deferred payments? Therefore, the only limit to the money power of a nation, is its own ability or willingness to pay taxes, whether for principal or interest,—and the faith of the lending world in the ability or willingness of the Government, and nation, and the value of the promise to pay.

Finance, therefore, is a question of ability to pay, and of willingness,—or of force. The logic of War is force. War always develops its logic, if the question be only lasting. If the object of the war be *national*, the nation that asserts its unity—its will, over the life, will always assert it over the pocket. Iron, if there be much of it, will always get gold, as long as there be any of *that.* It is the logic that Solon launched at Crœsus,—it was the laugh of Hannibal, at the merchants weeping for their money.

There was, however, a considerable delusion in England, about the effect of the *Premium on gold.* Paper money circulated as before; it was not too inconvenient, and the People believed in it. It is only when payments have to be made abroad, that the gold premium becomes a decisive question.

With regard to willingness, America has been always inexorably averse to tax-paying in time of peace, and in time of war, equally ready to pay. It is the spirit of Franklin, throughout, who was ready to spend nineteen shillings in the pound to defend the right to spend the twentieth shilling as he pleased. *Willingness* to pay, is, in fact, *a question of the spirit and power of nationality.* With regard to the ability to pay, or *National Solvency*, the *data* are in the national wealth. We have just given them.

It should however be added that what with agricultural and domestic products consumed by their producers, mechanical products individually below $500 per annum, labour in clearing and improving lands, building and repairing railways, canals, houses, manufactories, vessels, &c., none of which appear in the census, nearly half the annual yield is omitted therefrom.

Moreover, only about $1\frac{634}{1000}$ per cent. of land in Slave States has hitherto been brought into cultivation. Their largest production was 5,196,944 bales in 1860. Their capacity was from 50 to 100 million of bales annually. The Slave trade was, the Cotton trade is, in its infancy.

There are said to be two millions of square miles where *Petroleum* will probably be found, and Pennsylvania alone has reached an annual thirty millions of gallons.

Tests are either relative or absolute. The absolute tests are the actual capital and resources, and the proportion they bear to the debt. Relative tests are to be applied either to the exertion of America herself, in her past, or to those of other nations in great crises.

The question at issue, is, will Americans submit to pay interest on the debt, or to pay it off.

The popular character of the Government is a mighty element in this question, both as to productiveness and as to willingness. For all authorities agree that for any proper object, *willingness to bear taxation is in exact ratio to the freedom of the people.*

THE DEBT.

With regard to the *absolute test*,—of the amount of national capital, we desire to add nothing to the figures already given.

With regard to the *relative taxable power* of America, as compared with *other nations*, we will first take the amount of taxes borne by England in various years; premising that the fact that the annual taxes for the support of the English Government in time of peace, exceed $12 per head, whilst in America they have averaged less than $2 per head, only strengthens the taxable power of America in a crisis.

In 1801, they equalled 30 per cent. per head on incomes; in 1811, 42 per cent.; in 1815, 35 per cent; enabling it to cope with twice the number of Frenchmen for twenty-three years. A system of taxation on the North, *one-half* as rigid as that practised against Napoleon, would produce, in America, a fund equivalent to keeping one million of men constantly in the field. The cost of the Crimean and Italian wars was stated by Mr. Robb, to be together, to all the parties concerned, about fifteen hundred millions of dollars,—and this for wars, to most of the payers, merely of policy and foreign interest. English stocks, moreover, ordinarily at 90, have before now stood at 65, and fallen to 53, payable in depreciated paper.

Applying the relative test, from the past exertions *of America*, we find the following facts:—

The mere education or school tax imposed on New York City, for the year 1864—1865, was two millions six hundred thousand dollars.

The report of Mr. Cameron, the Secretary of War, in 1861, stated that in the war of the Revolution, Massachusetts had supplied troops to the extent of one in six of the entire population, at which proportion the loyal States could furnish *over three millions of men.*

A debt of $500,000,000 is *not one-fifth so large, in proportion to their means*, and not greater in proportion to their population, than their people have twice contracted and twice paid.*

Upon the adoption of the Constitution, the debt was $80,000,000; the population, 3,900,000. This sum exceeded $20 per head per annum.

In 1816, the debt swelled to $127,000,000; the population was 8,500,000; the rate $15 per head. The debt was paid in 1825. The application of steam to locomotion has been almost wholly created since then.

The increase of wealth is in three-fold ratio to that of population. Locomotive engines perform the labour of 50,000,000 horses. The machinery brought into use since 1816, is equal to the labour of 500,000,000 men. The capital of the Union in 1860, was more than sixteen thousand millions. Upon this sum the income, at 20 per cent., would

* This calculation is quoted by Victor from the European Circular of an eminent New York Commission House,—Sept. 1861.

be three thousand millions, and 33 per cent. thereon would nearly reach $5,300,000,000 per annum.

A rate per head equal to that paid by the people of New York for municipal and State purposes would produce $450,000,000, or a rate equal to that assessed upon the taxable property of the city, $550,000,000.

It is calculated that 50 million dollars per annum would pay interest on 500 millions, and create a sinking fund for its early redemption. Two hundred millions of taxes, would do the same for two thousand millions of debt, and that on a population of only 20 millions, would be only 10 dollars a head. This is half the rate paid in 1790. Further, the mere increase of property by 1870 will be eight times two thousand millions.

Finally, many now living will see the American population two hundred and fifty millions. The year 1890 will find it more than one hundred millions. The year 1900 will find the national wealth, at a minimum calculation, four hundred thousand millions of dollars. What sort of a debt must it be to burthen one hundred millions of souls possessing four hundred thousand millions of property?

The present debt of England is above eight hundred millions of pounds, or four thousand millions of dollars to about thirty millions of souls. That of America is much less to a considerably larger population.

That of all Europe is, according to Mr. Kolb, a German statist, twelve thousand millions of dollars in 1860. At present England owes per head, as compared with America, nearly three to two.

In the future the American debt can scarcely fail to bear a ratio of progressive diminution as regards the wealth, and to the population.

According to all probabilities and calculations, positive and relative, for America to bankrupt itself, is simply, *not possible.*

These guarantees of national solvency, this ratio of increase in national territory, wealth, and population, is, in fact, so vast and overwhelming as not only to stand out from all shadow of parallelism, but almost to outrun imagination.

FINANCE AND NATIONAL UNITY.

The manner in which Mr. Chase first evoked good from evil, by making financial schemes conduce to *national Unity*, as well as *financial success*, is also an essential part of the reconstruction of the American nation.

It must here be noted, as due also to the policy of Lincoln, the genius of Chase, and the freedom and loyalty of the people.

The Buchanan administration had increased the rate of interest on Federal loans from six to nearly *twelve per cent.* per annum in a time of profound peace.

In 1863, the average rate of interest was lowered to 3.89 per annum. The result was here gained by a system of which the main features were:—

1st. A loan to Government upon its bonds,

reimbursible in twenty years, or after five, at the option of the nation;—interest payable in coin.

2nd. The issue of the United States legal tender notes were fundable in this stock.

3rd. The authorization of certain banks, whose circulation would be secured by private capital, and adequate deposits of United States stock with the Government.

This system had to contend with the power of 1642 banks, but was carried through by Mr. Chase. The results immediate and ultimate were:—

1st. To reduce the rate of interest.

2nd. To reduce the premium on gold, for Federal currency fundable in this stock, from 73 per cent. to 27.

3rd. To add to the national Unity, and make future secession almost impossible, from the direct and universal interest in the national solvency of *every banker*, of *every stockholder*, of *every trader*, of *every holder* of universal paper currency.

Mr. Chase's own statement, in a speech delivered in Ohio, in Oct. 1863 is of permanent interest:—

"When I began the duties of my office, that great leader,—perhaps I should say that great follower of public opinion, the London *Times*, said that Mr. Chase would soon be coming over there to borrow money to carry on this wicked war with, and that when he came he would not get it. I said in reply that I *would'nt go there to borrow money*, but that they should come here to ask me to take their money of them, and if they waited till Mr. Chase went there to borrow money they would wait till their green isle sank in the ocean. I began then to borrow all the gold I could get in the country. I raised *one hundred and seventy-five millions*, and began paying it out, and it was soon observed that it didn't come back near so fast as it was paid out. Presently capitalists refused to furnish any more, unless at extravagant rates, which I would'nt pay. More money must be raised. *Eastern banks* proposed to take the notes of the Government for the amount we wanted, with six per cent. interest, and then go to work to manufacture the money to furnish us. So all things would have gone swimmingly for a time, but presently something would have happened. What would you have had me do with such a proposition? Just what I did, I think. It seemed to me that if I could get the *collective notes of all our citizens* they would be just *as good as the notes of every bank.* What should I do then but get those notes—the notes of the whole people. What, in short, but make *greenbacks?* At first many thought it a bold and hazardous experiment. Many bankers predicted its disastrous failure, and a disposition was manifested to break us down by discrediting *this currency.* Some refused to take it altogether. What was there next to do? What would you have done if you had been in my place? Precisely what I did. I think you would have told them, as I did when they refused it, that they would have to take either that or nothing. In other words, you would have made your *currency a legal tender.* That was the next step. After that we came to an *issue of bonds, paying the interest on them in gold.* We found we could get the gold to do it, and that we thus had our finances on a basis that entirely satisfied the public demand for security of investments. Now, what is there in this system that does not seem precisely what any one of you would have felt like doing? You have a currency which supplies all your wants, which is simply *the faith and credit of the whole people put into money.* One step more was needed. It was necessary to have the capital of the country engaged in this circulation to give it stability and permanence. To secure this we devised the *national banking system.* The whole financial policy of the administration thus became as plain as the alphabet. It required simply an honest purpose to know what was best and right to be done, and, having found this right, it only remained to ask God for courage to walk in it. *Common sense and courage* are the alpha and omega of the theory and practice of finance thus far."

Whatever has happened to the rate of interest

and the gold, the effect of the new banking system on national unity will remain.

The proposal to pay the debt in twenty-five years is perfectly feasible. Meanwhile their war expenditure only equalled the English Peace expenditure. For two millions a day, or seven hundred millions yearly, at two shillings the depreciated dollar, is £70,000,000.

The Nation, also, in following after principle and right, has fortified itself in all the elements and conditions of nationality.

§

THE MONROE DOCTRINE.

CANADA, MEXICO, EFFECT OF PANAMA TRANSIT, &c.

Next to questions of Principle, the question of the territorial reconstruction (or construction) of America, is the greatest. It is fivefold;—CANADA; the TERRITORIES; the GULF STATES; MEXICO; and PANAMA. The first, is a question of time only; the circumstances which will add Canada to the United States, must, in due course arrive. The basis of their union already exists. The second, is no question, for Slavery would be forbidden in present Territories by the laws of political economy, even if man-made law admitted it. As to the Gulf States, political economy, and the mighty material influences of the temperate zone, and the strategic and commercial value of the Mississippi, and the power of the national idea, guarantee the failure there of both Slavery and Oligarchy. As to Mexico (from which, by the bye, more than half of all the silver in circulation in the world has been produced), and the whole region south-west of the great river to Panama, it is less suited for white labour, and was more open to the enterprise of the Slave Barons. There was nothing to prevent its forming with the South one community, had the South succeeded. That it will ultimately form part of the United States, will result from two causes; first, the Monroe doctrine is a national idea; and second, from a commercial point of view, America *must* hold it. The project may be rather hastened, from the fact that Napoleon has seized the great strategic traditional centre, from which the isthmus and the whole region is to be commanded.

Should *the general acknowledgment of the Principle of Federation*, precede the advance of American nationality, the above results would be modified, but would not be hostile to American Unity.

Now, the whole region is almost roadless, and the enormous labour of developing its resources, is a great element in the question, and especially obstructive to Europeans.

With regard to these last two Divisions of Territory, Mexico and Panama, we propose to adduce certain facts, the momentous bearing of which is exceedingly obvious, and yet, generally speaking, except by Napoleon and the Americans, scarcely observed at all. The main facts are as follows:*—

* On the whole of the Panama transit question, see Commander Bedford Pim's "Gate of the Pacific." Reeve and Co. 1863.

The Panama route is now the only transit, and European commerce tends and will tend more in that direction, notwithstanding transhipment.

This is expected to give Americans the control of the whole Pacific commerce (and armaments)—British Columbia, East Australia, New Zealand, Japan, etc. We should be at an immense disadvantage in time of war, and in time of peace, the two weeks' shorter route, *in favour of the United States*, "*would throw into their warehouses and shipping, the whole entire commerce of the Pacific Ocean.*"

We propose to quote, in illustration of these positions, two authorities. The Emperor of the French, writing in 1847, and the Official Report to the American Congress, dated January, 1849, on Communications between the Atlantic and Pacific.

Of course, it were to the Interest of England, for all reasons (and, not the least, the revivification of Jamaica interests, &c.), to join in the ownership and making of some interoceanic canal, and in the neutralization of some transit route. This it should be the policy of America to promote. But whether done or undone, certain advantages must remain with the United States.

The Tehuantepec route, now in Napoleon's power, was formerly treated for between the Mexican and American Governments. He now proposes from his action in Mexico, certain advantages, amongst which are "security to his West Indian colonies;" and to prevent the United States from being "the only dispensers of the products of the New World."

This, with many other momentous subjects, was, from the year 1840, deeply pondered by the Emperor Napoleon, while a prisoner at Ham, and in the pamphlet written by him, in 1847, he shows historically, how certain countries have prosperity forced upon them by Nature, *provided* they avail themselves of her assistance. He then proceeds to say respecting the third Panama scheme:—

"There exists in the New World a State as admirably situated as Constantinople, and we must say, up to the present time, as uselessly occupied; we allude to the State of Nicaragua. As Constantinople is the centre of the ancient World, so is the town of Leon, or rather Massaya, the centre of the new; and if the tongue of land which separates its two lakes from the Pacific Ocean were cut through, she would *command*, by her central position, *the entire coast of North and South America.* Like Constantinople, Massaya, is situated between two extensive natural harbours, capable of giving shelter to the largest fleets, safe from attack.

"The State of Nicaragua can become, better than Constantinople, *the necessary route for the great commerce of the world;* for it is for the United States the shortest road to China and the East Indies, and for England and the rest of Europe, to New Holland, Polynesia, and the whole of the western coast of America. The State of Nicaragua is then destined to attain to an extraordinary degree of prosperity and grandeur: for that which renders its *political position more advantageous than that of Constantinople*, is, that the great maritime powers of Europe would witness with pleasure, and not with jealousy, its attainment of a station no less favourable to its individual interests, than to the commerce of the world.

"France, England, Holland, Russia, and the United States, have a great commercial interest in the establishment of a communication between the two oceans; but *England has more than the other powers*, a political interest in the execution of this project.

"England will witness with satisfaction the opening of a

route which will enable her to communicate more speedily with Oregon, China, and her possessions in New Holland. She will find, in a word, that the advancement of Central America will renovate the declining commerce of Jamaica, and the other English islands in the Antilles, the progressive decay of which will be thereby stopped." * * *

"War and commerce have civilized the world. The time for war is gone by; commerce alone pushes its conquests. Let us then open to it a new route; let us aproximate the people of Oceana and Australia to Europe, and let us make them partakers of the blessings of Christianity and civilization. To accomplish this great undertaking we make an appeal to all *religious and intelligent men*, for this enterprise is worthy of their zeal and sympathy. We invoke the assistance of all *Statesmen*, because every nation is interested in the establishment of new and easy communications between the eastern and western parts of the globe. Finally, we call upon *capitalists*, because whilst they are promoting a glorious undertaking, they are sure to derive a large profit thereby."

§

The report to Congress, in Jan. 1849, confirms and enlarges on the opinions of the Emperor, and shows the importance "of placing the future management of the Panama transit *in the hands of our* (their) *own citizens*."

"Great Britain is principally indebted to her skill in commerce and manufactures for her commercial ascendancy, but she is also indebted, in no small degree, to her *position*. She not only has the ports of the continent of Europe as her neighbours, but she is *fifteen hundred miles, or two weeks*, nearer than we are *to all other parts of the world, except the Atlantic ports of the American continent north of the Equator and the West Indies.* The cause of this is, that all vessels bound from our ports to places south of the line, or beyond either of the Capes, *cross the Atlantic* to the Azores or Western Islands, *for the purpose of finding favourable winds*, while vessels from British ports run down to the same latitude and longitude without the necessity of crossing the ocean to avail themselves of the same advantages. This difference in favour of British commerce, *running through our entire existence as a nation,* has been a most serious obstacle for our merchants and navigators to contend with, and has of itself been *a vast item in favour of the profits on British capital.* Lieutenant M. F. Maury, Superintendent of the Observatory, has within two or three years past proposed a more direct route for vessels bound from our ports to ports on the Atlantic side of the American continent, south of the Equator and beyond Cape Horn, which will save about one thousand miles of the distance to those places, but all vessels bound round the Cape of Good Hope will be compelled to pursue the old route.

" *The construction of the proposed railroad across the Isthmus, will not only do away with this advantage over us, now possessed by European commerce and navigation, but will turn the tide in our favour.*"

" The average distance from Liverpool, London, and Havre, to Panama, is 4700 miles; from New York the distance is 2000 miles; from Charleston, 1400; from Savannah, 1300; from New Orleans and Mobile, 1600—making an average distance from our principal exporting Atlantic and Gulf ports of about 1600 miles to Panama. If, therefore, we admit, for the sake of the argument, that European commerce with the Pacific Ocean, and the East India and China Seas, will take the new route across the Isthmus, *there will be a difference of* 3100 *miles in our favour.* Add to this the 1500 miles now against us, and we find that *we shall gain* by this channel of communication, in our relative position to those parts of the world, *a distance of* 4600 *miles, or of* 42 *days. In the voyage out and home,* we shall have the advantage of our European competitors of 9200 *miles and* 84 *days,* as compared with the present route.

" Our ports are on the very wayside from Europe to the Isthmus of Panama, and our lines of steamers and packet ships across the Atlantic will come laden with the freights for that channel of trade. The commerce, therefore, from Europe to the East Indies, China, and the west coast of this continent, will be forced to pursue the old route, *or fall into our hands.*

" It is thus shown that *the new route* across the Isthmus will bring us more than an average of 10,000 miles nearer to the East Indies, China, and the ports of South America on the Pacific, and will actually, for all the purposes of navigation and commercial intercourse, *bring the ports of the west coast of Mexico, California, and Oregon,* 14,000 *miles nearer to us* than they now are! With steamers on each side of the Isthmus that will go fifteen miles an hour—a speed ascertained to be quite practicable,—passengers, the mails, and small packages of light and valuable goods, may be conveyed from New York to San Francisco in fourteen days, and from our southern ports in less time: thus bringing these remote points, for all practical purposes, nearer than New York and New Orleans were twenty years ago."

The report then shows how European vessels would, for commercial reasons, sail to ports and *entrepôts* of the United States, and that American vessels would practically become the *carriers* thence of the transit cargoes. It then proceeds:—

"Let this railroad be completed, however, and *no part of the world will present as great advantages for the successful use of steam in ocean navigation as the Pacific.* Coal is found on all its borders, both American and Asiatic, in the greatest quantity and perfection. Its quiet waters seem to indicate steam as the proper agent to be employed in their navigation. The spirit and genius of the American people, and the extent of our territory on the west side of the continent, proclaims clearly enough that we are to become the legitimate heirs of a vast commerce that shall spread fleets of steam-ships over the bosom of this peaceful ocean.

"Steamers, with a speed of twelve miles an hour, would go from New York, *viâ* the Isthmus (throwing out the fractions):—

To Calcutta . . .	in 47 days.
To Canton . . .	36 ,,
To Shanghae . . .	35 ,,
To Valparaiso . .	17 ,,
To Callao . . .	12 ,,
To Guayaquil . . .	9½ ,,

To Panama . . .	in 7 days.
To San Blas . . .	12 „
To Mazatlan . . .	14 „
To San Diego . . .	16 „
To San Francisco . .	18 „

"This undertaking will place us so far ahead in the race for commercial supremacy, that they *can never overtake us.*

* * "European Governments and capitalists would not fail to perceive that its completion would *transfer the seat of commercial empire* to the Western hemisphere."

It will be observed that there is an enormous saving of time for steamers, a still greater saving for sailing vessels. This will tend to constitute *Americans* the factors of the whole of that hemisphere, extreme East as well as West. And the Suez route, though some ten days shorter from London to Calcutta, is longer to places six days east of that, besides being in the hands of France.

§

On the questions of political and commercial relationships, no better informed authorities exist than those we have quoted.

The principle of the foreign policy of Jefferson survives to this hour, though transferred from New Orleans to Mexico.

"*France*," said Jefferson, "*placing herself in that door assumes to us the attitude of defiance.* The impetuosity of her temper, the energy and restlessness of her character, placed in a point of *eternal friction* with us, &c. The day that France takes possession of New Orleans fixes the sentence which is to restrain her for ever within her low water-mark. It seals the union of two nations, who, in conjunction, can maintain exclusive possession of the ocean. *From that moment we must marry ourselves to the British fleet and nation.*"*

* *Jefferson's Works*, vol. v. p. 432.

Surely a policy of alliance between England and all her children would be complete, natural, and invincible.

And the advent of the Austrian to Mexico, renders rather *more* probable the final annexation of that territory to the United States. If the French and the Austrians may interfere, so, before all, may the Americans. Three thousand miles off, and with not even "the German Fleet," Austria is in poor case to contest with America. When the American nation shall be prepared to occupy these latitudes, they will have the country,—Mexico-Milian, or Napoleon, notwithstanding. Already have Americans extensively mixed their blood with the Black; it would be a contest of races, and even if the new Austrian Emperor could import an equal number of Austrians, their chances would be few. *Three-fourths of the slave population of America are believed to have their masters' blood in them.* The calculation may be excessive but it seems to us that they are precisely the race to spread over and conquer Mexico, and that the Austrian ideas, race, and archdukes, are of all possible importations, precisely those best calculated *not* to hold it against them.

With regard to Canada, the North American Review, of April, 1865, says;—

"If we succeed as we mean to succeed in making our institutions conform to our Principles, we shall become attractive. There will be no need to annex Canada by force. She will drift towards us by inevitable gravitation, or may be joined to the United States in a federative league."

PART V.

ITEMS OF RECONSTRUCTION.

FUTURE CAPITOL.

The general principles which decide the position of Capitols, seem undoubted. They depend upon considerations of Climate, Safety, ready communication, and centralised position.

These principles have already been recognised by American Statesmen. The report of the Secretary at War, Session 1861-2, observes:—

> "The Geographical position of the metropolis, menaced by the rebels, induces me to suggest a reconstruction of the boundaries of the States of Delaware, Maryland, and Virginia. Wisdom and true statesmanship would dictate that the seat of the national Government, for all time to come, should be placed beyond reasonable danger of seizure by enemies within, as well as from capture by foes from without."

In America the natural unity is more striking than in any other country.

Towards the fork of the Mississippi is the very centre, but St. Louis and environs seem at present to unite the greatest advantages. It is at the junction of the Missouri, and Mississippi, which, with its tributaries, touches thirteen States. It thus commands 46,000 miles of navigable water. The Illinois river and canal to Lake Michigan, will complete its communications with the whole water system of the Empire. Also the great Pacific Railway touches it. Its Isothermal lines are between those of St. Paul, which cut near Dublin and Sebastopol, and those of Washington and Richmond, which cut Rome and Egypt.

There was much truth in the words of Mr. Seward, when he took the stump at St. Paul's; but they seem to us to apply with more force to St. Louis:—

"Here is the central place where the agriculture of the *richest region of North America* must bear its tribute to the supplies of the whole world; on the East, all along the shores of Lake Superior; and on the West, stretching in one broad plain, in a belt quite across the continent, is a country where State after State is yet to rise. This is then a commanding field; but it is as commanding in regard to the *destinies of this continent*, as it is in regard to its *commercial future*, for power is not to reside permanently on the eastern slope of the Alleghany mountains, nor in the seaports. Seaports have always been overrun and controlled by the people in the interior. *The power of this Government is not to be established on the Atlantic or the Pacific coast.* The power that shall speak the will of men on this continent is to be located *in the Mississippi valley*, at the sources of the Mississippi and the St. Lawrence."—SEWARD, at St. Paul, capital of Minnesota, Sept. 18, 1860.

These ideas are familiar to Americans. But note the startling words of Sherman to Grant, 10th March, 1864; [Bowman's "Sherman and his Campaigns," Richardson, New York.]

"Now as to the future. Don't stay in Washington. Come West; take to yourself the whole Mississippi Valley. Let us make it dead sure—and I tell you the Atlantic slopes and the Pacific shores will follow its destiny, as sure as the limbs of a tree live or die with the main trunk. We have done much, but still much remains. Time and time's influences are with us. We could almost afford to sit still and let these influences work.

"Here lies the seat of the coming empire; and from the West, when our task is done, we will make short work of Charleston and Richmond, and the impoverished coast of the Atlantic."

THREE-FIFTHS VOTING CLAUSE.

The remaining "items of reconstruction," are the abrogation of certain arrangements *contrary* to the genius of the nation,* or their alteration by the natural force of a free Labor propagandism, or measures of mere detail and convenience.

The most prominent amongst the first, and probably one of the first items of Reconstruction, is the clause reckoning five negroes as three men. It openly defies the Principle of Equality. It gave a plurality of votes to Slaveholders. It vitiated also the Principle of Conservatism. The Constitution of electoral districts by *actual votes* might precipitate the reform.

This anomaly will probably be dealt with by the national Government. *Equality is the national Life*, and must override all traitorous interpretations of "State rights." And when Slavery and inequality were armed and organised by the strongest oligarchy in the world, it could not exclude free ideas and interests.

This three-fifths clause outraged the rights of property, if we take that stand-point, no less than the right of manhood; and of the Free States, as balanced against the Slave States.

According to the census of 1860, the *gain in*

* The anomaly of South Carolina for instance, which is the only State where electors are chosen by the Legislature. It also requires a considerable property qualification from members of the House of Representatives, one qualification being five hundred freehold acres and ten negroes; another, £500. free of debt. This conservatism has borne fruit.

population of the six New England States, Maine, New Hampshire, Vermont, Massachusetts, Rhode Island, and Connecticnt, in the decade, has been 407,185, or nearly 15 per cent.; while *the loss in number of representatives* has been four. In the middle States, New York, New Jersey, and Pennsylvania, the *gain in population* has been 1,566,972, or 26½ per cent.; and the *loss in members* of Congress has been *four*. New York has nearly *double* the *free* population of the six original Seceded States, and yet she has only *thirty-one* representatives *to their twenty-eight*. If the Slave States were apportioned representatives on free white population alone, their representation would *decrease about forty per cent.*, or taking the *property* basis, counting three persons for every five thousand dollars, the representation of the North would be immeasurably increased. Ohio, gaining about 400,000; loses three representatives. She has more free white population than the six States, South Carolina, Georgia, Alabama, Florida, Mississippi, and Louisiana, and yet has but *eighteen* representatives *against twenty-eight*.

South Carolina's representation in the Congress, 1860, was four to 398,186 free whites. That of Connecticut was four to 760,670; whereas the former was entitled, on the free white population, to about one-half of the latter. The seven original States of the Confederacy, had a white population of 2,656,481, and thirty-two representatives. The six New England States twenty-five to 3,135,301. A slave representation, adding to the South *fifty per cent.!*

No Peace is possible in America until Equality, the national ideal and life, is vindicated. If the uneducated negro cannot vote, neither can the South profit by its own wrong. The South must be held in some sort of subjection or Inequality, until the negro becomes politically Equal. Till the law can be brought up to the Principle, it must be brought down to the facts, and if the negro cannot vote, Southern representation must be reduced accordingly.

The negro suffrage will, as fast as it can be given, become an immutable material guarantee for the Americanising of the South.

THREE-FOURTHS AMENDMENT. DIRECT VOTING, AND JUDICIAL APPOINTMENTS.

Complete Popular Sovereignty, and Administrative Unity, are amongst the chief results of this contest. Popular Sovereignty, also, as claimed by some, demands an easier mode of amendment of the Constitution, and also a direct vote of the *People* for President.

We do not here advance our own opinions, but simply announce for what they are worth these demands of certain parties in America.

When the Constitution has been made one with the national conscience, it is said that it will also have to be made a more perfect and ready instrument and expression of the national will, and better adjusted to the national Genius. This will not be revolutionary, for there the People are, in effect, the Constitution; their destiny is in their own hands, and it is impossible to take it out of them. There, all have a stake in public security, and know that they could, on occasion, alter the alteration. They have property, knowledge, and power, and are therefore law-abiding, conservative, constructive, progressive, and content.

In England, the Constitution depends on Acts of Parliament. To alter it, public opinion has from question to question to fight against the *vis inertiæ* of wrong, against tradition, and all the associated force of feudality.

In America, the Constitution is a formal document, with provisions for alteration and amendment, to be carried through by a certain majority.

The North founded and settled the *Principles* of the Constitution. The South administered and moulded for 80 years the *Policy* of the nation.

The Principles, and the (internal) Policy became alien and hostile. The war will have once more *reunited them.* But now that the nation has reconquered their union, it will before long require complete *guarantees* of its continuance.

Those guarantees are two. The first, the destruction of the slave faction. The second, the formal and complete expurgation of three-fifths voting clauses, and all other recognition of Slavery, from the Constitution. A third is also debated, the substitution of some plan, more facile and practicable, for the present system of altering and amending the Constitution.

The first process is going on swimmingly. The second, the expurgation, is not doubtful, for words are apt to follow things. The substitute for the two-third amendment and three-fourth ratification, is a matter which has already taxed and occupied the forethought of American republican politicians. But whether the precedent of Secession will not show the advantage of these difficulties in alteration, and cause more conservative counsels to prevail, is much to be doubted.

As the Constitution now stands, the difficulty is first to get an amendment proposed, by two-thirds of both Houses, or by the Legislatures of two-thirds of the States, and then ratified by Legislatures or by Conventions in three-fourths of the States.*

The problem is the old, the eternal one in politics —how to combine conservatism with progress, and how to save popular initiative from becoming revolutionary, or Administrative Unity from becoming the vehicle of Despotism.

How this matter will be settled as to form, we cannot and need not divine. But this we doubt not, —that *Principles and Policy will again become one*,

* The text of the Constitution, on this point, is as follows: Article V. "The Congress, whenever two-thirds of both Houses shall deem it necessary, shall propose amendments to this Constitution, or, on the application of the Legislatures of two-thirds of the several States, shall call a Convention for proposing amendments, which, in either case, shall be valid as part of this Constitution, when ratified by the Legislatures of three-fourths of the several States, or by Conventions in three-fourths thereof, or the one or the other mode of ratification may be proposed by the Congress."

that Slavery will be expurgated from the national conscience and constitution, and that a free and living and progressive country cannot and will not be held back in its career, from adapting to its growth and expansion, or from altering or rejecting any form of words or of ceremonies, descended upon it from the olden (or rather from the younger) time.

Never and nowhere do forms stand against force, and in America the force is with the People and opinion.

§

Again, *the Constitution* says that the people shall not DIRECTLY ELECT the President, but that they shall elect his electors. But *the People* (and it was no new expedient) said to the electors, "Elect our man, and we elect you," and in an instant the trustees become delegates, and the parchment of the Constitution stretched and tore with the strain.

The People chose to make sure of their man,—Lincoln, and soon they showed that power is in living souls, and not in the cerements of tradition, or in the pigeon-holed and red-taped past. It is now proposed to legalise this direct election, and herein to bring the Constitution and the popular will into harmony.

Thus it is, and must increasingly be, with all Democracies that have tasted power.

It will be seen that the double process which constitutes American History—the advance to Administrative Unity and to Popular Sovereignty—is not contradictory nor hostile, but congruous and harmonious.

There is a fourth step recommended by some as necessary to the full measure of national administrative unity. At present *the national Government cannot attach an individual official of one of the States' Governments as such.* Article III, which regulates the Constitutional Judicial power, does not extend it to such a case. It is, however, doubtful whether this extension is compatible with the maintenance of State Governments as what Jefferson called them,—"the true barriers of our liberty."

The tendency throughout seems to be *to simplify forms and to give directness and energy to power.* If the People's power remains readily available, Judicial appointments may safely remain a matter of administration. General opinion advocates the appointment of State Judges by the Governors, to be confirmed by the State Senates, thus assimilating the State to the national usage and abrogating Judicial appointments by universal suffrage, or for a short term, as by a comparatively recent innovation, they now are in some few States.

SUNDRIES.

Certain matters of detail, remain. Prominent amongst these is Free Trade. A tariff *ad valorem* on imports *for revenue* will probably be maintained for some time. A discriminating tariff *for protection* will probably be abandoned.

Length of President's term, whether four years

as in the North, or six as in the South, and whether or no the one term principle shall be adhered to.

Appointments to office during good behaviour, instead of for President's term.

No removals for political reasons. This is of quite recent growth. In 1830 it was ascertained, in consequence of a resolution of Congress, that the practice of removal from office for political reasons had enormously increased. The total removals by the first six Presidents had been 74. For the last year there had been 491 in the office of postmasters alone.

We may also recall to mind, as the 13th, 14th and 15th resolutions of the Chicago platform, a demand for a complete and satisfactory Homestead measure; a protest against any impairing or abridging of the rights of citizenship accorded to immigrants; an approval of rivers and harbours improvements; and generally for the development of the national resources, &c.

§

Amongst the instalments of reconstruction virtually or actually made, are the following:—

Slavery abolished.

Future territories set apart for freedom.

The republican party demands the absolute equality of the negro; he must take his proper position in his triple right as Inheritor, Worker, and Conqueror.

His mere value as a labourer was, before the war, two thousand millions of dollars. His value as a man to the American nation can never be estimated. A few thousand families have hitherto spent the results of his labour.

The South is little used to the excitements and discussions and dangers of Freedom. It finds free negroes a nuisance, and capital, not employed in slave-driving, or slave-breeding, a danger. The incendiary element of Freedom lay in patches over the South, and remained harmless, for the trains could not be laid to connect them. Free negroes were under surveillance, and amongst the mean whites there was no element of manufacturing or commercial capital or skill, to counteract the overpowering influence of the Slaveholding caste.

Thus no middle class could be found to connect and to raise by gradations, either the mean white or the slave, either by the power of ideas or of money.

Free plantations will reverse all this, and reverse the results also. There will be a middle class, and the idea and money power, will be on the side of freedom.

This is the ransom "King Cotton" will have to pay to "King Labour," commonly called "Squatter Sovereignty." The South has to get itself reconciled to free trade in Cotton, and Labour—or to be extirpated and replanted. Southern ideas of property and robbery have to be reversed.

§

The last "Labour of Lincoln," so far, was to fix the fact of abolition. To take a parable from that invention that has almost worked a social revolution in America, he *locked* the stitches of Reconstruction, as he plied his needle of fate. Slavery should not survive to create future wars, if he could help it. Lincoln was Destiny on that, but left Free Will to Future Congresses on every thing else.

The Republican principle of Government which he has maintained by war in the greater part of the national Territory, his successor or the nation will uphold in reconstruction, by moral and constitutional sanctions and material support wherever there are any to take the Initiative. Rebellion attacked the People's rights with minorities. Johnson can assail the rebellion by active minorities, that will represent virtual majorities everywhere.

Lincoln would not alter the geographies of States. He could not alter the will of rebel chiefs. He provided a framework of reconstruction, and offered to the rank and file of Rebellion, pardon and freedom, and self-Government.

Thus the slave leaders will have lost for the South its Slaves, and for the Nation Slavery; and will have gained for themselves the reputation of the most conspicuous failure since Lucifer.

Lincoln will have secured for the nation, Freedom, Equality, Republicanism, Union,—in fact, true Federal Republicanism. For the South, a freedom of Ideas and Interests, which will create for it an almost miraculous future, make the debt a jest, and secure for the common heritage those splendid political qualities, which have won in the council and the field, an imperishable name.

Next in importance to Lincoln's policy of *Abolition* and *Reconstruction*, *the certainty of clearing the future course of the nation* and of extricating it from all doubts or half measures as to freedom, or decisions, favouring slavery, made *upon the Constitution*, is his crowning labour and glory. The declaration was not doubtful, if the constitution was, and if any part of the latter was rotten, or of doubtful interpretation, it must be cut out and remodelled upon the Declaration.

If Slavery was to be meddled with, it must be destroyed. A King, says Landor, should not be struck but in a fatal part. If Slavery were protected, it would destroy the political, social, and moral structure of the American nation.

Thus much did Lincoln, the first peasant emperor, one of the Fathers of nations,—one of the "friends of God."

§

The main value, in the present age, of the DECLARATION of Independence, consists in the fact, that it was, till 1860, the last great act of the People, and that it was the PREAMBLE OF THE REVOLUTION. The statement of Principles and intentions, upon which was invited and obtained the co-operation of the American People, and their victory over English thraldom, is the *root of the Title* of American nationality. Upon the faith of it they leagued together, and by the terms of it "the lives, and fortunes, and sacred honour," of the subscribers and their successors, were and are pledged for the independence of the nation, and "Freedom and equality in the pursuit of happiness," of the weakest and the poorest soul, if only it be untainted with crime, within the limits of the United States. To deny this is to lie in the face of God, in the front of the world, and in the van of civilization.

And the same idea was of the essence of all the movements of those days:—

The Virginian resolution of 1765 claimed for "*all his majesty's subjects since inhabiting, all* the "privileges, franchises, and immunities that have "at any time been held by the people of Great "Britain, as if born within the realm of England."

The Congress of 1774 recommended by the Virginian Convention of the same year, and at which Georgia alone was unrepresented, repudiated slavery, and passed *unanimous* resolutions respecting the rights of "the *inhabitants* to life, liberty, and property," based on the "*immutable* LAWS OF NATURE, *and the principles of the English Constitution.*"

Whosoever has taken, or would take, from any American subject the guarantee of equality written in the "Declaration," deserves to have taken from him all benefits and all sanctions secured by the revolution.

Whosoever would add to any Southern man-stealer powers denied by that declaration, as by "human nature," the "British Constitution," and the "Bible," deserves to have added to him and to his children the plagues and penalties of tyranny, treason, disunion, and national impotence, from which the revolution saved America.

The people sent up their delegates to do a certain thing, to adjust terms of national independence, and of individual equality. The ratifications were "in the name of the People, their constituents." If they ratified individual *inequality*, and class tyranny, their competency was none, their authority void, the Constitution so far was a juggle, the delegates from the Slave States were conspirators and the delegates from the Free States betrayed the trust held "for their constituents the People."

And the Declaration itself virtually provided against any such conspiracy. It declared "ALL MEN" free and equal. "That their rights were "life, *liberty*, and the pursuit of happiness. That "whenever any form of Government becomes "destructive of these ends, it is the right of the "people to *alter or to abolish it*, and to institute "new Government, laying its foundation on such "principles, and organizing its powers in such "form, as to them shall seem most likely to effect "their safety and happiness."

The men of that age were indeed little likely to deal "in glittering generalities," or to promulgate as "theories" truths which they would have to vindicate with their blood.

The original draft of this Declaration pointed at "Slavery" by name. The Committee of the whole House on the question of "Independence," appointed a Sub-Committee of Adams and Jefferson to draw the draft. It was actually prepared by Jefferson. This original draft of the Declaration thus indicts George III. and Slavery before the world, and clearly shows the popular ideas concerning Slavery.

"He has waged cruel war against *human nature* itself, violating its most sacred rights of life and liberty *in the persons of a distant people*, captivating and carrying them into slavery in another hemisphere, or to incur miserable death in their transportation thither. This piratical warfare, the opprobrium of infidel powers, is the warfare of the Christian King of Great Britain. Determined to keep open market where *men should be bought and sold,* he has prostituted his negative for suppressing every legislative attempt to prohibit or to restrain this execrable commerce."

So much for the man, who, as said the great Fox, being manifestly moved and possessed by the Devil, made war against two nations and republics, and drawing this nation after him, did his possible to prepare all the subsequent misunderstandings, collisions, and failures of England in both hemispheres.

Thus was the rough draft, by Jefferson, of the Constitution, * couched in terms of absolute reprobation of Slavery. But little and interested men, and abject and timid agencies, struck out his honest and impetuous denunciations, and forced the great men of the occasion to choose between disunion and compromise.

Nevertheless it was the King and the oligarchy of England that really forced them to keep Slavery as a compromise for the sake of Union, and safety against her attacks, and England, had she retained their allegiance, would probably have spread the institution more widely within their borders.

* This Draft is said to be in the American Philosophical Society, at Philadelphia, framed on both sides, as it was written.

In 1774 the People of England were thus appealed to against their Sovereign by Congress, "Permit us to be *as free as yourselves*, and we shall "ever esteem an union with you our greatest glory "and happiness; we shall consider your enemies "our enemies, and your interest as our own. But "if you are determined that your ministers shall "wantonly sport with the *rights of mankind*, we "must then tell you, that we will never submit "to be hewers of wood, or drawers of water, for "any ministry or nation in the world."

The excuse, and the only excuse, of American statesmen in retaining slavery, was the determination of the clodhopper maniac who ruled England, and of the oligarchy that united with him against democracy, to destroy the republic. There was no English nation then, Chatham was not supported, and the Republic had to fight the King, honestly if it could—but to fight him. *

And so because England denied freedom to America, America denied it to the slave, and the country must go back 80 years to the *abolitionist* Jefferson and begin *de novo*.

But Democracy is justified of her children. Results follow causes, and if the youth of the country be taught, and its manhood taught to as-

* "The King said to Lord Shelburne, 'I will be plain with you; the point next my heart, and which I am determined be the consequence what it may, never to relinquish but with my crown and life, is to prevent a total unequivocal recognition of the independence of America. Promise to support me on this ground, and I will leave you unmolested on *every other ground*, with full power as the prime minister of this kingdom.' The bargain was struck."—*Franklin's Works*, v. 5, p. 326.

semble in free Church and Assembly for worship and discussion, then all the elements of prosperity are in motion, and prosperity must follow.

SUMMARY OF RESULTS.

And if these powers of the School, Press, Assembly, and Church, have not yet done all their work, and have not yet quite expelled their opposites, it is only now a question of a decade or two. The whole People must rule, for they will be taught. The South now neither would nor could mop out the deluge of democratic propagandism, on which its future depends. But if it would, manhood development, association, and equality must run their career. *Labour and capital must penetrate, where the nation that supplies them cannot be bribed, intimidated, separated, or destroyed.*

We have followed the rise of popular power from the free School, Church, and Assembly, to the formation of a *nation* on principles of Equality.

Although till this was accomplished the world was put back, from epoch to epoch, of adverse teaching; there was *never* any doubt of the triumph of the principles, because God works by law, and works for progress. If the human soul, intellect, and body, are to be gradually better trained and more developed, they must be better and better able to associate; and if they associate, they must approach and possess Equality. Nation will now learn from nation, as formerly man from man.

Familiar traditions, touching the tendency of all executives, if strong, to despotism, and if weak to dissolution and destruction, taught historical students to discuss the alternatives of the blossoming of the great republic into empire, or of its utter de-centralisation and disunion. Recent events tempted men to conclude, as partisans of class Government with triumph, as philosophers with disgust, or as friends of the people with despair, that the great problem yet remained unsolved, even in the latest invention in statesmanship:—The problem how best to make a nation and consolidate it, how to balance the centrifugal and centripetal forces of empire,—how best to secure to *Government, its balance, stability*, and power, to the *Individual his rights* and freedom, and so to *Mankind* the conditions and guarantees of a perpetual *progress.*

But it is the essential fact and speciality of the American situation and struggle, that popular license and executive despotism, save as part of the Southern cause, were precisely the dangers that did *not* threaten. The Americans are proverbially a law-abiding nation. The danger that has assailed the State, began with that which assailed the Individual, the Unit of the State. The principle of individual freedom, was not made absolute and universal; and this one condition of national greatness being faulty, the whole glorious fabric has been shaken to its foundations.

But mark the giant strides of the North. In 1860, the question was non-extension of Slavery. In 1862, the question was its extinction; and already we see the principles of Freedom and Nationality, returning in triumph over the most powerful rebellion that was ever organized.

The eighty years' experiment of popular intelligence, freedom, and submission to self-imposed law, has *not* failed either in conservatism, individuality, power, or progress. So far from this, after a forty years' compromise of negro rights, forced on a strong abolitionist minority, that minority organized itself, and by the material, moral, and political progress of a free people, was enabled to defy the South in its attempt to make Slavery a national institution.

It is casting aside and off a ruling oligarchy of eighty years, maintains the national integrity, reverts to the first principles of the rights of man, puts the nation at one with principle and natural right, supplies the missing link between the free man and the complete nation, and now proceeds to set free the subject nation, which has grown up in bondage since the constitution was promulgated. It is the grandest and most definitive expression yet, of the conservative, progressive, and *recuperative energies of a self-governed people.*

The balance of power within the nation, was assailed, not by the people, nor by the executive, but by an *extraneous slave faction*, only too long borne with. The progress of the nation was arrested, but by that same felon Oligarchy, conservative only in wrong, and destructive of all rights, whether of their slaves, their equals, or their Government.

After the strain of battle, that from 1775 to 1782, had bound the then Thirteen States together in the work of Independence, was loosed, the prostration and reactions of peace brought with it internal questions, of which slavery ultimately became the greatest, and these again, parties and factions. The State wanted girders. For unification, the North abandoned the assertion *a l'outrance* of her Principles; it was thought best to admit Georgia and South Carolina on their own terms, and it is a great fact of historical retribution, that the Southern faction which demanded Slavery and compromise, has dared to deny that very Unity and centralised power for which the North had yielded them.

§

The great lesson of the war, and the great objects of 1787, as demonstrated by general consent to the principle and detail of the alterations, were two-fold:—

1st. *To centralise and nationalise the Government*, in order that commerce, trade, revenue, and export and import interests, might be developed and protected, and a foreign policy in commerce and war, created, directed, and controlled.

2nd. *To "form a more perfect union" of "the People"* of the United States, as contrasted with the old union of *States*, and the older one of the Confederacy.

The 1st would administrate and direct. The 2nd, cement, consolidate, energise, and render perpetual the union of the people. The practical effect, politically, was to bring up "the People" in greater power and prominence, and to diminish the power of the "States."

But the process, crowned by the achievement and declaration of American independence, did not what it appeared to do. The war was not long enough for that. It enunciated Principles, which it did not carry out, and left a riddle in the constitution respecting rights, which circumstances, and sectional interests, and the prudery and indecision of the North, have since elevated into importance. That riddle the North have had to read by the light of blazing towns.

The right of man to himself was clearly asserted in words, and plainly denied in practice; for black labour was too useful—the black man too insignificant. *The subordination of the parts to the whole*, was supposed to have been secured; but a principle remained in the constitution, destined to jeopardise it, and in the presence of the enemy, posterity was left to protect itself. The first omission raised the question of a *slave empire*, and of free or negro labour. The second, attacked the *national unity* by the assertion of an unbridled State sovereignty. The individual slave man is now recognised, and has got to be raised, and thus also the theory of citizenship perfected. The sovereignty of individual States must, on points of universal import, be submitted to the collective Sovereignty, before the work of "Independence" can be completed and the nation "made."

At the first Declaration of Independence, the value and freedom of the human soul rose upon the world with all the vividness of a new revelation, and has been declared and re-declared by their public manifestoes, and perhaps never abandoned by the majority; whilst the subordination in national matters of the "States" to the republic, constantly iterated, was manifestly the supreme condition of that Unity, without which a nation can neither feel, think, will, act, or be.

We grant at once, the truism of the sacred right of insurrection, and that a nation *cannot* revolt without oppression; but in this sense, it is the North that has really revolted, for the South, up to the recent growth of the Republican party, always carried on the Government, and directed the internal and external Policy. It was the mighty North-west that wrested by its growth the balance of power from the South, and resolved no longer to be the tool of her Policy, the accomplice of her crime, or the victim of the extension of her barbarous and desolating land system.

The North has now avoided the two equal dangers of leaving the Constitution, or tolerating Slavery.

The fault of the North was that it did not fight for empire until its independence was jeopardised. It neither overstrained its rights, nor interfered with those of the Sovereign States. It only interfered when its existence was at stake. The South had no claim here by Northern dereliction. The North did not put itself in the wrong by the manner of its action. It stood by the Principle of authority and the Principle of freedom; was the North wrong then in form or in substance? Has it violated the original compact, or natural right? If its empire was consistent with these, to taunt it with seeking to preserve it is the foolishest deliverance of a mind hide-bound by formulas, and given over to verbal delusions.

This battle point,—doubt it never,—is the hour of America's Manhood. Her years of nonage are gone, and the struggle prepared for and against for eighty years has come and gone. The great heart of that great nation never faltered, and this marvellous people achieved the marvellous task (as it would have been even for a consolidated country) of conducting a conservative resistance to the progress of a dominant party and policy, which were in the very nature of things bound beforehand to progress, expand, or die.

Although the Southern section was so strong as to succeed for a time even in tampering with mails, in depriving abolitionists of the *right of Petition* against slavery, and in gagging the press and the senators, so determined and true was the North, that after the ballot had decided once for all and for ever for freedom, and the South revolted against the decision themselves had courted, they waited for the first irrevocable overt act of treason, and have gone out by the million *to die* for the cause and the principles which with infinite patience they had never once by violence allowed to be put in the wrong.

Behold here the second and spiritual birth of the, as yet, completest nation under the sun. The sword of the spirit of the great American nation has not been drawn in vain. If such a nation is to die, History and her conclusions must die with it. The American nation is *made*, or we must unmake our philosophy, reverse our deductions, and begin the world of thought afresh; for, according to them, neither spiritually, morally nor materially even, is any other issue possible to it than success.

Its race, its strategical, commercial, and geographical unity, its mountain ranges, and river system, the splendour of its ideal, inflaming the hearts of the people, its magnificent moral attitude, its sacrifices, armies, and navies, its history, and its genius, all declare that this *people* shall continue to exist, as it was and is, one and indivisible.

For the intellect and just self-interest of the people appreciate too well to wish to change it for any of the old outworn condemned systems, this Government of themselves, which so well combines Conservatism with Progress. The existence of a mighty uniform class, with equal intelligence universally diffused, with no corporate interests springing from remote antiquity and ranged against the people, obstructing progress and aggravating opposition, with a general competency and stake, created a party too numerous, too intelligent, too independent to be overweighted by a section, led by the fanatical, or held back by the retrogressionists. This national party will always outnumber, outweigh, and overpower all who may attempt to rule for the few, or to ignore the rights of industry and intelligence. Let us repeat. *Knowledge, and power, and property are with the North, and they are always conservative, constructive, and progressive.* By the nature of men and of things, by absorption and conversion, if by no other or more summary process, the great and free North will destroy the slave faction, which bases the rights of the few on the wrongs of the many.

The destruction of the slave interest, false in statesmanship as in morality, is the only sacrifice required. The 190,000 slave-owners, with their 160,000 slave-brokers, their state properties, and mock presidents,their felon rights, founded on negro wrongs, and their dispensation of physical force, intimidation, treachery, and treason, are of course to be converted or eliminated in the process. These are the only men and theirs the only interests, irreconcileable with the supreme result which this struggle is to accomplish—THE MAKING OF THE AMERICAN NATION.

§

A nation, however created, can only be permanently sustained under two conditions. *The freedom and energy of the Individual*, and the *subordination of the Individual*, and of each corporate sub-organization, *to the general law*. A State that has not the first, has no strength or progress; a State without the last, has no conservatism. The one predicament tends to dissolution, the other to despotism. The enemies of the United States have therefore done wisely in their generation, to attack both in theory and by arms precisely these two things. They declared, contrary to all evidence, that America did not mean and shall not mean the freedom of the individual negro, and that the constitution did mean and shall mean the insubordination of each State to the central power. But the question was, not whether America should be two, or three, or four, but whether it should be one, or one hundred.

The North asserting, and the South denying, the two conditions of nationality, it could not have been difficult to perceive which was the true and which the false nation.

Lies and half truths may make factions, rebellions, treasons, failures, or empire even, but a "nation" and "independence," never. A nation *cannot* be begotten on a lie, nor held together by partial truths contradicted in practice. Still less can the world mistake the mighty action of an unprecedented class interest, for the *organic life* and *spiritual movement* of a People; or a faction-fight for political supremacy over one nation, and the power to destroy and degrade another, for the heroism and self sacrifice of Patriots, seeking, forsooth, "a country."

The freedom of the individual, the idea for the assertion of which America was created and colonised, and for which her independence was proclaimed, though perfectly conceived, was not clearly developed. But the hour of its manhood was surely coming, and it struck when, by the emancipation edict, the *idea of individual freedom was asserted fully and absolutely, together with that of nationality.*

The terms of contest were never yet so clear, logical, and antithetical. The Position is defined with awful distinctness, national life and individual freedom, on the one side, and sectional impotence, with personal slavery, on the other.

A nation is never *born* save under the stress.

and travail, and inspiration of some great idea,—the truth, consistency, depth, and universality of which is the warrant for its creation, and faithfulness to which is the pledge of its immortality.

A bastard nation, without the traditions, or inheritance, or vital energies of a nation, may be begotten of a sin upon a lie; but the monstrosity cannot live, the excrescence will be sloughed off, the morbid action will cease, and the parasitical life pass away.

If ever the immortality of a nation is won, it is won in the assertion of the special truths of its national and individual life, against armed assailants and infidel questionings, both from within and from without.

§.

The founders of the Union were at fault, inasmuch as they were only a great deal ahead of the rest of the world on the Slavery question, and did not formally and finally prohibit, that which the rest of the world was profiting by and encouraging. It was supposed on all sides, that the institution would be evanescent and die out, as it unquestionably would, but for its partially resting on Northern connivance, and chiefly on monopolies and artificial prices.

The vast majority of the legislature was at one with the popular ideal and will, and it is at one with it now. The people of 1774—the vast majority of them meant universal individual freedom as much, though perhaps not so intelligently, as the people of 1862.—They meant, and expressed, and proclaimed their meaning, but under the Confederation *Bye-Laws*, a majority of six States to three, and of sixteen members to seven, was not sufficient to carry the proposition of freedom in the States.

The madness of the South, which has torn the republic, concluded its inevitable cycle in despair. Barbarous in culture, infamous in morals, weak in its staple trade,—depending on protection for commercial, and on oppression for political existence, —with an organic disease in its "Constitution," and a lie in economics, and a mistake in statesmanship, for its "corner stone,"—the Slave empire and its composition, had indeed only got to be "recognised," to stand confessed an anomaly and an anachronism in the present epoch.

But the Union cannot die. It is founded on a rock, —on Truth, Nature, and the People, on the universal culture of the citizen, and on his freedom, not only in politics, but in religion also,—consummating the unity of the State, and the supremacy of the Law,—combining all the postulates of progress and of stable Government. It is precisely this struggle that completes the nation's manhood,—this antagonism within and without,—this divine white heat of conflict,—this enthusiasm of battle, that welds it into one, and that will make it immortal!

The salt of the earth is the few. The resolute disinterested good, are the minority in all countries and causes, and America is no exception. Its Puritan salt and savour saved America, and made the cause so good and strong, that it was impossible to ruin it. In what other age save Cromwell's, or in what other city in the world, would regiments march through, chanting godly battle hymns?—how often before, have Rulers said, and *meant*, intelligently, that "their only wish was to find and to do the will of God?"

Lincoln will stand grandly in history, though lately the butt of every *charlatan*. He made no mistake in policy, and it is by policy that the American battle was won. The old European imposture, that homely common sense and honesty cannot govern, has nohow been so well refuted as by Lincoln's government. But worse was said of Washington than of Lincoln. A long since extinct print the "Aurora," then the "leading Journal," declared—"If ever a nation was debauched by a "man, the American nation has been debauched "by Washington. An example to future ages, that "the mask of patriotism may conceal the foulest "designs against the liberties of the people."

Had Lincoln not been, comparatively speaking, the complete man he was—had he been a mere enthusiast, his enemies had forgiven him.

It was Lincoln who committed the North against Slavery. It is Lincoln, working in grand simplicity with the common sense of the people, who has swung the nation round the critical point of its whole history, bringing it from "non-extension" in 1860, to "abolition" in 1863, and, step by step, making it safe and sure *that the South could not return and bring Slavery with it.* It is Lincoln who kept the Border Slave States for Union, and prepared them and the Union to combine against

Slavery. It is Lincoln who went far enough and not too far ahead of public sentiment, who educated the mind of the North to abolition, till the Union and Freedom were one word.

Nevertheless, with John Brown at Harper's Ferry was, perhaps, more than with any other man, the turning point in the New World's history.

As to England, the North affirmed, and the South denied, the two main results of three hundred years of the blood, and sacrifices, and efforts, of the Anglo-Saxon race,—the principles and practice of freedom and of authority, of national and individual right, reconciled, and confirmed.

England has got through many struggles, with varying fortunes, and the mighty momentum of her Empire in the greatness of its way, has carried her through all the mistakes of her Statesmen. There was lately put to her the greatest question ever put to a country as a test of its use on Earth, or its value before Heaven. England should thank God for her democracy, for her oligarchy would fain have answered this great question the wrong way. Had she lifted a little finger against all her past, against her own sons and kindred, against the genius of authority, freedom, and national integrity and honour; against the great nation that has won the most glorious war of any age, that commands the largest territory, the greatest resources, the freest institutions, the most numerous armies and fleets, and soon the widest trade, and among living nations the most numerous population; that has had more military experience than all existing generals and troops elsewhere put together, that is three thousand miles from England's base of operations, and at the same time next door to Canada, and whose institutions are destined to change by their example the entire aspect of the world—had England moved against *this* nation, and aided *that other*, to "blow the billowy verge of everlasting night" across the precincts of civilisation—she had created the Nemesis which would have dismembered her empire, clouded all her past glories, and extinguished her future, and which would have so earned of the age, and of all ages,

> "A name which every wind to heaven would bear,
> Which men to speak, and angels joy to hear."

But the Democracy of England understood too well their interests in the great American popular "experiment," to allow of any further un-English experimentalising against it.

The solemn hour of America's manhood has struck and they keep the jubilee well. But had not America been equal to this work, had she been faithless to her MIGHTY UNKNOWN FUTURE, whose foundations are deep in democracy, whose heights are dim in the unfulfilled, whose principles are the life of nations—had she not been the martyr and saviour nation she *has* been, then Humanity must have turned once more towards the East, Democracy would have waited eighteen hundred years in vain for a precedent, and philosophy must have looked to other continents and to other civilisations.

America is now the grandest combination of Power, Stability, Unity, Freedom, and Happiness, the world has seen.

As a Nation it has, complete and sound, its material bases, its individuality, and its organic functions; and not only this, they are completer and sounder than has hitherto been thought possible. And more than that; they are based on principles which have some sort of *finality* in politics, for they reconcile an intense and concentrated executive, a legislature chosen by the whole national manhood, a balance of power between the sovereign parts and the sovereign whole, with *Equality the only Freedom as between Individuals, and the only guarantee of Freedom as regards the State.*

It has illustrated the great principle that complexity of relationships and inter-action whilst the result of Freedom, are not contrary to, but essential to, a complete national Unity, and that Equality of Individual right is the only thing that can *fulfil* the National Sovereignty and power.

As a Democracy it is based on that threefold freedom whose foundations can never be shaken, of School, Church, and Assembly.

As a Federation it has stood—and strengthened by it—the strongest test yet applied to Federations.

It seems almost as though there must be invented a new disease in body politics before the life of the American nation can be successfully assailed. The last assault delivered against it has ended, or is ending, in a propagandism of prosperity and freedom, that can have no limits save in the wants and emptiness of the nations. And both sections of America will have conquered; the North in the triumph of its principles, the South in appropriating their power.

Thus, this nation, made of the principle of Equality, unmakes for ever the Oligarchy of the West, and therewith all other oligarchies. Slavery, oligarchy, and other sectional, anti-national interests will be speedily assimilated or destroyed by it. Nations everywhere, like this Royal Anglo-American, will become royal, and manhood shall join hands around the earth.

From the moment of the victory of *that* system, *the principle of continued life and of political finality went visibly out of all others.* The Democracy of the West has prevailed to open the gates of the Future for all Peoples.

Before the first nation had been constituted upon a basis of Equality, the foundations of Society had not *settled*, and no superstructure could be safe,—the first principles of Association were not comprehended, and no system could endure. Till that foundation is laid and those principles acknowledged, in at least the political competency of the majority, Construction and Destruction must succeed each other interminably, and *organic* changes will shake the fabric of every advancing State: after that, the only questions will be those of administration, and of foreign policy. The development and organisation of the whole as to qualities, and the all as to numbers, is the only finality in politics. All progressive societies tend to one preponderating power, and the final preponderating universal power can alone be the People.

Now that the American nation is made, Equality thus closes the ERA OF DESTRUCTION, and it inaugurates the ERA OF CONSTRUCTION, upon a plan *final* in principle and *universal* in application. The precedent of the first complete nation gives the world assurance for all its future.

And the last gate of barbarism, the gate of "mixed" or monarchical Government, creaks now on its hinges. From the example of America, a world of United States may arise to unite universally the blessings of Unity and of Independence. Thus may she go on to perfect and to combine the means and the results of Government. Thus may the principle of her Unity prevail, and the orbit of her influence sweep wider and wider through the nations, showing how out of free School, free Church, and free Assembly,—Men, Institutions, Nations, Empires, and Federations are rightly made.

"To see, like some vast island from the ocean,
"The altar of the Federation rear
"It's pile i' the midst.—That mighty shape did wear
"The light of genius; its still shadow hid
"Far ships; to know its height the morning mists forbid.
"To hear the restless multitudes for ever
"Around the base of that great altar flow,
"As on some mountain islet burst and shiver
"Atlantic waves; and solemnly and slow
"As the wind bore that tumult to and fro,
"To feel the dream-like music which did swim
"Falling in pauses from that altar dim."

www.ingramcontent.com/pod-product-compliance
Lightning Source LLC
LaVergne TN
LVHW021243110826
845150LV00002B/399